A Fourth Way?

A Fourth Way?

Privatization, Property, and the Emergence of New Market Economies

Edited by
Gregory S. Alexander
and Grażyna Skąpska

Routledge
New York London

Published in 1994 by

Routledge
29 West 35 Street
New York, NY 10001

Published in Great Britain by

Routledge
11 New Fetter Lane
London EC4P 4EE

Printed in the United States of America on acid free paper.

Library of Congress Cataloging-in-Publication Data

A Fourth Way?: Privatization, Property and the Emergence of New Market Economies / edited by Gregory S. Alexander and Grażyna Skąpska.
p. cm.
Includes bibliographical references.
ISBN 0-415-90697-0 (HB).—ISBN 0-415-90698-9 (PB)
1. Privatization—Europe, Eastern. 2. Property—Europe, Eastern. 3. Privatization. 4. Property. I. Alexander, Gregory S., 1948– . II. Skąpska, Grażyna.
HD4140.7.F68 1993
338.947—dc20 93-1411
CIP

British Library Cataloguing-in-Publication Data

Fourth Way?: Privatization, Property and the Emergence of New Market Economies
I. Alexander, Gregory S. II. Skąpska, Grażyna
330.12

ISBN 0-415-90697-0 (HB)
ISBN 0-415-90698-9 (PB)

Table of Contents

Acknowledgments vii

Introduction: A Fourth Way? ix
Gregory S. Alexander and Grażyna Skąpska

PART I: THE TRANSITION TO PRIVATE PROPERTY—LEGAL PERSPECTIVES

The Challenge of Privatization in the Former East Germany: Reconciling the Conflict Between Individual Rights and Social Needs 3
Thomas Raiser

The Uneasy Breach with Socialized Ownership: Legal Aspects of Privatization of State-owned Enterprises in Poland 19
Stanisław Biernat

Pensioners in America: The Economic Triumph and Political Limitations of Passive Ownership 33
Gregory S. Alexander

PART II: THE TRANSITION TO MARKET ECONOMY—ECONOMIC PERSPECTIVES

The Transition to a Market Economy in Russia: Property Rights, Mass Privatization and Stabilization 57
Edgar L. Feige

Stabilization versus Privatization in Poland: A Sequencing Problem at Macro- and Microeconomic Levels 79
Andrzej Wojtyna

The Private Provision of Public Goods: Principles and Implications 95
Clayton P. Gillette

PART III: THE EMERGING SOCIAL ORDER OF THE NEW MARKET ECONOMIES

Privatization in Poland: The Evolution of Opinions and Interests, 1988–1992 119
Lena Kolarska-Bobińska

Private Farm Ownership in a Changing Poland: Myth and Reality 138
Krystyna Daniel

Social Consciousness in Transition: Toward a New Economic and Political System 150
Maria Borucka-Arctowa

Beyond Constructivism and Rationality of Discovery: Economic Transformation and Institution-Building Processes 163
Grażyna Skąpska

New Forms of State Ownership in Poland: The Case of Commercialization 182
Dariusz Chelmiński, Andrzej A. Czynczyk, and Henryk Sterniczuk

Has State Ownership Truly Abandoned Socialism? The Survival of Socialist Economy and Law in Postcommunist Hungary 198
András Sajó

Privatization as a Gender Issue 215
Joan C. Williams

PART IV: TOWARD A FOURTH WAY—PROGRAMMATIC STATEMENTS

Neither the Market Nor the State: Housing Privatization Issues 253
Duncan Kennedy

Limited Equity Housing Cooperatives as a Mode of Privatization 267
Duncan Kennedy and Leopold Specht

Republicanism, Market Socialism, and the Third Way 286
William H. Simon

Legal Theory and Democratic Reconstruction: Reflections on 1989 310
Karl E. Klare

Contributors 335

Acknowledgments

This book grows out of the Working Group on Privatization, Property, and the New Democracies that met in June 1991 in Amsterdam, The Netherlands, as part of the joint meeting of the Law and Society Association and the Research Committee on the Sociology of Law of the International Sociological Association. It is thus a product of the thought, will, and energy of those who made that memorable conference possible.

Several individuals merit special recognition. First among them is David Trubek, now Dean of International Studies at the University of Wisconsin-Madison. It was Trubek's idea to bring together in Amsterdam scholars from East-Central Europe and the United States to continue a dialogue that had begun earlier, when a group of American law professors visited Central Europe shortly after the peaceful revolutions. The Americans who made this trip were prominent figures in the Critical Legal Studies movement. Their goal was to discuss different perspectives on the transformations occurring in the countries of Eastern and Central Europe and the possibility of charting a realistic alternative to the "third way." The Amsterdam conference continued and broadened that discussion, and included economists and sociologists, both European and American, as well as legal scholars.

The Amsterdam conference was not without a clashing of opinions, hopes, and expectations, with each side no doubt perceiving the other as being slightly naive. Any hopes that the postcommunist countries would fashion a "Sweden" from the failures of state socialism were quickly dashed by the decidedly antistate, capitalist direction of the transformations. Still, scholars from East and West believed it worthwhile to challenge the most basic assumptions of the other side. However, there were also many common themes, as the essays in this book indicate. Significantly, each side agreed that the rules by which one may come to own, use, and dispose of private property will define much of the character of the emerging societies. Moreover, both sides repudiated top-down, centralized, economic planning as being both inefficient and undemocratic.

Invaluable help was also provided by William Felstiner, formerly Executive Director of the American Bar Foundation. The conference could not have occurred without his quick response to calls for financial help to defray travel expenses. Financial help for the preparation of this book was provided by the Cornell Law School. We wish to express our appreciation to Dean Russell K. Osgood for his generous support and encouragement. Karen Wilson, at Cornell Law School, provided invaluable secretarial help with patience and good humor. Carol Didget and especially Michael McIlwrath, members of the class of 1994 at Cornell Law School, provided outstanding research and editorial assistance. We are deeply indebted to them.

Our greatest intellectual debt is to our participating colleagues, including those who were unable to publish their contributions in this volume. This latter group includes Professors Gábor Hamza (Eötvös Loránd University, Budapest), Robert Kagan (University of California, Berkeley), Wiktor Osiatynskyi (University of Warsaw), Joseph William Singer (Harvard Law School), and Werner Gephart (Heinrich-Heine-University, Düsseldorf).

G.S.A.
G.S.

INTRODUCTION: A FOURTH WAY?

Gregory S. Alexander
Grażyna Skąpska

Even before the collapse of Communism in Europe, many scholars and political commentators both in the East and the West had called for a "third way." This phrase had several quite different meanings for different groups and in different places. For some, notably in communist Europe, it represented nothing more than a call to reform the communist system of centralized decision-making in ways sufficient to keep the system basically intact. Others used the term to express the romantic *Weltanschauung* of a utopian society characterized by face-to-face relations and small-scale economic enterprises. Yet another meaning is that of an economic system that combined the innovation and efficiency of market economics with socialism's ideals of fairness and the pursuit of social justice.

This last meaning is the one that has been especially appealing to progressives in the West. Nevertheless, critics, especially those from East-Central Europe, have argued that "market socialism," too, lapses into utopianism. As Ralf Dahrendorf, responding to western Progressives who associate the "third way" with Sweden, has stated:

> "Sweden" is not Sweden; it is a dream with no basis anywhere on the map of Europe. What is more, we must thank our lucky stars that there is no "Sweden" in the real world. . . . The real Sweden, fortunately, is a free country . . . with much of the untidiness and multifariousness, disorderliness and heterogeneity, conflict and changeability which allow the blossoming of human life chances, and of humans with them.[1]

Critics from former communist countries have pointed out that the actual experience under "third way" experiments in the past has been inefficiency and injustice. They argue that market socialist reforms such as those implemented in the former Yugoslavia during the 1960s resulted in economic inefficiency because they combined worker self-governance with bureaucratic control. These critics also emphasize their own past experiences when under the name of social justice, millions of economically active individuals, stigmatized as "bourgeois" or "kulaks," were exterminated. All of these experiences have led them to stress the axiological dimension of human action, particularly freedom of choice and individual responsibility. At the same time, though, they have also recognized the importance of democratic political control over economic reform.

We adopted the unfamiliar term "a fourth way" as the title to this book in an effort to avoid undesirable historical baggage that references to a "third way" carry for many people, particularly those in the postcommunist world. Several of the American authors in the volume continue to use the term, "a third way." In the context of the United States, that term has not taken on the same meaning that it has for Europeans.

The term, "a fourth way," is also intended to indicate that the proposals for particular legal and economic institutions that are offered by several of the authors in this book are more concrete and less utopian than are many discussions about a "third way." Its advocates reject state ownership as the primary form of property and economic relations, but look past the forms of liberal ownership and economic institutions that currently dominate in the West. Its guiding conviction is that neither the market nor state planning is adequate, in economic or moral terms, as the exclusive means to regulate the economy. Instead, as Fred Block has stated, "The fantasy of one royal road to rational decision-making must give way to recognition of the need for constant adjustment and adaptation to find effective ways to make choices."[2]

Where the third way (as it has been used in Europe) often laid down unrealistic goals, the notion of a fourth way must be more hardheaded. To be plausible at all, it must confront realities, recognize limitations, and offer concrete proposals that work within these realities and limitations. More to the point, it must acknowledge and learn from the experience of those who have actually lived under the statist regimes of the former Soviet bloc.

The essays in this volume constitute a dialogue about the prospects of a fourth way. As the essays indicate, the authors by no means share the same understanding of what the fourth way involves in all respects. While some understand it to mean an economic and legal system that seeks to democratize property relations while explicitly rejecting state socialism, others see it as merely democratizing the process of transforming centrally planned economies.

I. The Challenge of Post-Communist Privatization: Spontaneity versus Institutionalization

The challenges facing privatization in the postcommunist nations are of an unprecedented scale. The citizens of the new democracies expect privatization to eliminate the public immorality that Communism generated,[3] the selfishness of living at the expense of the future,[4] the problem of the "free-rider" syndrome, and questions of the legitimacy of the emerging property rights and relations. At the same time, they look to the state as both the agent of transformation in establishing the legal framework of change and as an ongoing participant in the social welfare.

In the economic context of the postcommunist transformations, privatization means the shift from a centrally governed and state-owned economy to a system based on the spontaneous interactions between autonomous private participants. But to define privatization so narrowly would be to ignore the magnitude of the transformations. Alexander Yakovlev, a Russian lawyer, likens the restructuring of the postcommunist societies to the destruction of a huge, unified, state factory built on Lenin's political ideals. Transformation requires not only the destruction of the state's monopoly of administrative machinery, but, more importantly, of the Communist party's monopoly of every sector of society.[5] In this sense, privatization means not merely the technical restructuring of property rights and property relations in order to make the economy more efficient, but the razing and rebuilding of the entire political process into institutions which permit and encourage public participation. Privatization, therefore, is understood both as an end and as a means of democracy.

A. The Moral Dimension of the Transformation

The most important context in which the emerging order in East-Central Europe is shaped is the moral dimension of social activity. Shifting political and moral responsibility to the individual has been an important theme of reform movements in East-Central Europe. The antidogmatic morality of human actions governed by individual rights and dignity informed the slogans of the Citizens' Forum, *Solidarność,* and the Civic Rights movements. For Václav Havel, such a morality stands in opposition to the self-momentum of the system, the "blind, unconscious, irresponsible, uncontrollable, and unchecked momentum that is no longer the work of the people, but which drags people along with it and therefore manipulates them."[6] For those who believe in the creation of a "civic morality," the moral character of change depends on conditions of full citizenship, with guarantees for individual autonomy in the decision-making process, and autonomy in the formation of interests that will foster responsible participation in public life. It further means repudiating the hubris of all monopolistic power structures that assume that all who disagree with their programs suffer from "false consciousness."[7]

B. The Systemic Dimension of the Transformation

The transformation from a state-command society to a market/democratic society has a second dimension as well. This is what might be called the systemic dimension of privatization. One of the most prominent characteristics of the modern world is the widespread resistance to the "system": bureaucracies, technologies, and other institutions that represent rational, impersonal, and often centralized power, of order imposed "from above."

After decades of official praise for government intervention and a scientifically rational system that imposed the ideal of progress through bureaucratic control over all aspects of life, the people of postcommunist countries are discovering the benefits of individual liberty and reliance on spontaneity. The same phenomenon can be seen in the West, although not as obviously. The growing environmental movement, the increased use of popular referenda, land invasions by impoverished "informals" and other aspects of the thriving informal economy in Latin American countries[8]—all of these developments reflect dissatisfaction with bureaucratic "apparatus[es] operating autonomously, over [people's] heads."[9]

Frustration with an often-reified "system" has led some to advocate a revival of laissez-faire ideas—deregulation, minimalist government, and individual self-reliance. In the context of the modern world, however, the vision of individual liberty based on unrestricted laissez-faire, deregulation, spontaneity, and resistance to the technological rationality of the "system" has a utopian character. First, there is the question of distinguishing the spontaneous (and technically illegal) activities of the poor from the spontaneous and unscrupulous activities of the rich and powerful. General rules limited to the protection of all modes of spontaneous activity in the modern, deeply differentiated world may eliminate those who do not have the power to participate. Second, there are limits to what an individual, acting alone, may accomplish in a world in which freedom of choice is intertwined with the desire for stable markets, foreign trade, and unprofitable activities such as education, research, and art. Consequently, a systemic dimension to the transformation will inevitably be called to both set the limits of individual liberty and adopt measures that maximize the ability of individuals to act within them. The tension between the desire for individual liberation from oppressive, top-down governance and the need for complex institutions can be reconciled through institutions that encourage individual expression and that protect a plurality of privatization paths while permitting democratic control over complex political, economic, and social processes of transformation.

II. The Fourth Way and the Paths of Privatization

The most important task faced by the postcommunist countries is the development of institutional structures that connect the moral dimension with the systemic one. A fourth way must therefore address not only the subjective, spontaneous, and individual aspects of economic and political life, but also the complex and organized—the "systemic" side of the transformation. Privatization is the most immediate nexus between these two dimensions.

The transformation of property rights and property relations is the critical aspect of the entire process of transformation. The form that property rights take will greatly influence the character of the societies that emerge from the process of privatization.

A. Contingency in Economic and Legal Transformation

> Contingency may provoke more anxiety in its failure to specify an outcome, but it surely embodies more hope in the power granted to people over their own futures. We are not pawns in a great chess game played by inexorable natural (and social) laws, but effective rooks, knights, bishops, kings and queens on a revolving board of alterable history with no set outcome.
>
> Stephen Jay Gould[10]

The first step is to recognize that the commitment to private ownership still leaves the actual results of the transformation highly contingent. Residents of the postcommunist countries of Eastern and Central Europe have an opportunity, virtually unprecedented, to create forms of property ownership that are both private and pluralistic. They are not confined to the nineteenth-century models of laissez-faire capitalism and state socialism, the "first" and "second" ways. Indeed, even before the revolutions of 1989, changes throughout the world had made these models anachronistic and largely irrelevant. In the communist world, dictatorship had made the democratic promise of socialism a cruel mockery. In the free world, many varieties of capitalism emerged (for instance, the Reaganite/Thatcherite capitalism of the U.S. and Britain, the MITI capitalism of Japan, the central bank capitalism of Germany), with their differences being nearly as important as their common characteristics.[11] The question is which capitalism, which market economy, which private property relations the postcommunist world wants.[12]

B. The Transformation: Evolutionary or Nonevolutionary?

It is crucial that policy-makers explicitly acknowledge that they are making deliberate choices among a wide array of options that can fairly be labelled private and market-oriented. This means repudiating the nineteenth-century doctrine of purely evolutionary social and economic change. There has been a tendency recently for some commentators to lapse into determinist evolutionary theories of history when discussing what role the state should play in transforming state-command economies to market economies. Echoing Hayek's critique of "constructivist" solutions to economic problems,[13] these commentators urge the citizens of East-Central Europe not to delegate the primary responsibility for privatizing the economy to state agencies. Even so distinguished an economist as Janòs Kornai, for example, has argued that relying on central authorities to privatize the economy, as Germany has done throughout the government *Treuhandanstalt* agency, simply extends the very *etatism* that privatization is intended to abandon.[14] This path to privatization, he contends, is self-defeating. The appropriate means to creating a private economy, he argues, is:

> an evolutionary process that selects among the institutions and organizations which emerge, causing the ones that are dysfunctional under the prevailing circumstances to wither away, and choosing as survivors the ones truly fit for their task.[15]

This argument overlooks the fact that several highly dynamic capitalist societies got that way not through the market's natural selection but as the result of central government policies that aggressively promoted capitalist enterprises (France is perhaps the clearest example). Examples of procapitalist government policies include subsidies for favored ventures or industries, and coordination of major investment decisions through central agencies. Related to this objection, the state is one of the many organizational actors doing the selecting, so it can hardly be said to be uninvolved or neutral.

Law in particular is one of the primary instruments through which the state acts to select particular institutions and types of economic organization. The rise of the modern corporation in the U.S., for example, could not have occurred without active encouragement by courts and legislatures.[16] As one American economist has stated, "There can be no neutral framework for competition to decide [which type of market economy emerges from the transformation]. Instead it must be answered by law and policy."[17] These choices must be made deliberately, and with a clear idea about what values are most important to the society. The initial choices, though not invariably dictating the future, will make change much more difficult. Political and economic interests that benefit from the initial choices will oppose change. Moreover, the initial choices may produce unanticipated and undesirable consequences that will seriously restrict the degree of flexibility that future governments have to adjust their policies and programs. An ill-considered decision to pursue a given policy today seriously risks popular backlash that prevents the government from implementing more sensible programs tomorrow.[18]

On the other hand, purely "constructivist" methods of economic transformation seriously threaten democracy, the openness of change, and individual freedom. The risk that political elites or powerful interest groups will subvert the formation of grass roots mechanisms of change in the interest of furthering their own agendas. This is precisely why fourth-way theorists, in addition to contending that economic and legal transformation is contingent and non-deterministic, stress the moral dimension of the transformation and the need for normative structures of transformation. It is no coincidence that the transformation process in East-Central Europe was begun through negotiation, round table agreements, and other open dialogic methods. These methods served as models for the future legal instruments of economic reform.

C. Multiple Forms of Private Property Ownership

Just as there is an array of different forms of market economy, so private ownership of property can take multiple forms. It is a great mistake to assume private ownership of property has just one meaning, the classical liberal idea of unlimited and absolute freedom by individuals to use, enjoy, or transfer their property as they wish, or that the general commitment to a market form of economic organization necessitates this form of property rights. The classical liberal form of individual ownership has probably never existed anywhere in the world at any time. It certainly does not exist today in the U.S., although its ideology still retains considerable force there.

To pick one important example, most investment capital in the U.S. is not controlled by individuals. Rather, it is controlled by large financial institutions, such as pension funds and insurance companies, which manage it on behalf of thousands of individual beneficiaries. Moreover, there are many forms of what might be called quasi-group ownership in which restrictions are imposed on individual owners to prevent them from using or transferring their assets in ways that would jeopardize the interests of other co-owners. These forms of co-ownership range from employee stock ownership plans (ESOPs), to producer cooperatives, to limited equity housing cooperatives, to partnerships.[19] All of these examples of co-ownership are private ownership institutions, despite the fact that they obviously deviate from classical liberal ownership.

The postcommunist world, then, has a historically unprecedented opportunity to create new market modes of economic organization and new forms of private ownership of property that avoid the weaknesses of both state socialism and corporate capitalism. The way to capitalize on this opportunity is to create legal and economic institutions that are designed to minimize three problems in particular: antidemocratic processes of decision-making, paternalism and passivity, and political and economic domination or exclusion based on race, religion, ethnic identity, or gender.

D. Three Goals of a Fourth-Way Form of Privatization

The first goal of a fourth-way version of economic transformation is genuinely democratic processes of decision-making. If the reinstitution of the market in the place of the command economy is to benefit the entire populations of the new democracies, and not just the already privileged classes, it must be accompanied by political freedom and truly democratic processes. Mario Vargas Llosa, in discussing the emergence of informal free markets in the Third World, points out that, whereas interventionism tends to perpetuate the corrupt and inefficient institutions of the past,[20] political freedom ensures the "evaluation, perfection, or rectification of any measure which does not work in practice."[21] The alternative form of economic transformation must be posed in the form of an open social order based primarily on responsibility for one's actions instead of government protection, on individual innovation instead of bureaucratic control, and on the critical evaluation of potentialities based on the knowledge and needs of individual actors instead of the administrative planning of social and economic policies.

The fourth way does not confine democratic decision-making to the political sphere. Fourth-way institutions strive to ensure that policy decisions regarding investment of private capital, labor-management relations, and other basic issues that directly affect the material conditions of people's lives are arrived at as democratically as possible. Far from being incompatible, economic transformation can in fact facilitate participatory property relations and encourage, through active participation, civic responsibility. The relationship between privatization, participation, and responsibility depends, as some observers have recognized, on what forms private property relations concretely take. The decisional structures of both the America-style corporation and the Communist party-government command structure centralized control over basic economic decision as much as possible. This was obvious in the case of communist agencies, of course, but it is true to some extent in the case of the American corporation, although there is a great difference of degree. Policy-makers in American corporations are, in theory, subject to diffused control through the so-called market for corporate control. If shareholders are unhappy with the direction in which corporate officers have taken the firm, they can initiate a hostile takeover and replace the decision-makers.

Theory and reality, however, here as elsewhere, rapidly part company. First, there are significant practical and legal constraints on the opportunities for disgruntled shareholders successfully to complete a hostile takeover. Second, the experience of hostile takeovers in the U.S. over the past decade suggests that their effects may be more socially harmful than beneficial. Third, gaining access to decisional authority is restricted to shareholders, leaving other groups, including employees and local communities, effectively powerless. These groups are often affected by corporate decisions as much, or more, as are shareholders.

There are, of course, sound practical reasons why the scope of democratization of control over the workplace or over pooled capital should not be unlimited. To the extent that decisional authority is diffused among a large number of individuals having diverse and often conflicting values, the familiar problems with collective action (high transaction costs, free riders, and so on) loom large. Moreover, overdemocratization would eliminate specialization and division of labor. Some degree of job specialization is essential to economic efficiency, although in a collaborative and cooperative form rather than in the traditional form of rigid hierarchies.[22] The important part, though, is that, in principle, confining democratic values to the sphere of politics is based on a false categorical dichotomy between the public world of politics and the private world of work and capital. The two spheres are interdependent. For one—politics—to be made and remain truly democratic, the other—work and capital—cannot be treated as totally separate.

Related to democratization is a second goal of fourth-way institutions: forms of private ownership in which individuals are as active in control of their assets as is feasible. Under "really existing socialism," society was the nominal owner of the means of production. In reality, the state-party apparatus left society powerless to affect the material conditions of life, prohibiting individual ownership of the means of production, nationalizing agricultural land, prohibiting or severely restricting private ownership of homes, and changing the legal structure of cooperatives in a way that practically nationalized their decision-making processes.

It is important not to recreate this regime of paternalism and passivity, either through state ownership or through certain private modes of ownership. A dominant characteristic of institutional ownership of investment capital in the U.S. today is passivity. Passivity exists at two levels. At the macrolevel, the institution investors that own investment capital, such as pensions, mutual funds, and life insurance companies, have little control over the policies of the firms in which they invest capital. At the microlevel, the beneficiaries of these institutional funds themselves have virtually no control over the funds to which they have contributed through deferred wages. Moreover, some institutions for pooling capital are also characterized by a high degree of paternalism toward beneficial owners.

State-owned assets and enterprises can be privatized in a way that confers not only beneficial ownership interests to individuals but also the power to control the material conditions of their lives. This form of privatization more fully realizes the classical liberal vision of individual autonomy than does a form of privatization that leaves individuals solely in the passive status as recipients of benefits, with no ability to influence how the capital that they have supplied is used. For example, capital fund owners should be able to determine whether their capital is invested with the exclusive objective of maximizing the economic return or for broader, noneconomic objectives (for instance, decreasing unemployment in a particular region or industry, decreasing pollution, or other social objectives).

It is not sufficient, then, merely to restore a regime of private property rights. The reintroduction of property rights must be accompanied by an extension of democratic control if the transformation is to cope successfully with the core problem of power. The question, as Fred Block has stated, is "not capitalism or socialism, but how a society can create economic institutions that give maximum scope to democratic participation."[23] At the same time, learning from the East-Central Europeans' experiences with worker self-governance, we also emphasize that the great challenge that the new democracies face consists precisely in developing institutional structures that simultaneously enable democratic control (at least of the processes of privatization) and rational conflict resolution that is necessary for economic activity.

A third goal of the fourth way is to avoid illegitimate forms of exclusion and economic and social domination based on gender and racial, religious, or ethnic identity. This means not simply that laws prohibiting discrimination in employment, housing, and other key sectors be enacted but that the free market not be used as a mechanism for perpetrating economic domination and exclusion. One example of this goal is the vulnerable status of women in privatizing economies. To the extent that privatization means terminating government-provided child care and other parental benefits, it will reinforce the economic subordination of working mothers, who, as American experience has shown, will be unlikely to afford private child care. Growing nationalism and ethnic hatred pose more visible threats to the fourth-way transformation. The most intense hostility is directed at the cheap labor force migrating from the East (from the former Soviet Union and Romania to Poland, Hungary, and Germany). Citizens in countries receiving large numbers of emigrants from the East worry about the threat of higher taxes due to extending welfare benefits to migrating workers. This anxiety has already produced mass demonstrations and even violent attacks on foreigners. It is absolutely crucial to the fourth-way transformation that this revival of nationalism, ethnicism, and xenophobia be staunched. These forces currently constitute the greatest threat to democratic political and economic transformation of post-communist Europe.

Europe's generally homogenous character in the past by and large immunized it from this problem. As population shifts make Europe more ethnically mixed, however, exclusion of minority groups will become an increasingly vexing problem for the new democracies. Privatization of public housing could lead to ethnically segregated residential patterns that confine minorities to the inferior housing stock. Of course, the same problem can occur through government action if popular majorities use their control of the political process to enact exclusionary land-use measures, such as the exclusionary zoning that is practiced in some parts of the U.S. The issue cannot be reduced to the simple choice between free markets or government control, then, but at a minimum it would be naive, if not irresponsible, to assume that in an unregulated market that is ethnically or racially diverse, price alone will be the basis for allocative decisions. At the same time, though, populist control over privatization processes may lead to anti-democratic, anti-liberal exclusion of "strangers" and "others" from participating in the transformation. Moreover, democracy and freedom could all-too-easily be replaced by dictatorship if ideologies based on hatred toward differentiated scapegoats underlay a vision of a segmented society.

Realizing these three goals requires that policy-makers explicitly articulate participation, democratic control, and social inclusion as values that motivate their choices of institutional forms of property relations. It is not sufficient merely to announce that they are pursuing the values of a market economy, for the market concept is too vague, and permits people to read into it a wide range of conflicting values. Nor is it sufficient to announce that the new political order is pursuing the goal of economic efficiency. There are many paths to efficiency, and not all of them require that participation, democracy, and inclusion be sacrificed. The new democracies were formed as the result of popular movements in which participation, democracy, and inclusion were dominant characteristics. The processes of privatization and democratization are not categorically distinct from each other, but are in fact closely intertwined. The same values that animated the turn to democracy are as relevant to the task of privatization. The point can be made more strongly: it is only through a privatized economy whose institutions are participatory, democratically governed, and socially inclusive that the ideal of democracy in the political sphere can be truly realized.

The essays that follow explore these and related themes. Our goal has been to reach a wide audience, including readers from both the West and postcommunist Europe. The authors and the topics discussed reflect our view that the whole subject of privatization, particularly its effects in the new democracies of East-Central Europe, must be addressed from an interdisciplinary perspective. To that end, this book includes essays by scholars in law, economics, management, and sociology.

The essays in Part I focus on legal aspects of the transition from state ownership to a private property regime. Thomas Raiser and Stanisław Biernat discuss the legal structures of the transformation from state ownership of enterprises to private ownership in the former East Germany and Poland, respectively. Turning to what forms private ownership of investment capital will take after the transformation, Gregory Alexander's essay considers whether institutional ownership and its attendant regulatory culture, along the lines of American private pensions, is an appropriate model for the postcommunist countries to follow.

Part II addresses specifically economic aspects of the transformation to a market economy. Edgar Feige and Andrzej Wojtyna both discuss the problem of the appropriate sequence of changes necessary to transform socialist economies to market economies. Wojtyna focuses on the sequencing problem in Poland's transformation to a market economy, while Feige discusses the sequencing dilemma with respect to Russia's changes. Clayton Gillette turns to the problem of what economists call public goods, such as national defense, clean air, and similarly nonexclusive goods. His paper analyzes whether the market or the government more efficiently provides this type of good.

The essays in Part III discuss several aspects of the social dimension of the shift to a privatized economy. Lena Kolarska-Bobińska's paper, which draws on several opinion polls conducted by the Polish Center for Public Opinion Research, of which she is the Director, discusses shifts in popular attitudes toward privatization in Poland since 1988. Krystyna Daniel's paper reports the results of empirical research she has conducted among Polish farmers since the fall of Communism.

On a more theoretical level are papers by Maria Borucka-Arctowa and Grażyna Skąpska. Borucka-Arctowa analyzes the problem of the social consciousness that more than four decades of Communism has shaped as an impediment to privatization. Skąpska argues that the most important lesson to be learned from the peaceful revolutions throughout East-Central Europe is that economic transformation is closely related to the deeper transformation in the societies' entire normative structures. That relationship has important consequences for choosing among competing strategies of privatization.

The papers by Dariusz Chelmiński, Andrzej A. Czynczyk, and Henryk Sterniczuk, and by András Sajó discuss how new forms of state ownership have been reintroduced in Poland and Hungary, respectively, as the results of aspects of the transformation processes in those two countries. Both papers, Sajó's especially, are somewhat pessimistic about the genuineness of economic change that has occurred to date in postcommunist Europe.

Finally, drawing on a wide variety of reports concerning the effects of privatization throughout Eastern and Central Europe, Joan Williams argues that privatization disadvantages women disproportionately by withdrawing state-supported child care and other parental benefits. She relates this emerging phenomenon to the situation that already exists in the United States, where children and working women disproportionately fall below the poverty line.

Part IV includes four programmatic statements about how a fourth-way (or as some of the authors refer to it, third-way) alternative might be implemented. Duncan Kennedy's first contribution is to describe the broad outlines of a fourth-way approach to privatization in the housing sector. Along with Leopold Specht, he then elaborates on that model in his second essay by detailing the terms of a concrete proposal that he and Specht made to transform state-owned multiunit housing in a particular district in Budapest into private cooperatives. In a paper that strongly complements Kennedy's, Karl Klare discusses how law can contribute to what he calls a postliberal reconstruction of democracy. The conception of democracy that he advocates illustrates the fourth-way theory's emphasis on extending the ideal of participation beyond the sphere of politics, narrowly defined. Also complementing both Kennedy's and Klare's papers is an essay by William Simon describing and defending a model of private property that is alternative to classical liberal ownership. He terms this model "social-republican" property, and he illustrates how that model already exists in various sectors of the American economy.

Our greatest hope is that these essays will indicate how much American and East-Central European scholars and policy-makers have to learn from each other. That message strongly emerged from our meeting in Amsterdam, and it suggests the urgent need to find ways of maintaining an open dialogue between East and West.

Notes

1. Ralf Dahrendorf, "Reflections on the Revolution in Europe," in *A Letter Intended to Have Been Sent to a Gentleman in Warsaw* (London: Chatto and Windus, 1990), pp. 2, 3.
2. Fred Block, *Postindustrial Possibilities: A Critique of Economic Discourse* (Berkeley: University of California Press, 1990), p. 198.
3. "Those who live in command economies have become aware that it generates immoral behavior." John Clark and Aaron Wildavsky, *The Moral Collapse of Communism* (San Francisco: Institute for Contemporary Studies, 1990), p. 330.
4. "For years the population was bribed with money that, under normal circumstances, would have had to be invested in new technology, research and development, energy-saving schemes—in ways and means of increasing productivity and the quality . . . of goods—but instead went to pay our modest social security. We lived, as is frequently and properly pointed out, at the expense of the future."

   Václav Havel, *Summer Meditations on Politics, Morality and Civility in a Time of Transition* (London: Faber and Faber, 1992), p. 64.
5. Alexander M. Yakovlev, "Transforming the Soviet Union into a Rule of Law Democracy: A Report from the Front Lines," *The Record of the Association of The Bar of the City of New York* 46: 129 (1991).
6. Id. at 166. For Adam Michnik, a prominent member of the Polish democratic opposition, transformation begins when the members of society begin to regard themselves as the subjects rather than objects of institutions, government, and history. Adam Michnik, *Letters from Prison and Other Essays* (Berkeley: University of California Press, 1985), pp. 58, 135.

7. "[The command economy] is an extreme expression of the hubris of modern man, who thinks that he understands the world completely—that he is at the apex of creation and therefore competent to run the whole world."
   Id. at 62.
8. See Hernando de Soto, *The Other Path,* trans. June Abbott (New York: Harper & Row, 1989).
9. Jürgen Habermas, *The Theory of Communicative Action,* Vol. 2: *Lifeworld and System: A Critique of Functionalist Reason,* trans. Thomas McCarthy (Boston: Beacon Press, 1987), p. 307.
10. Stephen Jay Gould, "Life in a Punctuation," *Natural History* (October 1992), p. 21.
11. Several mainstream American economists have similarly emphasized the significant differences that exist among the world's capitalist economies. See, e.g., Lester Thurow, "Communitarian vs. Individualistic Capitalism," *The Responsive community: Rights and Responsibilities* 2: 24 (1992) (contrasting Germany's "social market" economy with the United States's "market" economy); Robert Cooter, "Organization as Property: Economic Analysis of Property Law Applied to Privatization," unpublished paper delivered at a conference on "Transition to a Market Economy," Prague, Czechoslovakia, March 1991 (contrasting Japanese, German, and American models of capitalist corporate organizations).
12. For a careful discussion of the multiple possible forms of privatization in Central Europe (focusing on Hungary), see David Stark, "Privatization in Hungary: From Plan to Market or From Plan to Clan?" *East European Politics and Societies* 4: 351 (1990).
13. See Friedrich A. Hayek, *The Constitution of Liberty* (Chicago: University of Chicago Press, 1960).
14. Janòs Kornai, "The Principles of Privatization in Eastern Europe," unpublished paper delivered at the Tinbergen Lecture to the Royal Netherlands Economic Association, October 19, 1990.
15. Id. at 14 (citing works by Joseph Schumpeter and Armen Alchian).
16. See Morton Horwitz, *The Transformation of American Law, 1870–1960: The Crisis of Legal Orthodoxy* (New York: Oxford University Press, 1992); Martin J. Sklar, *The Corporate Reconstruction of American Capitalism, 1890–1916* (Cambridge: Cambridge University Press, 1988).
17. Cooter, supra note 11, at 36.
18. Stephen Cohen, a political scientist at Princeton University, recently expressed this fear in arguing against the "shock therapy" privatization strategy for Russia. Speaking on American television, Cohen stated, "[I see the shock therapy strategy as n]ot only threatening [progress toward democracy in the former Soviet Union], but condemning it to failure and not only in my lifetime but in the lifetime of my children." Remarks by Stephen Cohen, "Hard Times," *The McNeil/Lehrer NewsHour,* November 10, 1992, transcript no. 4495.

19. See William H. Simon, "Social-Republican Property," *UCLA Law Review* 38: 1335 (1991).

20. "The concept of liberty, in all its senses, has never been seriously applied in our countries. Only now, in the most unexpected way, through the spontaneous actions of the poor, is it beginning to gain ground, showing itself to be a more sensible and effective solution than any undertaken by our conservatives and progressives as ways of overcoming underdevelopment. Extremists of both persuasions, despite their ideological differences, agree to the strengthening of the state and its interventionist practices, which does nothing but perpetuate the system of corruption, incompetence, and nepotism that is the recurring nightmare of the entire Third World."

    Mario Vargas Llosa, "Foreword" to Hernando de Soto, *The Other Path*, p. xviii.

21. Ibid.

22. On collaborative and cooperative specialization, see Michael J. Piore & Charles F. Sabel, *The Second Industrial Divide: Possibilities for Prosperity* (New York: Basic Books, 1984).

23. Fred Block, supra note 2, p. 194.

I

The Transition to Private Property—Legal Perspectives

The Challenge of Privatization in the Former East Germany: Reconciling the Conflict between Individual Rights and Social Needs

Thomas Raiser

[*Editors' Synopsis:* The *Treuhandanstalt,* the government agency in charge of privatizing enterprises from the former East Germany, has faced several problems in fulfilling its role. The primary problems are unqualified management and employees; disagreement over how to privatize (restore to previous owners or sell to new investors); and a continuing debate over the exact role of the *Treuhandanstalt.* Nevertheless, new rules have facilitated the process and resulted in great progress in privatization in the former East Germany.]

Caught between the conflicting needs to provide housing and promote economic recovery on the one hand, and to restore the individual's right to property on the other, the unified Germany is confronted with some hard choices. The country must decide whether to keep inefficient businesses going, and how to recognize the ownership rights of those whose property was taken by the former regime. The urgency of the country's needs, combined with the process of trial and error, determines how Germany seeks to resolve the tension between individual rights and the need for social and economic recovery. The strategies the country has adopted for privatization reflect a pragmatic interpretation of Germany's constitutionally espoused theory of property.

This article seeks to demonstrate how Germany has attempted to overcome the many problems of privatization and restoration of ownership to those whose property was expropriated by the previous regime. The first part outlines the general plan for the transformation of the former East Germany to a West German market economy, and the fundamental role of the *Treuhandanstalt.* The second part describes various problems the *Treuhandanstalt* initially encountered under the privatization plan. The third part examines attempts to modify privatization efforts in light of those problems. The fourth part concludes that so far German privatization, in the hands of the *Treuhandanstalt,* has been a considerable success.

I. An Ambitious Plan for Transformation

Already under heavy pressure from West Germany to privatize, East Germany's last socialist government adopted the first transformation laws in March, 1990.[1] These laws ruled that collective combines (*Volkseigene Kombinate*) and VEBs (*Volkseigene Betriebe,* state-owned enterprises) adopt the legal form of either a public or a private company. They further established the *Treuhandanstalt,* a government-controlled public trust created to administer the shares of the new companies. Originally, the *Treuhandanstalt* was authorized, but not required, to sell shares to private investors. It could also restore ownership, but only to the former owners of small businesses that had existed under the legal form of single-owner enterprises or partnerships prior to expropriation. In general, the creation of the *Treuhandanstalt* was intended to privatize firms in form but not in substance. The *Treuhandanstalt* was the legal agency that administered state-owned firms that had merely changed to a private legal form. Genuine, fundamental reforms were not possible until after the first free elections of March 18, 1990.

The methods and the speed of economic transformation, previously much disputed for their political ramifications, were decided in June of 1990 when East and West Germany signed the first unification treaty.[2] This treaty set July 2, 1990 as the date for the monetary and economic union of the two Germanies, and imposed the West German legal system on East Germany. The German Democratic Republic ("G.D.R.") expressly agreed to abolish all laws and provisions of its own constitution relating to its former social and political system that were contrary to the treaty.[3] The treaty states:

> The basis of the economic union shall be the social market economy . . . to ensure the rights laid down in . . . this treaty, the [two countries] shall especially guarantee freedom of contract, freedom to exercise a trade, freedom of movement of Germans in the entire currency area, freedom to form associations to safeguard and enhance working conditions, and . . . ownership of land and means of production by private investors.[4]

The treaty did not, of course, mean that the East German economy had suddenly been privatized; it only imposed on the state administration the huge obligation to privatize. The government passed a law converting collective combines into public companies (*Aktiengesellschaften*) and all VEBs into limited liability companies (*Gesellschaften mit beschränkter Haftung*).[5] The law confirmed that the *Treuhandanstalt* should manage all shares of the new public companies. Because the public companies held the shares of the limited liability companies, the *Treuhandanstalt* indirectly administered the limited liability companies as well. The policy, however, was completely different.

The policy justification for the *Treuhandanstalt* was fundamentally changed from its former role. Upon unification, the *Treuhandanstalt*'s primary mandate became the sale of property to private investors. The law also contains other provisions to ensure privatization. For example, the agency must "facilitate the disentanglement and reorganization of those enterprises which stand a chance of competing in the market economy,"[6] make land available for profitable use, and contribute the proceeds of sales to the state budget. The *Treuhandanstalt* owns at least one million parcels of land and thirty thousand companies, including small enterprises and partnerships.[7] Considering its magnitude, such an accumulation could be highly dangerous without strong state and public control. A limitation on the government's acquisition of property protects against backsliding into socialism; only under certain exceptional circumstances may the *Treuhandanstalt* convey real estate or shares it holds to states, counties, or municipalities.

The privatization of the huge number of properties held by the *Treuhandanstalt* is an immense task. Seeking to completely privatize the firms as quickly as possible, the *Treuhandanstalt* has been continually expanded, and now employs several thousand people. Although it legally exists in the form of an independent administrative agency under the supervision of the German Minister of Finance, most of the *Treuhandanstalt*'s activities are in substance entrepreneurial. Recruitment of personnel is generally from private industry. The *Treuhandanstalt* delegates to subagencies many responsibilities; for example, the management of small firms, the sale of real estate, the privatization of farms, and the administration of large firms which must be restructured before they can be sold. These subsidiaries exist in the legal form of public and private companies.

The *Treuhandanstalt* itself is not bound to act as an entirely private or entirely public institution. In the capacity of share owner, the *Treuhandanstalt* follows the rules of private law; in the capacity of governmental agency it follows the rules of public administrative law. Often, what rule should apply to a given cause is a highly controversial matter. Some scholars have argued that the *Treuhandanstalt* should be treated as the parent company of a giant corporate group.[8] But because this would have had serious consequences for liability and judicial review, the law was amended explicitly to prohibit parent-subsidiary relations between the *Treuhandanstalt* and its companies.[9]

II. Initial Problems of the Transformation

A. Management of State-owned Enterprises and Combines: Privatization in Substance

The privatization of VEBs (state-owned enterprises) and collective combines is one of the most legally and economically complicated procedures. The law requires the newly formed companies to incorporate themselves;

to promulgate corporate by-laws; to add the words "in formation" to the company name; to reappoint former directors or elect new ones; to calculate "balance sheets" of their assets and debts; and to adapt themselves to the new economic conditions. In order to ensure that no company entered the new market economy with an unfair advantage, the *Treuhandanstalt* required firms to count dubiously granted "compensatory payments" of the former regime as debts owed to the state on their balance sheets.[10]

State-owned enterprises were inefficient and ill prepared to hold their own in a competitive market economy because of personnel and economic problems. Similar problems plagued agricultural production.[11] The decision to reduce the number of employees was a hard one for companies to make and the decision whether to reappoint former directors was no easier. Often the directors were either former communist officials the *Treuhandanstalt* wished to avoid, or they were incapable of managing under the new economic conditions.[12] Managing under these conditions was no easy task. Where a company managed to formulate a balance sheet, the new calculations of value frequently resulted in the company's having to file for bankruptcy, in accordance with the law, but this was an economically and socially unacceptable consequence of privatization. Acknowledging that a firm's opening balance sheet might not indicate its economic potential, the *Treuhandanstalt* included the effects of a possible reorganization in an evaluation of the firm's possible future viability and profitability. These extensive evaluations required a considerable amount of time, and before they were completed a firm could not go bankrupt. Interim continuation of firms avoided unreasonably high levels of unemployment and forced the *Treuhandanstalt* to procure loans to keep the firms running. Because loans were simply not justifiable for firms that clearly stood no chance of survival, the law authorized the *Treuhandanstalt* to make the painful decision to force such firms to shut down by refusing to approve credit.[13]

The fact that the law required the *Treuhandanstalt* to break up most state-owned enterprises into separate companies provided an additional hitch in the creation of new private companies. The combines urgently needed such reforms; in a market economy, different autonomous companies would likely produce the wide variety of goods manufactured by a combine. The enormous task of dividing and reorganizing the combines extended far beyond redistribution of assets, management and workers. The *Treuhandanstalt* was also confronted with the substantial problem of deciding which companies should be saddled with liability for the former combine's debts. Existing applicable laws lacked procedures for dealing with such unexpected problems. The process was made even more difficult and complicated when the government decided to restore ownership of as many of the firms as possible to their former owners.

B. The Great Dilemma: Restoration of Ownership or Sale to New Investors?

In the wake of the swift German unification a very significant question was initially left open: who should be able to own the property expropriated by the former regime, and under what conditions? An intense political controversy centered on how to prioritize the conflicting interests of former owners who wanted their property back and new investors who promised to rehabilitate businesses. Former owners and their heirs appealed to the principles ingrained in the property laws of the former West Germany in their claims that the socialist government had violated a fundamental human right to property by expropriating their property without adequate (or any) compensation.

Since its foundation in 1949, the Federal Republic of Germany ("F.R.G.") has sought to build a liberal state which strongly protects the right of individuals to own land and means of production. Article 14 of the German Federal Constitution establishes private ownership and the right to succession. Furthermore, the protection of private property plays an eminent role in German constitutional law; in fact the Federal Constitutional Court has frequently declared that property is not just a vehicle for obtaining wealth but a guarantee of personal liberty from public authority.[14]

Restoring ownership of expropriated property posed several problems, however. Many former owners were more likely to liquidate or exploit a business for its immediate value than to strive for its continued success. Others lacked the ability and expertise to make the company profitable. In either case, restoration would destroy the company's remaining productive power and would not generate state revenues, since former owners would not pay for the reacquisition of their property. Furthermore, if the government was going to restore property, it was not clear which period of expropriation it would use as a cutoff. During the war, and even the prewar period of Fascism, property had already been expropriated. Postwar expropriation in the G.D.R. occurred in several phases. In the first phase, 1945 to 1949, the occupying Soviet military government ordered the confiscation of all assets belonging to the National Socialist state and Hitler's National Socialist party, as well as property belonging to party organizations and leaders. The Soviets also forced the East German government to expropriate without compensation all farms larger than one hundred hectares and turn them into farming cooperatives, and to take all natural resources, mines, utilities, banks, and insurance companies, sometimes granting compensation, but at far less than market value. Later, the State confiscated the property of all those who had fled the G.D.R., often by appointing a trustee who would then sell the property to a third party. In the case of smaller businesses which were still privately owned, the State initially imposed itself as a limited partner, then, from 1972 on, forced out the remaining private associates.[15]

The shock of economic unification and the need for a rapid recovery urged a policy favoring new investments instead of restoring ownership. Selling the properties to new investors, it was argued, might salvage firms, secure existing jobs, create new ones, and generate sorely needed revenues for the state. As a condition of purchase, potential buyers could be required to submit and implement a reorganization and development plan that included their proposed financial investment.

Despite good arguments favoring new investment, the policy of restoring expropriated property to former owners or their heirs won out over a policy of new investment for two reasons. First, the legislature decided to recognize the legitimacy of the claims of former owners, and a policy favoring new investment would have deprived this group of their claims to ownership. Second, under a policy favoring new investment, the only ones with the capital to buy the enterprises would have been wealthy West German and foreign companies. As a result, East German citizens with legitimate claims to ownership would be enriching the Westerners at the expense of losing opportunities for themselves.

The initial laws of privatization, in the period leading up to unification, sought to undo only the post-1972 expropriations. In the negotiations for unification the mixed conservative-liberal government under Chancellor Kohl strongly favored a policy of restoration. Labor unions, the Social-Democrat party, and the government of the still existing G.D.R. all opposed restoration of ownership. However, with the West German government in a stronger negotiating position, the two countries agreed in June 1990 to prioritize restoration over sale in the privatization of all property expropriated by the government. Excepted from the agreement was all property seized between 1945 and 1949 under the direction of the Soviet military government, a concession which served to secure the Soviet Union's agreement to German unification. The Soviets were reluctant to reopen the potentially embarrassing postwar events and had threatened to block the unification process. The agreement restricted the former owner's right to restoration only in cases where it might jeopardize greater interests of public welfare, including the progress of the economic recovery.

The two countries codified this agreement in the Unification Treaty[16] but the exemption from restoration of property confiscated before 1949 under the Soviet military government stirred feelings of resentment among former owners of such property. These owners felt abandoned and were unwilling to accept the threat of a Soviet veto as an excuse for their having been left out of the process. The intensity of sentiment was understandable considering that often those who had had their property confiscated under the Soviet rule had suffered great hardships. The Soviets had often expropriated property by arbitrarily killing owners or expelling them from their inherited lands. However, Germany's highest court has ruled that the exemption was constitutional.[17]

The treaty provision was implemented by the *Vermögensgesetz*,[18] which specified when properties may be exempted from restoration. The policy on land and buildings, which the *Vermögensgesetz* distinguished from businesses or shares in them, was fairly straightforward. In principle, it gave priority to reversion to the former owner, but excluded land and buildings when:

(1) a third person had purchased the land in good faith;
(2) considerable investment since expropriation had changed the purpose or use of the property;
(3) the property had been dedicated to public use;
(4) the property is now part of a public housing project; or
(5) the property was now part of a commercial enterprise which reversion would severely impair.

The *Vermögensgesetz* also provided that former owners receive financial compensation where a request was denied or the owner simply preferred compensation to ownership. The German government currently must confront a dilemma over how to calculate such compensation. It is not yet clear what strategy the government will follow. The enormous financial burden privatization has placed on the federal budget has threatened the nation's economic stability, and the government may have no alternative but to keep compensation rates low. If compensation is significantly less than market value, rational owners who have no interest in using the land for themselves or in continuing the enterprise will wait for the market to improve, thus increasing the value of their property before selling it to new investors. A tax on those who choose restoration in kind would be unlikely to absorb the higher, actual value of the property. Already there is speculative trading in reversion rights; there are businesses that will buy the rights now in order to resell them at a profit in the future. Speculation of this sort prevents property rights from being quickly consolidated into the hands of definite owners who will invest in their properties. While politicians in Bonn are currently preparing a law on the subject, there appear to be no easy solutions to the problem.

The winter of 1991 saw renewed debate over the issue of restoration. Social democrats, labor unions, the *Treuhandanstalt*, and even many independent scholars advocated substituting reversion with a policy of granting former owners financial compensation only, the goal being to rebuild the economy and protect jobs by making real property and enterprises available to investors. The debate over reversion of enterprises and shares resurfaced for the third time beginning in March 1991. It was finally resolved in two lengthy amendments to the *Vermögensgesetz* of March 1991 and July 1992. Despite these laws, debate still continues over reversion. The continuation of this controversy demonstrates how dramatic and profound the problem is for the German economy.[19]

The debate must be understood in light of the economic and social conditions resulting from German unification, the uncertainties of ownership, and the different procedural and substantive problems posed by restoration. Unemployment was extremely high, and the economic recovery was occurring much more slowly than hoped. The population began to raise political objections to the program of economic reform.

From the beginning, restoration was a concept with questionable potential. First, as noted above, incapable or unwilling former owners (or their heirs) would likely jeopardize investment by speculating with their assets. Second, restoration would potentially split firms into their preexpropriation parts instead of efficiently restructuring them to meet present technical and economic demands (a situation that would arise each time a former owner's preexpropriation property constituted only a part of a VEB or combine formed after expropriation). Third, restoration could harm businesses whenever multiple former owners sought restoration but one or more would not cooperate in running the current business or simply preferred compensation to owning shares. In the latter case, because the *Treuhandanstalt* retained ownership of the shares after granting compensation, the agency theoretically would become a partner in the company with the other owners.

Restoration of property also posed significant problems of procedure. About 1.3 million claims to approximately 2.6 million properties, mostly real estate, have so far been registered. The total number of claims for farms may add up to between ten thousand and twenty thousand, but the exact number is unknown.[20] To handle these claims the *Vermögensgesetz* established 216 administrative boards (*Vermögensamter*) and six superior circuit boards (*Landesvermögensamter*).[21] More than 2,350 people have been assigned to staff these boards. There has been a severe delay in resolving the large number of claims caused by administrative and court procedures. A variety of factors are responsible for this delay, particularly at the level of the administrative boards hearing the claims. First, former ownership is a difficult thing to prove, the identities of former owners often having been stricken from public record. Second, the administrative boards were inexperienced; they had only existed since 1990 and were still being organized. Third, the boards were understaffed with personnel who were often unqualified. Fourth, the number of claims created an administrative backlog which effectively ensured there could be no quick resolution of any claim. Even greater delay was created by a rule providing for the appeal of all administrative decisions to the courts, a process which could easily take several years.

Because judicial rationale is based on former legal principles instead of economic needs, many believed that the *Vermögensgesetz*'s emphasis on principles of legality and judicial supervision was incurring overburdensome economic consequences.

Priority given to restoration and the unresolved questions of ownership were not the only things impeding privatization and the economic development of the former East German territory. Certainly, many outsiders must have balked at investing in the scant and quite uncertain economic prospects of many businesses. In addition, legal snags often made it difficult to buy and efficiently operate a business, or even to buy property at all. For example, despite the fact that Eastern firms employed an average of three times as many workers as their Western counterparts, German labor laws require the buyer of an enterprise to continue to employ the firm's entire work force (the change in ownership itself not being sufficient justification for laying off employees).[22] Because this law stems from a binding directive of the European Community, Germany could not suspend its application in the new state. Another legal snag was the fact that the local government usually laid claim to the property. It was not always clear whether a local government had a claim to a given property or whether it belonged to the *Treuhandanstalt,* with the obligation to privatize it. The legal resolution of such controversies is both burdensome and time consuming.

C. *No Priority for the Public Interest?*

The extent to which public institutions should be allowed to acquire private property and actively participate in the economy is a hotly contested issue, even in countries with traditionally capitalist economies. The decision to follow the West German model provided little guidance in cases where government entities of the former East German republic sought to continue or reclaim their rights of private economic activities. By the end of 1990, the *Treuhandanstalt* had received approximately fourteen thousand requests from local governments for property, mostly real estate. When the request regarded a specific public function or use, such as requests for town halls or public swimming pools, the *Treuhandanstalt* conveyed the property without encountering problems. The German legislature passed a law vesting communities with the right to acquire enterprises and real estate necessary for local government, including local transit systems, utilities, savings and loans, and waste disposal.[23] Municipalities could even acquire apartment houses formerly held by the state. While local governments also set their sights on commercial and industrial properties, the *Treuhandanstalt* generally did not grant such requests.

Public need for land and buildings is also protected by recent law on investment, the *Investitionsvorranggesetz.*[24] This law permits new investors to purchase real property for "particular purposes of investment," even when the former owner seeks to regain the property. The law defines such purposes as those serving urgent needs; for example, those which would create or secure jobs, alleviate the housing crisis, or rebuild Eastern Germany's decaying infrastructure. In most cases the *Treuhandanstalt* determines whether a potential investor may be granted the use of property for a particular purpose. Initially, all rejections of claims for restoration were subject to the judicial review of the administrative courts, a provision that was restricted in the March 1991 Amendments.

Serious public needs were less apt to be addressed in the privatization of businesses. As opposed to the restrictions on restoration of real property favoring common use and economic recovery, the first version of the *Vermögensgesetz* contained no comparable provisions for businesses. The *Treuhandanstalt* rejected former owners' claims for restoration only when the character of the enterprise was now entirely different from at the time of its expropriation. The law left the *Treuhandanstalt* with little opportunity to prefer promising investors to former owners. It was soon clear that restoration constituted a severe obstacle to the economic recovery of the F.R.G.'s new Eastern states.

III. Fine-tuning the System to Stimulate New Investment: The Amendments of March 1991

Given these many problems, one might question the wisdom of adopting restoration as a priority in the Spring of 1990. However, a switch to a system which generally excluded restoration would have been fraught with problems. Politically, this alternative strategy worried those who had a claim to a restoration under the Unification treaty, and the majority of the Federal Parliament opposed such a switch. As a practical matter, the possibility of a switch raised the difficult legal question of whether the former owners should be compensated if the government now took away the right to restoration the Unification Treaty had granted to them. If so, it was argued, the extremely high number of claims for compensation would overload the state's capacity to pay. Also, abandoning the priority of restoration would be a great departure from enlightened social policy. After all, economic recovery does not depend on all real estate and business ventures having new investors. There are other good reasons to return property interests to former owners. From the point of view of economic recovery, restoration is a suitable and satisfactory solution whenever former owners are able and willing to take over an enterprise and evidence indicates they will run it successfully. It was not surprising, therefore, that political forces favoring a switch to exclude restoration did not succeed in changing the government's policy favoring restoration.

Still, it was clear that the *Vermögensgesetz* needed reforming to stimulate new investments. In March 1991, the government amended the law, both by increasing the state's discretion to withhold certain specified property interests from former owners, and by reducing administrative and judicial constraints on the privatization process.[25] Specifically, the amended law authorized the *Treuhandanstalt* to bypass former owners of certain properties when it deemed new investment *proper,* not necessary, to secure or create jobs, or to improve the competitiveness of the enterprise. For example, the agency can now sell an enterprise to new investors if the former owner cannot guarantee that they will manage the business successfully. Furthermore, to reduce the number of bureaucratic snags, the amended law also freed the *Treuhandanstalt* from having to rely on recorded claims for reversion. The amendments reflect a compromise between the desires to protect private property and to advance public interests.

These new rules herald potential progress in three areas. First, the standards by which the *Treuhandanstalt* may prefer new investors to former owners have been redefined in a more open and flexible way and are consequently easier to meet. Second, the decisions to return ownership to former owners or to place property in the hands of new investors are concentrated in a single institution. This institution, the *Treuhandanstalt,* is now administratively competent and has substantial economic expertise. Third, the amendments reduce the interference and delay caused by judicial review: the law requires that the claims of former owners be heard *before* the *Treuhandanstalt* renders its decision. When former owners present a credible investment plan, they remain entitled to become interim owners of an enterprise. But if the government denies an owner's claim for restoration, the owner may only request compensation. If the property has been sold to a new investor, the owner may request the full amount the buyer paid. The *Treuhandanstalt,* through the administrative boards, will also deny the owner restitution if the property was sold to a third party after its expropriation in good faith, though the former owner may still sue the person who sold the property for compensation.

The amended law facilitates the process of privatization without being unfair to former owners, who have the chance to regain possession of their property and are ensured due process of law. If a decision is made against a former owner, he or she may still challenge the *Treuhandanstalt* in the administrative courts; however, the suit will not prevent the agency from transferring the property to the new investor. Usually, the administrative court's decision will be too late to stop the *Treuhandanstalt*'s interim sale of the property or to bring about its return, and the former owner may prefer simply to accept financial compensation rather than pursue the suit. In this case, the dispute shifts to the question of what amount is due the former owner, not whether he or she may prevent the new investor from acquiring title to the property. Thus, judicial decisions will no longer have any impact on either the functioning of enterprises or the economy as a whole.

Conclusion: The Success of the *Treuhandanstalt*

Privatization in former East Germany is an impressive example of a law responding to social forces, evolving out of a society's values and economic needs and taking on a definite shape through the process of trial and error. In application, both the *Vermögensgesetz* and the *Investitionsvorranggesetz* may now prove to be satisfactory legal acts. The German Constitutional Court is expected to hold that the duties of these institutions are compatible with the fundamental right to private property.

In light of the challenges it has confronted, the *Treuhandanstalt* must be regarded as an extraordinary success. By April 1992, more than twelve thousand out of the total fifteen thousand small businesses in Eastern Germany—shops, pharmacies, restaurants, hotels, and so on—had either been returned to their former owners or sold.[26] The sale of almost seven thousand large companies has secured more than 1.1 million jobs and the proceeds have contributed DM 19.8 billion (approximately $13 billion) to the German treasury. In addition, investments in purchased firms total roughly DM 130 billion (approximately $76 billion).[27] Foreign investors bought 248 firms, management and employees bought 894 firms, bankruptcy or liquidation proceedings terminated 856 enterprises, and former owners regained possession of 527 firms.[28] While the numbers of privatized firms have grown rapidly, so far only one company has been able to introduce its shares on the German stock exchange.

In the area of agriculture and forestry, private parties have bought 8,894 hectares (almost 22,000 acres) for a total of $238 million. In addition, the *Treuhandanstalt* has leased out 26,200 hectares (roughly 64,500 acres).[29]

An evaluation of the *Treuhandanstalt*'s initial success must not overlook the fact that buyers were more likely to purchase the most promising, competitive firms first. The enterprises that remain in the hands of the *Treuhandanstalt* increasingly are those that are too weak to be sold, forcing the agency to salvage and maintain them instead. Usually, this requires a major restructuring, drastic reduction of employees and substantial financial support.

Frequently, political pressure is brought to bear on the *Treuhandanstalt* to maintain an enterprise at taxpayers' expense, even though it realistically stands no chance of survival. The *Treuhandanstalt* resists such pressures as much as it can, but compromises between economic objectives and political pressures are inevitable. Well-known examples of such compromises are Zeiss AG, the world-famous producer of optical instruments in Jena (the company was taken over by the West German company of the same name but is still partly owned by the state of Thüringen) and the East German shipbuilding industry at the Baltic Sea.

The process of privatization in Eastern Germany can reasonably be completed within a few years.[30] The *Treuhandanstalt* has stood the test of privatization well. While the popular mood in the former East Germany is currently not very positive, problems relating to property are not the only reason. Unification is an extremely complicated process. Certainly neither the *Treuhandanstalt* nor any other state program can quickly resolve the problems that result from differences in private wealth between Eastern and Western Germans. But the privatization process should stimulate an economic recovery that will give Easterners an equal opportunity with Western Germans to earn high incomes. On the whole, then, the *Treuhandanstalt* serves as an effective model for other nations coping with similar problems of privatization.

Notes

1. The most important were the Gesetz über den Verkauf volkseigener Gebäude vom 7.3.1990 [Law on the Sale of State-owned Real Estate and Buildings of March 7, 1990], *Gesetzblatt* DDR I Nr. 18 S. 137 (G.D.R.); Gesetz über die Übertragung volkseigener landwirtschaftlicher Nutzflächen in das Eigentum von landwirtschaftlichen Produktionsgenossenschaften vom 6.3.1990 [Law Concerning the Transfer of State-owned Farmland in the Ownership of Private Producer Cooperatives of March 6, 1990], *Gesetzblatt* DDR I Nr. 17 S. 135 (G.D.R.); Gesetz über die Gründung und Tätigkeit privater Unternehmen und über Unternehmensbeteiligungen vom 7.3.1990 [Law Concerning the Foundation and Activities of Private Enterprises of March 7, 1990], *Gesetzblatt* DDR I Nr. 17 S. 141 (G.D.R.); and Verordnung zur Umwandlung von volkseigenen Kombinaten, Betrieben und Einrichtungen in Kapitalgesellschaften vom 1.3.1990 [Regulation Concerning the Transformation of State-owned Enterprises and Combines into Profit Corporations], *Gesetzblatt* DDR I Nr. 14 S. 107 (G.D.R.).
2. Vertrag über Schaffung einer Währungs-, Wirtschafts- und Sozialunion zwischen der Bundesrepublik Deutschland und der Deutschen Demokratischen Republik vom 18. Mai 1990 [Federal Republic of Germany—German Democratic Republic: Treaty Establishing a Monetary, Economic and Social Union of May 18, 1990], 1990 *Bundesgesetzblatt* [BGBl] II 537 (F.R.G.). Semiofficial translation by the Department of Foreign Affairs of the Federal Republic, reprinted in 29 I.L.M. 1108 (1990).
3. Id., Art. II(2).
4. Id., Art. I, II (1).
5. Gesetz zur Privatisierung und Reorganisation des volkseigenen Vermögens vom 17 Juni 1990, [Law Concerning the Privatization and Reorganization of State-

owned Property of June 17, 1990] *Treuhandesetz, Gesetzblatt* DDR I Nr. 33 S. 100 (G.D.R.). This act gave the agency the authority under East German law to dispose of state property.

6. Id., §§ 1 I, 2 I *Treuhandgesetz.*
7. This figure takes into account the requirement that VEBs and combines be broken up into separate, independent companies.
8. Norbert Horn, *Das Zivil- und Wirtschaftsrecht im Neuen Bundesgebiet,* p. 329 (1991); Robert Wiemar and Bruno Bartscher, "Treuhandanstalt und Konzernrecht," *Zeitschrift für Wirtschaftsrecht und Insolvenzpraxis,* p. 69 (1991).
9. Gesetz zur Änderung des Vermögensgesetz und anderer Vorschriften (Zweites Vermögensrechtsänderungsgesetz) 14 Juli 1992 [Second Amendment to the Law Concerning the Regulation of Open Questions of Property of July 14, 1992], Art. 11 § 5, 1992 BGBl I 1257 (F.R.G.).
10. Gesetz über die Eroffnungsbilanz in Deutscher Mark und die Kapitalfestsetzung vom 31.8.1990 [Law Concerning the Initial Balance in DM and Capital Arrangement of August 31, 1990], Anlage II Kapitel 3 zum Einigungsvertrag (DM-Bilanzgesetz) § 25, 1990 BGBl II 889 (F.R.G.). A number of companies had profited during the breakdown of the socialist economy by receiving compensatory payments which they now claimed as assets.
11. Under the former regime the Central Commission charged with all manufacturing and distributions decisions was heavily influenced by the Socialist party and tended to put political considerations over economic reasoning. VEBs and combines had the solitary goal of implementing the Central Commission's plan. Because the VEBs and combines were not independent units pursuing their own interests or acting at their own risk, they had no incentive to turn a profit or even the need to make realistic or reliable cost calculations. Often, raw materials and primary products were insufficient to meet the objectives of the plan; the ultimate goal of the VEBs and combines inevitably became their own existence. In addition, centralized distribution left consumers with no choice but to accept the only product available, making the marketing of goods unnecessary.
12. The *Treuhandanstalt* must find approximately eight thousand board chairpersons, thirty two thousand corporate directors, and hundreds of thousands of managers. Marc Fisher, "The Grinding Gears of Reunification," *Washington Post,* March 10, 1991, p. H1.
13. *DM-Bilanzgesetz* § 24, supra note 10.
14. The 1949 Constitution of the F.R.G. permits the government to expropriate property only when it is necessary for the public welfare and done with full compensation. While the Constitution explicitly authorizes the nationalization of land, natural resources and means of production (provided full compensation is given), this particularly constitutional provision has never been used.
15. Wilhelm Hebing, "Enteignung und Rückerwerb von DDR-Vermögen [Expropriation and Repurchase of Property in the GDR]," 16 *Betriebsberater,* (Supplement 21, 1990). Horn, supra note 8, at 157.

16. Art. 41 of the August 31, 1990 Unification Treaty, BGBL II 12889 (1990).

17. A group of people who had had their properties confiscated under Soviet rule brought suit against the F.R.G. in the Constitutional Courts. After a trial that was thick with emotional tension, the High Court dismissed the action on April 23, 1991. The Court held that the law did not violate the constitutional right to private property by failing to include properties confiscated before 1949 because the West German Constitution was not adopted until 1949. The Court gave several reasons for its holding. First, the Court explained that German unification did not mean that the Federal Republic had assumed responsibility for all socialist laws and actions of the S.E.D. (Sozialistische Einheitspartei Deutschlands—the German Communist party) or even the Soviet military government. Second, the Court maintained that, even if a natural right to private property exists above positive law, such a right mandates only compensation for property taken, not reversion in ownership. Finally, the Court pointed out that owners who had had their property confiscated before 1949 were not the only group to suffer irreversible injury at the hands of the Soviets or the S.E.D.-regime. Others had been imprisoned, had suffered damage to their health, and had seen their careers interrupted. The Court held that these former owners were entitled to no more than compensation for the loss of their property. Judgement of April 23, 1991, Entscheidungen des Bundesverfassungsgerichts, BVerfGE 84, 90 (F.R.G.).

18. Gesetz zur Regelung offener Vermögensfragen vom 3 Oktober 1990 [Law Concerning the Regulation of Open Questions of Property of October 3, 1990] 1990 BGBl 1159 (F.R.G.)

19. Gesetz zur Beseitigung von Hemmnissen bei der Privatisierung von Unternehmen und zur Förderung von Investitionen of 22 Marz, 1991 [Law Concerning the Elimination of Obstacles to Privatization of Firms and toward the Promotion of Capital Investment of March 22, 1991], 1991 BGBl I 766 (F.R.G.); Gesetz zur Anderung des Vermögensgesetzes und anderer Vorschriften vom 14 Juli 1991 [Law Concerning Modification of Property Laws and Other Regulations of July 14, 1992], 1992 BGBl I 1257 (F.R.G.).

20. *Frankfurter Allgemeine Zeitung,* March 23, 1992, p. 1.

21. Gesetz zur Regelung offener Vermögensfragen vom 3 Oktober 1990 [Law Concerning the Regulation of Open Questions of Property of October 3, 1990] BGBl II at 1159 (1990).

22. Civil Code, art. 613(a) (F.R.G.).

23. Kommunalvermögensgesetz vom 6 Juli 1990 [Law Concerning Municipal Assets of July 6, 1990], Gesetzblatt DDR I Nr. 42 S. 660 (G.D.R.).

24. Gesetz über den Vorrang für Investitionen bei Rückübertragungsansprüchen nach dem Vermögensgesetz [Law Regarding the Priority of Investment Over Claims for Restoration], 1992 BGBl I 1268 (F.R.G.).

25. Vermögensgesetz, Neue § 3a, 1991 BGBl I 766 (F.R.G.).

26. 9 Finanznachrichten des Bundesministers der Finanzen (January 27, 1992) p. 3.

27. *Frankfurter Allgemeine Zeitung* (May 8, 1992) p. 15.
28. 9 Finanznachrichten des Bundesministers der Finanzen (January 27, 1992) p. 3.
29. Ibid.
30. The president of the *Treuhandanstalt*, Birgit Breuel, has estimated that it will be possible to complete privatization of companies by the end of 1993. Supra note 28.

The Uneasy Breach with Socialized Ownership: Legal Aspects of Privatization of State-owned Enterprises in Poland

Stanisław Biernat

[*Editors' Synopsis:* The 1990 Polish Law on the Privatization of State-Owned Enterprises provides the legal framework for Poland's massive transformation from a command economy to a market economy based on private ownership of the means of production. Poland's privatization efforts have occurred because the Western capitalist ideas mix with social and economic remnants of the old system.]

Introduction

This paper discusses legal aspects of the privatization of state-owned enterprises. While many other property transformations are taking place in Poland currently, including privatization of state agricultural enterprises, of public utilities, and of property owned by cooperatives, by far the most important type of economic entity in Poland today is the state-owned enterprise. The privatization of these entities is crucial to the success of Poland's economic transformation to a market economy.

The first part of this paper discusses the organizational and legal environment of the Polish economy. The aim of this part is to map out the conditions within which the privatization process is taking place. The second part briefly describes the Polish Law on the Privatization of State-Owned Enterprises of 1990 (the LPSOE). The third part evaluates recent experience with privatization of state-owned enterprises and examines some general social problems connected with it.

I. The Origin and Organizational Structures of the National Economy

A. Postwar Nationalization of the Polish Economy

Immediately after World War II, the Polish government envisioned an economy consisting of enterprises that varied with respect to ownership structures: state-owned enterprises, cooperatives, and private businesses. However, the Communists, after stamping out the opposition, made the state economy dominant, following the Soviet example. Cooperatives lost their independence, and with respect to management, they became similar to bureaucratic state-owned enterprises. Private businesses were restricted by a new requirement to obtain business licenses and by a tough tax policy. The government had planned ultimately to eliminate them in accordance with the official political line of the Communist party. The forced industrialization of Poland in the early 1950s extended mainly to state-owned enterprises, which shortly became the dominant type of economic entities.

In 1946, the Law on the Nationalization of Industry[1] nationalized former German enterprises without compensation, while other mines and industrial enterprises as well as transportation and telecommunications were nationalized with partial compensation. The government set compensation levels quite low. Practically speaking, compensation was paid only to foreigners, not to Polish citizens, even though they were legally entitled to it. Most small private enterprises were not covered by the nationalization law, although towards the end of the forties, many small private enterprises were nationalized or taken over under the so-called mandatory governmental management, contrary to the nationalization law. The fact that some enterprises were taken over by the government against the law is important in the aftermath of Communism's demise because the former owners of these enterprises, or their legal successors, have a greater chance of recovery in the process of partial reprivatization.[2] The influence of the Soviet model—or, more specifically, the Stalinist political and economic system—was evident in the 1952 Constitution of the Polish People's Republic.[3] Subsequent amendments of the Constitution did not change either its character or the main features of the economic system. The Constitution was written in an imprecise language, more characteristic of the rhetoric of propaganda speeches than the language of legislation. Because of its general character, the Constitution legitimated the centrally planned economy and rigid planning, as well as minor reforms that only slightly moved toward a market-oriented economy.

The main features of the Constitution's economic provisions were as follows:

(1) *Socialization of the means of production:* The basis of all economic activity was supposed to be government-owned means of production, cooperatives, and other social organizations. The private economy was to be small and insignificant.
(2) *Central planning:* The entire economy was supposed to be conducted on the basis of central plans (annual and long-term ones). Directive guidelines of the plans became more specific at lower levels, including the plans of individual enterprises.

(3) *Active government role in the economy:* The socialist state "controlled the development of productive forces and the state's economy and strengthened the social ownership of the means of production"[4]
(4) *The Communist party dominant:* The Constitution provided that the party was "the leading political force in society on the road to Socialism."[5] Since the Constitution did not state in what way exactly the party was to fulfill this function, the party practically could interfere directly or indirectly with the national economy without any responsibility for the consequences of its commands. The most important means of influencing the state's political and economic systems was through recommendations of the *nomenklatura,* Communists who held executive posts.
(5) *Governmental monopoly of foreign trade:* Until the 1980s, bureaucratic state corporations had the exclusive right to conduct foreign trade.
(6) *Social and economic rights of citizens:* The Polish Constitution, similarly to constitutions of other communist countries, formulated an extensive catalogue of citizens' social and economic rights, including the right to employment, the right to the protection of health, and the right to education. Yet these rights were effectively meaningless since citizens had no right to sue for deprivations of their constitutional rights.

Beginning in the early 1980s, the government attempted to reform the Polish economy, as it became clear that the existing economic system was totally inefficient. In 1988, the Law on the Economic Activity[6] liberalized the laws permitting private persons and organizations to undertake and conduct economic activities. This statute also proclaimed a principle of equality of all economic entities as the binding legal norm, regardless of the form of property represented by them. The statute considerably stimulated private economic activity. About one and half a million new private firms have been created since its enactment.

The real turning point in the Polish economy began with amendments to the Constitution in December 1989.[7] They were introduced following the first partially free parliamentary elections and the creation of the first non-communist government in Poland. The effect of the amendments was to abolish all the aspects of a socialist economic system. In their place, the Constitution introduced the principles of economic freedom of all economic entities, equality of economic entities regardless of the form of ownership, and equal rights to the protection of property.

B. The Present Organization of the Polish Economy

The Polish economy currently is an amalgam of both socialist principles and recent transformations. State-owned enterprises continue to have a considerable significance, largely because of their economic potential, property value, number of employees, and other economic factors. In some branches of Polish economy, especially housing, trade, services, and small business, cooperatives have considerable significance. In reality, however, these organizations had very little in common with genuine cooperatives until very recently. In the centrally planned economy the legal and economic situation of cooperatives did not differ very much from the position of state-owned enterprises. The cooperatives remained under close supervision of the state, as well as of the bureaucratic central cooperative unions which were abolished in 1990. Presently, cooperatives are going through a crisis. Many of them are unable to face newly competitive economic conditions. In the near future privatization of their property will become more problematic, similar to the problem of privatization of state-owned enterprises.

Legal forms of private economic activity are currently varied. They include single-person enterprises, partnerships of physical persons, limited liability companies, or joint-stock companies. The private sector no longer plays a marginal role. Almost forty percent of the work force is employed in the private sector, while in some branches, such as trade or services or small businesses, private businesses dominate state-owned entities. Partnerships and companies exist not only in the private sector, but also in state-owned enterprises and cooperatives. An uncertain amount of business is done by the so-called "*nomenklatura*" partnerships, that is, partnerships set up by former executives of the Communist party or public administration who used their positions, contacts and access to information to start their own private business operations. Late in the 1980s, those executives took advantage of the liberalization of disposals of state-owned property to seize some assets belonging to state-owned enterprises and to create their own partnerships or companies. Erstwhile *nomenklatura* executives also sometimes preserved managerial positions in companies created by the state-owned enterprises with other entities, for example, in Polish-foreign joint ventures.

Until the mid-1970s, Polish law virtually ruled out the possibility of foreign enterprises conducting economic activities in Poland. In the 1980s, the possibility of foreign investment in Poland was recognized and gradually broadened.[8] Foreign investors may form limited liability companies or joint-stock companies, either by themselves or with Polish partners, on the basis of the 1991 Law of Joint-Venture Companies with Foreign Participation.[9] Contrary to former regulations, the present law generally does not require permission for creating such joint ventures from administrative agencies. Permission is required only when a Polish joint venture intends to operate in industries that are important for the national interest, or when the property of Polish state-owned enterprises is involved in such a company. Currently, over six thousand joint-venture companies are registered in Poland, but only about one thousand of them actually carry out business operations.[10]

C. *The Current Legal Status of State-owned Enterprises*

The current legal basis of state enterprises was created by two 1981 laws, the Law of State-Owned Enterprises, with amendments, and the Law of the Employees' Self-Government in State-Owned Enterprises.[11] This legislation was motivated by the desire to introduce some degree of independence of enterprises from the government and to broaden workers' participation in the management of enterprises. The reforms were nicknamed the "Three S's": for self-management, self-determination and self-financing (*samodzielność, samorządnośc, samofinansowanie*). State-owned enterprises are created by state administrative agencies called "founding organs." The organs supervise the enterprises' activities. The decision to divide a state-owned enterprise or to merge it with another one has to be made by the founding organ, with the consent of the employees' council. The enterprise may be liquidated only in circumstances strictly defined by the statute, one of which is privatization. The statutory principle of independence of state-owned enterprises means that decisions concerning enterprises are reached, as a rule, only by its organs. Interference by other governmental agencies requires special legal grounds. Enterprises sometimes abuse their independence in the disposal of their property and make inefficient economic decisions.

There are two employee self-government units of state-owned enterprises: the general meeting of employees, and a democratically elected employees' council. The organs of employee self-government take part in the decision-making process, pass opinions, initiate new undertakings, and inspect the functioning of the enterprise. Recently, the wide range of authority that the workers' self-government units exercise has aroused doubts. The self-government units have often abused their authority in order to defend the workers' immediate needs and to block initiatives aimed at raising the enterprises' economic effectiveness.

The government supplies the enterprise with the necessary financial means and equipment for its activities upon its creation. A crucial question is, who controls the enterprise's assets. The legal answer to this question has been uncertain in the past. Initially, the superior administrative organs, not the enterprise itself, controlled the appropriation of the enterprise's assets. Later, the enterprises themselves were gradually empowered to dispose of their property. However, fixed assets belonging to the enterprises generally could not be resold to private entities. Presently, state-owned enterprises are sole owners of their property, and only they can dispose of it.[12] They are free to transfer their assets to whomever they wish, including partnerships or companies.[13]

II. The 1990 Law on Privatization of State-owned Enterprises

On July 13, 1990, the Polish Parliament (*sejm*) passed the Law on the Privatization of State-Owned Enterprises (LPSOE).[14] A characteristic feature of the law is its open character. This is indicated by the fact that the law envisions a variety of ways and means of achieving privatization. Figuratively speaking, the act gives the public many keys which may open various doors; experience will determine which options will succeed. The open character of privatization of state-owned enterprises is reflected in several aspects of the statute: the decision whether and which enterprises will be privatized;[15] privatization procedures;[16] the organizational and legal shape of economic units resulting from privatization; provisions encouraging workers' participation in managing the firm following privatization;[17] the possibility of universal participation of all citizens in the privatization, in the form of the so-called employees' shareholding; and involvement of foreign capital in the ownership transformations. The LPSOE creates two basic privatization procedures, each of which has several varieties. The first procedure, called "capital or indirect privatization," takes place in two stages. The first stage consists of transforming a state-owned enterprise into a company solely owned by the state treasury (a joint-stock or limited-liability company). The only changes made at this stage are the organizational form of economic activity and the legal basis of its organization and functioning. For example, there is no employees' self-government in the state treasury company. The second stage, which in principle occurs within two years after the enterprise's transformation into a company, involves distributing shares to the public through sale. Strictly speaking, privatization occurs only at this stage.

The other procedure is the so-called "liquidation or direct privatization." The founding organ decides about liquidation of the enterprise and then decides about the distribution of its assets. Asset distribution may involve a sale of the enterprise or its part, as well as incorporating the enterprise or its part in a partnership or company. Moreover, the firm may be leased, again either entirely or in part, to partnerships or companies created by the employees of the liquidated enterprise.

The law does not mention in which situations it is more suitable to privatize the enterprise under the first or second procedure. Recent experience suggests that indirect privatization is best suited to cases of large, thriving enterprises with assets having considerable value. Such enterprises should not lose part of their capital as a result of privatization, but should be able to preserve the integrity of their assets. The liquidation type of privatization, on the other hand, is more appropriate in the case of smaller enterprises, or those in poor financial condition, whose capital does not have substantial value, and which can be easily bought out or leased out in their entirety or parts.

State authorities play a dominant role in the privatization process. The most important state functions are the following:

(1) Every year, the *sejm* sets the basic directions of privatization and defines what should be done with property acquired in this process. Moreover, the Sejm may decide to pass resolutions concerning the issuing of the so-called "free privatization coupons."
(2) The Council of Ministers gives permission to privatize some enterprises which are particularly important to the national economy, and consents to gratuitous distribution of shares in the state treasury companies.
(3) The prime minister may decide to privatize state-owned enterprises in cases where the enterprise's organs refuse to consent to such a move. (This constitutes an exception to the rule that privatization should be taking place at the suggestion or with the approval of the employees of a given enterprise.)
(4) The newly created Ministry of Ownership Transformations is responsible, among other matters, for the transformation of state-owned enterprises into the state treasury companies and for the public distribution of state treasury company bonds.
(5) The founding organs make motions and pass opinions concerning the transformation of state-owned enterprises into state treasury companies, and make decisions concerning the liquidation of state enterprises prior to their privatization. They also distribute the assets of liquidated enterprises and choose the organizational forms of the enterprises' subsequent economic activities.

III. The Political and Social Context of Privatization

A. The State's Changing Role

In the former politico-socio-economic system in Poland, the government performed two entirely different functions: first, economic functions, meaning that the government was the organizer of economic activities and the owner of the means of production; and second, the political functions of exercising public power, meaning that the state represented and protected public interests against various dangers posed by economic activities, such as, for instance, hazards to the natural environment, to health, to public order, and so on.

The relationship between these two sorts of functions was quite peculiar. In practice, the government's economic function as organizer of economic life and owner of means of production dominated over its political function as the guardian of public interest. This is especially apparent in the context of neglect of the natural environment in Poland. The government's course was to devote greater financial resources to industrial investment at the expense of protection of the environment.

After privatization of state-owned enterprises, the economic and public functions will be clearly separated. The government should be able to concentrate on its role as protector of the public interest. On the other hand, the Polish economy will not be entirely in private hands. The state-owned sector will remain relatively large in Poland. Nevertheless, even that sector will have to be organized on different principles from now. Moreover, the government will be able to invest its capital in economic activities on the same principles as private entities.

The legal provisions related to privatization are often criticized on the ground that the government's role in the process is too extensive and that the process is extremely bureaucratic. Some commentators argue that the Polish model of privatization leaves too little room for individual freedom and for spontaneity of citizens and economic entities. While this objection seems justified, one should remember that the task is the privatization of *state-owned* property. Therefore, it is virtually unavoidable that governmental agencies control and supervise the whole process. Moreover, the vast scale of the project requires extensive organization that seems feasible only through government coordination.

B. *A New Way?*

Does privatization mean that Poland is entering (or rather, after forty years, returning to) the familiar ways of contemporary Western economies? Or does it represent a search for some new, original way between the communist economy and the free-market one?

Attempts to answer this fundamental question differ depending on what aspect of Polish privatization one considers. First of all, it must be said that Polish lawmakers did not intend to create any new organizational and legal forms of economic entities. The economic units replacing state-owned enterprises are corporations. With respect to the methods of creating a new ownership structure, however, it is less easy to answer the question. Privatization has occurred through several different methods simultaneously. Moreover, the process is still far from completion, and new, unconventional ways may still appear. A crucial distinction in methods by which enterprises have been privatized in Poland is that between so-called equivalent and nonequivalent (or partially equivalent) participation in privatization. So far, privatization has proceeded on the basis of equivalence, meaning sale of stock or the enterprise's assets (depending on the type of privatization, capital or liquidation) to buyers at an undiscounted market price. The benefit of this technique is that it identifies new owners and ensures effective company management as well, obviously, as providing the government with the revenue from the sale of enterprises. It is questionable whether true equivalence in privatization is attainable, given the problems with asset valuation and pricing of shares.

Another major problem confronting equivalence is the limited purchasing power of most Poles. There simply are not enough buyers at equivalent values in Poland. Foreign investors, of course, are more likely to be able to pay prices that reflect equivalent value, but their role in privatization so far has been marginal. Poland and other countries of Eastern Europe, as well as the countries emerging from the former Soviet Union, are in need of foreign capital, and they strongly compete among themselves in this respect. As yet, the quantity of foreign capital is small, although the legal conditions of investment are more beneficial than before. Recent experience indicates that a consistent implementation of privatization based on the principle of equivalence would be a very long process. Not surprisingly, then, equivalence has been highly controversial in Poland.

The situation is different with respect to nonequivalent or partially equivalent privatization, that is, when the price of privatized enterprises, or that of their shares, is not a decisive factor. Nonequivalent privatization is primarily used to reach noneconomic goals, such as change of social structure and creation of investment opportunities for the society at large. The aspect of nonequivalent privatization that has been most controversial in Poland concerns which of the two methods of nonequivalent privatization to adopt; employee stock ownership or general massive privatization.

The idea of employee stock ownership was promoted mostly during the discussions before the adoption of the LPSOE. Its basis was the conviction that employees had some special rights to possession of their enterprises. Therefore, advocates of employee stock ownership maintained that privatization should be realized either through the transformation of enterprises into companies, whose shareholders would be their employees, or through passing the enterprise's assets to the employees and granting them (or rather granting managers nominated by the employees) the right to operate the new economic entities.

The idea of employee ownership was rejected both by the majority of discussants before the LPSOE was adopted and finally by the *sejm*. The idea of selling shares of privatized enterprises exclusively to their employees on credit or at lower prices, as well as other forms of appropriation, seemed to constitute an unjustified privilege. It cannot be said, particularly in the circumstances of a former planned economy, that only the employees of a given enterprise contributed to its development. Besides, getting a job in a particular enterprise is often accidental, especially if we consider the low social mobility in Poland, caused chiefly by the shortage of housing. The most important factor weighing against employee stock ownership, however, was a pragmatic one: the conviction that employee management is inefficient under existing Polish conditions. This conviction was shaped by experiences in recent years with enterprise management through employee self-government.

On the other hand, it is doubtless true that employees constitute a category of people who are connected with private firms in a special way. The employees' attitude towards privatization creates an atmosphere that can determine the success or failure of the transformation. Polish lawmakers took this fact into account in ensuring certain benefits for employees. Thus, in the case of capital privatization, employees have the right to purchase up to twenty percent of shares issued by the company established after the privatization of their enterprise, at fifty percent discount.[18] However, in the case of liquidation privatization, the proof of that tendency of lawmakers to provide benefits as a means of securing success is the creation of employee partnerships or companies.

The greatest opportunity for unconventional approaches to privatization exists with respect to so-called general privatization, also known as massive privatization. The 1990 LPSOE[19] provides in Article 22 that the *sejm* may (but is not obligated to) distribute among all Polish citizens free or credited privatization coupons. However, so far the *sejm* has enacted no resolution to that effect. Apparently it agrees with economists who argue that privatization coupons would not be successful. The whole operation would be very expensive: it would require printing and issuing to citizens millions of coupons which would have to be finally redeemed. Critics also expressed their reservations that many people who are not aware of the rules of capital market operations would be unable to make conscious investment decisions, that is, to use the privatization coupons deliberately to buy the shares of selected companies. Resulting disappointment could destroy the social and psychological benefits of the whole project. The implausibility of privatization coupons does not close the door on general privatization, nor does it exclude a search for other methods to implement that idea. But there is simply no agreement on the subject at this point.

The very idea of general privatization has encountered strong opposition. Critics emphasize that the distribution of privatization coupons, or other securities representing rights to the privatized enterprise assets, will not produce the desired social effects, such as release of the "spirit of entrepreneurship," and thus will not contribute to the creation of a strong middle class, which Poland now lacks. That skepticism is based on the projection that many coupon owners would be indifferent to long-term investment, and instead would sell their rights as soon as possible to gain immediate benefits. The opponents of general privatization maintain that all hopes connected with the idea are ungrounded because the value of the property which could be designed for the needs of general privatization is too limited to become a significant part in the property of individual citizens.

Some of the proposals for implementing general privatization are very radical and unrealistic. Among these is Lech Wałęsa's idea to grant every Polish adult citizen a loan of about ten thousand to be paid off in twenty years. During the first ten years the loan would not bear interest, and after that period the annual interest would be ten percent, several times less than the current inflation rate in Poland. The loan could be used for the purchase of privatized assets of state-owned enterprises and communal enterprises, shares of state-owned corporations, or for some other investment purposes, as well as for the purchase of apartments. Economists generally agree that President Wałęsa's plan, at least under present circumstances, is unrealistic. In many cases the loans would not be fully paid at the end of twenty years, due to ineffective investments. In effect, then, it would be a subsidy which the country, with its substantial budget deficit, can hardly afford.[20] Moreover, issuing the credit coupons would unavoidably contribute to inflation. Privatization credit coupons would play the role of artificial money put on the market in great quantities.

The Ministry of Ownership Transformation's general privatization plan is quite different from President Wałęsa's proposal. It identifies around six hundred large and medium-sized state-owned enterprises to be changed into shareholding companies. Ten percent of the shares would be designated for employees and 30 percent would belong to the state treasury. Sixty percent of shares would be made available for twenty specially created National Investment Funds. The goal of these funds is to restructure former state-owned enterprises and to provide them with effective management. Professional firms, both Polish and international, selected by bidding, would manage the funds. All Polish adult citizens would have the right to obtain shares in National Investment Funds for a small fee. Such shares could be traded at the stock exchange.

The Ministry's plan is intended to ensure effective and professional management for the former state-owned enterprises, as well as to provide all adult Poles with a source of profit expected from the National Investment Fund shares.[21] What is characteristic here is the complete separation of the passive role of citizens from the active position of the National Investment Funds. Some commentators recognize this feature as an advantage, while others criticize this solution. On the one hand, the benefits of professional management by specialists, ensuring constant profit to citizens, is frequently emphasized. People are not interested in directly influencing the economic decisions that companies make. On the other hand, doubts are raised as to whether the management of a large number of companies by the National Investment Funds will be effective. There is also a real danger of the monopolization of the national economy. One can also argue whether the completely passive attitude of citizens will not destroy both the social and psychological benefits of the general privatization, such as the establishment of investment habits and making individual economic decisions. Returning to the question of whether any of the proposed methods represent an innovative approach to privatization, one can certainly say that there is nothing new or original about privatization based on the principle of equivalence. Additionally, the notion of involving employees in ownership or even management of privatized enterprises is a fairly conventional solution, intended to grant certain preferences to the people who are the most interested and affected by the privatization process.

Some aspects of Polish privatization, however, do represent significant departures from conventional methods of privatization. The high popularity of employee companies taking over the property of liquidated enterprises by leasing or buy-out, for example, creates a new economic and social situation. People act in two roles simultaneously in this situation, as both shareholders and employees of the same firm. This is especially true of companies created from smaller state-owned enterprises. The primary risk for this method of privatization is that the liquidated enterprises are often in a poor financial situation, which in turn constitutes a bad start for the employee companies' activities.

The proposals for general privatization, covering potentially all adult citizens, also involve innovative solutions to privatization. They can be considered as new methods of changing ownership relationships and, more generally, the entire social structure. However, we should expect that general privatization will be used only on a limited scale. It will not apply to most state-owned property. However, it seems unlikely that the government will withdraw from equivalent privatization, which provides an important source of income through the sale of shares or assets of the privatized enterprises at market prices.

Generally, one can say that, so far, conventional solutions dominate in Polish privatization. This conclusion should not be surprising. After over forty years of the communist system, which failed as an economic, social, and political experiment, there is a noticeable lack of willingness within the government and the population to create and promote unknown and unproved economic solutions. To the contrary, the dominant sentiment is that Poland should use models originating from the developed Western democracies and market economies to the greatest possible extent. The real question is whether systemic and ownership transformations can be implemented to obtain economic effectiveness of the developed countries based on free market economy, avoiding undesirable social consequences. But that is another story.

Notes

1. *Dziennik Ustaw* 1946, No. 3, Item 17, as amended.
2. Reprivatization is the subject of considerable public discussion and legislative activity. Several draft bills have been prepared, but the Sejm has not yet adopted any of them. The primary areas of dispute concern: the scope of reprivatization, that is, whether it should relate to the entire property seized by the government or only certain parts; and whether reprivatization should cover property independently of the method of its occupation in the past, or only in cases of nationalization carried out contrary to the laws then in force. The form that reprivatization takes is also controversial: should the physical property be returned, compensation be paid, or securities be granted, for instance, of privatized firms? See Alberto M. Aronovitz and Mirosław Wyrzykowski, "The Polish Draft Law on Reprivatization: Some Reflections on Domestic and International Law," *Swiss Review of International and European Law* 2: 223 (1991).
3. *Dziennik Ustaw* 1952, No. 33, Item 232, as amended.
4. Cf. Art. 5, Items 3 and 4 of the 1976 Constitution. *Dziennik Ustaw* 1976, No. 7, Item 36.
5. Cf. Art. 3.1 of the Constitution in the form established in 1976. We should add here that both the quoted provision and the one mentioned in the previous footnote are not in force any more.
6. *Dziennik Ustaw* 1988, No. 41, Item 324, as amended.
7. *Dziennik Ustaw* 1989, No. 75, Item 444. The official name of the country is presently "Rzeczpospolita Polska" (Republic of Poland).
8. The legal grounds were subsequently the following: the Law of 1982, *Dziennik Ustaw* 1982, No. 19, Item 146, as amended; the Law of 1986, *Dziennik Ustaw* 1986, No. 17, Item 88; and the Law of 1988, *Dziennik Ustaw* 1988, No. 41, Item 325.
9. *Dziennik Ustaw* 1991, No. 60, Item 253.
10. Cf. Janusz Lewandowski, "Pięć mitów prywatyzacji" (Five Myths of Privatization, *Gazeta Wyborcza,* April 30–May 1, 1992, No. 102.
11. *Dziennik Ustaw* 1981, No. 24, Items 122 and 123, as amended. The Law of State-Owned Enterprises was published again in *Dziennik Ustaw* 1991, No. 18, Item 80, as amended.
12. When there is a danger of unjustified disposal of the enterprise's property, however, especially when the property is gratuitously transferred, the enterprise must obtain permission from the supervising administrative entity or the founding organ.

13. The buy-out of some of the enterprise property and assets is treated as "small privatization" (as opposed to proper privatization defined in the provisions of the 1990 LPSOE).

14. *Dziennik Ustaw* 1990, No. 51. Item 298, as amended.

15. The statute does not require universal, automatic privatization of state-owned enterprises. It entitles state administrative organs and those representing the enterprises in question to initiate and implement the privatization procedure.

16. These are differentiated according to methods of privatization.

17. Although there were proposals for creating employee-owned enterprises, the LPSOE rejected these. This question will be discussed below in III. B.

At the same time, the law takes into account the employees' special ties with their enterprise and provides for certain preferences which would make it easier for the employees to participate in the privatization process. The preferences are different in the case of indirect (capital) privatization, and different still in the case of direct (liquidation) privatization. Namely, the employees have the right to preferential purchase of up to twenty percent of shares in the resulting company. Preferences consist of reducing the price of shares by half. However, employees may purchase further shares beyond the twenty percent limit. If the enterprise is liquidated, its entire property or part of it may be sold, rented out, or leased to a company formed by the employees.

18. Practically, employees find it difficult to buy such assigned shares, despite their lower price. This is why some have suggested offering ten percent of shares to employees free of charge.

19. General privatization was discussed even prior to approval of the 1990 LPSOE.

20. Cf. Krzysztof Dzierżawski, "Kredyt czy darowizna" [Loan or Gift], *Gazeta Wyborcza,* June 4, 1992, No. 131.

21. We should also add that general privatization, at least in the government's proposed format, is justified less by social reasons than by pragmatic considerations. The purpose is to accelerate the process, to reconstruct the national economy, and to provide effective corporate management in the companies created as a result of privatization.

Pensioners in America: The Economic Triumph and Political Limitations of Passive Ownership

Gregory S. Alexander

[*Editors' Synopsis:* One of the many open issues in the transformation to a private property regime is what forms of private ownership will be permitted. More specifically, if, as seems likely, one form of ownership that will exist is one in which private institutions own capital for the benefit of large numbers of individuals, how will the state regulate the relationship between owners and beneficiaries? An important Western example of this form of capital ownership is the American corporate pension system. American law renders pension beneficiaries passive and treats them paternistically. The American private pension system thus in certain respects resembles the paternalism and passivity of state socialism. Postcommunist countries must decide whether this form of institutional ownership is compatible with their political and social culture.]

Introduction

Economic paternalism is a notable characteristic of life in state socialist societies, where the government provides for each citizen's basic needs. Critics of state socialism say this paternalism turns citizens into passive recipients of government favors, producing mass cynicism (an attitude of "Where's mine?") instead of a sense of responsibility for themselves or others. This view of protective life under state socialism contrasts strongly with the popular image of life in capitalist societies, particularly the United States, where the classical liberal model stresses active ownership of property and self-reliance instead of an egalitarian distribution of property. In reality, however, the dominant modes of owning capital in the United States—corporate shareholding and pension funds—suffer from many of the same problems of passivity and paternalism that plagued the countries of state socialism, in addition to the problems of antiegalitarianism that mark capitalist economies.

Although the institutions of passive ownership first emerged in mature capitalist economies with the rise of the modern corporation,[1] the corporate pension system has greatly exacerbated this situation. In many respects it is a private version of paternalistic social policy, in which individuals have no opportunity to practice responsible ownership. Pension owners do not decide how to invest the capital they contribute through deferred wages, nor do they vote the stock they hold in pension funds or choose who will manage pension assets.[2] Important decisions, despite considerable social impact, are not made by the group of participants in the fund, plan trustees, or society as a whole but by investment specialists who do not democratically represent the fund owners or society. The laws governing pensions in America, fiduciary laws, are strongly paternalistic; participation is largely involuntary. Furthermore, the corporate pension system as presently constituted is inegalitarian. The corporate pension system provides coverage for those who are least in need and virtually ignores those at the bottom of the economic ladder.

The comparative implication for East-Central Europeans is to illuminate some of the problems raised by institutional ownership of capital. Many participants in the debates over privatization in postcommunist Europe have argued that pensions should play an ownership role there similar to the one they play in the United States and other Western countries. It is important to the debate in Europe, then, to understand the problems that the American mode of pension ownership creates. These problems are not inevitable in pension ownership. Western countries have quite different systems of pensions and pension ownership. It is a fundamental error to suppose, as some economists and other observers do, that the current mode of pension governance in the United States or any other country in the West developed through an evolutionary process according to some immanent logic of the market. Such an evolutionary view ignores the constitutive (not merely facilitative) role of law: the American pension system, like others, is the product of an explicit collective choice; it is created by a set of legal rules. The aim of this paper is to indicate how specific legal choices can either ameliorate or exacerbate the political problem associated with large institutional ownership of capital through corporate pensions.

The principal thesis of this paper is that the passive and paternalistic mode of ownership that the pension system has created diminishes the degree of personal responsibility that classical liberal ownership required all individual owners to take.[3] The second part describes both the pension economy and the corporate pension system, and briefly refutes the thesis of "pension fund socialism." The third part explains how the system of American pensions fosters paternalism and passivity. The fourth part develops the paper's major normative premise: that an active, participatory form of individual ownership is usually desirable because it enables individuals to develop a sense of both personal and civic responsibility. The fifth part considers practical constraints on realizing a more participatory form of pension ownership. The concluding section, the sixth, argues that the developing market economies of East-Central Europe can draw important lessons from the American experience.

I. Ownership Under the Modern Pension System

A. An Overview of the Pension Economy

Prior to the end of World War II, pension funds were relatively unimportant institutions in the United States.[4] Their importance to the American economy today is suggested by their enormous size. In 1950, when General Motors first created its influential employee plan, pensions held less than one percent of all equity securities and only thirteen percent of all corporate debt.[5] In 1983, 56.2 percent of the nonagricultural workforce was covered by an employer-sponsored pension plan.[6] If the employment base is adjusted to exclude part-time workers, self-employed workers, workers under the age of twenty-five, and workers with less than one year on the job, the coverage rate rises to about seventy percent.[7] By 1988, the combined assets in public (excluding federal) and corporate pension funds had reached $2.1 trillion.[8] This includes nearly a quarter of all equity securities and half of all corporate debt. Pension funds are the largest source of investment capital for the American economy.[9] Indeed, American pension funds now constitute the largest single fund of private capital in the world.

At the same time, however, the current pension system is highly inegalitarian. Coverage varies significantly according to industries and according to employees' annual earnings. Coverage is highest in the public sector and, within the private sector, in the communications and utilities industries (81 percent each in 1987). Excluding agriculture, it is lowest in nonunionized occupations such as retail sales (29 percent in 1987).[10] Pension coverage also strongly correlates with employee earnings. As of 1983, while nearly eighty-four percent of employees earning fifty thousand dollars or more annually were covered by some private pension, among those earning five thousand dollars or less annually, only twenty-four percent were covered.[11] These variances according to income level raise important wealth-distributive concerns.

Other factors that correlate with pension coverage also tend to undermine the democratic character of the pension system. Gender, for example, substantially correlates with pension coverage. Women have lower levels of both coverage and benefits than men.[12] Unionization is another important factor. In the private sector the percentage of unionized workers covered is nearly double that of covered nonunion employees.[13] Also related to unionization, firm size strongly affects coverage. Large firms (above five hundred employees) are far more likely to have pension plans than small firms (less than one hundred employees).[14] This is explainable on the basis of the greater probability that most or at least many employees in large-sized firms are unionized.

It is no exaggeration to say that the current pension system benefits those who need it least. A truly democratic pension system would provide retirement security across all economic levels, but it would particularly focus on benefitting employees at the lower end of the wage scale.

B. The Corporate Pension System

Pension plans are classified in several different ways under American law. They are public (that is, for government employees) or private; contributory (that is, employees contribute along with employers) or noncontributory; individual corporate or multiemployer; defined benefit or defined contribution plans.

The distinction between defined benefit and defined contribution plans is the most important from the perspective of democratic political theory. Defined benefit and defined contribution plans structure benefits in fundamentally different ways. Under defined benefit plans, participants receive fixed specified benefits upon retirement. By contrast, defined contribution plans obligate employers going into the fund rather than going out, that is, to make only a specified contribution into the fund, rather than a specified amount as benefit. These two types of plans differ with respect to allocation of the investment risk. Under a defined benefit plan the employee is entitled to receive a stated amount upon retirement, usually a monthly payment of a fixed amount for life. Thus this type of plan allocates the investment risk to someone other than the employee. If the invested pension fund fares poorly, the employer, the employer's insurer, or a federal agency, the Pension Benefit Guaranty Corporation, must make up the difference. Conversely, if the investment performs better than expected, the employer's contributions will decrease. Under defined contribution plans employees do not receive a stated amount upon retirement. Rather, benefits are based on the amount that the employer has contributed to the plan. Employer contributions to defined contribution plans are made to individual accounts for each employee; the employee bears the risk for investments of her or his own account funds.[15] This feature is frequently cited as the reason why defined benefit plans are more advantageous to employees. However, defined benefit plans also restrict mobility; give their participants a false sense of security, as the asset-reversion boom during the 1980s indicated;[16] and, through final pay arrangements, backload benefits to a disturbing extent.

Defined contribution plans are more consistent with the democratic model of pensions than are defined benefit plans. They permit the beneficial owner to be more active—through his own contributions to 401(k) plans—in managing his own retirement funds. Moreover, by allocating the investment risk to the employee, who is, after all, the beneficial owner, defined contribution plans give the owner greater responsibility over his own life and over affairs that affect the community (here, of employee-participants) to which he belongs. In this respect, defined contribution plans are also more consistent with classical economic theory, which holds that risk and control should be concomitants of ownership. Return is the market's compensation for the owner's risk-taking, and to manage that risk owners should have control. Because they do not bear the investment risk, employers with defined contribution plans theoretically should be willing to contribute more in the pension fund.

Most private pension plans are single-firm, or corporate, plans, rather than multifirm plans. A corporate plan is one that a single employer firm sponsors for its employees only. Single-firm plans more commonly exist in heavily concentrated industries with a few dominant firms. Multifirm plans, where several firms contribute to a common plan, are more typical among industries in which employment patterns are irregular, such as the construction industry. "Multis," as they are called, tend to be quite large. It is not uncommon for a multi to have ten thousand or more active participants.

C. The Pension Fund Socialism Thesis

The pension fund thesis is that the pension fund system is socialist, insofar as one defines socialism as an economic system in which workers own the means of production. Since employee pension funds now own a command position in virtually every sector of the American economy, this means that the United States quietly became socialist even while its foreign policy was largely developed around the goal of fighting state socialism. A further irony is that it has become socialist completely through private means, without nationalizing any of its industries. The pension fund socialism thesis basically claims that the corporate pension system is a privatized form of socialism.

This thesis is mistaken at both ends. At one end, the corporate pension system is not thoroughly private. Major aspects of it are nonconsensual and paternalistic. At the other end, the pension system is not socialist in any nontrivial sense of the term. It does not extend the ideal of democratic participation to the domain of employee-provided capital.

Three distinguishing features are commonly attributed to the American private pension system. The system is said to be employment-based, tax-encouraged, and consensual, that is, private.[17] There is little room for disputing that the corporate pension system is employment-based and tax-encouraged, but the description of corporate pensions as consensual is somewhat illusory. Corporate pensions are, like other important resources including land, privately owned but inherently social.

From both the employer's and the employee's perspective, the highly favorable treatment of pensions under American tax laws[18] itself suggests that the government is not neutral about the employer's decision to offer or the employee's decision to accept (to the extent employees have any choice) a pension plan as part of the compensation arrangement. The corporate pension plan system, although formally private, is a key component in government policies on retirement and other employee benefits, supplementing the American retirement system, social security, for a large percentage of the work force.

More importantly, pensions involve a set of decisions over which employees usually have little control. The most important among these is the decision to join the plan. According to the prevailing theory, pensions are a form of deferred compensation.[19] It is more accurate to describe them as a system of compelled savings. The employee contributes to the plan in the form of reduced wage compensation. In general, neoclassical economic theory predicts that, other things being equal, most people would rather receive the same amount of compensation as after-tax wages than as employment benefits.[20] The compulsory character of pensions thus raises familiar issues of collective paternalism.[21] Characterizing corporate pensions as a privatized form of paternalism would both directly threaten the liberal ideal of individual owner autonomy and undermine the argument that corporate pensions are a system of employee benefit entirely distinguishable from government welfare benefit programs.

The decision to forego present consumption in favor of saving for retirement (or other benefits) typically is not made by the employee but by the employer, either acting alone or, in unionized firms, together with a collective bargaining unit. Of course, it is possible that if employees were free to choose, they would opt for saving rather than increased income, but this is far from certain. From the perspective of a political theory that emphasizes responsibility, as the civic and communitarian theories do, the case for pensions as a form of paternalism is somewhat uneasy. The one step away from individual self-control that the pension system takes the precommitment device idea is a substantial step.

What the pension fund socialism thesis really focuses on is the fact that pension funds, by pooling vast amounts of capital, now hold dominant ownership positions in all sectors of the economy. Workers indirectly own most of the investment capital—the means of production—in the American economy. But this is social ownership of the means of production only in a formal sense. Classical socialism sought to vest ownership of the means of production in workers so that workers would control the use of capital. This is exactly the characteristic that the corporate pension system lacks.

II. Fiduciary Law and the Legal Construction of Passive Ownership

The rise of the corporate pension system exacerbates an important paradox of capitalist development. As capitalist economies become more advanced, that is, more successful, the owners of capital have less control over it. This attenuation of control from benefit undermines the basic political vision inherent in liberal, as well as classical republican, property theory;

individual autonomy secured through private ownership of property. In advanced capitalist societies, the individual owner becomes only a capital supplier. Financial intermediaries assume a role loosely analogous to that of the state under state socialism, making decisions for the individual.

What explains the greater distancing of owners from control, even participation, as capitalist economies become more advanced? One theory that has been offered to explain this phenomenon is Dean Robert Clark's theory of natural evolution of capitalist institutions.[22] Dean Clark argues that the increasing division and concentration of discretionary control over capital in capital management and investment specialists reflects the efficiency advantages of role specialization and the awareness of these advantages by key individuals who are responsible for creating institutions like corporate pensions. According to this thesis, law plays only a responsive role, developing different regulatory strategies that seem appropriate to the peculiar problems posed by novel nonlegal institutions emerging with each successive stage of capitalist development.

The basic weakness in the evolution theory is its failure to acknowledge the creative role of fiduciary law in explaining the increasingly nonparticipatory character of capital ownership. American fiduciary law structures the relationship between beneficial owners of pension capital and pension managers not simply as a response to efficiency problems that new forms of financial intermediation create, but according to a social and political vision of capital ownership as passive. Specifically, American fiduciary law assumes that the appropriate role of pension owners is that of passive investors, rather than self-governing and responsible owners, and it realizes that assumption by constructing a pension governance structure whose purpose and effect is to inhibit participation by equitable owners.

Fiduciary law's paternalistic policy on the issue of whether to allow employees the opportunity to opt out of participation in a pension plan does not necessarily justify paternalism with respect to internal governance issues. The Employee Retirement Security Act (ERISA), the federal statute that regulates corporate pensions, constructs the fiduciary office in a way that concentrates control over internal matters exclusively in the trustee and other pension fiduciaries. But participants do not need trustee protection on some internal issues. On many of these issues, participants do not act alone, but act through a group, most notably (given the high correlation between pensions and unionization) a union. If the union itself is democratically structured, the participant can exercise voice through collective action.

Apropos governance issues, an important example of ERISA's paternalistic approach to the fiduciary office concerns the trustee's exclusive control over investments. Participants cannot direct the trustees to limit their investments to particular industries or geographic areas. The trustees are required to act for the exclusive benefit of the participants. The meaning of benefit is limited to maximizing returns to the fund. The upshot of this definition is that trustees are forbidden to take into account noneconomic considerations, such as encouraging unionization, promoting employment in the area, or saving the jobs of plan participants,[23] even if the plan participants express their approval of such factors. An approach that allowed trustees to be guided by a vote of all the participants would add an important measure of democracy to pensions without unduly jeopardizing the fiduciary office.[24]

Another important issue of control concerns voting rights. In defined benefit plans, the trustee or investment manager, not the participant-owners, exercises the right to vote stock in matters such as election of corporate directors, election of auditors, and organic corporate changes, including mergers, stock exchanges and asset sales. Plan fiduciaries hold and vote the shareholders' proxies. Voting proxies is a fiduciary act, as to which trustees are under a duty to act for the exclusive benefit of plan participants, but this does not require them to consult with the participants.

A countervailing consideration concerning voting rights is that in employee-owned firms, and firms whose plans own significant employer securities, individual voting may lead to results that are contrary to the employees' best interests as a group. Conflict of interests among participants is an important problem in most pensions (for example, younger versus older employees, current workers versus retirees, high-income versus low-income employees), and these different subgroups, voting their own interests, may vote in different ways if individual voting is permitted. The employees' best interests might be served by block voting, which does not dilute their voting power, particularly if outside shareholders or management have substantial holdings in the firm. Currently, the most control that participants-employees, as equitable owners of the firm, can have in the firm's management is to elect directors and approve major changes involving the firm's capital structure. They lack voice as to all other basic policy issues, including investment and marketing strategy, labor policies, and the like. A genuinely democratic and participatory form of employee ownership would confer control over these matters to the participants.

A final legal factor that creates pension ownership as passive and nonparticipatory is the authority of the sponsoring firm to select as plan trustees or investment managers its own officers.[25] The American law gives pension beneficiaries no right to directly participate in decisions about the use of pension assets. Neither does pension law give beneficial owners indirect voice, such as by recognizing a right to participate in decisions about the selection of persons who control pension assets.

III. Property and Responsibility

The claim that particular forms of property ownership facilitate development of moral and political personality better than others is not unfamiliar.

Classical liberalism stressed moral as well as the economic benefits accruing from the model of individual ownership that consolidates control over resources in individual hands. Adam Smith, for example, argued that individual property rights create wealth by reducing fragmented ownership, which impedes economic efficiency.[26] Many economists today no longer accept this critique of fragmented ownership. In fact they regard the consolidated control mode of ownership as incompatible with wealth creation insofar as it inhibits specialization.[27] The economic critique of the consolidated control model of ownership, however, does not respond to Smith's other argument in favor of keeping individual ownership consolidated. Smith, along with civic humanists like James Harrington, thought that consolidated individual ownership promotes certain personal traits that are morally desirable.[28] Among these is a sense of responsibility. Passive forms of ownership provide no opportunity for individuals to experience responsibility, one of the great problems of state socialism. The theory of state socialism, that all citizens are owners of the means of production and are represented by the state, mocked the real experiences of the citizens of East-Central Europe, where the individual was relegated to the role of a passive receiver of whatever few benefits the state chose (and could afford) to drop his way.

While some aspects of pension law's model of passive ownership exhibit a paternalistic outlook, other aspects of the model do not involve paternalism. Arguments against the model of passive ownership, then, must distinguish between objections to the model's paternalism and objections that focus on owner passivity as such.

Passivity does not necessarily entail paternalism, though paternalism usually involves passivity. A passive ownership regime is one in which individuals lack the power to practice self-governance, either because they have consensually delegated that power to others, or because the state has denied them that power on the assumption that they are unable to calculate what is in their best interest. Only the latter reason for denying individuals decisional power involves paternalism.

Some aspects of the private pension system quite clearly are paternalistic. The state does not compel employers to create pension plans, although it does offer them powerful tax incentives to do so, but once an employer has decided to create a plan, employees are not free to opt out. The basic reason why pensions deny employees the exit option is the judgment that "[l]eft to their own devices, many people will not save enough for their old age."[29] Temporally inconsistent preferences, preference changes due to adaptation to new circumstances, and simple myopia create a systematic pattern in consumption and savings behavior to sacrifice long-term self-interest in favor of short-term individual satisfaction.[30]

This rationality gap creates good reasons for compelling individuals to participate in plans that bind them to saving for retirement security.[31] The restraint against opting out of a pension plan is a classic example of a precommitment device.[32] But this rationale does not require paternalism or passivity in all or even most internal aspects of the plan's governance. One might rationally conclude that while good paternalistic reasons exist for denying participants the opportunity to exit from the plan, participants should still have substantial "voice" in internal governance decisions. Indeed, as Albert Hirschman's study powerfully demonstrated,[33] a major reason for denying exit is that doing so tends to make exercise of the voice option crucially important.

The idea of civic responsibility, although more frequently encountered today in communitarian discourse than in liberal discourse, with its nearly exclusive focus on individual rights, is not necessarily incompatible with liberalism. Indeed, if liberalism is understood as focusing above all on individual freedom, the concept of responsibility is at the core of liberalism. Individuals cannot be self-governing unless they exercise responsibility. To act without responsibility is to act in such a way that others control aspects of one's life. The person who acts without a sense of responsibility believes that others are accountable for his actions. He effectively cedes power to others. As any child will attest about his relationship with his parents, those who are accountable for another's actions have a measure of power over him. This is precisely what makes legal paternalism seem objectionable to many people, including both communitarians and liberals. The person who lacks a sense of responsibility does not experience his life as free, nor is he truly free. Practicing responsibility is a liberating experience because it allows the individual to realize his full personality and to develop those personal qualities of character that justify self-respect and self-love.

A sense of civic responsibility grows out of the experience of personal responsibility. Living a life of personal responsibility impresses one with an awareness of one's interrelationships with others. When one acts responsibly one accepts accountability for one's decisions, that is, bears, and realizes that he will bear, the consequences of his actions just because they are *his* actions. Being accountable encourages deliberation. A person takes into account the possible consequences of his decisions on others in the decisional process when he realizes that he will bear the consequences of his actions. It's much easier to ignore the consequences of individual acts on others ahead of time when one knows that those acts will not be treated as one's own. A person who has developed a robust sense of personal responsibility feels a greater sense of obligation to others. He particularly feels a deep sense of obligation to the communities with which he identifies himself. He feels committed to those communities and wants to contribute to their well-being.

A sense of responsibility develops only when a person has the opportunity to act responsibly. Having the opportunity to act responsibly means that one is empowered to make decisions and to practice self-governance. Responsibility, in short, requires activity. When one is denied the power to participate in those decisions that affect one's life, one cannot feel committed. To live a passive life, that is, a life in which one is only a receiver, rather than a creator, is to experience dependency and degradation. Commitment requires individual empowerment, a sense that one has a measure of control over those decisions that affect one.

Individual ownership of property creates the potential for individuals to be active and self-governing. It can enable them to practice personal responsibility and ultimately creates the necessary opportunity for citizens to learn civic responsibility.[34] Realizing that potential, however, requires a particular form of individual ownership. It requires that individual owners have substantial and meaningful control over the use of their assets. This vision, then, is antagonistic to certain forms of fragmented ownership. What is crucial is that the owner be given the obligations along with the benefits of ownership.

So long as virtually all property was owned according to the classical liberal mode of ownership, there was little occasion to worry about the relationship between specific forms of private ownership and responsibility. Private ownership was highly (though certainly not completely) individualized, and individuated ownership facilitated a sense of responsibility. It is only as new modes of private ownership—in which the traditional "bundle of rights" is disaggregated and the authority to manage property is spun off from ownership—have been developed that the link between private ownership and responsibility has come to be seen as problematic. The emergence of the corporate pension system is only the latest stage in a long process of disaggregating individual ownership and weakening the connection between property ownership and responsibility.[35]

No one would suggest that individuals should actively control all aspects of all areas of their lives. It is appropriate to ask, then, whether an active, participatory form of ownership is at all appropriate in the workplace, and specifically for pensions. Most people are happy to delegate decision-making responsibility to others in some aspects of their lives. Health care decision-making, for example, is an area that has traditionally been characterized by a high degree of paternalism, although a more participatory model of the doctor-patient relationship has gained force in recent years. Still, few people are prepared to accept full responsibility for decisions regarding their health.

There are several reasons to reject passivity in the pension context, however, even if one accepts it as valid in other contexts. The argument for creating a meaningful opportunity for pension participants to exercise voice relates pensions to the broader goal of infusing the principles of democracy in the economy and the workplace.[36] The goals of economic and workplace democracy are founded on the commitment to protecting employees and their communities from the multiple insecurities of the market, especially in the late capitalist environment of deindustrialization and deregulation.[37] Workplace democracy would indirectly protect employees from the dislocations of plant closings, job relocation, and wage reductions that deindustrialization and deregulation have caused, by giving employees a meaningful role in the decisions that directly affect their lives, rather than directly protecting them through guarantees concerning the substantive terms of employment. Workplace democracy reflects the pragmatic judgment that employee participation best responds to the justified concerns of employees, and the communities to which they belong, for greater job security and investment stability, without unduly inhibiting the ability of firms to respond flexibly to changing market conditions.[38]

Pensions could potentially contribute toward the realization of the vision of greater democracy in the workplace by giving capital ownership a directly participatory role in the investment process. Pensions could use their huge capital accumulations to affect firms's decisions that directly affect their employee's lives by investing a substantial portion of the plan's assets in stock of the sponsoring firm. Fiduciary law, however, constrains most pension plans from realizing that potential.

IV. Constraints on Internal Pension Voice

One problem with giving pension participants greater control in their internal governance, including investment decisions, is that they lack necessary expertise. This point justifies the passive model of ownership insofar as it protects the beneficiaries' economic stakes better than the democratic model of pension would. Investment is a highly specialized activity, and few employees have the expertise or the inclination to devote the resources necessary actively to participate in pension investment decisions. With respect to who should have the power to select and control investment specialists, the employer or the employee, the employer may be said to be in the better position to select and monitor third-party specialists.[39]

It is sometimes thought that the efficient capital market hypothesis (ECMH) diminishes the importance of investment expertise. In fact, this is not so; the ECMH simply changes the sorts of expertise an investment specialist must possess. The efficient capital market hypothesis holds that a sound investment strategy is to invest the equity portion of a portfolio in index funds, which are designed to match market performance, and leave it there. Selective investing increases transaction costs and, in the overwhelming number of cases, results in submarket performance. The ECMH strategy does not eliminate the need for investment expertise, though. Instead of the ability to pick particular stocks that are undervalued, investment advisors must be able to assemble diversified portfolios and to hedge investment risks using sophisticated dynamic hedging strategies such as index arbitrage.

The decisional structure that American fiduciary law creates may economically disadvantage beneficial owners at times. Investment managers, who owe their positions and remuneration to the firm's officers, have strong incentives to invest in ways that are calculated to win the approval of the firm's top managers. The theory of virtual representation does not answer the concern about whether investment decisions satisfy the beneficial owners. Corporate managers do not always share the same objectives as the beneficial owners, so that rent-seeking behavior by outside investment specialists may make the owners worse off.

Specialization is largely illusory in some contexts, however. Defined contribution plans are usually considered riskier for employees than defined benefit plans since the employee bears the investment risk and the plan is not federally insured. Despite the fact that the employee bears the investment risk, the employer often controls investment decisions. Large firms typically hire investment specialists or let employees choose among several mutual funds. In small firms, however, where defined contribution plans greatly outnumber defined benefit plans,[40] the owner commonly manages the pension fund.[41] Small business owners may not possess much greater expertise about managing portfolio risk than employees, and may not have any knowledge about their fiduciary obligations.

A related problem is that small business owners may be tempted to use pension funds to bail out their failing business or as a source of needed capital for their own enterprises. Even if the owner is expert in managing risk and is aware that such uses of pension funds breaches his fiduciary duties, that knowledge may not deter him from misuse.

A more serious impediment to the democratic model of pension ownership is the familiar problem of rational apathy. The collective-action problems that are widely thought to make shareholder voice ineffectual in the corporate setting apply in the pension setting as well.

The stock story of why shareholder voice fails as an effective response to the agency problems associated with the separation of management and equitable ownership asserts that shareholder passivity is inevitable. Even where they are given voice—legal power to control managers or to participate in decision-making processes, for example, through proxy rules—shareholders rationally conclude that it is not worth their time and effort to exercise the voice option. The problem is not that these beneficial owners do not value participation at all. Rather, it is that the costs of participation exceed the benefit to them individually. Participation is not costless, and participation costs are especially high if there are many other investors in the firm. They own only a small fraction of any single firm's stock, so the gains to the individual investor's holdings in the firm from participation usually do not justify these costs. Collectively, the value of multiple beneficial owners having similar interests may well be high enough to justify active participation, but collective-action efforts to capture these potential gains face coordination obstacles. Collective action is not costless, and its benefits are nonexclusive. Consequently, individuals have incentives to free-ride off the efforts of others. Since all of them share this incentive, the result is that no one makes the effort. So passive ownership is not the contingent result of legal rules, but the result of the logic of rationality.[42]

This story is used to explain both why institutional investors such as pension funds rarely attempt to influence corporate policy, and why within pension funds themselves individual plan participants are apathetic about the use of the plan's capital. Part of the reason for apathy in both situations—by pensions as shareholders and by participants within individual pensions—is dispersion of ownership. Most pensions do not own large stakes in any single firm. Rather, pension portfolio managers invest the plan's capital in a variety of assets, representing both equity and debt of a large number of firms. Because they lack significant control over any single firm, pensions as institutional shareholders lack incentives actively to participate in any firm's affairs. Similarly, individual participants have little reason to invest resources in monitoring the plan fiduciaries. Pension participants and shareholders obviously differ with respect to the percentage of the entire portfolios that the investment represents. The individual pension participant's stake in a pension fund usually is not small in relation to his overall portfolio, while the shareholder's investment in any single firm rarely constitute anything like a substantial portion of his entire portfolio. Pensioners own interests in only one fund, while stockholders usually own shares in many firms. For many Americans, their pension constitutes the second or third largest single asset in their entire estate, after the family residence and life insurance. Pensioners have greater reasons to care, then, about the fund's management than most shareholders do about the management decisions of any single firm. Moreover, it is easier for participants to monitor plan managers than it is for shareholders to monitor the firms in which they invest. Unlike shareholders, they have only one fund to monitor and can concentrate their efforts, rather than deciding which of several firms to monitor.[43]

Nevertheless, participants lack incentives actively to participate in the management of the fund, even if they had the legal power to do so. This is especially obvious in the case of highly diversified plans, which are analogous to mutual funds. The experience of diversified plans that have beneficiary-elected trustees tends to confirm this prediction. Voter participation rates are low, and candidates rarely run on substantive platforms. At a minimum, then, increasing pensioner participation requires that plans not be highly diversified.

Nondiversification is a necessary but not a sufficient condition of overcoming apathy. Even assuming that nondiversification were legally and practically acceptable, it would not be enough to make the democratic model of pensions a reality. This is because each participant's equitable ownership of the fund constitutes only a small fraction of the plan's total fund, so that his efforts are unlikely to have much effect. To offset that problem, plans would have to target their investments in institutions that most affect the participants. Creating conditions that would increase the incentives for participants to exercise voice requires concentration of ownership. Just as pensions might become more active shareholders if they owned larger stakes in single firms, so plan participants might take a greater interest in the governance of their pensions if the plan's capital were concentrated and control was decentralized among the participants, rather than, as it is now, centralized in the fiduciaries.[44]

As I have already indicated, collective-action theory appears to suggest that apathy is a more serious problem for large, diversified plans. This is not necessarily the case, however. A pension can be limited to union members, and block voting on important issues, including selection of plan trustees, can become part of the internal political life of a union. To some extent, this solution involves sacrificing participatory democracy to representative democracy, but within the union itself prospects for participation seem to be stronger than they do for direct participation within highly diversified pensions. The key is in assuring that unions are genuinely democratic. In a democratic union in which people participate, block voting on important pension issues could facilitate a more active form of pension participation.

The most important problem with creating a form of equitable pension ownership that is robustly participatory is the trade-off between voice and risk. Substantially increasing pensioners's control over internal management of pension capital to some extent sacrifices the beneficiary's economic welfare. Funds that concentrate a participant's pension investment in the workplace increase his risk by failing to diversify his total investment. The concern about the level of economic risk seems especially acute with respect to retirement investment; most individuals planning for retirement have a low tolerance for risk. This risk profile argues strongly for diversification of pension funds. Modern finance theory establishes that, other things being equal, a diversified portfolio will have less variance in returns for the same average return than an undiversified one. Nondiversified plans generally expose participants to greater risk, and this exposure would be magnified if the plan invested heavily in the workplace. Participants already have substantial investments of human capital in the workplace, so reducing their economic risk requires that their pension capital not be unduly concentrated in the same firm.

How much concentration should be permitted depends on making trade-offs among several factors. There are, as I have already indicated, political advantages to a fund that concentrates investment in the workplace. An economic advantage is that concentration theoretically should increase the employee's productivity incentives. Moreover, while it increases one form of risk, it decreases another, that is, the risk of job loss. (Employee-owners may still lose their jobs, of course, if the firm fails.) In fact, it is arguable that diversification economically harms rather than helps employees. Because workers are so underdiversified in relation to their human capital investment, which is the primary life investment for most workers, arguably they need better ways of monitoring that investment than the law currently allows.[45] Consequently, if workers become significant shareholders in their employer firms, they can more effectively monitor their main life investment—their jobs.

Related to these points is a macroeconomic factor: The appropriate level of concentration for a particular fund depends to some extent on the level of risk in the relevant industry.[46] Diversification becomes more important for firms within industries that have higher levels of risk. Nobody would, or at least should, suggest, though, that anything close to a majority of their retirement funds be invested in the pensioner's employer. The more basic point is that the democratic model of pensions has to reckon with an unavoidable trade-off between participation and investment diversification, voice and economic welfare.

Conclusion

Following their "peaceful revolutions," the countries of Central and Eastern Europe have begun to explore alternatives to the regime of state socialism that created enormous misery for their citizens. Anxious to repudiate the past half century of oppression, which they associate with state ownership of capital, they have eagerly embraced "privatization" as the appropriate path for reorganizing their economies in a way that simultaneously protects individual liberty and increases social and individual wealth. But privatization may take many different legal forms, and not all of the private legal forms in the West may implement the political and social values that East-Central Europeans have in mind when they say they want to "privatize" their economies.

Corporate pension plans in America have blurred the line between privatized and socialized capital. Pension plans have the potential for enhancing the participatory and civic responsibility of private ownership of capital, but this potential has been frustrated by aspects of American fiduciary law which treat the beneficial owners of pension capital suppliers as passive investors who have no responsibility for how pension capital is used. The social vision underlying American fiduciary law has blocked the opportunity for pension owners to participate in decisions regarding the use of the vast amount of capital collectively held in pension funds. In adopting a more participatory legal structure for pension decision-making than the American system, the postcommunist societies would permit individual pension owners to experience greater self-governance and a sense of civic responsibility. But in the end, they must decide what type of society they want to create.

Notes

1. The classic discussion is Adolph A. Berle & Gardiner C. Means, *The Modern Corporation and Private Property* (New York: Macmillan, 1933). Paradoxically, some commentators describe this shift in terms that are consistent with the core tenets of classical liberalism, while others have described it as a form of socialism. See John H. Langbein & Bruce A. Wolk, *Pension and Employee Benefit Law* (Westbury, N.Y.: Foundation Press, 1990) p. 24 (characterizing beneficial pension ownership in contractarian terms); Peter F. Drucker, *The Unseen Revolution: How Pension Fund Socialism Came to America* (New York: Harper & Row, 1976). Drucker first articulated his pension fund socialism thesis in an essay, "Pension Fund Socialism," *The Public Interest* 3 (Winter 1976). Neither of these characterizations is accurate. Beneficial interests in pensions deviate in crucial ways from the conceptions of ownership under both classical liberalism and classical state socialism. The form of beneficial ownership of capital that the pension system represents fails to realize the political and moral visions embedded in classical liberalism's and socialism's model of ownership. Berle and Means, on the other hand, argued that the problem that the separation of control from ownership created was economic. The interests of managers and shareholders in the modern corporation diverge, and, they argued, this divergence diminishes the overall efficiency of the modern economy, dominated as it is by large corporations. I argue that passive ownership as current pension law constructs it creates a problem that is less economic than political and moral.

2. As part of the struggle to improve workers' compensation after years of wage restrictions during World War II, American union leaders in the coal industry demanded that employers contribute to a union pension fund that would be managed entirely by the union. In enacting the federal Labor-Management Relations Act of 1947 (the Taft-Hartley Act), which applies to multiemployer plans, Congress directly rejected this demand in order to ensure that labor did not control the enormous supply of capital that both sides realized was at stake in the creation of the pension economy. See William Graebner, *A History of Retirement: the Meaning and Functions of an American Institution, 1885–1978* (New Haven: Yale University Press, 1980) pp. 220–221.

3. See Deborah Weiss, "Paternalistic Pension Policy: Psychological Evidence and Economic Theory," *U. Chi. L. Rev.* 58: 1275, 1279–85 (1991).

4. The modern era of pensions begins with the series of pension plans negotiated for union workers in various industries, including mining, steel, and automobiles, after World War II. Wage and price controls during the war deflected compensation demands into benefits, and this shift in how employers competed for workers contributed to the enormous growth of corporate pensions after the war. Pensions were first created earlier, though. Historians usually cite the plan established in 1875 by American Express Company (which then was primarily involved in the railroad industry) as the first formal corporate pension plan. See William C. Greenough & Francis P. King, *Pension Plans and Public Policy* (New York: Columbia University Press, 1976) p. 27. The classic history of premodern pensions is Murray W. Latimer, *Industrial Pension Systems in the United States and Canada* (New York: Industrial Relations Counselors, 1932).
5. Richard A. Ippolito, *Pensions, Economics, and Public Policy* (Homewood, Ill.: Dow-Jones Irwin, 1986) pp. 123–24.
6. Emily Andrews, *The Changing Profile of Pensions in America* (Table III.1) (Washington, D.C.: Employee Benefit Research Institute, 1985) p. 49.
7. Lee A. Shepard, "Toward a Rational Pension Policy," *Tax Notes* 37:235 (1987).
8. "Investment of Pension Fund Assets," *EBRI Issue Brief* (Washington, D.C.: Employee Benefit Research Institute, July 1988) p. 3.
9. See Jeremy Rifkin & Randy Barber, *The North Will Rise Again: Pensions, Politics and Power in the 1980s* (Boston: Beacon Press, 1978) p. 10. The increasingly dominant profile of pensions is true in other Western countries as well as the United States. In Britain, for example, as of 1987, 32 percent of corporate shares were held by pension funds, and the percentage must surely be higher today. See M. Schaffer, "On the Use of Pension Funds in the Privatization of Polish State-owned Enterprises," mimeo (London: London School of Economics, 1990).
10. Id. at 235.
11. Emily Andrews, *The Changing Profile of Pensions in America* (Table III.2) (Washington, D.C.: Employee Benefit Research Institute, 1985) p. 52.
12. This can be attributed to lower earnings levels among women, the pattern of interrupted participation by women in the work force (due largely to child rearing practices in the United States), and greater concentration of women employees in industries that have lower levels of pension coverage, such as retail sales. Id. at 62–69. Pension recipiency among women is expected to increase in the future as a result of legal changes and demographic changes in the workplace.
13. This means that nonunionized employees may be doubly exposed to economic insecurity, lacking job and wage protection through collective bargaining and retirement income security. Ibid.
14. Id. at 49 (Table III.1).

15. Defined benefit plans are the dominant form, but defined contribution plans have become increasingly popular with employers. Different classes of employees may have different preferences about the type of plan offered. Younger, higher-paid employees, who have more expendable income, likely prefer defined contribution plans that allow them to take advantage of a tax advantage (under IRC § 401(k)) of augmenting employer contributions with their own contributions of pretax dollars. Older, long-term employees prefer defined benefit plans, which use a formula that gradually accumulates guaranteed retirement income, and provide a high degree of retirement income security.

16. See Langbein & Wolk, supra note 1, at 647–48. The wave of asset reversion touched off a political controversy. Organized labor and its supporters tended to oppose the ability of employers to recapture plan assets. The Reagan Administration, on the other hand, supported asset reversions, subject to a nondeductible ten percent excise tax. See Norman Stein, "Taxing Reversions from Pension Plans" *Tax Notes* 35:1131 (1987).

17. See Langbein & Wolk, supra note 1, p. 24.

18. The principal tax advantage of pensions are, first, that employers may, subject to certain limitations, deduct from their taxable income their contributions to the pension trust (Internal Revenue Code § 404(a)(1), (2), (3)), second, the pension trust (which is a taxable entity) is exempt from tax on its investment income (IRC § 501(A)), third, the employee (or other beneficiary) is subject to income taxation only when amounts are actually distributed to her rather than when the employer contributes to the plan, and, fourth, employees increase their savings (for health insurance, child care, or other tax-exempt or tax-deferred fringe benefits) by saving with pretax dollars.

19. See Langbein & Wolk, supra note 1, p. 15. This is the feature that most significantly distinguishes pensions from other employee benefits, such as health care, life insurance, and disability plans. These benefits all represent employee-purchased services, rather than forms of deferred compensation. This is not to deny that such benefits are an important part of the wage-and-benefit package that employers offer to employees as compensation—they are. But they are not truly interchangeable with wages, either from the employer's or the employee's perspective. Employer pension contributions, on the other hand, represent compensation that the employer presumably would otherwise have paid as current wages to the employee. This distinction becomes important in explaining why the vision of participatory ownership does not extend to these employee benefits.

20. See Daniel S. Hamermesh & Albert Rees, *The Economics of Work and Pay*, 4th ed., (New York: Harper & Row, 1988) p. 341.

21. See Weiss, supra note 3.

22. See Robert Charles Clark, "The Four Stages of Capitalism," *Harv. L. Rev.* 94:561, 568–69 (1981).

23. See Ian D. Lanoff, "The Social Investment of Private Pension Plan Assets: May It Be Done Lawfully under ERISA?" *Labor L.J.* 31: 387, 389 (1980). A notable

case deviating from this view is Donovan v. Walton, 609 F. Supp. 1221 (S.D. Fla. 1985), aff'd per curiam, sub. nom. *Brock v. Walton,* 794 F.2d 586 (11th Cir. 1986), rehearing en banc denied without opinion, 802 F.2d 1399 (11th Cir. 1986) (multiemployer plan's investment of plan assets intended in part to create jobs for union members held not to violate ERISA's exclusive benefit rule since that rule "does not prohibit a party other than the plan's participants and beneficiaries [i.e., the union] from benefitting in some measure from a prudent transaction with the plan." Id. at 1245.).

24. If the trustees themselves decided to invest plan funds to save the employee's jobs, they would open themselves to the charge that breached their duty of impartiality by effectively transferring wealth from retirees and older participants-employee to younger participants-employee. An example of such an action was the Teachers Retirement System's decision to purchase over $2.5 billion in municipal bonds from New York City at a time when the city was on the brink of bankruptcy. In *Withers v. Teachers Retirement System,* 447 F. Supp. 1248 (S.D.N.Y. 1978), aff'd mem., 595 F.2d 1210 (2d Cir. 1979), the court approved the trustees' actions under common-law trust principles (ERISA does not apply to public pensions). For a criticism of this decision, see Daniel Fischel and John H. Langbein, "ERISA's Fundamental Contradiction: The Exclusive Benefit Rule," *U. Chi. L. Rev.* 55:1105, 1144–46 (1988).

25. ERISA § 408(c)(3).

26. Anticipating the problem that economists today call agency costs, Smith contended that the directors of stock companies could be expected to behave as efficiently with other people's money as they would with their own. See Adam Smith, *The Wealth of Nations* (Everyman's Lib. ed. 1971) vol. 2, p. 229.

27. See, e.g., George Stigler and Claire Friedland, "The Literature of Economics: The Case of Berle and Means," *J. L. & Econ.* 26:237 (1983); Eugene Fama and Michael Jensen, "Separation of Ownership and Control," id. at 301.

27. Contrary to a common view that sees them as complete antagonists, Adam Smith's commercial man and James Harrington's fee simple landowner, although differing in other important respects, shared at least one aspect of a common vision concerning the relationship between individual ownership of property and the sociology of virtue: individual ownership as nurturing certain desirable qualities of personal character. The most important of these qualities was awareness of one's own social character and of the fact that obligations grow out of being enmeshed in social webs. As Harrington (but not Smith) realized, since the social welfare depends on a propertied citizenry, the ideal of civic responsibility can provide the basis for an egalitarian program of property distribution, at least initially. The same line of thought historically has appeared in American political thought as well. A clear example is Thomas Jefferson's proposal for privatizing government land through an egalitarian program of distribution. See Gregory S. Alexander, "Time and Property in the American Republican Legal Culture," *N.Y.U. L. Rev.* 67:273 (1991).

29. Weiss, supra note 3, p. 1275.

30. The best systematic explorations of these problems in rational-choice theory are by Jon Elster. See Jon Elster, *Sour Grapes: Studies in the Subversion of Rationality* (Cambridge: Cambridge University Press, 1983); Jon Elster, *Ulysses and the Sirens: Studies in Rationality and Irrationality* (Cambridge: Cambridge University Press, 1979).
31. See ibid.
32. On the role of precommitment devices generally, see Jon Elster, *Ulysses and the Sirens,* supra note 30, pp. 36–111.
33. See Albert O. Hirschman, *Exit, Voice, and Loyalty: Responses to Decline in Firms, Organizations, and States* (Cambridge, MA: Harvard University Press, 1970).
34. Jeremy Waldron has sketched an argument that largely, though not exclusively, coincides with this tradition. According to his argument, individuals are more apt to act responsibly and to develop a sense of enduring commitment to others under circumstances in which their subsistence depends on ownership of private property over which they have sole responsibility. See Jeremy Waldron, *The Right to Private Property* (Oxford: Clarendon Press, 1988) pp. 310–13.
35. See generally Berle and Means, supra note 1.
36. Of course, it may not be appropriate to extend the participatory model of ownership to certain employment benefits such as health care and life insurance. For reasons that I have already indicated, the voice model is most appropriate with respect to defined contribution plans rather than defined benefit plans.
37. On the potential of pensions as a vehicle for implementing a more democratic vision of capital ownership, see William H. Simon, "The Prospects for Pension Fund Socialism," in *Corporate Control and Accountability,* eds. Joe McCahery, et al. (forthcoming 1993); William H. Simon, "Social-Republican Property," *UCLA L. Rev.* 38:1335, 1380–82 (1991). On the potential role of labor law in implementing this vision, see Katherine Van Wezel Stone, "Labor and the Corporate Structure: Changing Conceptions and Emerging Possibilities," *Chi. L. Rev.* 55:73 (1988); Katherine Van Wezel Stone, "The Legacy of Industrial Pluralism: The Tension Between Individual Employment Rights and the New Deal Collective-Bargaining System," *U. Chi. L. Rev.* 59:575 (1992).
38. See William H. Simon, "Contract versus Politics in Corporation Doctrine," in *The Politics of Law,* ed. David Kairys (New York: Pantheon, rev. ed. 1990) p. 404.
39. See, e.g., Langbein & Wolk, supra note 1, at 30.
40. See Slater, "Retirement Plans that Quietly Melt Away," *Wall St. J.* (June 6, 1991) sec. C, p. 1, col. 3.
41. Ibid.
42. The locus classicus on collective-action problems, of course, is Mancur Olson, *The Logic of Collective Action: Public Goods and the Theory of Goods* (Cambridge, MA: Harvard University Press, 1965). Bernard Black has recently published a remarkable critique of this thesis, which he calls the "passivity story." His article discusses the phenomenon of passivity by pensions as institutional

shareholders. Despite their enormous holdings of corporate equity, pensions historically have played little role in corporate governance decisions. (This phenomenon might be called the external aspect of pension passivity, to be distinguished from internal pension passivity, i.e., voicelessness by participants of the internal management of pensions.) Black persuasively argues that this passivity might not be the inevitable result of collective-action problems, but the contingent effect of legal rules that strongly inhibit institutional shareholders from being more active in corporate decision-making. See Bernard Black, "Shareholder Passivity Reexamined," *Mich. L. Rev.* 89:520 (1990).

43. A countervailing consideration, however, is that economies of scale may make it easier for some shareholders, especially institutional investors, to monitor multiple firms. See ibid.

44. The so-called "wage earner funds" that exist in Sweden and Germany provide a more promising model for using pensions as a vehicle for redistributing wealth, but these plans are not designed to enhance pension democracy as such. See generally Peter Swenson, *Fair Shares: Unions, Pay, and Politics in Sweden and West Germany* (Ithaca, NY: Cornell University Press, 1989).

45. See Stone, "Labor and the Corporate Structure," supra note 37.

46. See Simon, "The Prospects for Pension Fund Socialism," supra note 37.

II

The Transition to Market Economy—Economic Perspectives

THE TRANSITION TO A MARKET ECONOMY IN RUSSIA: PROPERTY RIGHTS, MASS PRIVATIZATION AND STABILIZATION

Edgar L. Feige

[*Editors' Synopsis:* Most economists today agree that privatization and stabilization should precede liberalization in transforming a centrally planned to a market economy. Professor Feige has argued in favor of a theory of "socialist privatization," under which egalitarian redistribution of state-owned assets and monetary and fiscal stabilization measures would be implemented before control of prices is liberalized. Testing this theory in this paper, he concludes that recent experience in Russia supports it. Hyperinflation, which constitutes the single greatest threat to the success of Russia's reform program, has occurred because the government liberalized prices before privatizing state-owned assets or stabilizing the economy.]

The problem of how to transform a centrally planned economy into a market economy has emerged as one of the most compelling and challenging issues of our time. The question is salient because the republics of the former Soviet Union and the nations of Eastern and Central Europe are in the midst of a transformation process that seeks to capture the claimed efficiency advantages of market mechanisms for their economies. It is complex because a rapid transition from socialism to a market economy is historically unprecedented, and requires a fundamental restructuring of a nation's economic, political, social, and legal institutions, as well as its physical infrastructure. Not surprisingly, there are differences of opinion concerning the scope of reforms and the speed with which they should be undertaken. Murrell suggests "that slowness of transition might be a virtue."[1] An evolutionary path of transition is justified on the grounds that rapid and radical adjustments are likely to cause major short-run disruptions while yielding only modest offsetting benefits. According to this view, a program of gradual reforms is more likely to produce a stable transition by maximizing the flow of output over the entire transition period. At the other extreme is Ericson's claim that reforms must be "trenchantly negative" and "disruptive on a historically unprecedented scale."[2] This revolutionary view acknowledges that the rapid displacement of an entire system of interdependent central planning institutions inevitably causes painful economic disruptions. But unless these severe costs are borne in the short run, the entrenched structure of the centrally planned system will not be overturned, and the reform process will remain susceptible to reversal. To assure the irreversibility of reforms, the old system of central planning must be scrapped and replaced by a new system of legal, administrative, commercial, social security, fiscal, and monetary institutions capable of supporting a market economy.

Most economists now agree that an appropriate transformation program must combine elements of stabilization, privatization, and liberalization. In theory, each of these reform components reinforces the other, and therefore they should ideally be introduced simultaneously in one "big bang" reform. However, private property rights must be created, distributed and credibly enforced before exchange in these rights can take place in markets. Since the efficiency of exchange is greatly enhanced when exchange is conducted in a stable macroeconomic environment, privatization and stabilization should typically precede liberalization reforms. In practice, it has proved impossible to initiate a "big bang" reform strategy. The time and practical difficulty of implementing privatization and stabilization measures has forced governments to liberalize first and only then to undertake stabilization and privatization initiatives. The improper sequencing of reforms is likely to have a significant impact on the stability of the transition to a market economy.

As conceptual reform strategies are put into practice, however imperfectly, the costs of rapid structural adjustment become more visible and widespread. The threat of closure of large state enterprises and the experience of unemployment and hyperinflation produce a political backlash against the advocates of rapid and radical reform. The realization grows that simple prescriptions for transplanting market mechanisms into formerly planned economies are unlikely to succeed unless the institutional prerequisites for a market economy are securely in place. These legal, commercial and administrative institutional precursors of market economies took generations to evolve historically, and can not be readily created *de novo*. Long-standing expectations and behaviors generated by regimes of central planning are difficult to change. The time required to establish the credibility of a reform program, as well as the institutions required to assure its success, may well exceed the political horizon allotted to reform leaders.

There remains an enormous gap between transition theory and practice. The theory of reforms is continuously being reassessed in the light of experience with the actual reform programs. This paper examines the theory of reforms in light of the experience of the recent reforms which preceded and followed the dissolution of the Soviet Union. The first sections review the essential components of reform strategy concerning the nature, sequence, and speed of the reform process. The paper goes on to describe the major political cycles that have characterized the reform process before, during, and after the dissolution of the Soviet Union. The most radical reforms have only recently been initiated in Russia but these reforms are already being seriously challenged. The Russian reforms now appear poised at a critical juncture, one that may well determine whether, and in what form, the transformation to a market economy will proceed.

I. The Conceptual Framework of Transitional Reform

Transformation strategies typically define the final objectives of reform and the nature, sequence, and timing of reforms most likely to achieve the designated objectives. Reform objectives include stability, efficiency, equity, and economic growth, and these objectives are believed to be most readily attainable by the establishment of a market economy. To be successful, a transformation program must be comprehensive, coherent, credible, and dynamically stable. A comprehensive program of reform must contain elements of stabilization, privatization, and liberalization. To be coherent, these elements must be properly sequenced and mutually reinforcing. Credibility requires the consistent management of the reform program such that the expectations and commitments created by the reform plan are in fact fulfilled, and thereby reinforced. The necessary, although not sufficient conditions required to satisfy a stable transition to a market economy include:

(1) The creation and enforcement of an efficient system of property rights governing the ownership, use, and exchange of real and financial assets over time and space, and the distribution of state property to the public.
(2) Fiscal and monetary institutions that promote macroeconomic stability.
(3) Industrial reorganization to promote entry and exit; demonopolization, and the conversion of military production to consumer-oriented output.
(4) Liberalization of economic activity that permits market-determined prices to provide the information and incentive signals required to allocate factors, products, and assets to their highest valued uses, including price linkages that permit integration with the world economy.
(5) The creation of a social safety net to cushion the economic dislocations that are sure to accompany radical reforms.

In several earlier papers[3] I have outlined a specific transformation strategy for the former Soviet Union consisting of a sequenced set of stabilization, mass privatization, and liberalization reforms.[4] This integrated program was designed to attain many of the aforementioned conditions for a stable transition from a command economy, with a preponderance of state-owned property, to a market economy with private property. In brief, the transition strategy, referred to as "socialist privatization," envisioned combining a massive egalitarian redistribution of the state's custodial assets to its citizens with monetary and fiscal stabilization as the prelude to a complete liberalization of the price mechanism.[5]

The effort to establish a market economy in an economic environment devoid of market institutions and a political environment overtly hostile to market activities presents a major challenge. The Soviet economy was organized by a huge central planning bureaucracy that controlled state property representing ninety-five percent of all property. Soviet political ideology viewed "private property" as anathema, and Soviet law dictated that many elementary market activities, such as arbitrage, were economic crimes subject to severe punishment[6]. Under these extreme circumstances, the challenges of the transition from socialism required a radical program specifically designed to take account of the particular political, social, and economic circumstances of the Soviet Union. The unprecedented scale of state property, the absence of asset markets for valuing the property, and the lack of private savings to acquire that property implied that conventional forms of privatization[7] were totally inadequate as a means of creating and distributing property rights.

II. The Critical Importance of Property Rights

The essence of every market economy is the exchange of rights to various forms of property, broadly understood to include goods and services as well as real and financial assets. The creation of a market economy is unthinkable in the absence of valued property rights. Property rights refer to the institutional arrangements that govern the ownership, use, and disposal of property. The value of property rights is ultimately determined by their exclusivity in use and their transferability in exchange. When property rights are vaguely defined, they have little value. When the transactions costs of exchanging property rights are very high, the rights themselves have little value. In the republics of the former Soviet Union, the exclusivity of property rights are at best vaguely defined because of the legal fiction of state ownership. It is therefore not surprising that the stock of capital is so poorly maintained that its productivity so rapidly diminished. In the absence of *de jure* ownership, use, and transfer rights, the terms on which property can be used or transferred is arbitrarily set by state planners. *De facto* rights are distributed by the "privilege system." Under these circumstances, the "privileged" have a single incentive, namely to rapidly exploit their tentative *de facto* rights through rent-seeking behaviors.

The absence of real property rights is largely responsible for the system's inefficiency in production and exchange, and its poor maintenance of capital stocks and natural resource endowments. Exclusive rights to property create the incentives to utilize property efficiently. The right to own and exchange all forms of property avails the economic system of the efficiency advantages of unfettered exchange. But efficiency also demands that exchange be conducted with relatively low transaction costs. A necessary condition for low transactions costs is the existence of credible monetary institutions capable of establishing a monetary medium of exchange with a stable value. Finally, if exchange is to be universal, the establishment and equitable distribution of valued property rights must be one of the principal cornerstones of any reform program. Property rights must be distributed to citizens and other legal entities in an orderly and transparent manner. These rights must include both exclusivity in use and transferability in exchange. Exclusivity must be established by the privatization of state assets, while transferability must be assured by the establishment of a fully functioning monetary and payments system.

III. Privatization Mechanics

Socialist privatization calls for a constitutional grant of private property rights to all citizens, and for the state to relinquish its stewardship of the means of production. The nation's real wealth is to be supplemented by the creation of financial assets capable of representing physical wealth in more fungible form. State enterprises are converted into joint-stock companies whose shares convey title and property rights. State assets are redistributed in two stages: an open-market sale of small-scale state assets, including apartments, shops, storefronts, land parcels, vehicles, and so on, and a large-scale mass privatization in which as much as half of all existing state assets are freely and equitably distributed among the population in the form of "citizen's shares." Citizen shares, as distinct from vouchers,[8] are shares in a state holding company whose assets in turn consist of a bundled portfolio of equities in large state enterprises. A citizen share is analogous to a claim on a mutual fund portfolio representing a broadly based index fund such as the Standard and Poor 500 share index. Citizen shares represent a generalized residual ownership claim on the earnings of the pooled assets of large state enterprises.[9]

Mass privatization can take the direct form of a free distribution of citizen shares, or the indirect form of distributing vouchers (privatization checks) to citizens, who in turn convert them into specific forms of state property. The indirect use of vouchers is advantageous for the purpose of small-scale privatization at the local level. It effectively gives each citizen an economic vote in the election of small-scale state assets. Some knowledge concerning small-scale asset choices is available to most citizens and therefore an equitable distribution of these economic voting rights is likely to result in a more equitable distribution of property rights. However, vouchers are entirely inappropriate for large-scale privatization. Voting rights can only be effectively utilized in combination with information concerning the values of alternative choices. When these values are unknown, and perhaps unknowable[10] for the public at large, vouchers can not effect efficient property distribution. When relevant information is only available to a privileged few, vouchers can not effect an equitable distribution. A highly skewed information distribution will bring about a highly skewed property distribution even when votes (vouchers) are initially distributed equally.[11]

For large-scale privatization, the direct distribution of temporarily inconvertible citizen shares circumvents these problems. Distribution of these shares does not require valuation of the underlying equities. As reforms progress and asset markets are established, citizens can then exchange their citizen shares into shares of newly established private mutual funds. Mutual funds can acquire pools of citizen shares which they would unbundle in order to specialize their own portfolios. Mutual funds would be expected to specialize their portfolios so as to achieve concentrations of ownership in particular enterprises. Institutionalized concentration of share ownership would provide additional incentives for efficient management of enterprise assets and production decisions.

Under the socialist, or people's privatization proposal, fifty percent of all bundled equity shares would be equitably distributed among all citizens. Of the remaining shares, (ten percent) would be allocated to the central government, another (twenty percent) would be allocated to local governments, and the remaining twenty percent would be unbundled into enterprise-specific shares and auctioned off to workers, managers, and foreign investors associated with particular individual enterprises.[12] This final twenty percent concentrates ownership in specific enterprises and thereby provides efficiency incentives for improved management.[13]

The proposed mass privatization program would distribute state assets by means of both sales and free giveaways. Asset sales provide an immediate source of budget revenues during the critical transformation period when the fiscal system is likely to become dysfunctional. The sales also create initial asset markets in which tentative asset prices are established by the forces of supply and demand. Preferential sale options available to managers, workers, and foreign investors are designed to capture the efficiency advantages gained when entrepreneurial skills are matched with existing capital assets. The program permits sufficient concentrations of ownership in specific enterprises to provide incentives for asset preservation and enhancement. It simultaneously converts *de facto* property rights into *de jure* property rights.

The giveaway component of the mass privatization program is motivated by both political and economic considerations. The widespread egalitarian distribution of property rights to citizens creates a constituency for further reforms. Its economic intent is to create an extensive pool of private savings that can eventually be channeled into investments in the emerging private sector. The government's share of bundled equities provides it with a long-term source of revenues with minimal collection costs.

IV. Privatization, Stabilization, and Liberalization

In order to capture the positive synergism between privatization and stabilization, the revenues obtained from asset sales are sterilized in order to eliminate the monetary overhang. To further strengthen stabilization, state subsidies to consumers and firms are phased out, and hard budget constraints are imposed on the state sector. Military expenditures are cut back to regain fiscal balance. The reduction of fiscal deficits in turn reduces the need for further monetary expansion. Thus, the sterilization of the initial monetary overhang and the reduction of fiscal deficits reduce macroeconomic stock-and-flow imbalances, tempers inflationary expectations, and acts as a brake on the price level. Once the economy is stabilized, price liberalization (decontrol) can be completed without the threat of initiating inflation.

The distribution of income-yielding citizen shares creates a natural income and wealth safety net for the populace at large to help weather the short-term transitional costs of structural reallocation of resources.[14] The distribution of citizen shares also creates a broad base of private savings and a diversified consumer market. The bundling of enterprise equities, and their wide distribution among citizens and government agencies, serve to pool the risks and rewards of the transition process. Governments and citizens retain similar stakes in the success of the reform package. Rapid, equitable, mass privatization reinforces stabilization and liberalization, and creates a broad political constituency for reform.

The liberalization reform frees the power of the market to allocate resources more efficiently. Since all citizens become *residual* holders of a substantial portion of pooled equity shares, they participate equally in both the gains and losses that result from resource reallocations and structural changes. Many state enterprises that were constructed and rationally managed under the central planning regime emerge as value-subtracting enterprises when their outputs and inputs are evaluated at market prices that reflect true scarcity values. Given the irrationality of continuing to produce outputs that are worth less than the sum of their inputs, it is essential that nonviable value-subtracting firms be rapidly closed. The closing of nonviable enterprises creates short-term hardships for their workers, but it is socially preferable to provide these displaced workers with unemployment compensation and relocation aid than to continue to subsidize value-reducing production.

Many of the essential features of this type of reform strategy are now widely accepted by policy-makers in formerly planned economies. It is generally recognized that, ideally, all of the key components of the reform strategy should be introduced together, so that each can benefit from the reinforcing effects of the other. This synergy provides the theoretical justification for the "big bang" approach to reform, which calls for all elements of the reform package to be simultaneously put into effect. Unfortunately, these ideal circumstances can not be realized in practice, because each of the reform components (stabilization, privatization, and liberalization) requires a different length of time to implement. Price liberalization requires the shortest period of time to implement, while privatization requires the longest period.[15] The time period required for stabilization to effectively take hold may be quite long and highly variable. Under these circumstances, it is best to immediately initiate privatization and stabilization, and allow full liberalization to follow only after prices and budgets have been brought under control. Destabilizing expectation effects can be minimized by announcing all components of the reform strategy at once and then scrupulously maintaining the announced programmatic schedule, so as to gain credibility for the reform process.

The emerging consensus on the essential requirements of a reform strategy has yet to be confirmed by empirical evidence accumulated in the wake of successful historical experiments with radical transitions to market economies. Actual reform experience suggests that the process of achieving a sustainable and stable transformation to a market economy may be lengthier and far more difficult than was initially supposed. In order to appreciate the complexities of the process, and to learn its lessons, it is useful to review the experience of the Soviet Union during the past few years as it vacillated between reform impetus and retrenchment.

V. Reform Cycles in the Soviet Union

Prior to its dissolution, the Soviet Union faced a constitutional crisis,[16] the threat of civil war, and massive economic dislocation. To appreciate the gravity of the situation one must imagine the United States *simultaneously* confronting its three major domestic historical challenges: the constitutional crisis of the Federalist period, the bloody civil war fought to resolve the crisis over state rights and property rights, and the Great Depression.

The constitutional crisis in the former Soviet Union was manifest in the "war of laws" in which legislative bodies at all levels of government scrambled to assert the supremacy of their enacted legislation over that of the central government. At issue were fundamental questions concerning ownership and control of property, land, and mineral resources, as well as republics' claims to fiscal revenues and their assertions of independent control over monetary affairs. The breakup of the Soviet Union into independent republics broke the control of the "center," but left unresolved the problem of property rights between and within the republics. Complex issues of fiscal federalism and monetary union remained unsettled. Ethnic strife within and between republics occasionally flared into armed conflict, and continues to threaten a wider civil war. Symptoms of the economic crisis included sharp reductions in output and labor productivity, inflation, huge budget deficits, sizable diversions of state resources into the underground economy,[17] and a flight from currency into costly barter transactions.

A. *Step-by-Step Perestroika*

With the initiation of *perestroika* in the mid-1980s Gorbachev signaled a willingness to undertake "step-by-step" economic reforms. These included the antialcohol campaign, the Law on State Enterprises and the Law on Cooperatives. Each of these partial reforms produced unintended consequences. The antialcohol campaign deprived the government of a major source of revenue, stimulated criminal bootlegging, and caused a shortage of sugar. The centerpiece of the reforms was the Law on State Enterprises, which conveyed greater decision-making authority to enterprise managers, and abolished mandatory output targets. Central planners and ministries remained responsible for long-term strategy and state procurement contracts continued to dominate enterprise production orders. The loosening of controls led to greater diversions of state property to the underground economy, and permitted enterprises to raise real wages in excess of productivity increases. The Law on Cooperatives created a fledgling "private" sector with greater flexibility to lease property, hire outside labor, and attract capital. Yet by 1990, the cooperative sector accounted for less than four percent of the labor force and the economy continued to flounder.[18] Step by step liberalization loosened government control over budgets and monetary emissions, and thereby created even greater macroeconomic imbalances. It was not until the summer of 1990 that it appeared that Soviet leaders were finally prepared to revitalize the moribund economy by abandoning central planning, and by initiating more radical policies to effect a painful but necessary transition to a market economy.

B. *The Shatallin-Yavlinsky Reforms*

The "500 Day Plan,"[19] fashioned by the reform-minded economists who then served as principle advisors to Gorbachev and Yeltsin,[20] formulated a comprehensive political and economic program for transitional reforms. It adopted the radical principle of distributing state property to the people[21] by implementing a mass privatization program. The introduction to the 500 Day Plan was bold in style and libertarian in sentiment:

> the state was wealthy while the people were poor, . . . the program sets forth the task of taking everything possible from the state and giving it over to the people. . . . Everybody has a right to choose, guided by his own wishes and capabilities, whether to become an entrepreneur, an employee of the state apparatus or a manager at a stock company, to engage in individual labor, or to become a member of a co-op. The reform grants citizens the right to economic self determination, setting the rules which will prevent certain people, groups of people, enterprises and regions from infringing upon the economic rights of others while pursuing their own interests. It is freedom of choice which makes the basis for personal freedom of the people, for the realization of the creative potential of a personality. . . . The right to property is realized through denationalization and privatization, giving over the state property to citizens. By giving property back to the people the social orientation of the economy will manifest itself. This is not a revenge act, but an act of social justice, a form to fix the right of man to his share in present and future national wealth. . . . The program gives equal chances to everybody. But this equality of opportunity should not be seen as a mirror reflection of egalitarianism.

The political aspects of the program called for the devolution of central powers through the establishment of a "new Economic Union" comprised of "sovereign states united voluntarily" with a view to "stop disintegration of inter-republican links" in order to "create new incentives for economic integration based on the free will of all Republics and due regard for their interests." The powers not explicitly ceded to the "center" were to be reserved for the Republics. The 500 Day Plan acknowledged the systemic failure of the central planning system and candidly recognized that the nation was facing:

> a general crisis of the socio-economic system, including the national structure and ideology—a crisis that has exposed the non-viability of the existing structures.

The *Transition to the Market* report went on to analyze the alternative options available to Soviet policy-makers. It foresaw that a continuation of the government's "half measures and gradual economic reforms" would bring on the "disintegration of the economic system" and the "final collapse of the Union." The report also warned that a realistic alternative was the reactionary scenario, a reversion to the old system of centralized planning. This option would necessitate "large scale political repression" which would return the nation to the "suicidal" course that "has driven the country to the curb of world progress." The option advocated by the authors of the 500 Day Plan included "the preparation and implementation of a radical economic reform aimed to create the foundations for a market economy." The radical reform option was justified by the empirical evidence of Western experience, which supported the superior efficiency of a market economy. The report argued that if the Soviet Union ignored the "universal nature of laws of economic and social development," it would do so at its own peril. The plan envisioned a rapid and radical transformation toward a market economy that included an overly optimistic timetable for implementing macroeconomic stabilization, privatization, and liberalization.

Despite Gorbachev's initial endorsement of the 500 Day Plan, and its rapid adoption by the Supreme Soviet of the Russian Republic, Gorbachev replaced it with a diluted set of "Basic Guidelines" [22] which he submitted to the USSR Supreme Soviet for adoption. The "guidelines" eliminated many specifics of the original plan, including the timetable for implementing reforms, but still asserted that:

> The choice of transition to a market (economy) which has historic meaning for the fate of our country has been made. The question now lies in how to implement the choice.[23]

Gorbachev's "Basic Guidelines" called for the "the improvement of finances and the money supply by reducing the state budget deficit and suppressing the issuance of money." The plan envisioned the maintenance of a single currency, controlled by an independent central banking authority modeled on the U.S. Federal Reserve System.

In the context of Soviet politics, the most controversial aspect of the 500 Day Plan was its explicit call for "the destatization and privatization of property, and the implementation of land reform."[24] The advocacy of destatization and privatization was hailed by Western economists as an explicit acknowledgment that a market economy could only be built on the basis of the institution of private property. However, more careful scrutiny of the political interpretations given to the terms "destatization" and "privatization",[25] revealed that they meant very different things to Soviet leaders than to Western economists. Destatization was broadly interpreted in the West to mean the conversion of state property to private ownership. In Soviet circles it meant a continuation of the program of "self-financing" of state enterprises that had begun with the new laws on state enterprise. The meaning of destatization was clarified in a presentation to the USSR Supreme Soviet on October 18th, 1990 by Academician Abel Aganbegyan,[26]

> First, I would like to say that destatization is a fairly general process, the essence of which is the separation of the function of economic management from the function of state administration. This is a policy of granting independence to enterprises and economic bodies which are responsible themselves for their own revenue and their own expenses and, consequently, enjoy a wide range of rights of self-financing and many other rights.

Aganbegyan, regarded as one of the founders of *perestroika*, revealed the depth of the ambivalence still felt toward private property when he publicly observed:

> Privatization is not a good word. . . . *Privatization is not a switch to private property.* It is a more general term, connected with a change of owner. . . . *We should not think that the authors of the program believe that private property should prevail in our country,* and so on. This section states firmly that the right of private property is recognized, and that is all.[27]

As Gorbachev sensed opposition to reform mounting, he withdrew his support from the reformers, and thereby encouraged the opponents of reform to initiate policies that destroyed whatever credibility the promise of reforms had sought to establish. The first such move was the clumsy recall of fifty- and one-hundred-ruble denomination notes, along with the imposition of strict limits on withdrawals from saving bank accounts. Under a presidential decree, the K.G.B. was granted new powers to seize the accounts of cooperative (private) enterprises. The government went on to decree significant increases in the prices of goods and services, representing yet another attempt on the part of the central planners to "get the prices right," rather than to allow prices to be determined by market forces. The confiscatory nature of these policies served only to further devalue the fragile set of tentative property rights created by earlier reforms, and to set back whatever credibility the government had gained as a champion of reform. The rejection of the economic aspects of the 500 Day Plan also led to the postponement of its critical political component, namely, the agreements that had been reached by the republics concerning the terms on which they would continue to support the Union.

The adoption of the Union Treaty was finally scheduled to take place on August 20th, 1991. On August 19th, conservative forces attempted to preempt its passage with a coup that failed. The attempted coup brought about the dissolution of the Soviet Union and abruptly swung the political pendulum back toward an agenda of more radical economic reform. Under the leadership of Russia's President Yeltsin, the newly formed Gaidar government moved rapidly toward implementing key elements of market reforms.

C. The Yeltsin-Gaidar Reforms

On January 2, 1992, Russia, the largest and most influential member of the newly created Commonwealth of Independent States (C.I.S.), embarked on a closely observed economic experiment whose consequences are shaping the nation's political and economic future. The Russian leadership opted to mimic the Polish "shock therapy" model. Without the benefit of prior monetary and fiscal stabilization measures, the government committed itself to the administratively easy, though politically costly, measure of decontrolling most prices. Following the Polish model, they postponed stabilization, demonopolization, and privatization until after the price liberalization action. Yeltsin explained the flawed sequence of reforms as follows:

> The most difficult and the most urgent measure was the deregulation of prices. No doubt it be preferable first to patch up the hole in the budget, and to cease endless emission, to stabilize money supply and to carry out the whole of privatization, as it should be done in a civilized way, and only then to set prices free. Yes, that is the textbook option. But, regrettably, we already have missed the opportunity for this option because the people's trust has reached its limit.[28]

The first consequence of price liberalization was to bring the previously suppressed inflation into the open by permitting state prices to reflect the demand pressure exerted by the "ruble overhang."[29] In the past, shortages of consumer goods had been rationed by queues and by black market prices in the underground economy. Since the "ruble overhang" represented the stock of excess cash waiting to be spent, its release into the official markets caused a once-and-for-all rise in the official price level. The initial price shock increased the average price level fourfold.

Second, and with more lasting consequence, the liberalization reform eliminated the planned economy's traditional macroeconomic policy instruments, namely price and wage controls. The macroeconomic task of the former planners had been to set the average wage rate and the average consumer price level so as to achieve an exact balance between the total wage fund and total consumption expenditures. When the wage fund exceeded total consumption expenditures, consumers found themselves with excess cash balances whose cumulated sum formed the "ruble overhang." Setting the average wage rate was analogous to collecting an income tax from workers. Fixing the average consumer price level was similar to the imposition of a sales tax. Relinquishing both wage and price controls effectively eliminated the government's ability to collect taxes. Having surrendered its traditional implicit tax base, the government levied an explicit value added tax (VAT). Inadequate administrative preparation, along with high VAT rates, made noncompliance commonplace, depriving the government of sorely needed tax revenues. Despite serious efforts to cut expenditures, the government found it impossible to restore fiscal balance.[30] The government, incapable of financing the deficit with either taxes or borrowing, was left to passively finance the deficit by running the printing presses. What emerged was a textbook receipt for accelerating inflation.

The price liberalization program, unconstrained by stringent fiscal and monetary stabilization, unleashed further inflationary expectations and increased the fragility of the monetary system. The liberalization program did not induce the hoped-for supply response in production. In fact, measured output fell off precipitously. The actual decline in production is difficult to assess, because output measures may themselves be flawed, underestimating increased output in the emerging private sector and overstating output decreases in the public sector. Actual declines in output reflected decreased demand for military and export goods, and production bottlenecks created by a disruption of traditional channels of supply. The breakup of the Soviet Union into independent republics initially gave each republic the ability to increase fiscal expenditures, and thereby export inflationary pressures to all other republics. Efforts to control this practice created export controls that significantly reduced interrepublic trade and thereby compromised channels of supply.

The partial nature of the price liberalization program also contributed to the reduction of output. Although most retail and wholesale prices were decontrolled, energy prices continued to be controlled at levels that were a fraction of world prices. Given the expectation that energy prices would eventually be raised to world levels, rational managers restrained oil output in anticipation of profiting from future price rises. The extraordinary degree of industrial concentration, and the absence of domestic or foreign competition, permitted large state enterprises to fully exploit their monopoly positions by raising prices and actually reducing output. With the collapse of state orders and the breakup of the Union, interenterprise trade suffered, and distribution bottlenecks became more prevalent. Finally, in the absence of a developed capital market and an effective interenterprise payments mechanism, large-scale state enterprises began to issue and accumulate debts to other enterprises. The buildup of interenterprise arrears resulted from the inadequacy of the payments system, and from incentives and information distortions.[31] The potential financial failure of a major segment of state-owned enterprises, and the concomitant threat of widespread unemployment, have created great political pressure from the military and industrial enterprise interests on the central bank to issue vast new credits to offset the massive accumulation of interenterprise arrears.

The central bank, an institution beholden to the Parliament, is yielding to enterprise interests by expanding noncash credits to accommodate the interenterprise arrears with newly created credit. Interenterprise arrears increased from 40 billion rubles to more than 3.2 trillion rubles during 1992. By accommodating interenterprise debt the central bank avoids the immediate consequences of enterprise failures, but it effectively reinstates the "soft budget" constraints demanded by leaders of the enterprises. The central bank justifies the accommodation of interenterprise debt as being necessary to provide working capital to enterprises. Without this working capital, the enterprise sector could implode, leading to massive unemployment and a radical collapse of output. The growth of interenterprise arrears has made it increasingly difficult to distinguish viable from nonviable enterprises. As such, imposing hard budget constraints might force the shutdown of enterprises which are illiquid but solvent. To accommodate interenterprise arrears destroys whatever credibility the reform program had established in attempting to force state enterprises to respond to market rather than central planning incentives. The accommodation of arrears will lead to another round of money supply creation and bring the economy closer to a hyperinflation that could bring about the collapse of the entire monetary system.

The rapidly accelerating inflation has resulted in part from the monetary expansion arising from the maintenance of a ruble zone without adequate monetary controls. Each republic in the ruble zone has the incentive to capture short-term concentrated gains from public expenditure. The inflationary consequences of the monetization of these budgetary deficits is widely diffused over all the other republics.

Fiscal deficits continue to be financed by the creation of cash and noncash components of the money supply. This monetary expansion, and *not* the reforms themselves, has created a monetary system exhibiting symptoms of acute dysfunction. The ruble is not viewed as a viable store of value, and is rapidly being displaced as a medium of exchange by goods and foreign currencies. The real rate of interest on monetary instruments is negative, and there is a growing concern over the moral hazard in the newly emerging system of "private" commercial banks. The high inflation rate swamps the relative price information conveyed by the emerging price system, and thereby robs it of its allocation function. The monetary instability reduces the likelihood that the ruble can attain the status of a convertible currency, and thereby denies the economy the benefits of international trade and competition. Finally, the macroeconomic instability calls into question the ability and desirability of maintaining a common currency zone for the

C.I.S. In short, unless monetary stability and a functioning monetary system are rapidly reestablished, the entire reform movement may be dealt a setback from which it is unlikely to recover.

The inappropriate sequencing of reforms diminished the salutary effects that price liberalization had hoped to achieve. Without the benefit of prior stabilization and privatization, relative price changes were overwhelmed by the inflationary erosion of domestic purchasing power. In the absence of domestic and foreign competition, limited entry and exit into existing markets, and the extraordinary degree of industrial concentration and monopolization, freed prices did not reflect true scarcity values. With inflation rampant, it became impossible to create the preconditions for establishing the ruble as a convertible currency.[32] The inability of the government to impose adequate fiscal and monetary restraint has also cost the government the long-sought aid of international organizations. The International Monetary Fund had scheduled aid on the order of twenty four billion dollars, but to date only a small fraction of the promised aid has been forthcoming. The original plan to create a stabilization fund to make the ruble an internationally convertible currency has been rendered inoperative by the failure to stabilize the currency domestically. As hyperinflation becomes more likely, the continued erosion of the ruble's value, both domestically and internationally, appears inevitable. Despite government denials, a radical currency reform similar to that undertaken during the New Economic Policy of the early 1920s may be the only solution for reestablishing stability once hyperinflation has taken hold.

The postponement of privatization deprived most citizens of rights to real property that could have served as an asset shield from the inflation tax. The major impact of the inflation has been a massive redistribution of income from holders of monetary assets to holders of goods and real assets. Since the holdings of durable goods and assets were highly skewed toward the old *nomenklatura*, the major consequence of the inflation tax has been to redistribute existing wealth in a highly regressive manner. The inflationary asset redistribution has wiped out the monetary savings of many citizens. Faced with lower real wages and growing prospects of unemployment, popular support for the reforms is eroding. Another cycle of reforms appears to be coming to an end as pressures mount for a drastic slowing of the reform process.

VI. Evaluation

When viewed from the perspective of seventy years of authoritarian centralized control over all facets of political and economic activity, the scope and speed of the recent reforms initiated in the Soviet Union are nothing less than extraordinary. Within a short span of years, political leaders have adopted, and large segments of the public have accepted, an entirely new agenda for their economic and political future. The fundamental decision to abandon central planning and replace it with market mechanisms for organizing economic activity has been made, and will be difficult to reverse. A variety of transitional reforms have been attempted with varying degrees of success.

Domestic liberalization, in the form of price decontrols and decentralization of decision-making, has been widespread. A critical exception is the maintenance of controls over energy prices, which are still maintained below world prices. The freeing of prices has reduced queues and has increased the variety of goods available in a limited sector of the market. But in the absence of successful stabilization and privatization, liberalization has not achieved the goal of increasing the supply of output. The failure to stabilize the economy merits particular attention because hyperinflation now presents the single greatest threat to the continuation of the reform process.

The failure to achieve macroeconomic stabilization during the process of transitional reform resulted from a variety of interconnected causes. Most important among these was the inheritance of a monetary overhang, a repressed inflation, and a large budget deficit from the era of central planning. The monetary overhang and the repressed inflation could have been eliminated by a privatization program that exchanged state property for excess rubles. Unfortunately, the needed privatization program required a lengthy time period to initiate, and its introduction during the early phases of *perestroika* was politically untenable, given the widespread ideological resistance to any notion of "private property." The inability to sterilize the ruble overhang assured that a once-and-for-all rise in the price level would accompany any price decontrol liberalization program. This initial burst of inflation set off further destabilizing expectations, and created strong political demands for fiscal expenditures to compensate workers for lost purchasing power. The distributive burden of the inflation fell on the shoulders of money holders, namely the vast majority of Soviet citizens, whose only legal form of savings were ruble hoards and savings accounts at state banks.

Continued inflation resulted from the government's inability to bring the fiscal budget under control. In the absence of a market for government bonds, all government expenditures had to be financed by taxes or through money creation. Once price and wage controls were relaxed the government lost its conventional tax base, and was forced to rely on new and unfamiliar taxes, which became increasingly difficult to collect. Under these circumstances, fiscal stringency required slashing government expenditures. The reduction of consumer subsidies and military expenditures had to be supplemented by the imposition of credible hard budget constraints on large-scale state enterprises. In short, any government that hoped to provide the appropriate microeconomic incentives for enterprises to adjust to market conditions had to establish a stable macroeconomic environment, in which market information signals were explicit and uncontaminated, and a property rights system that gave property owners the opportunity to profit by following market incentives.

In the face of an initial tightening of financial subsidies to state enterprises, the enterprises themselves created a pyramid of interenterprise debts which they hoped would be repaid by yet another relaxation of hard budget principles. At the critical juncture, where fiscal credibility might have been established at the cost of some major enterprise failures, the central bank circumvented the government's attempts at restrictive policy by bailing out the credit-hungry enterprises with more state subsidies. The benefits of this action were highly concentrated in the military-industrial complex, whereas the costs were diffused over the entire population through another round of inflation taxation.

Another difficulty in the stabilization effort resulted from the maintenance of a common ruble zone in various republics without an institutional centralization of monetary authority. Each member of the ruble zone maintained the ability to inflate at the expense of all the other members of the ruble zone. Once again, the direct benefits of inflationary expenditures were concentrated in each republic, whereas the inflationary costs were diffused over all republics. This failure of interrepublic financial arrangements will most likely force the abandonment of a single monetary unit. Separate republican currencies will shrink the present ruble zone. Even Russia will be forced to replace the current ruble through a fundamental monetary reform unless some means can be found to forestall the threatened hyperinflation.

Recent applications of game theory to transition problems[33] reveal the interdependence between distribution issues and stabilization reforms. Stabilization reforms are often delayed, and efficiency-enhancing policies often fail to be adopted, both because of the uncertainty concerning the distribution consequences of the reform policies, and by wars of attrition between groups hoping to acquire a disproportionate share of the gains. If stabilization reforms are to succeed, their distribution consequences must be more transparent and must benefit a broad political constituency. What is required is that the implicit redistribution of wealth, which is now accomplished by inflation, be replaced by an explicit program of wealth redistribution through privatization—the creation and distribution of valued property rights.

Privatization programs, like stabilization programs, will be delayed so long as their distribution implications are poorly understood. What is needed is a transparent mass privatization program that can be rapidly implemented. The program must contribute to fiscal stability by providing the government with a source of revenue that is collectable at low cost. It must provide efficiency incentives to produce new wealth rather than to simply redistribute existing wealth, and it must credibly demonstrate that the conversion of state property into private property conforms with distribution norms of equity. Conventional privatization, that is, the enterprise-by-enterprise sale of state assets, requires too much knowledge and too much time to be an effective means of creating a functioning market economy. Socialist privatization, on the other hand, combines the rapidity and equity of privatization from above (the free distribution of a sizable portion of the pooled residual claims to large-scale state property to the entire population) with the evolutionary and efficiency orientation of privatization from below (the sale of small-scale state property to private owners at the local level and the auction of the unbundled portion of large-scale enterprise shares). Employing both methods assures that the transfer of state property into private hands need not be postponed until the valuation of that property becomes feasible. Valuation of the large-scale properties must await the resolution of the interindustry debt crisis and the establishment of credible hard budget constraints.

The cyclical pattern of observed reforms suggests that political time horizons are considerably shorter than the time horizons required to create and maintain a credible reform program. A necessary if not sufficient condition for lengthening the political lifetime of reform-minded policy-makers is to create a broad political constituency for reform. One important constituency for market reforms will be the emerging private sector of the economy. To facilitate the growth of this private sector, mass privatization is essential and it must be accomplished rapidly.

Notes

This paper, originally presented at the Law and Society Meetings in Amsterdam in June, 1991, has been updated to include a discussion of the reforms adopted by the Russian government after the dissolution of the Soviet Union.

The author wishes to thank Kent Osband and Michael Burnstam for helpful discussions. Research support from the Graduate School of the University of Wisconsin is gratefully acknowledged.

1. Peter Murrell, "Big Bang Versus Evolution: Eastern European Reforms in the Light of Recent Economic History," *PlanEcon. Report* (June 29, 1990).
2. Richard E. Ericson, "The Classical Soviet-Style Economy: Nature of the System and Implications for Reform," *J. of Econ. Perspectives* 5:11 (1991).
3. Edgar L. Feige, "A Message to Gorbachev: Redistribute the Wealth," *Challenge*, May–June 1990, p. 46; Edgar L. Feige, "Perestroika and Socialist Privatization: What is to be Done? and How?" 32 *Comp. Econ. Studies* 1 (1990); Edgar L. Feige, "Socialist Privatization: A Rejoinder," id. at 71; Edgar L. Feige, "Perestroika and Ruble Convertibility," 10 *Cato J.* No. 3 (1991).
4. Liberalization involves both domestic and foreign components, including price decontrols, currency convertibility, and integration with the world economy.

5. A summary and comparison of various privatization proposals suggested by Feige, "Perestroika and Socialist Privatization," supra note 3; Oliver Blanchard, Rudiger Dornbusch, Paul Krugman, Richard Layard, and Lawrence Summers, *Reform in Eastern Europe* (Cambridge, MA: MIT Press, 1991); Roman Erydmon and Andrzej Rapaczynski, "Markets and Institutions in Large Scale Privatization," in *Adjustment and Growth: Lessons for Eastern Europe* eds. Vittorie Corbo, Fabrizio Coricelli, and Jan Bossak, (Washington, D.C.: World Bank, 1991) David Lipton and Jeffrey Sachs, "Privatization in Eastern Europe: The Case of Poland," 2 *Brookings Papers on Economic Activity* (1990), is found in Eduardo Borenzstein and Manmohan S. Kumar, "Proposals for Privatization in Eastern Europe," 38 *IMF Staff Papers* no. 2 (1991).
6. F.J.M. Feldbrugge, The Soviet Second Economy in a Political and Legal Perspective, in *The Underground Economic* ed. Edgar L. Feige (Cambridge: Cambridge University Press, 1989).
7. Conventional privatization schemes rely on the public sales of state assets on an enterprise by enterprise basis. This is the type of privatization undertaken in the United Kingdom and in parts of Latin America.
8. Voucher schemes distribute certificates which entitle the bearer the right to bid for and acquire property put up for privatization by the state. The voucher may have a specific nominal value such as the ten thousand ruble vouchers now being distributed in Russia, or a point value such as those distributed in Czechoslovakia.
9. Financial assets permit ownership rights to be unbundled from use rights and therefore permit the separation of ownership from control.
10. In Russia it may be impossible to determine the value of an enterprise whose assets include large receivables from other state enterprises. Given the magnitude of interenterprise arrears, and the uncertainties concerning the liquidation of particular enterprises, it becomes impossible to determine the likelihood that the receivables of any one enterprise are actually collectible.
11. When vouchers can be freely exchanged for cash the asymmetry of information creates the "carpetbagger" problem referred to by Feige, "Perestroika and Socialist Privatization," supra note 3.
12. It should be noted that the creation of a broad class of citizen "shareholders" can take place rapidly, since the bundling of shares precludes the necessity for valuation to precede distribution. The unbundled shares that are intended to be placed in the hands of the enterprise's future entrepreneurs will take time to distribute in a more evolutionary manner. As such, socialist privatization combines aspects of both Murrell's (supra note 1) and Ericson's (supra note 2) approaches with respect to the speed of the transformation.
13. Morck, Shleifer and Vishny report that for Fortune 500 companies, "performance of firms with management ownership between 5 and 20 percent, as measured by profitability or by the ratio of market value to the replacement cost of assets, is indeed better than the performance of firms with management ownership between zero and five percent." However, they also find "that

performance deteriorates as management ownership rises beyond 20%." R. Morck, A. Shleifer, and R. J. Vishny, "Management Ownership and Corporate Performance: An Empirical Analysis," *NBER Reporter* (Fall 1989) p. 9.

14. Given the magnitude of the required structural transition, unemployment is likely to rise significantly and most likely be of longer duration. Since income payments from citizen shares will be insufficient to compensate for lost labor income, additional targeted safety-net policies are required. These include job retraining and unemployment compensation programs. The most effective means of reducing unemployment is to create incentives for the rapid development of the private sector, and improved labor mobility.

15. The experience of the United Kingdom and Eastern Europe suggests that the time required to complete enterprise-by-enterprise privatization sales must be measured in decades rather than in years.

16. The constitutional crisis was precipitated by what is now referred to as the "war of laws," the conflicting claims of various legislative bodies to the supremacy of their own enacted legislation. The most dramatic cases involved the confrontations between the Republican Supreme Soviets (the Baltic and the Russian Federation) and the Supreme Soviet of the USSR. Under Soviet law, the judicial powers of the Supreme Court were insufficient to adjudicate these disputes. To complicate matters, the Committee on Constitutional Supervision of the USSR, which was itself appointed by the legislative branch of government (the Supreme Soviet of the USSR), had the powers to suspend presidential decrees believed to be unconstitutional and could suspend or call to the attention of the Supreme Soviet that fact that some of its own legislation was unconstitutional.

17. Shatalin cites various estimates of the size of the underground economy suggesting that it approached twenty percent of GNP. S. S. Shatalin, *Transition to a Market Economy* (Moscow: Avkhanagelskoe, 1990) p. 97–98.

18. A full analysis of the economic events of this period can be found in Marshall I. Goldman, *What Went Wrong with Perestroika* (New York: W. W. Norton, 1991).

19. Shatalin, supra note 17.

20. The main authors of the 500 Day Plan included Stanislav Shatalin (Member of the Presidential Council), Nikolai Petrakov (Personal Economic Advisor to the President), Grigory Yavlinsky (Deputy Prime Minister of the Russian Federation) and Boris Fedorov (Minister of Finance of the Russian Federation).

21. Feige, "A Message to Gorbachev," supra note 3.

22. "Basic Guidelines for the Stabilization of the National Economy and the Transition to a Market Economy" published in *Izvestiya* (October 18, 1990) pp. 1, 3.

23. As reported in the *Wall Street Journal* (October 17th, 1990) p. A15. The "Basic Guidelines" represents a compromise between the 500 Day Plan and the government's earlier program *on Regulated Market Economy Structure and Mechanism Formation* (identified with the former Council of Ministers Chairman N. I. Ryzhkov). The Ryzhkov plan argued that "the Soviet Govern-

ment considers the entire package of measures taken to transform the economic system as aimed at the introduction of a socially-oriented market economy," and speaks of the "destatization of property—a full-scale process of transforming state property into other forms" (*Program on Regulated Market Economy Structure and Mechanism Formation* (September 1990) pp. 2, 8, and 9).

24. On October 9th, 1990 the CPSU Central Committee plenum published its reactions to the Supreme Soviet's adoption of Gorbachev's proposals concerning the transition to a market economy. The CPSU's support for the continuation of central planning is made clear by its statement:

"The CPSU Central Committee insists on effective actions by governmental bodies to maintain economic ties, to observe contractual discipline" and, "While supporting diversity of form when withdrawing enterprises from state control, the CPSU Central Committee at the same time advocates priority for collective forms of ownership" and "does not support the idea of handing over or selling land to private ownership." (FBIS-Daily Report-SOV-90-199 [October 15, 1990] pp. 27–28.)

25. FBIS SOV-90-203 (October 19, 1990) p. 33.

26. FBIS SOV-90-203 (October 19, 1990) p. 33.

27. FBIS SOV-90-203 (October 19, 1990) p. 33 (emphasis added).

28. FBIS-SOV-92-009 (January 14, 1992) p. 34 (statement of January 11, 1992).

29. For a full explanation of the "ruble overhang" and how it was originally generated see Feige "Perestroika and Ruble Convertibility," supra note 3.

30. The 1991 budget deficit was roughly twenty percent of GDP.

31. Summers provides an overview of the payments mechanism in Bruce J. Summers, "Russian Payment Institutions and the Medium of Exchange Function of the Ruble," paper presented at the Conference on Institutional Economics and the Transition to a Market Economy in Russia, Madison, Wisconsin, 1992. Ickes and Ryterman explain how the institutional arrangements concerning payments and credit allocation provided incentives for enterprises to make loans at negative real interest rates to other enterprises whose solvency was itself virtually impossible to determine. Barry W. Ickes and Randi Ryterman, "Inter-enterprise Arrears and Financial Underdevelopment in Russia" (mimeo, 1992).

32. Feige and McKinnon describe preconditions for external convertibility and its relationship to domestic reforms. Feige, "Perestroika and Ruble Convertibility," supra note 3; Ronald I. McKinnon, *The Order of Economic Liberalization* (Baltimore: Johns Hopkins Univ. Press, 1991).

33. Raquel Fernadez and Dani Rodrik, "Resistance to Reform: Status Quo Bias in the Presence of Individual-Specific Uncertainty," *Am. Econ. Rev.* 81:1146 (1991); Alberto Alesina and Allen Drazen, "Why Are Stabilizations Delayed?" *Am. Econ. Rev.* 81:1170 (1991).

Stabilization versus Privatization in Poland: A Sequencing Problem at Macro- and Microeconomic Levels

Andrzej Wojtyna

[*Editors' Synopsis:* Poland has hit a large roadblock impeding development. Debates not only over the manner and speed of privatization but also the problem of sequencing of changes have hindered progress and prolonged economic stagnation. At issue in the problem of sequencing is conflict between privatization and stabilization of the economy.]

Introduction

Two and a half years after launching the Balcerowicz plan, a program of sweeping economic reforms aimed at stabilizing the economy, Poland is once again at a crossroads. There has been a clear deterioration of performance at both the macro- and microeconomic levels, threatening not only to reverse progress made by the country's economic stabilization plan, but also to undermine the currently fragile political stability. The country must find answers to fundamental economic questions, but the fact that Eastern European economists are at work in the dark is by now a virtual cliché. Many essential problems are yet to be addressed, and given Poland's lack of previous experience of market economy, a high degree of uncertainty logically accompanies the transformation process. This uncertainty is much higher when efforts to stabilize rampant inflation are implemented, as they now are in Poland, simultaneously with profound systemic changes (such as privatization, demonopolization, deregulation, liberalization, and so on). Lessons learned during the early phase of the reform process have led to a better understanding of the inherent dilemmas faced by postcommunist societies, the most important being that the transformation process is much more complicated than was expected just two years ago.

The task confronting the economies of Eastern Europe is only now becoming clear. A severe and persistent recession has fueled, rather than cured, inflation, putting privatization at the top of economists' agendas.[1] While it is true that the role privatization plays in the transformation process is much more vital to economic recovery than was initially assumed, Polish economists now tend to stress privatization as a panacea for all of the country's economic ills.[2] A "Murphy's Law of Reforms" would state that reforming an internally consistent economic system makes things get worse before they get better.[3] But this is an oversimplification. The reality of the situation in Poland, as I will discuss in this paper, can be summarized as follows:

(1) Recession leads to a budget deficit, which adversely affects stabilization efforts and perpetuates the recession.
(2) The deficit encourages the government to privatize by selling stock in state-owned enterprises (as opposed to a free distribution of shares in privatized firms), but the recession limits the demand for these stocks.
(3) If the government attempts to finance its expenditures in a noninflationary manner through bond issues, the bonds will compete with stock offerings for scarce savings.
(4) Shifting privatization to commercial terms slows down the entire process of ownership transformation.
(5) Because of budget constraints, the government might also be forced to abolish tax incentives for investment in the private sector. This would slow privatization down even further, in the long run leading to a lower rate of growth and consequently a lower tax base.

Hindsight indicates that a different approach to the problem of sequencing economic stabilization and privatization might have helped at least to alleviate, if not avoid, some of the roadblocks to economic reform in Poland. While history cannot be reversed, a better understanding of the interrelationship between stabilization and privatization can lower future costs of transformation and bring the Polish economy closer to self-sustained growth. This paper argues that both privatization and stabilization policies must consider the effects one will have on the other, and the inherent conflicts between immediate needs and long-term goals of legal certainty and economic stability.

I. Controversy over the Sequencing of Economic Reform

The sequencing of economic reform has only recently emerged as a topic of theoretical discussion. During the 1980s, academic discussion focused on the order in which capital controls, domestic financial markets, and trade barriers should be liberalized, and modeled upon developing, market-oriented countries. Sebastian Edwards concluded:

> the first, and perhaps the only generally accepted principle of reform sequencing, is that international capital controls should only be lifted after the domestic financial market has been reformed and domestic interest rates have been raised. In turn, interest rates should be liberalized only after the fiscal deficit is under control.[4]

While the economic principle Edwards invokes may be valid for the relatively homogeneous group of developing, market-oriented countries, it is of only limited value to the postsocialist economies. In developing, market-oriented countries sequencing has a much broader meaning, since economic liberalization is only one part of the systemic transformation. "[I]f liberalization from classical socialism is to succeed, moves to dismantle the apparatus of central planning, decontrol prices, privatize property, and so on need to be supported by a proper sequence of fiscal, monetary and foreign exchange measures."[5] Within this "seamless web of the transition process"[6] are two interconnected dimensions of sequencing:

—time relationships between the major building blocks of the reform (stabilization, liberalization, privatization, and so on);

—time relationships between the steps taken within each building block (for instance, privatization).

Overemphasizing the first of these dimensions may lead to reforms that are too abstract and academic, while overemphasizing the second may lead to a situation in which logically consistent proposals in one area (such as privatization) wreak havoc on the economy as a whole. Debate is split between those who argue for an optimal sequence and those who maintain that sequencing is not an issue worth worrying about. Those who argue the value of sequencing believe that existing transformation strategies are incomplete, and that debate should be fostered in order to avoid further deterioration of the economic situation, and to prevent government from making stupid mistakes in the future. But how much time should the country spend debating the issue before adopting one of several sensible proposed strategies?[7] For an economist, speaking in abstract terms of a hypothetical economy, the question of whether economic stabilization should come before or after systemic changes is more complicated and obviously less urgent.[8] However, when one is confronted with the prevailing economic situation in a given country, such sequencing decisions are unavoidable. Each country offers a unique economic and political platform for reform, and is likely to develop a unique mix and sequence of transition measures.[9]

This is precisely where hyperinflation enters the picture. Most economists agree that the existence of hyperinflation compels the selection of a "stabilization first" sequencing pattern.[10] Given the damaging consequences of hyperinflation, it is not surprising that most Polish economists favored the "stabilization first" approach, even though they were divided on the exact nature of the reforms and the speed of their implementation. While the Balcerowicz economic stabilization plan itself gives rather sparse details regarding the sequencing of reforms, it explicitly states that "effective implementation of the economic stabilization program is the necessary prerequisite for success in pursuing fundamental systemic changes, because such changes cannot be carried out effectively if accompanied by rampant inflation."[11] This picture is less clear if one considers other parts of the Balcerowicz plan, especially Part IV, which states:

> parallel with efforts to counteract inflation and stabilize the economy, the Government will take steps leading to a breakthrough change in the economic system. This will consist of introducing market economy institutions which have proven themselves in the developed Western countries. Instrumental to that will be: ownership changes, making the structure of ownership similar to that in the industrially developed countries. . . .[12]

Although the Balcerowicz plan made no explicit commitment to a specific sequencing pattern, the spirit of the plan and its later implementation indicate that a policy of "stabilization first" prevailed.[13]

There are three general features of Polish sequencing under the Balcerowicz plan. First, hyperinflation forced the government to make stabilization a top priority in the early phase of the program's implementation. Second, complexities of the stabilization phase, and difficulties with achieving targeted rates of inflation, resulted in government's preoccupation with instruments of macroeconomic policy. This brought about further delay in launching the privatization part of the plan. Third, this delay in privatization is one of the factors prolonging Poland's recession, which in turn makes the goals of stabilization even more difficult to achieve.

II. Stabilization and Privatization: Possible Connections

Both mainstream economic theory and the empirical experiences of market economy stabilization plans indicated that inflation could be eliminated through a mixture of monetary, fiscal, currency exchange, and taxation policies. Therefore, during the first phase of the Balcerowicz plan there were good grounds to believe economic stabilization was possible even before any progress had been made in other areas of the transformation. Most observers felt that the real difficulties would be encountered in the second phase of the plan. "Massive marketization of an economy has never been tried before and the technical problems are daunting."[14] However, as the recent Polish experience shows, the most difficult phase of transformation in postsocialist countries may actually be economic stabilization, because it is so fraught with unexpected challenges and complications.

The experience of the Polish stabilization plan has forced Polish economists to look at the relationship between stabilization and privatization from a new angle. The traditional, cause-and-effect view of transformation regarded stabilization as a prerequisite to privatization.[15] The emerging view, however, is that stabilization measures are not always good for privatization, even if the causal sequence must still be perceived to run from the former to the latter. A "stabilization at all costs" policy may harm rather than encourage changes in ownership. According to this new view, the progress of privatization (or lack of it) affects stabilization efforts. A country that does not provide the sort of incentives which motivate private firms may encounter great difficulty in attempting to lower inflation to single-digit annual levels. This is one of the most important feedbacks of the transformation process, although, as this paper discusses, stabilization and privatization are inextricably connected in many other ways.

III. Privatization and the Credibility of Stabilization

The uncertainty surrounding the privatization process in Poland has contributed to the passivity with which enterprises have responded to the new economic conditions, which in turn fuels the recession. According to the new conventional wisdom, commercialization and privatization can remedy the problem of the passive adaptation of state enterprises to the new circumstances by providing firms with private incentives.[16] I use the term "new conventional wisdom" for this view (not without pejorative coloring) not because it is wrong *per se,* but because it relies on the wrong time horizon. The conventional wisdom (which really is the efficiency argument of private incentives) is probably the most persuasive rationale favoring privatization, at least in the abstract. Few economists in Poland (or elsewhere) today doubt that privatization (with private incentives) is the only mechanism that will lead to long-term improvements in productivity at the microeconomic level.[17] Consequently, no controversy surrounds the question of whether privatization will have a positive long-run impact on macroeconomic stabilization.[18] But while it is easy to say that privatization is necessary for the success of stabilization efforts in the mid- to long term, my own view is that by reinforcing the credibility of stabilization efforts, privatization can also contribute substantially to resolving the immediate problem of the recession. This positive contribution is achieved not by providing the incentives inherent in private ownership, but by reducing persistent microeconomic uncertainties over the durability of the reforms. If people doubt either the sustainability or irreversibility of the reforms, economic actors will begin to speculate, generating forces that can endanger the reforms themselves. Privatization reduces this problem.

> Macroeconomic and structural reform measures introduced simultaneously are likely to reinforce each other, provide confidence and momentum, and reduce the risk that the process will be reversed [which in turn will] contribute to the credibility of the transformation process.[19]

The law on privatization was passed only six months after the Balcerowicz plan had been launched, a remarkably short period given the complexity of the task. However, during this six months the country was also undergoing other dramatic changes, including price liberalization and a shift from soft- to hard-budget constraints, which considerably increased uncertainty. Due to a lack of private ownership during these six months, these changes combined with the restrictive demand policy to bring about a hybrid system of incentives that effectively paralyzed enterprise decision-making. Surprisingly, passage of the law on privatization did not significantly reduce the public's uncertainty over the reforms.

Given the inherent public uncertainty over the transformation process itself, the law on privatization, when enacted, left several methods of privatizing open to enterprises and government. This flexibility has both positive and negative aspects, depending on whether one speaks of privatizing in the long or short term. Because Parliament will not be called to frequently amend the law, flexibility is a virtue; it ensures that the law itself retains its integrity and relative stability over time, and hence the legislature's commitment to privatization will be more credible in the long run. But because the law does not pin the government down to a given form of privatization, flexibility can only fuel the public's uncertainties over the present privatization process. In the end, the best way to establish credible reforms is by creating institutions that prevent the government from implementing abrupt changes in policy.[20]

In the transition from socialism to capitalism, privatization may be a stronger anchor than the recommendations suggested by the International Monetary Fund. These recommendations included the so-called nominal anchors: devaluing the exchange rate, making it convertible and stabilizing it at the newly depreciated rate, and implementing a tax policy that is designed to limit wage increases in state enterprises. While neither actual privatization nor its laws will be able to perform this function in the near future, there may be other ways to significantly reduce uncertainty and thus to encourage enterprises to adapt to the new circumstances.

A promising measure to establish a degree of certainty is a proposed "legal map" of privatization, which would supply state enterprises with a clear picture of their situation *vis-à-vis* the government's intentions. This legal map has been promised since June 1991, but the interim Polish governments have yet to produce one. In order to plan its operations, each enterprise should know at a minimum whether it will remain a state enterprise either permanently or at least in the "foreseeable future," whether it will undergo commercialization (incorporation),[21] whether the decision to privatize the enterprise will be made by a government authority or by the enterprise itself, and whether it will have a free hand in deciding the most appropriate methods of privatization. Surveys conducted in enterprises reveal that such a map is sorely needed to address the current short-term bias in decision-making (a "wait and see" strategy) of state-owned enterprises, and to encourage the enterprises to adapt to the new economic conditions by reducing costs, modernizing, searching for new markets, and so on.

There are, of course, many other ways in which the issue of credibility can influence the relationship between privatization and stabilization. For example, the public may expect future currency devaluation even if the government seeks stable exchange rates (which functions as a nominal anchor) as a way to establish the credibility of stabilization efforts; rational actors will therefore reduce their savings or even go into debt in order to buy imported goods while they remain "cheap." Increasing imports would reduce the available funds which could be used to buy stocks, handicapping efforts to privatize firms by offering them for public sale. This scenario is quite possible in Poland, where the actual value of the firms proposed for sale is much greater than the public's ability to purchase their stock. This is the subject of the following section.

IV. The Problem with Privatization through Public Sale Offerings: The Impact of Recession on Purchasing Power

The Balcerowicz plan's results actually overshot some of its goals. Among these goals was eliminating inflation, by liberalizing prices and at the same time constraining the money supply with a tight fiscal and monetary policy. The purpose of this policy was to encourage the market to shift away from consumption and towards production. In practice, however, it constrained privatization efforts by eroding forced and voluntary savings, leaving resources for private investment in short supply. This is one of the traps that appear when draconian stabilization measures precede privatization, but it could have been avoided. If the stabilization and privatization phases of the Polish transformation process had been better synchronized, people would have been more inclined to invest their savings in privatized enterprises.

Due to both the traditionally low savings rate in Poland and the consequences of an anti-inflationary tax imposed in late 1989 and early 1990, the financial capital currently in the hands of the public is a small fraction of the value of the enterprises to be privatized. One study, which assumes that the market value of enterprises is a multiple of their annual earnings,[22] concludes that, given even the lowest calculated price-earnings ratio of six, the estimated market value of the largest five hundred enterprises is roughly two and a half times the current savings of private households (that is, hard currency and bank deposits). Experts at the National Bank of Poland believe this estimate to be overly optimistic, that in reality the relation of savings to the market value of the enterprises is far more disproportionate.[23] Even under the most favorable estimates, however, it is clear that an initial public offer cannot be the primary method of privatization in Poland.[24]

Only one hundred and thirty thousand people purchased stocks in the first five enterprises to be offered for public sale at the end of 1990. Demand for stock in these five enterprises exceeded supply by a mere seven percent. Public expectations were at least partially responsible for this lack of demand. Despite the fact that money balances held by the public actually increased in real value during 1990,[25] a December 1990 survey found that sixty-seven percent of Polish households expected they would have to decrease their savings; twenty-seven percent anticipated no change, and only 3.8 percent expected their savings would increase in the near future. From January to December, 1990, the average money balance rose from thirty-eight day expenditures to fifty-one days, though it was still far below pre-hyperinflation levels (ninety-one days in July, 1989).[26]

Poles appear to be overwhelmingly opposed to privatization through the sale of stock in state-owned enterprises. One author estimates that only ten percent of Polish adults support privatization through a public offering.[27] Another survey aimed at examining Polish attitudes found that eighty percent of the public opposed the purchase of stocks and seventy-two percent were against the purchase of bonds.[28] A 1992 survey of public attitudes towards mass privatization through vouchers was more optimistic. More respondents favored a government policy of selling shares in investment funds (forty-three percent) rather than giving shares away (thirty-two percent). Thirty-one percent said they would sell their shares, sixty-three percent said they would keep them, and six percent said they would buy more shares.[29]

There may be some validity to the argument that in gauging actual behavior one should be wary of opinion polls as measures of preferences. My point, however, is that considering even the most optimistic of these polls, one would have to conclude that the lack of willingness to invest in privatized firms presents a nearly insurmountable hurdle to privatization, at least if privatization is to proceed by offering to sell state enterprises at market or near-market value. For example, at Jotes, a medium-sized state enterprise in the electromachinery industry, over eighty percent of the employees favored liquidating the firm in order to arrange a management/employee buy-out.

Roughly a thousand Jotes employees pledged a total of one billion Złotys towards this purchase, a figure that fell short of the twenty percent of the enterprise's value required for such a buy-out.[30] Under this requirement, employees would have each had to invest twenty million Złotys in the company's stock, twenty times more than they had voluntarily pledged to contribute. The same is true of Próchnik, one of the five enterprises offered for public sale. Employees there have been slow to purchase the twenty-percent share to which they are entitled.

The examples above illustrate the fundamental constraints on creating a capital market in Poland, and they are only the tip of the iceberg. One must not overestimate the short-term adverse impact of a prolonged recession on both available capital and public attitudes. In comparison with other postcommunist countries, Poland was characterized by a low savings-to-income ratio long before the transformation process started, further diminishing the ability of Poles to invest in private enterprises under adverse economic conditions. Equally important, and also equally unfavorable from the point of view of establishing a capital market, is the structure of savings characterized by a low concentration ratio.[31]

Public support for privatization has also diminished. In the three months from November 1991 to January 1992, the percentage of those who favor accelerated privatization fell from fifty percent to just over twenty percent.[32] At the same time, opposition to foreign investment rose from twenty-four percent in September 1991 to thirty-seven percent in February 1992.[33] The shift in public attitudes is a symptom of "adjustment fatigue syndrome," characteristic of economies during the late stages of transformation.

V. Different Methods of Privatization and their Effect on the Economy

In considering the relationship between stabilization and privatization, one must remember that privatization is not only denationalization of existing state-owned firms, but also the founding of entirely new private companies. Under current economic conditions, "stabilization" means much more than simply disinflation in Poland. Private investors perceive stabilization in terms of the entire sociopolitical, legal, and economic framework within which they make their investment decisions. Lack of stability gives rise to decision-making that is biased towards the short term. In Poland, such shortsightedness has brought about relative overinvestment in wholesale and retail trade (where new private firms are mushrooming) and underinvestment in production. In this sense, Polish privatization has involved a certain amount of deindustrialization, and one can hardly expect private companies to invest further into the future before fundamental regulatory mechanisms appear more stable (for instance, taxes, customs duties, and foreign exchange). Stabilization in a narrow sense (disinflation) also plays a very important role in the decisions of private investors, because both interest rates and their volatility heavily influence the amount of investment. In 1990, Poland's restrictive financial policy not only discouraged the founding of new private firms in the production sector, but also brought many existing firms to the verge of bankruptcy.[34] The adverse impact of the widespread lack of stable economic factors on investment decisions poses yet another serious threat to the future of privatization in Poland. With recent liberalizations in foreign transactions, it is very likely that investment capital will migrate to more secure foreign markets. This process has actually already started,[35] and it is accompanied by a shortage of foreign capital flowing into Poland. The result is a "crowding-out" effect in which investment capital is diverted from private firms, a situation that can only get worse if denationalization proceeds on commercial terms (for example, through an initial public offer).

The restrictive monetary measures of the stabilization process have affected how firms choose to become privatized. For example, during most of 1990 the two most popular forms of privatization were leasing and liquidation with management/employee buy-out, because they offered enterprises the fastest way to avoid paying the *popiwek* (a highly progressive tax imposed on excess wages). However, a November 1990 regulation[36] made these two methods unattractive by attaching high nominal interest rates to the principal of the buy-out or leasing price.[37] In all twelve enterprises under one study the five-year cumulative burden of these interest payments would be two to eight times higher than if the enterprise remained state-owned and paid the dividend tax. Fortunately, in May 1991, the government modified the regulation by setting maximum nominal interest rates to protect new companies from unexpectedly high inflation.

The relationship between stabilization goals and the methods of privatization can be something of a vicious cycle. For example, a highly restrictive demand policy erodes savings, and hence places practical barriers on the commercial sale of state-owned enterprises. Under these conditions, free distribution or sale of stock at prices below market value are the only viable methods of privatization. However, distribution on these terms would likely result in rapid increases in wealth and liquidity that could overinflate aggregate demand in consumption. From the point of view of short-term macroeconomic stabilization, such a situation would be disastrous. Borensztein and Kumar claim that distributing enterprise ownership on these terms would triple consumption over current levels.[38] They point out that even if consumers spent only ten percent of their increased wealth, private consumption would increase by thirty percent. Although part of the resulting increase in consumer spending could actually substitute for government safety-net spending, it might be necessary to curb private consumption at the risk of jeopardizing the stabilization effort. Consumption diverts scarce savings from investment, crowding out capital from private firms. Because of Poland's high propensity to import goods, scarce capital is not only momentarily diverted from private firms, but forever migrates to other countries.

In 1991, the Bielecki government knew that privatization vouchers could bring about inflationary pressures which would endanger economic stabilization. The government planned to tighten its financial policy whenever necessary to control undesirable increases in consumption.[39] However, in the first half of 1992, the Olszewski government delayed its plans for mass privatization, which involved the free distribution of vouchers that could be used to buy stock in investment funds. Although the voucher system potentially threatened economic stability, much stronger inflationary pressures now come through a cost-push mechanism.

VI. Privatization and the Budget Deficit

Privatization affects both government revenues and expenditures. An oft-cited reason for selling state enterprises is to relieve a deficit aggravated by subsidization of state-owned enterprises. Most responsible economists, however, agree that privatization should never be used as a tool to achieve even the most urgent short-term policy objectives (such as balancing the budget), but rather must be a way of establishing a viable, long-term economic order. It is indisputable that privatization will clearly increase revenues in the long run by expanding the government's tax base.[40]

Initially, short-term budgetary considerations were not considered an important issue in the privatization debate. The reason for this was the unexpected budget surplus,[41] a favorable situation that was completely reversed by the first quarter of 1991. In all likelihood, this decline in revenues significantly affected the government's privatization policy. The prolonged recession pushed the 1991 budgetary goals out of reach. In planning the government's budget, Parliament had assumed there would be a four percent increase in gross national product and a maximum rate of inflation of thirty-two percent (it was soon obvious that neither of these targets would be met), and had also relied on an early prediction that the sale of state enterprises would generate fifteen trillion Złotys in revenue. Parliament had even decided how it would spend these revenues. Instead, actual revenues from privatization were below three trillion Złotys. In the 1992 budget (which Parliament did not ratify until June of that year), Parliament stated that revenues from privatization should amount to 10 trillion Złotys, but given the sluggish rate of privatization under the Olszewski government, this goal is probably much too optimistic.

Due to the fact that the recession has reduced the value of the state enterprises offered for sale to domestic and foreign investors, government revenues are lower than anticipated. With fewer funds at its disposal, the

Ministry of Ownership Transformation is currently able to prepare fewer enterprises for privatization. At the end of January 1992, for example, the Ministry owed 27.4 billion zlotys to consulting firms in the West and in Poland. In the first quarter of 1992, the Ministry is scheduled to pay about one hundred billion Złotys for services already rendered, but will probably be able to reimburse the firms for only a third of this amount.

The growing budget deficit has forced the government to search for new, noninflationary ways of financing government expenditures. The issue of government bonds (begun June 1, 1992) got off to a good start. However, like so many other aspects of the stabilization plan, these bonds compete with stocks for scarce savings and hence have an adverse impact on privatization.[42]

Conclusion

It is too early to predict how the complicated short- and long-term interrelations between stabilization and privatization will develop. Future political developments will, no doubt, play an important role. Parliament is highly fragmented, and does not offer a climate of political stability and continuity, which is so important for both economic equilibrium and privatization.[43] It is vital that political discourse in Poland take into consideration the following principle: although a rapid move to a market is indeed risky, a slower, graduated process may ultimately prove even riskier.

Notes

1. As *The Economist* recently observed, "[A] year ago [the idea of putting privatization in front of economic stabilization] could not have been taken for granted. Some Western advisers believed that market economies could be created merely by freeing prices . . . ; private enterprise was desirable, of course, and would come, but there was no need to rush." "From Marx to the Market," *The Economist* (May 11, 1991) p. 11.
2. Interestingly, while many economists now view privatization as the top priority, this view is not reflected in government policies, where privatization is actually occurring more slowly than in the past. The shift away from the "big bang" theory of privatization to a more gradualist approach reflects a growing wariness of "experimentation."
3. See William D. Nordhaus, *Soviet Economic Reform: The Longest Road,* Brookings Papers on Economic Activity (1990) 1:300.
4. Sebastian Edwards, *The World Economy* The Sequencing of Economic Reform: Analytical Issues and Lessons from Latin American Experiences, 1:3 (1990).
5. Ronald I. McKinnon, "Financial Control in Transition to a Market Economy," unpublished paper delivered at Stanford University (February 20, 1991) p. 2.

6. David Lipton and Jeffrey Sachs, *Creating a Market Economy in Eastern Europe—The Case of Poland,* Brookings Papers on Economic Activity 99 (1990) 1.
7. Michael Marrese, "Report of June 1990" (Rapporteur's first draft), Economics and Statistics Department (ESD) Seminar on the Transformation of Planned Economies, OECD, Paris (June 20–21, 1990) p. 3.
8. In such a context the issue is also less clear, and there are convincing arguments in favor of each case. For further discussion on this important theoretical and practical problem, see Manuel Hinds, *Issues in the Introduction of Market Forces in Eastern European Socialist Economies,* Rep. No. IDP-0057, Internal Discussion Paper, Europe, Middle East and North Africa Region, The World Bank, Washington (1990).
9. Gary H. Jefferson and Peter A. Petri, "From Marx to Markets," *Challenge* (September–October 1990), p. 5.
10. Western authors have commented on the Polish situation. Stanley Fischer, for example, has written that "for an economy facing hyperinflation, as Poland did at the end of 1989, the first step has to be macroeconomic stabilization. The structural measures come next, with transformation of the industrial structure, including ownership, the prime goal." Stanley Fischer, *Comments,* 1 Brookings Papers on Economic Activity (1990). This view has not been universally accepted, however. Lawrence Brainard, for example, believes that it is a mistake to undertake radical economic stabilization until key structural reforms are ready to be implemented. Lawrence Brainard, "Strategies for Economic Transformation in Eastern Europe: The Role of Financial Market Reform," paper prepared for ESD seminar, OECD, Paris (1990). Murrell also strongly criticizes the pattern of sequencing adopted in Poland. Peter Murrell, "Big Bang versus Evolution: East European Economic Reforms in the Light of Recent Economic History," *PlanEcon Report* 26:5, 8 (1990).
11. Janusz Bugajski, Poland's Anti-Communist Manifesto, *Orbis* (Winter 1990), p. 112.
12. Ibid., p. 113.
13. Domenico Nuti offered a comparison of the three Polish economic plans proposed in 1989, those associated with Soros, Sachs and Balcerowicz. With respect to timing, Nuti calls the Balcerowicz program "sequential," the Soros program "simultaneous," and the Sachs program "parallel." However, Nuti distinguishes the Balcerowicz plan of September 1989 from that of January 1, 1990. He characterizes the timing of the latter as a "simultaneous stabilization package to be followed by a further round of policy measures" and explains that "the Poles (and the IMF) have put the end of inflation as their primary and only concern for the first four to five months of 1990." Domenico M. Nuti, Privatization of Socialist Economies: General Issues and the Polish Case," paper prepared for ESD seminar, OECD, Paris (1990) pp. 180–81.
14. Janusz A. Ordover, "Economy in Transition," *Business Economics* (January 1991), p. 27.

15. See Lipton and Sachs, supra note 6 ("[T]he private sector will emerge only if the proper price signals exist"); John M. Montias, "The Sequencing of Reforms," *Challenge* (September–October 1990) ("[P]rivatization also hinges on the attainment of equilibrium prices. If prices are far removed from the mark, no one knows what productive assets are worth."); D. M. Nuti, quoted by Marrese, supra note 7, p. 9 ("[T]he sale of shares in state enterprises should occur after stabilization has been attained and fiscal reform has been implemented. This sequence would minimize the extent to which state assets are sold at below-market prices.").

16. Stanislaw Gomulka, "Rozluźnienie zdusiloby rozwój" [Loosening [the macroeconomic policy] would choke development], 120 *Gazeta Wyborcza* (1991).

17. Or at least it is the only approach not guaranteed to fail.

18. Lipton and Sachs summarized this last point: "Most important, Poland must begin a rapid process of privatization of state firms, not only to assure efficient resource use in the future, but to prevent the collapse of the stabilization itself in the medium term. Experience around the world, plus the logic of the soft budget constraint, strongly suggests that it will be difficult to maintain the financial discipline of the state enterprises beyond the short run, especially if the state enterprise sector remains the dominant part of the economy. Eventually, wage pressures and lax investment decisions are likely to undermine the financial health of the state firms." See Lipson and Sachs, supra note 6.

19. Guillermo A. Calvo and Jacob A. Frenkel, "From Centrally Planned Market to Market Economy," IMF Staff Papers (1991) No. 2.

20. Edwards, supra note 4.

21. See generally Dariusz Chelmiński, Andrzej Czynczyk and Henryk Sterniczuk, in this volume.

22. Lipton and Sachs, supra note 6. They consider three price-earnings ratios of six, eight, and ten.

23. The Bank's experts estimate the market value of state enterprises at one hundred fifty to two hundred trillion zlotys and the maximum total demand for stock in these companies at 9.4 trillion zlotys. Jacek Tittenbrun, "Sprzecznośi prywatyzacj" [Contradictions of privatization], *Polityka* 20:6 (1991).

24. This is true, even though the market for privatized firms is far from clear; empirical evidence is scant, flimsy and mostly anecdotal.

25. Katarzyna J. Malysz, "Kondycja gospadarstw domowych" [The conditions of households], *Życie Gospodarcze* 2: 8 (1991).

26. Marian Górski and Dariusz Jaszczyński, "Makroekonomiczne uwarunkowania i skutki polityki stabilizacyjnej w Polsce" [Macroeconomic determinants and consequences of stabilization policy in Poland], paper presented at conference organized by Instytut Finansów [Institute of Finance] and Ministerstwo Finansów [Ministry of Finance] (Warsaw, April 24–26, 1991) p. 24.

27. Edward Golachowski, "Procesy prywatyzacyjne w krajach postsocjalistycznyc," [Privatization processes in postsocialist countries], paper prepared for

conference organized by Instytut Finansów [Institute of Finance] and Ministerstwo Finansów [Ministry of Finance] (Warsaw, April 24–26, 1991).

28. Marian Ber, "O dochodach, akcjach i obligacjach" [On incomes, stocks and bonds], *Życie Gospodarcze* (1991) 8:10.

29. Pawel Wujec, "Prywatyzacja powszechnie platna" [Privatization universally paid for], 35 *Gazeta Wyborcza* (1992).

30. The firm was valued at 105 billion Złotys; the employees' offer to buy the firm was therefore less than one percent of the firm's value, or five percent of the capital required for an employee buy out. " 'Jotes' państwow lub . . . pracowniczy" ['Jotes' owned by the state . . . or the employees], *Życie Gospodarcze* (1991) 20:5.

31. Jan Czekaj and Andrzej Sopoćko, "Rynki finansowe w okresie przejściowyn, uwarunkowania, zagrożenia, perspektywy" [Financial markets in a transition period: determinants, threats, prospects], paper presented at conference organized by Instytut Finansów [Institute of Finance] and Ministerstwo Finansów [Ministry of Finance] (Warsaw, April 24–26, 1991).

32. Piotr Pacewicz, "Koniec pogody dla reformy?" [End of good weather for reforms?], 29 *Gazeta Wyborcza* (1992).

33. "Coraz bardziej obcy kapital" [Foreign capital more and more alien], 56 *Gazeta Wyborcza,* (1992) p. 5.

34. This development took place even though the private sector in 1990 distinctly benefited from the government's preferential treatment of new private firms, at least as far as the tax policy was concerned. Izabela Bolkowiak and Ewa Relewicz, "Reformy systemu podatkowego w warunkach rynkowych przekształceń gospodarki" [Tax system reforms in the process of the economy's marketization], paper presented at conference organized by Instytut Finansów [Institute of Finance] and Ministerstwo Finansów [Ministry of Finance] (Warsaw, April 24–26, 1991) p. 19.

35. Zdzislaw Sadowski, "Niezależne spojrzenie na prywatyzację w Polsce" [An independent look at privatization in Poland], *Gospodarka Narodowa* (1991) 3:6.

36. Ministry of Finance, November 10, 1990.

37. Henryk Zalewski, "Wykańczalnia" [A finishing device], *Życie Gospodarcze* (1991) 20:5.

38. Eduordo Borensztein and Manmohan S. Kumar, "Proposals for Privatization in Eastern Europe," IMF Staff Papers, No. 2 (1991).

39. "Memorandum Rządu Polskiego w sprawie reformy gospodarczej i średnioterminowych kierunków polityki gospodarczej" (1991–93) [Memorandum of the Polish Government on Economic Reform and Directions of Economic Policy (1991–93)] unpublished material available from author (Warszawa, March 25, 1991) p. 5.

40. That is, "[if] the economy moves to a higher growth path as a result of privatization and taxes are thus higher than they would otherwise be." Farid

Dhanji and Branko Milanovic, "Privatization in Eastern and Central Europe," Working Papers, The World Bank, WPS 770 (September 1991).

41. The lack of emphasis on current budgetary needs may also have been due in part to a quest for "ideological purity."
42. In the public mind, the lack of progress in privatization is only a minor cause contributing to the large budget deficit; according to one poll, only thirteen percent of Poles surveyed cited lack of privatization as a cause of budgetary problems. See Pacewicz, supra note 32.
43. Twenty-eight parties were seated following the October 1991 election.

The Private Provision of Public Goods: Principles and Implications

Clayton P. Gillette

[*Editors' Synopsis:* Liberal economic theory conventionally assumes that society cannot rely on the market to provide public goods and, therefore, that such goods must be provided by the government. This assumption implies that the concept of public goods provides an inherent limit to the scope of economically optimal privatization. Professor Gillette argues that no such clear categorical distinction can be maintained consistently with the goal of economic efficiency. Determining whether goods are more efficiently provided by the market or by the government requires a particularistic analysis of the comparative institutional advantages and disadvantages of the market and the government.]

Introduction

Worldwide debate about privatization has focused primarily on the sale of state-owned firms that in capitalist systems are owned privately, and whose operation is dictated by market forces rather than by government fiat. Thus, discussion has centered on the sale of airlines, telephone systems, and industrial plants, for which production levels and prices were previously set by the state rather than through the forces of supply and demand.

I wish to explore the propriety of privatization by investigating a different segment of the economy, goods and services that are traditionally or frequently supplied by government even within capitalist systems. These include activities such as education, garbage collection, and pollution control. I do not want to overstate this distinction between public and private sectors—indeed, much of what I have to say stems from the belief that private and public providers are more interchangeable than the theory of privatization (or some theories of privatization) suggest. Thus, I want to avoid any rigid classification of activities as inherently governmental or inherently private, even in a society that seeks to achieve efficient production and provision. My thesis, instead, is that we can learn a great deal about the appropriate scope of privatization, and the ability to achieve an optimal division of public and private functions, from an examination of public provision in capitalist systems. In particular, the use of the public sector to overcome obstacles to collective action may reveal human frailties that foretell difficulties in any attempt to install a privatized regime.

Proponents of privatization often assume that government should be entirely displaced in the provision of goods and services. Recent writings (almost anarchist in nature) suggest that goods long thought to require government-managed provision if they are to be provided at all—the category known in economics literature as public goods—will ultimately evolve even in the absence of government, as groups of citizens cooperatively solve the strategic puzzles that initially induce all to forgo what each one desires.[1]

The possibility that market transactions, over time, can replicate centralized solutions to strategic behavior is, however, only a first step in the argument from public provision of public goods to privatization. The necessary next step in the argument is an economic theory that suggests public goods will be provided more efficiently by profit-maximizing private enterprise than by public officials. In this paper, I will accept that we should assign the obligation to provide any particular service to whichever sector, public or private, is more likely to provide an efficient amount of that service. I then want to explore some of the assumptions that underlie the belief that privatization will best achieve this objective. I suggest that, even accepting the efficiency objective, wholesale adoption of either public or private provision of goods is inappropriate. Rather, comparative institutional analysis must proceed in a very particularistic way with respect to each good or service. This analysis reveals two lessons for societies facing privatization. First, debate about provision of goods and services should focus on the need for interplay between public and private sectors rather than on a binary choice between them. Second, to the extent that both public and private provision suffer from different and often incommensurable imperfections, the choice between government and private production is more one of politics and ideology than of economics.

I. Markets and their Discontents

I begin with a brief review of the economic argument for government participation in the marketplace. A reasonable question to ask if one is advocating a shift of provision from government to the market is, why should the government *ever* be involved in the production and provision of goods and services? The starting place of the analysis is the standard economic assumption that individuals are rational and self-interested in their marketplace transactions. That is only to say that they will act sensibly to further their own welfare when involved in economic exchange. Thus, when faced with scarcity, individuals will bid against each other to drive the price of a resource up to the maximum value that they can obtain from it. This value may be determined in terms of personal pleasure or, more importantly, by using the resource to produce new goods that can be resold to others. The prices generated by this bidding process signal producers how much they should spend producing any specific good. The result is that scarce resources end up in the hands of those who can use them most productively. (It encourages production of goods and services that are preferred by society.) It is essential to recognize that personal or monetary gain from the transaction is the motivation for our rational, self-interested actors to engage in this process. If, for example, I could not capture, through market prices, some of the surplus value that my activity creates for others, I would have no self-interested incentive to engage in that activity.[2]

Neoclassical economic theory suggests that government intervention skews this allocative process, by obscuring the price signals for production that would otherwise be conveyed through market transactions. If, for instance, one is otherwise indifferent between eating meat and fish, but market forces lead to a state of affairs in which fish costs a dollar a pound to produce, while meat costs two dollars a pound, a rational actor will eat more fish and less meat. But if government subsidizes meat prices and reduces the market price to fifty cents a pound (notwithstanding its production cost), a rational actor will eat more meat and less fish. Hence, fish will be underconsumed and meat overconsumed, relative to preferences (demand) that exist independent of government action, and relative to the cost of supplying the goods at issue. Meat will be scarce, and prices will not provide a sufficient amount of resources (relative to demand absent the subsidy) to catch fish.

This basic theory about allocation of resources explains why, in general, government planning should not replace market transactions as a guide to production and price. It also explains how government pricing generated shortages and inefficient production in East European economies. It does not mean, however, that government intervention should be excluded from the marketplace. Indeed, traditional economic theory tells us that government is needed to supply some goods, commonly referred to as public goods or social goods, that individuals will not supply, notwithstanding substantial demand for them.

In their pure form, these goods share two characteristics. First, they are *nonrival,* meaning that my partaking of them does not preclude your doing the same. A pair of shoes exhibits rivalness—you and I cannot wear them simultaneously. Mosquito spraying does not. Even if you spray your property, I will obtain some benefit from reduced mosquito infestations. Second, public goods (again in their pure form) are *nonexcludable.* That is to say, I cannot (without great cost) exclude you from the benefits of the good, even though you have made no contribution towards its production. Again, if I purchase a pair of shoes, I can exclude you from their use or benefit. But if I pay for lighting on the street on which we both live, I cannot (without difficulty) exclude you from the benefits, notwithstanding your failure to contribute to the cost.[3]

These characteristics can be incorporated into our understanding of how markets work. Typically, I am willing to purchase a good in the market for any price up to the value that I believe that the good is worth to me. Presumably, I will obtain a scarce good if I am willing to pay more for the good than are other potential purchasers. Allocative efficiency is achieved when goods find their way into the hands of those who value them most highly. In the case of the public good, however, this logic does not work. If, due to its nonrival and nonexcludable nature, I can get the same benefits from a good without paying for it as I can by purchasing it—as long as you are willing to make the payment—then I am better off awaiting your action than bidding for it out of my own resources. Should you make the payment necessary to produce the good, my strategy is successful and I can free-ride off your efforts. You will be unable to preclude my enjoyment of the good. You, of course, will have the same set of incentives to free-ride, and thus await my bid. Therefore, the transaction will take longer to come about, if it materializes at all—a most inefficient state of affairs.

The traditional resolution of this problem has been to create some entity that can identify demand for the public good, make arrangements for its provision, and impose a form of payment on beneficiaries. Ideally, that entity is government, which can infer constituent preferences from voting behavior, direct communication, and residential patterns. Government has the power to contract for actors to perform the desired tasks,[4] and impose taxes or other fees on constituents to pay for the desired projects. Thus, the role for government, taken from public goods theory, is to provide public goods in order to prevent their undersupply.[5]

Describing the government task in this manner, however, beclouds the issue of how to classify a wide variety of goods and services. While many goods exhibit some characteristics of publicness, the search for the pure public good has been futile. Individuals enjoy goods to different degrees, and at times the disparity may be so great that one actor would be willing to pay for the good, notwithstanding secondary benefits enjoyed by noncontributors. Common ownership may produce disparate benefits even to those who pay similar amounts (think of municipal golf courses supported by property taxes, or the different benefits obtained by military contractors versus citizens with respect to national defense). Notwithstanding the "publicness" of these goods, some beneficiaries may gain so much from their production that there are tendencies to have them over-, rather than undersupplied.

To demonstrate the haziness of the public/private good distinction, consider the common example of a public good: the lighthouse. Economists have often suggested that this enterprise is the quintessential public good because all ships can take advantage of the signal it casts, whether they have contributed to its maintenance or not. But Ronald Coase demonstrated that lighthouses can also function as a private good.[6] In England, lighthouse services were provided and paid for through market transactions for hundreds of years. Note that Coase is not arguing that lighthouses *should* be provided by the market, only that they *could* be. Privatization was possible because, even if some ships passed in the night and escaped paying a fee, a sufficient number that benefited from the lighthouse signal were willing to pay that the enterprise was profitable.

Even the classic example of a pure public good—clean air—does not return equal benefits, and allows for free riders. Asthmatics benefit more than those without respiratory disease, and hence would likely be willing to pay more for it. Environmentalists similarly are more willing to pay for clean air than others, even if it means that those others can enjoy the results without making any contribution. Of course, the reaction of some contributors may be to attempt to privatize the benefits that were originally public. Technology assists these individuals by allowing greater exclusion of goods that were previously available to all. A recent news story reports that in Mexico City, considered by some to be the dirtiest city in the world, booths are being built where citizens can enter and receive, for the fee of approximately two dollars, a minute's worth of pure oxygen.[7] In a similar vein, if individuals stopped funding police patrols, they might be replaced by burglar alarms installed in individual homes and businesses, and monitored by private companies.

Nevertheless, goods of a wide variety display sufficient characteristics of publicness that public provision would be appropriate, if not inevitable. At the same time, goods and services that we consider public produce sufficient private benefits that some private firms find it worthwhile to offer them, even though these firms cannot capture rents from all beneficiaries. The question, then, becomes not what is privatizable (virtually everything is, albeit to different degrees); rather, from the perspective of institutional design, the question is, which sector can produce any particular good most efficiently?

II. The Inefficiencies of Government Provision

Implicit in the theory of efficient provision is the assumption that self-interest motivates individual action. Hence, economic actors will be inclined to produce a good or service only if they capture a substantial share of its benefits. The possibility of maximizing these benefits (which generally take the form of profit or price gleaned in excess of production costs) provides incentives to self-interested producers to keep costs low. Those who have an interest in the profitability of the firm (shareholders) have incentives to monitor the performance of officers and other employees, and the employees have job-related incentives to serve the owners' interest. The fact that a particular policy advances or retards public interest, apart from the coincidence of that interest with personal benefits, is irrelevant to the actor's decision about what tasks to perform and how to perform them.

Much of the argument for privatization proceeds from the assumption that government actors do not have the appropriate incentives to maximize profit, because they receive little or none of the benefit that their conduct produces. At the same time, government actors may have substantial incentives to act inefficiently. Activity that appears to be wasteful from a social perspective may maximize some personal objective of the employee. Because they receive few rewards from efficient production, and often have self-interested motivations not to act efficiently, government actors are unlikely to reduce costs related to their activities.

This is not to say that public provision of a good or service is without advantages. If public entities properly calculate collective demand for a public good, they can presumably charge prices resembling those that would otherwise prevail in the marketplace. Government provision under these circumstances theoretically could be superior to private provision, since government action on behalf of its constituents could achieve economies of scale in production, and reduce transaction costs. Additionally, many of the difficulties of monitoring may be attributable to particular forms of government control, rather than endemic to the enterprise. For instance, advantages attributed to private entities, such as incentives and opportunities for advancement, are transferable to the public sector, and could be even more transferable if public employment took on some of the characteristics of the private sector, for example, a weakening of civil service employment security. Thus there is no structural reason why public providers could not adopt characteristics of private producers that tend towards efficient provision. The question is whether there is any incentive to do so.

Finally, as we investigate these problems of monitoring and agency costs, it is important to keep in mind that the problem with government supply is not necessarily the fact that it is government that is providing these goods and services, but that it is a monopoly that is doing so. Government may be inefficient not because government employees are by nature more prone to slack than private employees, but because any firm—public or private—that has a monopoly has less incentive to be efficient. Two points follow from this observation. First, if monopoly is the true problem, privatization of itself probably will not be a cure, if that phrase means only handing the enterprise over to a single, unregulated, private entity. Second, if private monopoly is to be constrained by government regulation, that is, if privatization means government hands the enterprise over to the private sector but regulates prices or activities of those firms, then the problems of government intervention persist, but in the process of regulation rather than production. Regulators may have incentives to act in a manner that maximizes their personal interest rather than public interest, and thus regulation will not necessarily enhance social welfare. With these thoughts in mind, I want to examine the alleged deficiencies of government provision more carefully.

III. The Incentive to Monitor: Residual Value and Monopoly

The self-interest of actors poses problems for both public and private producers. It means that, even if all parties are agreed on what the public or private enterprise should do, the employees who are to implement that policy may have reasons to do otherwise. Self-interested employees may wish to advance something other than the firm's welfare. For instance, they may wish to maximize their leisure time, in which case there will be substantial slack in production. Managers may wish to maximize their department budgets, in which case they may find it worthwhile to act inefficiently or to demonstrate that their costs of operation are higher than they need be. Alternatively, employees may wish to maximize their power within the firm or agency, or gain opportunities for subsequent employment, characteristics that are not necessarily coextensive with being productive.

If employees have incentives to act in an inefficient manner, then the choice between public and private provision of public goods may rest on which sector is best able to counter those incentives through monitoring. If efficiency is our goal, some reason exists to prefer monitoring by private owners rather than by public officials. In a system based on individual property rights, owners of the private firm have an entitlement to the residual value of the firm, that is, to the profit that remains after costs of production have been incurred. The owners, therefore, have self-interested incentives to create as much residual value as possible.[8] They are, therefore, likely to seek and monitor managers who will, in turn, monitor employees. The existence of a market for managers itself provides incentives for effective monitoring at this level. This cycle filters down, in theory at least, to employees who can command higher wages and better working conditions by demonstrating a willingness to act in accordance with the interests of the owners, rather than through maximization of leisure or alternative objectives.

Owners of firms whose residual values are translated into shares that are themselves marketable also have mechanisms for registering discontent with the firm's performance. Shareholders of publicly traded companies can signal their dissatisfaction with relative ease: by selling their shares. Decreased performance is likely to be reflected in decreased share values. Thus, the market for shares facilitates monitoring, and provides a strong signal of the level of efficiency that a producer has achieved. Where a potential owner believes that he or she can provide a good or service more efficiently than is being done under current ownership, the market for shares provides a mechanism through which the firm itself can be bought and sold. Since new owners can hire or fire employees, or change production methods, the constant threat of takeovers gives greater incentives to current managers to provide services at lowest cost.

Monitoring itself, of course, has the characteristics of a public good. My monitoring reduces your need to monitor. Hence, one might contend that the policing activity that provides the private sector with a theoretical advantage is unlikely to materialize in fact. If the interest of each owner in the firm were sufficiently small that the costs of monitoring outweighed the benefits to each owner, free-riding would pose a difficult problem. But here, again, disparate benefits ensure private provision of the good that initially seems purely public. A few shareholders whose stake in the firm is sufficiently large that it is worth their while to monitor may perform that function, notwithstanding that others who contribute nothing to the effort receive the related benefit.

These monitoring devices have only imperfect analogues in the public sector. Public officials (or managers in firms where performance is not driven by market mechanisms) are not entitled to the surplus that they create. As nonowners, they receive no property right in the residual value of the public goods they produce. They thus have less reason to ensure that the good is delivered at the lowest cost. Indeed, doing so may interfere with other objectives that they can pursue, such as maximizing budgets, doing favors for particular constituents that impose greater than necessary social costs, or engaging in conduct that maximizes their employment opportunities in the private sector when they leave public service. Further, even if officials wanted to monitor employees, they are constrained in their capacity to provide either the carrots or the sticks necessary to encourage public-regarding performance. Government employees often receive pay raises according to preset scales, and are protected against redress for improper performance by civil service rules that make sanctions and firing difficult, if not impossible. Only the rules of American universities, which provide lifetime tenure after three to six years of successful service, provide so much benefit without continuing demonstration of worth. The effect is to dull the incentives otherwise provided by market forces.

This is not to say that the desire to do a good job disappears. Reputation, personal pride, and other nonmonetary incentives may all operate to induce even self-interested managers and employees to perform at a high level. The point is only that, as compared to a system in which slack can lead to demotion, dismissal, or reduced pay, nonmerit systems are unlikely to generate additional efficient production.

These diminished incentives for "managers" of the public enterprise are exacerbated by the difficulty the "owners" (voters) have in monitoring the activities of officials (again, relative to the capacities of private owner/shareholders). Because they have no ownership share in the enterprise to sell,[9] the primary ways in which these "owners" can register discontent or signal poor performance are by exiting the jurisdiction, or by voting the offending officials out of office.

At first glance neither of these monitoring mechanisms seems effective. Exit costs are quite high, even where we are speaking of public goods provided at the local level. They are obviously substantial where the public good is provided at the national level. Some people may move out of a jurisdiction if the schools are considered below an acceptable level. (Or they may opt for a privatized solution, such as a boarding school.) Some might even move if refuse collection is inadequate. But few will leave a national jurisdiction on the grounds that the level of spending for national defense is too low or too high. These costs may be increased artificially by legal impediments to emigration or immigration.

That leaves voting as a monitoring option. We can consider political voting to be the functional equivalent of voting shares, by which competing candidates for office bid to take over the public enterprise. Competition from potential candidates for public office does provide some incentive for current officials to provide public goods and services efficiently. Nevertheless, voting a public "owner" out of office is an imperfect substitute for the threat of takeovers in the private market. The problem with monitoring through electoral politics is that it occurs only at isolated intervals (as opposed to the constant exchange in the market for shares), and is binary in nature. A voter who can only vote for or against election of an official will likely cast a vote that reflects a view of the official's performance on balance, and will have no electoral opportunity to express opinions on individual policies. Elected officials, however, are likely to interpret a vote as an endorsement of all their policies. Hence, partial discontent is unlikely to be registered at all.

The relevant ineffectiveness of voting as a measure of constituent satisfaction suggests that the free-riding problem associated with monitoring is likely to be more prevalent in the public sector than the private. As indicated above, it is possible that some shareholders will have sufficient stakes in the firm to make monitoring worth their while, notwithstanding their desire that others monitor. In the public sector, it is less likely that individuals with a sufficient stake to overcome the free-rider problem will emerge. Given the costs of investigating government entities, few would obtain the benefits necessary to warrant monitoring. Those who seek political office or who seek profits from reporting government misbehavior (for instance, newspaper editors) would arguably monitor those aspects of the government considered most salient to the public. Few, however, will consider supervising or publicizing the more mundane elements of government.[10]

But I do not wish to understate the power of the voters or overstate the power of the marketplace. Even if exit is more costly at the public level, and voting can fail to express views on different goals, other mechanisms exist for voters to express discontent. Letters of complaint, telephone calls to representatives, and—at least at the local level—direct contact with representatives all provide means by which the push of consumers may interact with the pull of owners to monitor performance. Of course, consumers of private goods similarly have the ability to complain, and there is some reason to believe that complaints about public goods will be less than for private goods. A complaint about my automobile will redound only to my own benefit,[11] but a complaint about insufficient police response time will aid all residents. Complaint, in short, itself may have the characteristics of a public good, and is most likely to have those characteristics when the target of the complaint is a public good. If others complain about a governmentally provided service, I have less need to, since any remedy will tend to benefit all beneficiaries of the service.

Nevertheless, complaint is likely to remain a powerful monitoring mechanism for all goods. Criticism about numerous such goods associated with government provision—education, water supply, garbage disposal—may confer sufficient personal benefits to make personal complaint as worthwhile as it would be in the case of purchasing a defective automobile, ill-fitting shoes, or rotten food. Few other residents receive the same benefit from repair of the pothole in front of my house, or the removal of the city-owned tree that has fallen on my yard. Thus I am unlikely to await their action in order to avoid the costs of complaint. Others may benefit if I complain about insufficient policing of the park where my children play, or of playground equipment in disrepair, or wandering dogs. But in each of these cases, the safety of my children will be sufficiently important that I will not await action by others just to avoid their free-riding on my efforts. Finally, the amount of remedy may vary with the number of complaints. Hence, if adding my voice to protests about a service incrementally increases the governmental response, I should be willing to complain as long as the increment exceeds the cost of my contribution. The issue of monitoring, in short, may depend more on how much benefit an individual gets from a public good, and on how susceptible those who provide the good are to personal rebuke, than on the public or private identity of the provider.

I have alluded to one additional source of monitoring, the existence of competition, which is perhaps the most powerful motivator toward efficient production.[12] Where firms face no competition (where they have a monopoly) they are able to impose prices on consumers, and have far less incentive to reduce costs in order to maximize profits.

Where the state owns or plans all the means of production, it is necessarily a monopoly. This fact has led to claims that government can tie goods that serve the public interest to other goods that serve only special interests.[13] To the extent that privatization simply means handing the state's assets over to a privately held firm and granting that firm the same exclusive right of production that the state formerly had, there is little reason to believe that the firm will perform better than the state. For instance, the bilateral monopoly features of long-term contracts between governments and private providers can be expected to suffer, and to enjoy all the characteristics of long-term supply contracts between private parties.[14] Again, the efficiency of performance will depend on the incentives for adequate performance implicit and explicit in the relationship between parties: their level of interdependence for survival, and their options for exit should dissatisfaction arise. There is no reason to believe that the artificial labels of public and private will dominate these elements of the transaction.

IV. Multiple Objectives and Measures of Success

Even if those affected by a service—as owners, managers, or consumers—possess sufficient incentives to monitor performance, they can perform this task only if they have a reliable measure of success and failure. The inability to define a uniquely proper objective for public officials may inhibit the constituents' ability to monitor public officials. While I have been assuming for purposes of this paper that the proper bench mark is efficient provision, even within government agencies there is bound to be disagreement about what policy satisfies that criterion. Does efficient schooling mean that the same number of dollars are spent on each child, that average test scores are at a particular level, or that teachers achieve a wage comparable to some private sector employment? This debate varies substantially from the same issue in the private sector, where success or failure is measured by the bottom line. While there is substantial debate about whether the bottom line that counts should be a short-term or long-term one, or about how to accomplish the goal, no one doubts that the objective for the private organization is single-minded: to maximize profits. This provides both incentives for managers to monitor the performance of employees to avoid waste, and the capacity to measure performance.[15] Public enterprises that are not charged with returning a profit, however, have more difficulty defining a "good" job.

As with monitoring, however, various advantages of the private sector in defining the appropriate objective may be overstated. Numerous governmental activities are performed by agencies or departments that are as solitary in their objective as is the market. We may be uncertain whether public housing should be provided in some amount that reflects what markets would provide, or whether everyone is entitled to a certain level of housing even if that produces inefficiencies. Nevertheless, services such as check collection, railroad and airline operation, or weather forecasting seem removed from conflicts between fair distribution and efficiency. If a service is being provided by government solely out of fear of market failures, rather than to ensure a particular distribution, government should be capable of imitating what market prices would otherwise be. Indeed, a great many government services are provided through user fees that purport to accomplish just that objective: they charge prices that correspond to what would be charged were the same service provided by a private firm.[16] The issue, again, is not one of how public inefficiencies are magically translated into private efficiencies. Rather, the issue is whether the particular service is surrounded by constraints in either sector that make its provision susceptible to measurement.

Assuming the possibility of a single metric, one would imagine that if private provision were in fact more efficient than public, empirical support could be found. Indeed, studies of the relative cost of the same service provided by the private and public sector do exist. Like beauty, however, efficiency may be in the eye of the beholder, so interpretation of data may be tainted with an ideological lens. One summary of approximately fifty studies concludes as follows:

> In only two, in which the quality of service was held constant, were public firms found to be more efficient than their private counterparts. In over forty studies public firms were found to be significantly less efficient than private firms supplying the same service. The evidence that public provision of a service reduces the efficiency of its provision seems overwhelming.[17]

An alternative reading of the same studies by John Donahue is less conclusive. Donahue finds, for instance, that studies of refuse collection by public and private entities reveal that costs will vary with size of the firm, financing arrangements, level of competition, and levels of consumer information, more than a clean breakdown between public and private. With respect to some of these features, government has an advantage; with respect to others, the market does.[18] The least expensive arrangement appears to be one in which governments contract out to private firms, rather than allow open competition. Contracting out does, of course, entail some level of privatization, but it also entails the use of government as a clearinghouse for information, an auctioneer on the part of the public, and an active participant (if not sole provider) in the marketplace.

Moreover, Donahue finds that in some areas, water supply and electrical supply, studies support the conclusion that publicly owned utilities are more efficient than private ones.[19] Again, however, the conclusion does not follow inexorably from the fact of public ownership. Rather, greater efficiency is related to a complex mix of organizational structure, regulatory incentives for certain types of investments, financing, and the likelihood of collusion to keep prices artificially high where an industry is occupied by a small number of firms (emphasizing once more that competition may impose greater discipline than the form of ownership).[20]

The preferability of private to public provision, then, becomes a far more complex inquiry than is suggested by advocacy of government divestiture. The message is not that government will be as efficient as the market, but that the choice of provider be made only after the tendencies of each sector are applied to the individual case. Any effort to resolve the efficiency issue with a quick appeal to surrogates such as the different objectives of the public sector, or superior monitoring capability, will yield unwarranted results if applied across the board.

V. Externalities and Public Provision

Much of the preference for private provision stems from the assumption that self-interest coincides with public interest. Yet economic theory also recognizes that government intervention becomes essential in the area of externalities, where self-interest deviates from public interest. If private firms, more than public, are prone to impose adverse effects on those to whom they are not accountable through economic or political markets, the desirability of privatization must be questioned, at least where the probability of external effects is high.

Assume, for example, that a firm produces a good through a mechanism that pollutes the air of people living downwind of the firm's plant. Reducing pollution is technologically feasible, but costly. Given my starting point of self-interest, we would not expect that the firm, left to its own devices, would engage in substantial pollution reduction. The reason is simple. If pollution affects downwind residents but not customers or employees (assuming minimal overlap among them), then the firm has no market-based incentive to reduce pollution. Indeed, it has substantial market-based incentive not to do so. Any pollution reduction mechanism will raise production costs, and hence the prices that the firm will have to charge its customers. Since the customers (other than downwind ones) receive no benefit from this added cost, they will be unwilling to pay for it and the firm will make fewer sales and less profit by investing in pollution reduction.

There is some reason to believe that a public provider would internalize certain externalities. Because different public entities exist—cities, states, countries—it is possible to assign the production task to the jurisdiction that receives both the benefits and costs of production. Thus, geographical externalities can be avoided by having a level of government that contains the affected territory undertake the task.[21] Presumably, a jurisdiction that represented both downwind and upwind residents would, unlike the private firm, take into account the interests of each in deciding how much to invest in pollution control. Failure to do so would lead to the processes of voting, exit, and complaint that I have discussed above. While each of these is imperfect, government may be *relatively* able to address the externality issue. Firms whose constituencies transcend jurisdictional boundaries are less likely to be concerned with the geographically concentrated pollution that they cause.

This is not to say that the public entity will necessarily make the correct decision, or actually take all relevant interests into account. The environmental devastation created by state-run industries in Eastern Europe belies that assertion. But there is reason to believe that public officials, at least those that face competition in elections, are more likely to consider externalities created by some firms than are the firms themselves.

The existence of externalities, therefore, might be considered as a counterweight to the arguments for privatization. But that seems too quick a conclusion. The threat of externalities may justify governmental intervention into market transactions, but not necessarily government ownership. In the above example, government could induce the private owner to take external effects into account without displacing the owner's position. Government could impose a series of fines on the firm sufficient to bring about the same result as if the firm had, of its own volition, considered the interests of downwind residents. Alternatively, the government could assign to residents at risk a right not to suffer the adverse effects of pollution, and either provide a forum for seeking redress when the firm violated that right, or enforce trading of rights between polluters and victims. A large part of contract and property law in common-law countries consists of these types of government intervention into the market. Finally, the government could create a market for clean air (or for polluted air) and auction off the rights to that asset to the highest bidder. In each of these situations the government is intruding into the market in order to ensure that an optimal level of a resource (clean air) is maintained.

These forms of intervention suggest several points. The first is that what we mean by privatization is inherently ambiguous. Forms of privatization such as contracting out, assigning rights to monopolies and then regulating the recipient (as with broadcasting along the radio spectrum), or selling assets under tightly constrained conditions, all require continued interaction between the public and private sectors. The question, at least in interesting cases, is not whether the particular function should be allocated to government or the market, but instead, how to strike the appropriate balance between them.

The second, perhaps more crucial point, is that while government can address the issue of externalities, it is not necessarily the case that it will do so. Again, pollution in Eastern Europe indicates that state-owned firms were no more attentive to consequences outside their confines than private firms would have been. To understand why that might be the case under any governmental regime, let us return to the assumption that a rational firm, left to its own devices, has no market-based reason to consider external effects, and substantial reason to resist attempts to impose pollution-reducing regulations on it. Consider also that adverse effects of pollution are likely to be diffuse and trivial with respect to any one person, although substantial in the aggregate. The total costs of pollution may exceed the firm's additional profits made from avoiding abatement; but for any one person, pollution costs are unlikely to be as great as the costs of monitoring either the firm or the public officials charged with regulating those firms. Hence, little monitoring through nonmarket mechanisms is likely to be accomplished, as it is in virtually no one's self-interest to do so. (Compare this incentive to monitor with the incentive of the person whose children use the park to keep that facility free from danger.) The firm, on the other hand, has an intense, concentrated interest in avoiding regulation or prohibition of its profitable activities. It is within the self-interest of the firm, therefore, to undertake tasks directed at avoiding harsh regulation, as long as those tasks do not cost more than the expected profit from avoiding regulation. On the one hand, then, we have regulators being urged by firms with substantial resources and incentives to avoid regulation. On the other hand, we have potential victims in need of regulation, but unwilling to incur the costs necessary to contend for it. Thus, while regulation as a control of externalities may serve as a counterweight to total reliance on the market to produce efficient levels of production, serious questions remain about just how frequently that counterweight will be employed.

VI. Implications for Privatization

Essentially all the preceding comments relate to the tendency of individuals to pursue self-interested goals in a manner that may deviate from what would be necessary to achieve publicly endorsed objectives. This tendency, if endemic in human nature rather than indicative of members of capitalist economies alone, has important implications for the level of privatization that can be achieved and the proper structure of any privatization effort. The same tendencies that warrant some form of government intervention for the provision of public goods in capitalist economies, in short, will interfere with privatization of industries that display high degrees of rivalness and excludability, and are susceptible to market pricing and distribution. Unfettered endorsement of privatization may too readily seize on characteristics that render government intervention problematic, without asking how those same characteristics affect any retreat from public provision.

Let us begin by recognizing that the firms currently being privatized have been operating as state-owned enterprises up to this point in time. As a result they have employees and managers who have a natural interest in maintaining their positions. Privatization, however, threatens the continuation of many of those positions, for the reasons that I have discussed. Increased efficiency is likely to require substantial reduction of production costs, a phenomenon that is likely to translate into vast job reductions within the targeted firms.[22]

The consequences of this phenomenon flow from the discussion of the asymmetric interests of pollution producers and victims. Recall my assertion that we would likely have a greater than optimal level of pollution because producers have substantial, discrete interests in avoiding pollution reduction, while victims have only diffuse and limited self-interest in requiring it. This same analysis should tell us something about the likelihood of achieving a desirable level of privatization, even if we could identify that level. If we consider that current employees have a large stake in their employment, a stake that far outweighs any *pro rata* share of the social benefit that they will obtain from privatization, it would seem likely that it will be worth their while to oppose privatization of industries, even if privatization would return net benefits to the public at large. At the same time, those benefits will be quite small for any member of the larger population. Hence, members of the public are unlikely to bring pressure to privatize any particular firm or industry, and some firms that should be privatized will not be.

The only exception would be the potential owners of the firm. Other things being equal, one would imagine that potential owners would serve as an effective force for privatization. There will be occasions when employees are insufficiently organized or threatened to resist the push for public goods to be placed in the hands of private providers. Here, the intense interests of potential owners who anticipate large personal profits from privatization should dominate. Thus, there are reasons to suspect that, in some instances, we will see privatization where public provision would be more or equally appropriate. That the supplying of our military rests in the hands of private firms that extract huge profits may explain a great deal of why we spent such a great percentage of our budget on the public good of national defense.

Note, however, the caveat that the inducements of private owners will dominate only if other things are equal. The tendency in East-Central Europe over the coming years, I would propose, will lean in the direction of insufficient privatization, as current conditions inject substantial uncertainties into the calculus. The large number of firms susceptible to privatization dramatically increases the costs to potential purchasers of obtaining information relevant to a prospective purchase. Accounting systems of firms that have a long history of inefficient operation, and that are not standardized, cannot be expected to provide reputable data; records cannot be expected to be accurate; profit and loss statements and balance sheets—the basic information needed in a market exchange of assets—are likely to be nonexistent. It is largely for these reasons, for instance, that the Trust Agency (*Treuhandanstalt*), which has been charged with privatizing eight thousand companies representing the economy of the former East Germany, has been able to sell only a small percentage of the industrial, retail, and service businesses that are available for purchase.[23] As a result of inadequacies of information, companies are sold without any warranties or representations by the *Treuhandanstalt* as to the correctness or completeness of financial data, or stability of the firm.[24] The result is entirely predictable in an environment where potential owners of firms are unlikely to be as strong a force for privatization as might otherwise be, while employees are likely to be rigorous in their opposition.

Moreover, those entities that are successfully privatized will not necessarily advance social welfare, at least in the short term. Where only a single firm within an industry survives the privatization process, its monopoly position will leave it as undisciplined by market forces as its governmentally owned predecessors. The discussion above suggests that even those firms that do not enjoy monopoly status are likely to act in a manner that deviates from the social ideal if they are not monitored by sophisticated shareowners. This raises some questions about the proper form of privatization. In some plans, those of Poland and the former Czechoslovakia in particular,[25] privatization entails the donation of vouchers to every citizen to provide them with a stake in the outcome of the privatized venture. To the extent that this plan substitutes for investment of capital in the enterprise, one must wonder whether the donee is likely to prove as rigorous of a monitor of firm performance as one who has placed capital at risk. My suggestion is not that donees will fail to monitor at all, simply that they are likely to be less active. Given capital shortages in nations that are now entering the privatization movement, it may be that gifts of shares do not displace investment by others who would monitor more rigorously. But dependence on monitoring by donees cannot be expected to provide the same rewards as monitoring by those who place previously gained assets at risk.

Finally, I believe a more important problem exists in the current rage of privatization in these countries. The phrase privatization is being waved like a shibboleth over the unsettled waters of bankrupt economies. As I have tried to demonstrate above, it is not the placement of assets in private hands alone that brings the order of market efficiency to an enterprise; rather it is the environment in which that placement occurs that generates the desired effects. Even the competitive privatized firm will not possess the necessary incentive to consider adverse effects of its activities on those who are neither customers nor employees. Negative externalities can be controlled only by some external check, whether by the assignment of legal rights to the injured, or by direct regulation by some form of government. Even where external effects are minimal, privatization can be expected to have positive effects only where owners are disciplined by competition, where market forces provide sufficient information for potential owners to determine whether they can improve performance in firms owned by others, where regulations require attention to negative externalities, where monitoring is both possible and likely. Each of these processes is dynamic and incremental. Efficiency does not arise immediately with the creation of something called a market; it develops through a time-consuming process of give and take, trial and error, in which relatively efficient firms survive, and inefficient ones fall by the wayside, as firms mimic the procedures of successful firms, and eschew the errors of insolvent ones.[26] The revolution from a nonmarket to a market economic system cannot replace an evolutionary process by which markets achieve intended results. Thus the expectation that privatization will immediately lead to efficient production and provision must be resisted. If markets are to develop, they must be preceded by the generation of reliable information, by the emergence of interest groups that force debate about government involvement, by the creation of legal rules that permit and encourage exchanges of scarce resources, internalization of externalities, and the maintenance of residual values.

Market economies work by virtue of individuals taking calculated risks about payoffs that can be received from making investments. The emphasis in that sentence, however is on "calculated." Entrepreneurs need to have sufficient information to predict costs of production and demand for the goods and services produced. Bidders for existing firms must have useful information about the current economic posture of those firms, the integrity of receivables, the certainty of title to property. In a system that has no conception of private property, these are difficult tasks.

All of the above suggests caution about placing too much faith in any particular economic arrangement. The vicissitudes of history and politics reveal that the movement towards privatization is not the culmination of economic development, but a way station on a road that has no single destination, and that each generation must travel on its own. A single story makes my point. Thirty years ago, the Idaho Supreme Court was asked to approve the use of capital by a municipality to acquire industrial property that would then be leased to a private firm. The purpose of the plan was to attract industry, and thereby increase employment in the area. The court refused. Its reasoning was not rooted in the economic rationale of allocating responsibilities between the public and private sectors. Rather, the court considered the proposed plan to be an abrogation of political choices that had been made in creating the state and the nation. The court concluded:

> If the state-favored industries were successfully managed, private enterprise would of necessity be forced out, and the state, through its municipalities, would increasingly become involved in promoting, sponsoring, regulating and controlling private business, and our free private enterprise economy would be replaced by Socialism. The constitutions of both state and nation were founded under a capitalistic private enterprise economy and were designed to protect and foster private property and private initiative. Socialism is as foreign to our constitutional, political and economic system as our private enterprise system is to the socialist system of Russia.[27]

This language seems odd today not only because of recent developments in socialist countries, but because the scheme for governmental assistance to aid private industry rejected thirty years ago in such confident language has subsequently been adopted in virtually every state in the capitalist United States. Jurisdictions compete for new plants by offering tax subsidies, localities issue bonds and use the proceeds to construct industrial parks that are leased to private firms at below-market rents, private property is condemned for sale to other private owners.[28] We seem to be reaching some sort of convergence in which public and private systems intersect. I do not mean to suggest that there is a single, optimal relationship to which all nations will gravitate and then remain. To the contrary, I believe that this relationship will continue in flux, with occasional extreme swings to the public and private sector as people express dissatisfaction with the system in place at any given time.[29] The lesson to be learned is that the relationship of the public and private sectors is not immutable or inexorable. The way we strike the balance at any given time should reflect current devices for monitoring, structuring incentives, and designing organizational form. Beyond efficiency, however, the balance we strike will inevitably reflect other values, and our satisfaction or dissatisfaction with the status quo. In short, decisions about privatization neither will nor should be dictated wholly by vague generalizations improperly extracted from the dismal science of economics.

Notes

1. See Michael Taylor, *The Possibility of Cooperation* (Cambridge: Cambridge University Press, 1987); Gregory Kavka, *Hobbesian Moral and Political Theory* (Princeton, NJ: Princeton University Press, 1986); Jean Hampton, *Hobbes and the Social Contract Tradition* (Cambridge: Cambridge University Press, 1986);

Anthony DeJasay, *Social Contract, Free Ride: A Study of the Public Goods Problem* (Oxford: Clarendon Press, 1989).

2. Here, I am assuming that individuals are motivated entirely by rational self-interest. I do not mean to deny that individuals act out of other motivations, or that they balance other motivations, such as altruism, against self-interest in deciding on a course of action. See, e.g., Howard Margolis, *Selfishness, Altruism and Rationality* (Cambridge: Cambridge University Press, 1982). But adopting this simplifying assumption is useful to understand the basic theory of both markets and privatization, especially since I will demonstrate that reliance on free markets is limited even on its own terms.

3. Again, I have used a simplified model. Examples of "pure" public goods are rare. See infra notes 4 to 6 and accompanying text.

4. Contracting may take the form of employing personnel or contracting with other firms to provide the work. This latter device (contracting out) is itself a weak form of privatization. See, e.g., Ronald A. Cass, "Privatization: Politics, Law, and Theory," *Marq. L. Rev.* 71: 449 (1988).

5. This is not to suggest that government is a panacea. Government is itself a public good and thus poses its own collective action problem. Since any resident would benefit from some other resident incurring the cost of government, it is likely that only those who obtain some special benefit will actually become involved in the process of governing. Only when those special benefits are taken into account will personal benefit from governing exceed personal cost. All too often, those special benefits come in the form of rents that advance the self-interest of the governor without advancing the interests of the governed. For an elaboration of the view of government as a collective action problem, see *De DeJasey,* supra note 1; Clayton P. Gillette & James E. Krier, "Risk, Courts, and Agencies," *U. Pa. L. Rev.* 138: 1027 (1988).

6. Ronald H. Coase, "The Lighthouse in Economics," L.J. & Econ. 17: 357 (1974).

7. "Pay to Breathe," *The Economist* (February 16, 1991), p. 35.

8. See Michael H. Schill, "Privatizing Federal Low Income Housing Assistance: The Case of Public Housing," *Cornell L. Rev.* 75: 878, 883 (1990).

9. This overstates the case at least a bit. Privatized surrogates for ownership shares of the jurisdiction may induce monitoring. For instance, homeowners within a jurisdiction have reasons to monitor officials' performance in order to keep home values high. See John Yinger, "Capitalization and the Theory of Local Public Finance," *J. Pol. Econ.* 90: 917 (1982). Nevertheless homes are less liquid than shares in firms. Furthermore, if the homeowner is not contemplating a sale for several years, the incentive to keep values high in the immediate future is somewhat reduced.

10. Some might consider it worthwhile to monitor agency behavior in order to determine whether government action is consistent with their own interests. Where the monitor's interest differs from that of the public, this possibility provides little solace for to those who fear that free-riding will cause unproduc-

tion of supervision. The possibility that self-interested monitors and others will have similar interests seems quite strong in the case of private firms, since all stakeholders seek a common objective, that is, profit maximization of the firm. In the public setting, however, self-interested monitors may have quite divergent interests. The class of persons whose personal stake in government action might be sufficient to induce monitoring, for example, those subject to government regulation, or those who seek government regulation to protect a monopoly position, may have interests that diverge substantially from the constituents at large. In addition, as noted below, even constituents who agree that the government should advance public interest may have divergent views of what that objective entails and how it should be met.

11. I am assuming the problem is not a defect which affects a whole group of cars.
12. Note that my allusion to the need for multiparty politics suggests that competition is conducive to efficiency in both political (public) and economic (private) markets.
13. See, e.g., Albert Breton, *An Economic Theory of Representative Government* (Chicago: Aldine Pub. Co., 1974); Anthony Downs, *An Economic Theory of Democracy* (New York: Harper, 1957); Gordon Tullock, *Toward a Mathematics of Politics* (Ann Arbor: University of Michigan Press, 1974).
14. See, e.g., Clayton P. Gillette, "Commercial Rationality and the Duty to Adjust Long-Term Contracts," *Minn. L. Rev.* 69: 521 (1985); Victor Goldberg, "Price Adjustment in Long-Term Contracts," *Wis. L. Rev.* 1985: 527 (1985); Tracy Lewis, Robin Lindsey, and Roger Ware, "Long-Term Bilateral Monopoly: The Case of an Exhaustible Resource," *Rand J. Econ.* 17: 89 (1986); Robert E. Scott, "Conflict and Cooperation in Long-Term Contracts," *Cal. L. Rev.* 75: 2005 (1987).
15. See Cass, supra note 4, p. 483.
16. See Clayton P. Gillette and Thomas D. Hopkins, "Federal User Fees: A Legal and Economic Analysis," *B.U.L. Rev.* 67: 795 (1987).
17. Dennis C. Mueller, *Public Choice* II (Cambridge: Cambridge University Press, 1989) pp. 261–66.
18. John D. Donahue, *The Privatization Decision* (New York: Basic Books, 1989) pp. 58–68.
19. Id., pp. 73–77.
20. Id.
21. There are other types of externalities, primarily intertemporal ones. There is some reason to believe that firms will better internalize intertemporal externalities than government because share prices take into account a longer period of the firm's future performance than is considered by political actors, whose time horizon is limited to the next election. On the other hand, recent critiques of American enterprise have suggested that too much emphasis is put on short-term results at the expense of long-term planning, e.g., Robert H. Hayes & David A. Garvin, "Managing as if Tomorrow Mattered," *Harv. Bus. Rev.* 60: 70 (May–June 1982).

22. Consider the fact that in 1985 East Germany had approximately 3,500 companies in the production sector with an average of 925 employees each. At the same time, there were approximately 48,000 companies in the production sector of West Germany with an average of 151 employees. Jörg Soehring, "Privatization in East Germany and the Functions of Treuhandanstalt" (manuscript on file with author).
23. "Privatization in East Germany is Mired in a Collapsing Economy," *N.Y. Times* (March 12, 1991) p. A1.
24. Soehring, supra note 22.
25. See "Everything Must Go," *The Economist* (November 17, 1990) p. 88.
26. See, e.g., Armen A. Alchian, "Uncertainty, Evolution and Economic Theory" *J. Pol. Econ.* 58: 211 (1950).
27. *Village of Moyie Springs v. Aurora Mfg. Co.*, 82 Idaho 337, 350, 353 P.2d 767, 775 (1960).
28. See, e.g., *Poletown Neighborhood Council v. City of Detroit*, 410 Mich. 616, 304 N.W.2d 455 (1981). On government aid to industry, see Robert S. Amdursky and Clayton P. Gillette, *Municipal Debt Finance Law: Theory and Practice* (Boston: Little, Brown, 1992) pp. 84–157.
29. See generally, Albert O. Hirschman, *Shifting Involvements* (Princeton: Princeton University Press 1979).

III

The Emerging Social Order of the New Market Economies

PRIVATIZATION IN POLAND: THE EVOLUTION OF OPINIONS AND INTERESTS, 1988–1992

Lena Kolarska-Bobińska

[*Editors' Synopsis:* Privatization provides a glimpse of how economic strategies and public opinion affect each other. Public attitudes have driven economic change in Poland since the prerevolution days of the mid-1980s, and remain an important factor in the country's current choice of economic strategies. Of course, "public attitude" is a misleading term. In reality, attitudes shift among various social groups according to whether group interests are affected by proposed changes, and among individuals according to whether the effects of change will be felt directly or indirectly. Professor Kolarska-Bobińska points out the significant inconsistencies that exist in a postsocialist environment between people's expectations, fears, and experiences of the economic transformation. Privatization sheds light on how these inconsistencies take the form of "What is good for my country may not be good for me."]

Introduction

The collapse of Communism and the introduction of a market economy in Poland will usher in a series of changes affecting the entire social as well as the economic system. Several groups' positions in the social structure will change. The change to a market economy may result in the emergence of new and unanticipated economic divisions within Polish society, and these divisions will indirectly influence access to noneconomic goods such as political influence, power, and prestige. The upshot of these changes may well be the emergence of a new class structure.

Historically, social change has usually been supported by the "have-nots," who hoped for a more equal distribution of wealth, power, and prestige throughout their societies. The "haves," to put it crudely, favored maintenance of the status quo and with it, their privileged positions. But the logic of the transition from state socialism to market economy is different from that of previous social changes. It will lead to greater inequality in the distribution of income, power, and prestige. This raises several questions: Which social groups will profit from the change to a market economy in the long and short runs and which will support those changes? What factors shape the interests of the various groups at a time of transition, when the "old" is being transformed into a "new" system, with its blurred identity?

The changing structure of industrial ownership, growing unemployment combined with rapid expansion of new private enterprises, the unprecedented growth of the commercial sector, the growing number of bankruptcies, and the influx of foreign capital—all of these factors have contributed to significant changes in public attitudes in Poland toward privatization. But while it is clear that attitudes have changed, the opinions and interests of various social groups have not yet crystallized. In the fluid, new socioeconomic structure social groups find it difficult to assess what changes would benefit them in the long term, and even in the short term.

While some Polish sociologists have acknowledged the undefined character of social interests in postcommunist Poland, others have argued that the old interests that existed under "real" socialism have simply continued.[1] Bearing in mind the persistence of old ways of thinking, questions about the effect the change to a market economy on social attitudes and interests in Poland must be placed in the broader context of the evolution of attitudes that occurred during the 1980s, prior to the fall of communism. Present attitudes toward the transformation are the result of previous opinions and expectations as well as recent experiences.

Privatization provides the best context for examining these questions. Obviously, privatization is a key feature of the change to a market economy, and the form that privatization takes in Poland and the principles undergirding that form will determine Poland's future social structure. Additionally, the means by which privatization is implemented, in particular its human relations aspect, may significantly influence public attitudes toward the entire transformation. These are the bases on which people build their visions of Poland's future and of the place of the socioeconomic structure.

I. Introducing Market Reforms: Attitudes before the "Great Leap"

Public attitudes towards privatization must be viewed in light of the political and social atmosphere which shaped them. During the early 1980s, privatization, long regarded as antithetical to the best interests of the state, began to gain official as well as popular acceptance in Poland. This shift occurred during the Communist government's discussion of economic reform. The government's initial strategy was not to privatize the overall economy; rather, it was to inject competition into the state-run sector. Eventually, however, it proved difficult for state leaders to praise market mechanisms while suppressing the private sector.

The government's change in strategy coincided with shifting popular attitudes towards privatization. A 1984 survey reflected the public's ambivalent attitude toward privatization: eighty-two percent of those responding favored the introduction of a competitive market economy, but only fifty-nine percent wanted to expand the private sector.[2] Many, including the media, treated small businesses entrepreneurs contemptuously. Social acceptance of privatization came late in the 1980s, as the government increasingly consented to private sector growth. By 1988, the vast majority of those surveyed supported expansion of the private sector.

Poles at this time did not perceive the private sector as a source of socioeconomic differences and injustice. Many did not consciously associate the existing private sector with a market economy, which at the time was to them simply an abstract notion. Nor did they widely equate private ownership with nonegalitarian principles of distribution. Rather, they looked on the private sector as an escape from the injustices and inconveniences of the party and state system.

A continuing economic crisis fueled this shift in public attitudes. Many begin to view state-owned industries as unreformable, inefficient, and incapable of offering employees a satisfactory wage. In 1988, sixty-two percent of respondents indicated they would accept a job in the private sector given the opportunity.[3] While financial gain was given as the primary motive, respondents also stressed many nonfinancial reasons for preferring the private sector as employer. Among these were better organization of work, relation of earnings to efforts, the chance to demonstrate one's worth, and greater independence. An additional factor explaining the shift was that the lack of meaningful job opportunities in the state sector had forced many workers to move into the private sector. But, curiously, given a choice between a private-sector job and a state-sector job that offered satisfaction and good prospects for development, eighty-seven percent of those surveyed said they would prefer a satisfying job in the state sector. Only fifty percent said they would want such a job in the private sector.[4]

By 1988, then, the public was prepared for some form of economic change. There were two main views of how change should occur: through the introduction of market mechanisms into the state economy, or through the privatization of state-owned industries. Both views supported development of the private sector, but they regarded the relationship between the private and state sectors quite differently. The first viewed the private sector as operating only on the periphery of the state, complementing but not replacing the state economy. The second school of thought abandoned the state economy and linked all hopes to the private sphere.

The Communists' fall from power in 1989 made the second approach—total economic liberalization—the only available option. The question was, through what means would this transformation occur. The country's political liberalization made democratic negotiations among competing interests an obvious strategy through which to pursue the economic transition. But political interests and attitudes remained, by and large, as they had been defined during the communist era. Consequently, rather than leaving reform to interest-group politics, a group of professionals formerly connected with the forces of opposition defined the strategy for economic change. This group outlined a plan to transform the economy into a capitalist economy in the shortest possible time: the Balcerowicz plan.[5]

The plan had two stages: economic stabilization, followed by economic restructuring based on privatization of state-owned enterprises. The stabilization plan shook the economy in the first half of 1990. Privatization on a large scale should have immediately followed this first stage, but the process proved to be much more complex than anticipated. Only five large firms had been privatized by the end of 1990.

Privatization lacked political legitimacy in the 1980s, and the public lacked any concrete experience with privatization. The government's commitment in 1990 to privatizing state-owned enterprises resolved the legitimation problem. However, while a portion of the population began to form concrete opinions about privatization by following discussions in the mass media, many people had no opinion at all, or had opinions that were shaped by the likely privatization of their own jobs. Stereotypes, hopes, and fears of privatization propelled the opinions of this second group. The deep recession of 1990 only added to this group's anxiety. To understand this, we cannot abstract public opinion from the actual effects of economic change, nor from the underlying system of values and social aspirations.

II. Expectations and the First Experiences: 1990–1992

The first step in the move toward a market economy was the national plan of economic stabilization, which went into effect on January 1, 1990. This plan made deep cuts in government subsidies, drastically devalued the Polish currency (which, subject to certain limits, may now be converted), and removed price controls. At the same time, very strong restrictions on wages were introduced. The plan resulted in a significant decline in consumer demand.

Polish society accepted the drastic measures out of a sense of trust in the noncommunist government, and belief in the need for quick, wholesale reform, rather than pinpoint surgery on the existing economic system. The majority of the public accepted this reform, which did not favor any particular group.

The stabilization plan successfully reduced inflation to eight percent per month, stabilized the exchange rate, shifted relations between prices and income, restricted state subsidies, and increased exports, which now exceed imports. However, this success also caused the living conditions of many groups to decline, resulting in an ambiguous public perception of the change.

In 1990, people were much more apt to view favorably the transformation of the entire economy than they did its impact on their lives. It was as if they said, "I lose, but the country's economic situation improves." The data in Table 1 reflect this dissonance:

Table 1. Opinion of the economic stabilization plan[6]

Has the plan caused more good than harm?	More good	About the same	More harm	No change	Unsure
For the economy	23.9%	34.1	21.5	5.0	15.4
For society	13.7	32.3	38.5	2.5	12.7
For you personally	11.4	25.6	37.5	14.7	10.5

A similar discrepancy of reception was found to exist in how respondents feel about change in different spheres of life. Respondents' approval of change at the national level diminished greatly when the question regarded their personal situation, as Table 2 indicates:

Table 2. Perception of how change has affected various areas of life.[7]

How has change affected the following area?	For the better	For the worse	No change	Unsure
Relations with other countries	68.0%	11.0	9.2	11.8
Politics	54.0	21.0	12.7	11.9
Economy	39.0	38.5	18.3	4.1
Community (local milieu)	20.0	25.0	51.0	3.8
Family	23.5	34.4	40.4	1.2
Workplace	24.0	41.0	27.8	6.2

How can we explain this gap between assessment of the effects on one's country and on one's own welfare? The discrepancy results from the seemingly paradoxical facts that the country appeared to be improving while the quality of people's lives deteriorated. Shops were full of goods, but many people could not afford to buy them. In November 1990, sixty-seven percent of respondents claimed that the cost of running a household had increased over the last two years; thirty-one percent said health care had deteriorated; and fifty percent said they had less free time.

The gap may also be explained as indicating a tension between public values and private interests. When people speak of the economy on a national level, they express a general set of values: Changes are good for us, necessary, and so on. When they discuss the effects of economic policy on their jobs, however, they express the interest of their particular socio-occupational group or their personal fear of being laid off, having to change habits, work harder, and so on. The ambiguous perceptions toward change were reflected in different attitudes toward privatization of the economy, on the one hand, and of one's own workplace, on the other.

On the eve of the government's planned massive shift to private ownership of the means of production, privatization meant to the Polish people a bundle of contradictory values, hopes, and fears. The hopes were mostly for the economy as a whole, and the fears were for what change would spell for people's individual lives. The Polish public identifies the private sector and privatization with the positive qualities of self-determination, individual autonomy, greater chance for personal fulfillment and higher earnings, good organization and discipline of work, efficiency, and modernization. But the public also associates privatization with unemployment (nearly fifty percent of employees believe their jobs are threatened) and increased rivalry among workers and loss of benefits.[8]

Respondents were inclined to view privatization as helping the country but adversely affecting their own lives. For example, in April 1990, sixty-six percent of those responding to one survey stated that the privatization of most state-owned enterprises was or would prove necessary to stimulate the economy.[9] In November, another study revealed that only nineteen percent of the respondents wanted the government to abandon privatization of industries.[10] In a privately funded study, seventy-two percent accepted privatization while eighteen percent rejected it.[11] However, as more specific matters were addressed, respondents were less likely to speak favorably of privatization. Kuczyński and Nowotny concluded that in fact only about fifty percent of the population favors privatization, while twenty-one percent opposes it. The April 1990 CBOS survey revealed that the percentage of respondents who favor privatization on ideological grounds, that is, regardless of its context, was only thirty-seven percent, while an almost equal thirty-six percent opposed such a strong conception of privatization.[12] When asked about private ownership of their workplace, by either a Polish or a foreign business, the number favoring privatization was markedly lower than those who favored privatization "in general." Only twenty-seven percent of respondents preferred their place of work to be privately owned; fifty-eight percent opposed privatization of their workplace.[13] But this response changes dramatically when the category "employee ownership" is introduced (see Table 3).[14]

By 1990, people feared not just losing their jobs, but losing control over their lives. These anxieties over loss of job and control of one's life were particularly discernible among professionals, and those with a higher education. While they, along with individual owners, are the most ardent advocates of the privatization process, they are the least likely to want the organization or business where *they* work to become private property.[15] Autonomy is highly valued in this group and is part of their work ethos. This is why professionals choose to establish their own firms rather than work in privatized firms.

It is, to put it mildly, not an insignificant fact that for forty years communist propaganda portrayed private property and capitalism as the public's princi-

Table 3. Type of ownership preferred

What type of ownership would you prefer?	State-owned (as before)	Private ownership	Employee ownership	Unsure
Laborers	36.3%	13.2%	35.3%	15.2%
Managers	20.6	20.6	46.6	12.2
Executives	13.3	37.3	37.3	12.0
Self-management	10.6	23.4	55.3	10.6
Solidarity (trade union)	9.6	21.3	58.5	10.6
OPZZ (trade union, popularly called "the old one")	39.6	10.4	41.7	8.3

pal enemies. Many people perceive the individual, private owner as a ruler of life and death. Others recall the form of capitalism that existed in prewar Poland. These facts help explain why so many would prefer to work for themselves or for the state rather than taking a job in a privately owned firm. Thirty-three percent of those employed outside agriculture in the autumn of 1990 declared their intention to work for themselves; twenty-seven percent said they intended to work in a state-owned industry; and only twelve percent said they would seek work in a privately owned business (of which they were not the owner).[16]

Those who prefer work in the state sector generally feel that the state provides a better guarantee of job security and benefits. More than half of those who would prefer self-employment hope for a greater chance of autonomy and self-fulfillment. Only twenty-five percent identified "better financial opportunities" as the reason for preferring self-employment. Similar results were reached by another study, in which fifty-two percent of respondents said that, given the same wages, they would prefer state employment. Only 30 percent said they would prefer employment in a private enterprise.[17]

In light of the fact that many businesses in the state-owned sector are currently headed for bankruptcy or liquidation, this belief in state-sponsored job security is quite surprising. The uncertain legal status of Polish trade unions in the private sector is one reason so many people still prefer state employment. Because elimination of a firm's self-management employee council was a prerequisite of privatization of that firm,[18] employees feel they are left with no one to defend their interests.

III. Privatization of Various Sectors

Attitudes toward privatization vary greatly according to socioeconomic spheres. Support is greatest in the following areas of the economy: retail, service industries, construction, small factories, and the mass media. Resistance to privatization is greatest in areas affecting social welfare: health services, insurance firms, railways, and the postal system (followed by large enterprises). Table 4 illustrates these different attitudes.

From this information, we can draw the following conclusions:

(1) Support for privatization is increasing in Poland. This support, however, is mostly for limited, controlled privatization. Poles fear the uncertainty of the privatization process and its consequences; they prefer a mixed model of ownership in which private property would coexist with a strong state sector. Those employed in the industrial sector, however, are more apt than the general population to support more widespread privatization.[20]

(2) Many factors have shaped Polish attitudes towards privatization, and the communist allowance of private property into certain parts of the economy has played an essential role. Support for privatization is greater in those areas in which private property had already existed in Poland for a number of years, such as agriculture and the service sector.

(3) Under Communism, Poles rejected the role of the state as an economic and political player, but they accepted it as their protector and guarantor of social welfare. Support for privatization weakens in areas reserved to the state under communist doctrine or in pre-1939 Poland, that is, social services or large enterprises.

(4) People support privatization in those areas where public resentment of the centralized state's incompetence and inefficiency was greatest, such as food production, housing, retail, and other areas related to basic needs.

IV. Domestic Versus Foreign Investment

One might imagine that, after a history of having their nation partitioned among the three neighboring countries, Poles would be inclined to reject foreign investment. Recent surveys, however, do not confirm this expectation. Polish attitudes to foreign investment largely parallel attitudes to privatization (see Table 4). In November 1990, between ten and twenty percent favored unrestricted foreign investment in certain areas of the economy, and almost half the population favored limited foreign investment.[21] Only ten to twenty percent expressed opposition to any foreign investment at all. More recently, this attitude has not changed, as a 1992 survey indicates.[22]

Although popular attitudes towards privatization are less enthusiastic when the workplace is involved, the reverse is true in the case of foreign

Table 4. Attitudes Toward Privatization, 1988–1990.[19]

Area	Privatized without restriction			Privated with some restriction			Should not be permitted to privatize			Unsure		
	1988	1990	foreign capital	1988	1990	foreign capital	1988	1990	foreign capital	1988	1990	foreign capital
Housing Construction	29.5	28.1	16.3	39.7	38.4	45.3	18.6	17.3	23.0	11.6	15.5	16.0
Farm services companies	31.2	37.0	19.0	37.8	36.0	47.0	14.8	12.0	20.0	15.5	14.0	13.5
Urban transport	16.4	21.4	13.0	33.2	34.4	40.0	35.4	28.2	31.0	14.5	15.5	15.0
Banks	10.6	22.0	13.0	24.3	41.4	48.3	44.4	19.0	22.3	20.4	17.2	15.6
Hospitals	11.4	10.4	10.3	25.8	32.0	40.2	51.3	47.6	40.0	11.0	9.0	11.0
Mass media	15.9	34.0	16.1	28.8	33.0	41.0	35.9	15.0	26.0	18.9	17.3	16.3
Large industrial enterprises	12.2	12.5	8.2	32.4	49.0	56.0	40.1	23.3	23.5	15.2	15.16	11.8

[19]Because the category "no answer given" is not presented, percentages do not total one hundred percent. Data comes from the surveys *Poles 88* and *Poles 90*.

investment. Support for the purchase of one's workplace by foreign capital is much greater than support for foreign investment in the economy. Thus, it is not the attitude toward foreign capital that is crucial, but the rejection of privatization of one's workplace. The percentage of those who would like to work in a foreign-managed firm is even higher. People simply "want to work in a prosperous and well-managed firm, which would guarantee good earnings without the risk related to the transformation of one's workplace."[23]

In a 1990 survey of industrial workers, thirty-three percent said they would like to work in a foreign-owned business; thirty-four percent said they would not. Twenty-seven percent of industry managers said they would like to work in a foreign owned business; thirty-four percent said they would not.[24] Another 1990 survey indicated that twenty-eight percent of those with a basic vocational education wanted their workplace to become a foreign-owned business, while fifty-eight percent did not.[25] The degree of rejection is greater in the case of those having a higher education. It should be noted that roughly the same percentage would not like their workplace to fall into the hands of private Polish businessmen. The wider acceptance of foreign investment at the level of firms than at the level of the general economy indicates that people notice the opportunities and advantages that foreign capital may bring to individuals, yet are also aware of the possible threats to national interests.

V. Privatization as a Distributive Process

Most Poles know very little about the methods and principles of privatization. Roughly half the population knows nothing about the subject,[26] even though knowledge of different methods might well influence their thinking about privatization. This reflects not just the complicated nature of the privatization process, but also the failure of those in power to explain what privatization means, and to formulate a straightforward plan of privatization.

Studies indicate that people's attitudes toward how to implement privatization are confused. One report concludes that over eighty percent of respondents favor privatization through selling shares, while only nine percent favor the free distribution of such shares.[27] However, another study revealed that the free distribution of capital bonds which could then be exchanged for shares in certain firms is more popular than the sale of shares.[28]

The socially accepted criteria of distribution of national wealth are much clearer than the methods of privatization. The communist system, with its obscure and intangible bases for allocating privileges to certain groups, has produced in the population a dislike of privileges. Interestingly, Polish citizens appear to object not to privileges *per se*, but to criteria that create *illegitimate* privileges. Certain criteria are perceived as consistent with a just distribution, rights that society owes to certain groups, such as miners, due to their dangerous work, and teachers, because of their responsibility. What is clear is that people believe the allocation of privileges should be based on social, rather than economic or political, criteria. The process of privatization, therefore, must take into account social perceptions of justice. Respondents in one survey recommend the following criteria as the bases for preferences:[29]

—economic efficiency: 30.3 percent
—individual justice: 37.4 percent
—no new privileged groups: 29.4 percent

Respondents in the same study favored giving preferences to the employees of privatized firms, employees with seniority, and those with the lowest earnings. The majority of respondents opposed the sale of shares to former members of the party apparatus as the exclusive buyers, and to convicted criminals.

Poles appear to be generally unaware that their criteria may be self-contradictory. A private study revealed that nearly two-thirds of the respondents said that a firm would be better managed by its owners (sixty-one percent) than by its employees (twenty-seven percent).[30] The authors of the study concluded:

> [T]he population acknowledges the essential advantages of privatization of state-owned firms and recognizes the need of an "owner" who would run the firm better than the state and better than the employees would manage. At the same time, the majority feels that employees should be given as many potential advantages as possible. People do not adequately recognize the conflict between these two sentiments.[31]

In 1990, the general public thought that employees should have the right to buy the entire enterprise. But at the same time only eight percent of them declared that they would like to buy shares.

Employees' inclination to own shares in their own firm tends to vary with the individual's position in the firm. In response to the question, "Would you buy shares in your firm if you had the opportunity in the near future?" fifty-five percent of workers, sixty-four percent of middle managers and seventy-six percent of executives answered yes.[32] The desire to buy into one's own workplace reflects not only a fear of the future, but also the sense that the workplace really does belong to its employees, even though employees have generally treated their firms as belonging to no one. The sale of state-owned enterprises apparently has triggered this dormant sense of ownership, which previously did not create a corresponding concern for common property. Polish workers have long valued autonomy and self-determination. While workers often did not take active part in projects of self-management and trade unions (with the obvious exception of joining Solidarity in 1980 to 81), they did not like the decisions that were made on their behalf but without their consent. According to one study, sixty-four percent of employees questioned said the decision whether to sell a firm to its employees should be made by the employees themselves. Only thirty-four percent said state authorities or banks should have this right. The very low degree of interest in the general purchase of shares, coupled with a relatively high interest in buying stock in one's own place of work, indicates a possible strategy for accelerated privatization.

VI. Group Opinions and Interests: Growing Divergence

In the mid-1980s, I wrote about the formation and consolidation of the promarket alliance.[33] The market symbolized several prized but unrealized economic and political values. By 1988, Poland's nonegalitarian mood, which had increased throughout the 1980s, ended as the economic crisis intensified. The economic stabilization plan of 1990 lowered the living standards of many groups even more, differentiating the population not only on the basis of purchasing power, but also on the degree of job certainty and attitudes toward the impending privatization.

The most egalitarian-minded groups in 1990 were skilled and unskilled workers, workers doing mixed manual and mental work, and farmers.[34] Nonegalitarian principles had their strongest advocates among business people, professionals, and those with higher education, followed by technicians and white-collar workers. Farmers represent the most dramatic shift in opinion. In 1988, their attitudes generally were rather inegalitarian.

The opinions of the various socio-occupational groups underwent an interesting evolution during the 1980s. In 1980 there was considerable similarity of opinions among all groups. Since then we have witnessed a process of differentiation and change of intergroup alliances. The reform alliance of the mid-1980s consisted of groups with strong nonegalitarian sentiments, that is, professionals, technicians, and some skilled workers. This alliance began to fall apart in 1988. The growing economic crisis and decline in the standard of living accounted for the fact that the nonegalitarian sentiments of some workers had shifted; their opinions were now closer to those of unskilled workers. This similarity between the opinions of skilled and of unskilled workers, which probably reflects common interests of the two groups, manifested itself quite clearly in 1990, as Table 5 indicates.

Meanwhile, the gap between professionals and workers is growing, and

Table 5. Evolution of egalitarian opinions of selected occupational groups between 1981 and 90.[35]

Table 5A: Support for a ceiling on the earnings of the highest earners (answers "favorable" and "mostly favorable")

OCCUPATIONAL GROUP	1981	1984	1988	1990
Professionals	68.8%	41.4	37.0	33.0
Technicians	71.0	52.6	52.0	48.4
Skilled workers	71.6	57.4	63.0	60.0
Unskilled workers	—	73.5	70.0	59.0

Table 5B: Support for a full employment policy (answers "favorable" and "mostly favorable")

OCCUPATIONAL GROUP	1981	1984	1988	1990
Professionals	48.7%	47.0	39.0	49.0
Technicians	—	—	57.0	50.0
Skilled workers	62.0	56.2	63.0	73.0
Unskilled workers	65.6	69.3	68.0	76.0

the introduction of the market economy will make the interests of these two groups even more divergent. To many representatives of the intelligentsia, workers are no longer romantic, simple, strong, and righteous fighters for a common cause against Communism. Rather, they are a threat to the changes necessary to create a market economy, which professionals and intellectuals generally favor. This evolution of attitudes is illustrated by a statement made during an interview by A. Celinski, an advisor to Lech Wałęsa and Solidarity during the period when that movement was the manifestation of a mass protest:

> To put it most mildly, precisely the strength of big industry workers has become the factor which blocks change, the more so as the working class has its own representatives. [T]he links between work and its financial effect have ben broken. . . . Big industry workers are thus not a group dominated by creative attitudes, entrepreneurship, and above all responsibility for one's decisions, understood as acceptance of such rules of the game in accordance with which one not only wins but can lose as well. This is combined with the great drama of the collapse of the ethos of work. I am afraid that for many people irreversible changes in mentality have taken place, so that claims have become disassociated from one's responsibility and one's work. . . . The historical responsibility of Solidarity, and its leading elites in particular, is to carry out a program of change which would ease social tension above all by

> enabling many workers to escape to other social positions, for example, services provided by their own businesses, even those organized on a self-employment basis.[36]

Moreover, the cohort comprised of professionals and persons with a higher education is dividing into those who will remain employees of state-financed institutions and those who will find themselves in the private sector. This group's opinions will become increasingly polarized. One might hypothesize that following privatization, employment in either the state or the private sector will influence opinions and interests more than educational background or membership in a given socio-occupational group. Already today, egalitarian opinions are more readily found in the state sector than in the private one.

The growing divergence of opinions and interests among economically differentiated groups is also reflected in changing attitudes toward self-management. In 1980, self-management involved more than employee participation in the management of the firm. Rather, it was one of the few available mechanisms for protecting workers from the arbitrariness of the central planner. Guaranteeing the autonomy of the firm, self-management became one of the pillars of reform, one of the "Three S's": self-management, self-determination and self-financing. Moreover, although self-management tends to be rooted more strongly in egalitarian views about economic distribution, even nonegalitarians valued self-management.[37] The likely reason for this broad support is that the concept of self-management, understood as the free and active status of employees, was a synonym for democracy, a value that Poles at that time ranked very highly. Indicating the high level of popular support for self-management, eighty-five percent of the respondents in a 1980 survey stated that they supported employee management of the firm.

Many economists have pointed out that self-management was a useful solution to a firm's ills within a centrally planned economy, but that self-management is incompatible with the market mode of economic organization. This view is now reflected in the process of commercialization, the first step to privatization. Commercialization involves the conversion of state-owned firms into limited liability companies, with the treasury holding all shares until the firm is sold to private investors. When a firm is commercialized, its self-management employee council is eliminated.[38]

Support for self-management presently varies according to socio-occupational groups. Skilled workers, who have the greatest sense of conflict with their bosses, are among those who most strongly advocate self-management.[39] Within firms themselves, alliances are somewhat different: the attitudes of technicians, white-collar employees, and skilled workers are markedly different from owners of private businesses, who generally oppose self-management.

Support for self-management also varies according to attitudes toward full-employment policies, with full-employment advocates tending strongly to support self-management. Seventy-two percent of full-employment policy advocates favor self-management, while only forty-nine percent of those firmly opposed to a full-employment policy support self-management.[40] The acceptance of self-management is also combined with the support of the principles of market economy and privatization in all fields, except for very large firms. Self-management enjoys the support of seventy-three percent of those respondents who would like full privatization of banks and of sixty-four percent of those who would not. A portion of the respondents probably regard self-management as a guarantee of employee interests in the privatized firm, which explains why it is accepted by advocates of privatization as well. For some people, self-management is a symbol of freedom and autonomy, the same values that many identify with the market economy.

We appear to be witnessing the adjustment of an institution initially shaped in the environment of a centrally planned economy to a new socio-political order. Self-management used to guarantee autonomy and independence from the central planner. Under the new regime, however, employees will use self-management to secure their active status and autonomy *vis-à-vis* the new private owners.

To summarize, at the present time, privatization is supported mainly by those with a higher education, professionals, private owners, managers, and young people. These groups are optimistic about the new situation, and perceive possibilities for improving their social and economic position. Fifty percent of professionals responding to one survey said they would like to start their own business, compared with twenty-six percent of skilled and twenty percent of unskilled workers. Workers and technicians are those who are most aware of the social costs involved in privatization, and fear losing their jobs more than any other group. Within firms as well, highly educated elites, including managers and union activists, are most likely to support privatization.

The growing alienation of workers from other groups, both within firms and in society as a whole, is a very unfortunate development, since the goal of privatization is to evolve not only a market economy, but also a democracy which better represents the various interests. The balanced development of both sectors, state and private, if at all possible, should guarantee the stability of transition.

Conclusion

Attitudes toward privatization in Poland have changed very significantly since the reforms were launched. The new, noncommunist authorities and their economic program at first enjoyed strong support, but this has gradually declined. During the initial period, privatization was treated as an immanent part of the change and was widely accepted, at least as far as general slogans are concerned. Later, as the hardship of reform set in, privatization began to be associated not only with progress, efficiency, profit, and catching up with Western Europe, but also with unemployment and the decline workers' economic status, the group that Communism privileged.

As the following table indicates, by 1992 privatization enjoyed less and less support:

Table 6. [41]

Will privatization be for the Polish economy:	Replies of respondents by dates of studies							
	9/90	1/91	2/91	4/91	6/91	8/91	5/92	11/92
advantageous	43	47	42	31	32	25	18	32
advantageous and disadvantageous	24	27	26	30	31	26	34	30
disadvantageous	8	5	11	9	17	27	30	19
hard to say	24	20	21	19	20	21	18	19

As Table 6 indicates, from September 1990 to June 1992, the percentage of the respondents who believed privatization to be advantageous for the Polish economy dwindled systematically.[42] By 1992, Poles were far more attentive to the dangers to the economy resulting from changes in ownership than they were to the advantages.

Poles, however, still cannot estimate or predict the consequences of privatization. Neither economists nor the ordinary people are able to say how quick privatization will be, what the size of the state sector will be, what the dynamics of the private sector will be, and hence how all that will affect the structure of the labor market, the scope of unemployment, social differentiation, or the number of the rich and the poor. Even though privatization is now no longer a myth, its scope is very limited. Moreover, its forms are greatly differentiated. Many people fear privatization, but when asked about its consequences for them personally they answer, "I don't know."

The declining support for privatization is accompanied by the common belief that the pace of privatization is too slow. The number of people who think it is too slow is twice as large as that of those who think it is too quick. (The number of people who think so has increased since 1991.) This reflects what is really taking place: privatization in Poland so far has proceeded very slow. But how are we to explain the simultaneous decline of the acceptance of privatization and the opinion that the latter is advancing too slowly? It would be reasonable to suppose that those who fear the consequences of privatization would be interested in a slowing down of the process, and would claim that privatization is too quick. Yet attitudes towards privatization are full of contradictions, and reflect the main ways in which Poles think about the change taking place in their country.

The reduced support for reforms and privatization is now accompanied by a process whose consequences are the exact opposite of rejection: adjustment to the new situation. Many people voice their dissatisfaction with the change and express pessimism. They complain about their deteriorating condition, and deny support to the basis process of the transformation, but at the same time, they seek new solutions for themselves and their families. After having lost their jobs in the state sector, they find new ones in private firms. Some of them set up businesses of their own, frequently small and not very profitable, but still their own. The adjustment of ways of thinking and behaving to the new situation manifests itself in various ways and contributes to the new situation. The process is neither as rapid nor as conflict-free as had been expected at first, but it is nevertheless quite visible.

Notes

This article is a modified version of a paper that was prepared for a program organized by the United Nations Research Institute for Social Development (UNRISD) on "Participation and Changes in Property Relations in Communist and Post-communist Societies." The original paper will appear in a forthcoming UNRISD Publication.

1. See, e.g., E. Mokrzycki, "Social Limits of East European Economic Reforms," *Krytyka* No. 36 (1991).
2. "Preferred Social and Economic Order," in *Poles 84,* W. Adamski, K. Jasiewicz, and A. Rychard, eds. (Warsaw: Warsaw University Press, 1986).
3. Kolarska-Bobińska, "The sense of injustice and conflict and the preferred economic order," in *Poles 88,* eds. W. Adamski, K. Jasiewicz, L. Kolarska-Bobińska, A. Rychard, and E. Wnuk-Lipiński (Warsaw: Polish Academy of Sciences, 1989).
4. Rychard, "Visions of the future and the chances of reform in public opinion," in *Poles 88,* supra note 3.
5. For a description of this plan, see Chelmiński, Czynczyk, and Sterniczuk, "New Forms of State Ownership in Poland: The Case of Commercialization," in this volume.
6. Center for Public Opinion Research (CBOS)," *How to Privatize the Polish Economy* (June 1990).
7. CBOS, "*Social Perception Changes in Poland*" (March 1991).
8. Kolarska-Bobińska, "Groups and their Interests in the Economy," in *Poles 90,* W. Adamski, J. Bietecki, K. Jasiewicz, L. Kolarska-Bobińska, A. Rychard, E. Wnuk-Lipiński (Warsaw: JFis and JSP Pan, 1991); CBOS, "New Economic Order," April 1990.

9. CBOS, supra note 8.
10. Kolarska-Bobińska, supra note 8.
11. P. Kuczyński and S. Nowotny, *Report on the studies concerned with the privatization of enterprises in Poland, March 1990* (Warsaw: Demo skop, 1990).
12. CBOS, supra note 8.
13. CBOS, supra note 6.
14. I discuss the issue of employee ownership infra at pp 129–133.
15. Asked whether they thought privatization would help the national economy, seventy-nine percent of those with higher education said yes, compared with sixty-four percent of those with vocational education. When asked whether privatization would raise the standard of living of a majority of the population, sixty-four percent of those with college degrees said yes, compared with fifty-five percent of those with a vocational education. But forty two percent of those with higher education said they did not believe wages in privately owned industries would always exceed wages in state-owned industries, compared with twenty-four percent of those with vocational education. CBOS, supra note 8.
16. Kolarska-Bobińska, supra note 8.
17. Kuczyński & Nowotny, supra note 11.
18. See Chemiński, Czynczyk, and Sterniczuk, in this volume.
19. Because the category "no answer given" is not presented, percentages do not equal one hundred percent. Data comes from the survey *Poles 88* and *Poles 90.*
20. See M. Jarosz, M. Kozak, A. Jawłowski & P. Kozarnewski, *Social Consequences of the Economic Reform* (Warsaw: Institute of Economic Sciences, 1990); *Poles 90,* supra note 8.
21. See *Poles 90,* supra note 8.
22. See CBOS, June 1992.
23. Jarosz, et al., supra note 20, p. 24.
24. Ibid.
25. CBOS, supra note 8.
26. CBOS, supra note 6.
27. See Kuczyński & Nowotny, supra note 11.
28. CBOS, supra note 6, p. 5.
29. Ibid.
30. Kuczyński & Nowotny, supra note 11.
31. Ibid.
32. Jarosz et al., supra note 20.
33. Kolarska-Bobińska, supra note 3.

34. Kolarska-Bobińska, supra note 8.
35. Kolarska-Bobińska, supra note 8.
36. A. Celinski, "The New Reality," *Życie Warszawy* (September 1989), p. 3.
37. Kolarska-Bobińska, 1991, supra note 8.
38. See Chelmiński, Czynczyk and Sterniczuk, in this volume.
39. Kolarska-Bobińska, supra note 8.
40. $p = < 0.001$, $V = 0.24$, Kolarska-Bobińska, supra note 8.
41. *Opinions about Privatization,* CBOS, June 1992, November 1992.
42. A slight excess of negative over positive forecasts was first recorded in August 1991. The distribution of the answers in May 1992 indicates a marked change in the public climate connected with privatization.

PRIVATE FARM OWNERSHIP IN A CHANGING POLAND: MYTH AND REALITY

Krystyna Daniel

[*Editor's Synopsis:* One of the ironies of economic transformation in East-Central Europe is that Polish farmers' demands for absolute private property rights hamper the shift to a market economy by obstructing any regulation in the public interest. The irony is even stronger when one considers the fact that Polish farmers have long held to traditions that teach the public responsibilities of private property. The privatization of Polish farmland illustrates the problems new democracies encounter when private interests clash with the public good. Professor Daniel argues that the laws establishing private property must address the specific insecurities produced by decades of unstable rights of ownership, but without abandoning protection of the public good.]

Introduction

This article discusses the effect of the Communist regime's halfhearted preservation of private farmland on the formation of farmers' attitudes, and the impact of these attitudes on current policies aimed at revitalizing Polish agriculture.[1] Among the countries of so-called "true socialism," Poland was unique in maintaining a limited system of private ownership of certain means of production, including agricultural land.[2] By the end of the 1940s, as a result of land reform and legislative measures, approximately ninety-three percent of all agrarian land in Poland was owned by the farmers who worked the land.[3] Beneath the Communist government's apparent commitment to individual ownership of agricultural land, however, the reality of ownership was quite different.

Because private ownership was tolerated within a context of socialized ownership and pressure for progressive collectivization, farmers never felt secure in their rights, and now feel the need to overcome these past insecurities. They are extremely hostile to any action in the public interest which even minimally encroaches on the rights of private ownership, including measures essential for protecting the environment or safeguarding farmland. Their sense of individualism and desire for autonomy is a significant impediment to the country's plan to rebuild its villages by creating larger, more efficient private farms that depend on hired labor.

Although private ownership of farms doubtless will produce benefits for Poland, some legal regulation of farm land-use practice is necessary to protect the public welfare. The key is to persuade farmers to accept government solutions to farming issues. Agricultural policies that take into account the attitudes of Polish farmers stand a far greater chance of success.

I. Historical Background: The Communist Government's Recognition and Erosion of Private Ownership of Farm Land

One must have some knowledge of the tradition of agrarian land ownership and Polish land policies since the end of the war in order to understand current issues of private farm ownership. The fact that Poland had never experienced a capitalist system of land ownership determined the relationship farmers would have to their land under the communist system. Polish farmers did not value land solely for its economic value. To them, land symbolized independence and freedom, the guarantee of a peaceful existence, security, and desirable social status.

A 1944 decree of the Polish Committee of National Liberty (PKWN) was the primary regulation of the postwar system. The law was enacted "specifically to ensure that the farming system in Poland [would] rest upon strong, healthy and productive farms, being the [private] property of the farmers."[4] The Communist government's motivation in introducing such a law, and others like it later on, was to gain sympathy and support in rural areas.[5] Communist legislators could not treat lightly the attachment of Polish farmers to their lands, and their psychological involvement with ownership. The preservation of private farms was a pragmatic but significant concession to capitalism necessary to secure the farmers' acceptance of the communist system.

In December 1925, the Polish legislature began breaking up large private estates, a process interrupted by the outbreak of World War II. Wartime reforms gave farmers land from these large estates, and farmers fully expected the process of enfranchisement to continue after the war's end. Polish farmers had decisively rejected the Soviet collectivist model of farming introduced in the other communist countries, and were demanding that opportunities for farmers to own their farms actually be expanded.

The first years after World War II saw the liquidation of great land estates, resulting in a twenty-five percent increase in peasant farms, and the enlargement of a third of preexisting small farms.[6] On the whole, of all the land farmers would eventually own, thirty percent came from the postwar land reforms. The ascending communist system even expanded private land ownership to include more people. All told, more than ninety percent of the land belonged to private farms, and a sizable number of farmers soon acquired deeds of ownership.[7] The situation of private ownership in Poland, therefore, was exceptional and unparalleled in other communist countries, where all farming was eventually collectivized.

However, farmers' trust in the government's laws regarding private land ownership was quickly shaken. State actions beginning in 1948 and increasing in the 1950s irrefutably indicated to farmers that private ownership was a mometary mechanism, and that the ultimate goal was agricultural collectivization. The state initiated a campaign to collectivize rural lands, raising the number of cooperatives to ten thousand by 1956. In order to facilitate the liquidation of large, prosperous farms,[8] the state overburdened the owners with exorbitant taxes. The government harassed large farm owners in other ways as well: they were not allowed to hire employees, and severe restrictions were imposed on purchasing equipment. When these measures did not fully succeed, the government charged prosperous farmers with tax evasion and other political crimes. During this same period (from 1951), farmers were required to supply products such as grain, milk, meat, and potatoes to the government at deflated prices.[9] New regulations required that an administrative office approve any transfer of land, officially suspending the processes of sale or transfer of land. Particularly significant for farmers was the newly ratified Constitution of 1952, which established the favored status of socialized ownership. The new Constitution did not secure the inviolability of peasant ownership, promising instead to merely protect and preserve private farms.[10]

Farmers' discontent over such steps to facilitate collectivization ultimately caused an economic fiasco, which forced the political leadership to pursue its plan to "socialize" rural areas through more gradual means.[11] The government attempted to make farmers bear much of the brunt of postwar redevelopment. Under the so-called obligatory supply of farm products action, farmers were required to sell their goods for a substantially discounted price. Predictably, the result was a substantial decline in agricultural output, as well as a decline in farmers' incomes.

The lack of constitutional guarantees of the stability, inviolability, and equality of private ownership paved the way for a series of laws facilitating the state's takeover of farms during the 1960s and seventies. The government passed laws providing for confiscation of land for outstanding debts in 1962[12] and for compulsory state purchase of unused land in 1968.[13] In practice the government rarely used these regulations to take land from farmers, but their very existence created an atmosphere of uncertainty and threat to farm owners. Beginning in 1962, however, the widespread application of retirement laws did allow the state to gain ownership of a significant amount of farmland. These laws conditioned the right of farmers to retire on their surrendering ownership of their farms.[14] The vulnerability of Polish farm owners under such a system is obvious; not only could the government easily take their property, farmers also had little ability to control their farms or the goods they produced, since they were forced to sell the bulk of their goods to the state. By 1989, only 71.2 percent of farmland was in private farms.[15]

Private farm owners also perceived the glaring inequality between how the government treated them and how it treated the favored collectives and state farms. For example, a state farm or collective might leave considerable tracts of land uncultivated without suffering any repercussions from the state. On the other hand, a private farm owner could potentially lose his land for letting it lie fallow. And while unprofitable state farms and collectives had the benefit of subsidies, loans, and tax exemptions, private farmers were not even allowed to buy new farm equipment until 1971.

The situation of the farmers grew progressively worse as continually harsher government regulations limited the transfer of land. Formalistic, complicated rules of territorial limitation made it nearly impossible for farmers to adjust the sizes of their farms to suit their needs. For example, the regulations used eight hectares (twenty acres) as the basic norm for farm sizes. A farmer who owned an eight-hectare farm could not reduce its size. Farmers did not have much opportunity to enlarge their farms, either. The regulations set the maximum size of farms at fifteen acres for cultivation or twenty acres for breeding livestock.

Regulations against the division of farms resulted in a proliferation of technically illegal informal land sales,[16] to the point where it was becoming difficult to distinguish ownership from mere possession of land.[17] Even when farmers managed to legally obtain the deed to their farms, their use of the land was excessively hampered, and they were under the constant threat of losing their ownership. These regulations, like the others on farms and farm production, led many farmers to believe that eventually farming would be collectivized, along with the rest of the land in Poland. The uncertain and transitory sense of ownership continued to have a negative impact on private farm production.

II. Failed Policies and New Legal Strategies

If private farms were to survive, changes were needed to strengthen farmers' sense of ownership. An Act of 1971 was one of the first measures seriously to address the concerns of private farms. The Act legitimated status quo ownership by granting and recording the deeds of those who had obtained their land through informal trade.[18] So ingrained were farmers' insecurities at this point that some farmers were distrustful of even this seemingly innocuous law. To them, recording was a trick to collectivize land. These farmers feared that, when they died, the deeds would entitle the state to take the land of the "enfranchised farmers" without regard to heirs. The fact that such opinions existed, even if not widely held, illustrates the legal awareness of Polish farmers and how extremely sensitive they were to changes in their legal status.[19]

A mass migration of young farmers to the cities, and the increasing abandonment of rural areas and farms (in the east and south of Poland and in Dolny Slask), was clearly the result of the loss of confidence in private land ownership, the disapproval of excessive legal interferences in private farming, and the weak economy of the 1970s. Empirical studies have revealed that, because of the uncertain future of private farms and the difficulty of running one, farmers would discourage their children from remaining on the farm.[20] Thus the government's policy of expanding legal ownership to include significantly more private farms while simultaneously restricting the owners' rights was an inadequate method of ensuring the continued existence of private farming.

In light of their dire situation, farmers in the 1970s proposed legal changes to secure their private property rights—all in agreement with the public interest, of course. First, farmers proposed a constitutional amendment which would guarantee the certainty and continued stability of private property, as well as clearly establishing the conditions upon which the government could appropriate their property. Under legal rules in force until March 1982, the state could easily deprive a farmer of ownership of part or all of his farm. Specifically, if a farmer increased the size of his farm beyond certain defined limits, the state could expropriate the excess without paying any compensation. The state was also authorized to take over insolvent or mismanaged farms, giving the farmer a small pension as compensation. Even after 1982, a farmer could lose his land if he did not cultivate and live on it for two consecutive years.

Second, farmers proposed a broad law granting them the ability to freely exercise the rights of private ownership, including the right to profits derived from the land. These proposals, which had the immediate support of the Church[21] and later of Solidarity, led to progress favoring farmers. Most important were changes in the Civil Code (1982)[22] and the Polish Constitution (1983)[23] granting much-needed stability and equality of rights to owners of private farms. Accompanying these changes was the repeal of several laws which had previously enabled the state to acquire private land, in addition to the simplification and liberalization of the rules regulating the sale of farmland. Size limitations on farms were also abolished.[24] The majority of farmers desired and accepted these changes as part of a new process to remove real and imagined barriers to the development of individual farming in Poland.

III. The Pendulum Keeps Swinging: Expanding Private Rights While Limiting Social Responsibility

The expansion of farmers' rights of private ownership, and farmers' growing confidence in those rights, has evolved alongside a disconcerting tendency to minimize the social responsibilities that come from owning land. Farmers believe that they should have complete and unlimited freedom of trade and freedom to use the land as they wish. They reject any form of state intervention, even measures intended to safeguard the public welfare, such as protecting the environment, encouraging efficient farm sizes, and ensuring the productive use of the land.

Most farmers believe they should have the unlimited ability to enlarge their farms. Currently, the average farm is a little more than five hectares.[25] Farmers do not see any need for state intervention when land is mistreated or lies fallow. The only restrictions that most farmers accept are laws forbidding the sale of farmland to foreigners (primarily to Germans or Russians).

Land and the laws of ownership are closely tied to a society's values, both in the economic sphere and beyond. The product of a consciousness shaped by the previous period, farmers' predominantly selfish attitudes are antithetical to a prosocial, Christian ethic. Farmers seek to advance the interests of their own business or close family members. My research indicates an individualistic tendency bent on making private land ownership absolute.[26] This attitude is somewhat surprising, since contemporary Catholic social doctrine emphasizes the social functions of private ownership, and the Church has traditionally been a strong influence on the attitudes of Polish farmers. Since the 1930s, the Church has emphasized the dualistic individual-social nature of ownership as a vehicle for benefitting society as well as the individual, and has clearly taught that private ownership is a social function.[27]

It seems reasonable to say that the most popular conception of private land ownership in Poland is closer to the classic conceptions of Roman law and the Napoleonic Code than to the modern conceptions which dominate Western Europe. In Western European countries what is controversial today are the problems raised by the business of farming, not agricultural land itself. In France, for example, the effectiveness and stability of farms are most crucial. Reflecting this concern, agricultural laws provide various guarantees for farm managers, regardless of whether they are owners or lessees, so that they have maximum freedom to manage the farm. These guarantees include long-term leases until the lessee retires, the right of preemption, and the right to transfer the lease. The aim of these laws is by no means to weaken private ownership. To the contrary, the commitment to stable private ownership of land remains strong in France, as indicated by the fact that French lessees tend to buy their leased land whenever possible.[28]

In Poland, on the other hand, problems concerning land ownership remain unresolved and acute. Poland today is experiencing a noticeable counterreaction to previous government policies of far-reaching control, strong paternalism, and limitations on private ownership. Within Polish society, the process is universal. It results from the conflict between two competing tendencies: the simultaneous expansion and limitation of owners' rights. A similar situation occurred during the French Revolution and the rejection of feudal ownership. As a result of the peasants' attachment to land and the regulation of owners' rights in the period preceding the revolution, the Napoleonic Code emphasized the free exercise of individual rights in the ownership of land.

Similarly, after years of governmental attempts to collectivize all of Polish agriculture, an enormous change has occurred in Polish land law. Not only has private land ownership been stabilized, but the government has introduced excessive liberalization measures. For example, restrictions on transfers of farmland designed to limit the size of farms, have been completely abolished. The government also abolished the requirement that farm purchasers must be qualified to farm.[29] Requirements designed to assure the effective use of land were also kept to a minimum.

Polish farmers themselves very much approved of these changes. Their approval, however, probably reflects the fact that, freed of restrictive governmental control, farmers simply did not consider the value of public regulations securing effective land use, providing an efficient land-ownership structure, and protecting against concentrations of land ownership that would threaten the peasant family farm.

Results of empirical research that I conducted in 1990 and 1991 indicate that farmers still tend to mythologize private ownership, opposing measures in the public interest which do not favor owners' rights of absolute autonomy. Comparing the mediocre production of the old regime's favored state farms with the success of disfavored private farms only fuels the myth of private ownership.[30]

The fact that farmers resent any state acts which interfere with their ability to exercise their rights as owners does not mean they are entirely insensitive to the social responsibilities that accompany ownership. Farmers are simply distrustful of legal regulations. The majority believes that farmers themselves know best how to reconcile conflicts between individual profit and public welfare, and experience indicates that farmers may very well be justified in holding such a belief. For example, the rigorous limitations placed on the transfer of farmland undermined the policy of efficient land use by discouraging adaptation of farm size and structure, a situation somewhat ameliorated by the fact that farmers often disobeyed the regulations by engaging in informal land transfers. Today, the institution of a system liberalizing such transfers has seen a slow but steady growth in the creation of larger, more efficient private farms.[31] It is difficult, however, to foresee this process occurring without regulatory laws creating the conditions necessary to stimulate improvements in the agrarian structure.

IV. Agrarian Attitudes Toward Ownership: The Key to Success for Poland's Agricultural Policies

Currently, few Polish farmers lease land. There are two likely reasons for this. First, there is little Polish law regarding such leasing. Second, the characteristic preference of Polish farmers to work on land that is their own extends to leased land.[32] Encouraging farmers to lease land through modern, long-term, possibly inheritable leases would have a positive effect on Polish agriculture. Many farmers who are too old to farm will not relinquish ownership of their land. Leaving the owner with title to the land and appropriate profits, but bestowing the lessee farmer with a sense of security in his right to peaceful possession of the land, would have the effect of immediately freeing land for useful cultivation. Such leasing would also work to concentrate farmland into larger, more efficient farms faster than the enlargement of farms by means of outright purchase.[33]

Another agrarian attitude that has an important bearing on the issue of private ownership, although little discussed, is the community traditions of Polish farming. The common use of woods and meadows by inhabitants of one or more villages has long existed as a Polish custom. The so-called "land communities," which farmers commonly owned and freely governed, served this purpose.[34] The point is that farmers do not reject community forms of land ownership where they are allowed to freely use and govern the property. For example, the Communist government inherited a system of joint ownership of properties from the previous regime, which the Communists attempted to maintain. Farmers could become co-owners of these properties, but the land was subjected to far-reaching state administrative control. Because farmers refused to participate, the government parcelled out some of the joint properties and left some to decay. Only in places where farmers fought for real independence from government control, such as in southern Poland, did the system of joint ownership work effectively.[35]

The task facing Poland today is the need to rationally regulate the country's two million, seven hundred thousand private farms, while at the same time overcoming the weight of farmers' mistrust. Farmers' expectations will spell the success or failure of the country's agricultural policies. For example, the country's policy of strengthening family farms through advantageous tax credits is likely to succeed because it stresses the work of the owner himself and his immediate family. On the other hand, a policy that is unlikely to succeed is the attempt to rebuild the country's villages through the radical plan of "farmerization," that is, the creation of conditions for the development of large private farms based on hired labor. This policy ignores farmers' attitudes regarding ownership. Not only will this policy quickly lead to the economic ruin of smaller, inefficient farms, evoking great dissatisfaction in the owners, but it may take years before other areas of the economy are able to absorb the displaced farmers.[36]

Modifications in the laws regulating private farms which seek to promote the public welfare cannot rest solely on conceptions of the public character of land ownership. To be effective, Polish agricultural laws must give weight to and come to terms with the liberal conception of individual autonomy that Polish farmers prefer. Otherwise, the government must find a way to persuade Polish farmers that some degree of government involvement with their land use is desirable, both for themselves and for society.

Notes

1. Land is an excellent reference point for any analysis of changes in the realm of ownership. As a well-known Italian lawyer put it, "Ownership of land is an area of experimentation upon which we build our laws of property." S. Romano, "Sulla Nozione di Proprieta" (On the Notion of Property), *Revue Trimestrielle de Droit Civil* 337 (1960).
2. The Constitution of the People's Republic of Poland, July 22, 1952, regulated the different types of ownership. Dz.U. No. 33, pos. 233, Articles 7–14 and Article 70, §§2.72 and 77, paragraphs 1–2.
3. See J. Lubin, *Komuniści na wsi polskiej 1944–1986* (Communists in the Polish Village, 1944–1986) (Kraków: Wydawnictwo Myśli Niezaleźnej, 1988).
4. Article 1, paragraph 1, sentence 1 of the decree of September 6, 1944. Dz.U. no. 4, pos. 17; homogeneous text from 1945, Dz.U. No. 3, pos. 13.
5. Interestingly, doubts that private farms would endure were regarded as hostile, anticommunist propaganda during the early postwar period of agrarian reform. Jan Ptasiński, *Ze spoktań z W. Gomułką* (from Meetings with Gomułką), Rzeczywistość, 41/1983.
6. Although the Communists claimed to have granted land to farmers for free, this was not entirely true. Farmers had to pay about a third of the land's value over a period of ten to twenty years. During the period of enforced collectivization, 1948 to 1956, the government insisted on accelerating payments.
7. A September 6, 1951 decree authorized the regulation of deeds of ownership for settlers possessing farms in the western and northern lands. Dz.U. No. 40, pos. 340. A June 18, 1955 decree authorized the regulation of farms where the owner-farmers did not possess a deed of ownership. Homogenous text 1959, Dz.U. No. 14, pos. 78.
8. Large farms, the so-called "*kulaks,*" were farms of more than 10 to 15 hectares (25 to 37 acres).
9. The obligatory supply of farming products was introduced in 1951, partially limited in 1957, and completely abandoned in 1972. *See* Paweł Bojarski, *Przyczynek do zagadnienia dostaw obowiazdowych i kontraktacji* (Introduction to the Problem of Obligatory Contract and Supply), *Państwo i Prawo* (January, 1965).
10. Article 10, pos. 1 and Article 12 of the 1952 Constitution. Compare J. Lubin, note 3 supra pp. 25–26.
11. The turning point was a declaration at the Communist party's Eighth Plenum of the Central Committee in October, 1956. This declaration was the primary political document ending the period of Stalinist reprisals, and inaugurating

the period of distinctly Polish socialism. The document guaranteed the end of compulsory collectivization and announced that private land ownership would continue. Other significant changes included the cancellation of trade limits, reduction of obligatory supply quotas, higher prices for farm products, and the like.

12. Act of 28 June 1962, Dz.U. No. 17, pos. 130.
13. Act of 24 January, 1968, Dz.U. No. 14.
14. Act of 28 June 1962, Dz.U. No. 38, pos. 166, and primarily the Act of 24 January 1968, Dz.U. No. 3, pos. 15, and the Act of 29 May, 1974, Dz.U. No. 21, pos. 118.
15. *Mały rocznik statystyczny* (Abridged Statistical Annals), Primary Government Statistics (1990).
16. Act of 29 June 1963, Dz.U. The principles of this act limiting the division of farms were incorporated in the Polish Civil Code on 23 April, 1964. Dz.U. No. 16, pos. 93. In practice, the law forbid the division of farms.
17. According to data received by the Ministry of Agriculture in December 1980, the unregulated ownership that resulted from these informal land sales accounted for approximately eighty percent of all farms.
18. Act of 26 September 1971, Dz.U. No. 27, pos. 250. See Jósef S. Piatowski, "Uregulowanie własności gospodarstw rolnych i zmiany w kodeksie cywilnym" (Regulating Ownership of Farms and Changes in the Civil Law"), *Państwo i Prawo,* (1971) pp. 8–9.
19. Krystyna Daniel, *Poglądy rolników na cele i skutki regulacji własności gospodarstw rolnych* (Farmers' Opinions on the Goals and Results of the Regulation of Farm Ownership), Wrocław (1987).
20. See Eugenia Jagiełło-Łysiowa, *Zawód rolnika w świadomości społeczej dwóch pokoleń wsi* (The Farmer's Occupation in the Social Consciousness of Two Generations of Villagers) (Warsaw: Książka i Wiedza 1969); Bronistawa Kopczyńska-Jaworska, ed., *Stosunek mieszkańców wsi kujawskiej do ziemi* (The Villagers' Attitudes Toward Land) (Łodż: Ossolineum, 1974).
21. The Conference of Polish Bishops, during June 26 to 27, 1975, had a large impact. In an official document, the Church supported private ownership, and expressed worry that more and more land was being taken by the state. In 1981, the Primate of Poland appealed to the government to accept Solidarity of Individual Farmers, which was established May 12, 1981. Compare Andrzej Micewski, *Kardynał Wyszyński, Prymas i maz stanu* (Cardinal Wyszynski: Primate and Statesman) (Paris: Editions du Dialogue, 1982) pp. 348.
22. Act of 26 March 1982, Dz.U. No. 11, pos. 80.
23. Constitutional Amendment of 22 July 1983, Dz.U. No. 39, pos. 175.
24. Acts of 26 March 1982, Dz.U. No. 11, pos. 79, 81, 82, and the recent Act of 28 July 1990 changing the Civil Code, Dz.U. No. 55, pos. 321.
25. Research for this section was conducted in 1989 with farmers from the areas of Warsaw and Tarnów (southern Poland) and Jelenia Góra (western Poland).

Legislation enacted in 1982 limited the maximum size of farms to one hundred hectares (two hundred and fifty acres). In 1990, the government abolished all restrictions on increasing farm size.

26. This attitude is by no means unique to farmers in Poland. For more on this topic, see Father Janusz Mariański, *Moralność w procesie przemian—Szkice socjologiczne* (Morality in the Process of Change: Sociological Sketches) (Warsaw: Publishing Institute PAX 1990) pp. 191–124.

27. In the *Encyclical Quadragessimo Anno of Pius XI* (1931), the Church stresses the need for private ownership to benefit society, and not just the individual. The *Encyclical Mater et Magistra of John XXIII* (1961) states even more clearly that private ownership is a social function, as do the *Populorum Progresso of Paul VI* (1961) and the *Laborem Exercens of John Paul II* (1981). Jerzy F. Godlewski, *Katolicka myśl kościelna o prawie i państwie* (Catholic Thought Regarding Law and State), (Warsaw: State Scientific Publishing House, 1985).

28. See Joseph Hudault, "Ewolucja stosunku miedzy gospodarstwem rolnym i jego wlasnoscia w prawie rolnym" (The Evolution of the Relationship between the Farm and Its Ownership in French Law), *Prawo Rolne* (July–September 1991).

29. This last action is particularly significant because traditionally Polish farm owners have done all their own farming.

30. 1992 data from the Ministry of Agriculture indicate that only 870 out of 2236 state farms are run efficiently and are profitable.

31. Id. In 1980, 4.3% of private farms had more than fifteen hectares (thirty-seven acres). By 1989, that number had grown to 6.1%.

32. Farmers not only prefer to work their own land, they also tend to produce more when the land is their own. For example, while state farms constituted nineteen percent of farmed land in Poland in 1979, they accounted for only seven percent of agricultural production, ninety-three percent being supplied by private farms. J. Lubin, supra note 3, p. 51.

33. Compare Aleksander Lichorowicz, *Dzierźawa gruntów rolnych w ustawodawstwie krajów zachodnieuropejskich* (Leasing Farmlands in the Legal System of Western Europe) (Kraków: Universitas Iagellonica Acta Scientiarum Litterarumque, Schedae Iuridicae, Fasciculus CXVIII, 1986).

34. Land communities serve as pastures for breeding animals and sources of wood and firewood. According to the Ministry of Agriculture, the area of land possessed by land communities in 1981 was more than 160,000 hectares (400,000 acres), which were mainly pastures, woods, and uncultivated farmland. See Michat Ptaszyk, *Spółki do zagospodarowania wspólnot gruntowych - sytuacja prawna, funkcjonowanie, perspektwy* (Cooperatives for Using Land Communities: The Legal Situation, Functions and Perspectives), (Kraków: Universitas Iagellonica Acta Scientiarum Litterarumque, Schedae Iuridicae, Fasciculus CXXIX, (1989). See also Ludwik Jastrzębski, *Wspólnoty gruntowe i ich przyszłość* (Land Communities and Their Future), *Państwo i Prawo* (July, 1963).

35. Joint ownership is evidence that Polish farmers do not reject all forms of common ventures. It is only when joint ownership is excessively controlled by the government that farmers object. At the same time, however, one must emphasize that joint ownership does not currently constitute a significant form of land ownership in Poland.
36. Compare Marian Błażejczyk *Pozycja prawna chłopskiego gospodarstwa* (The Legal Status of the Peasant Farm), Zagadnienia Ustroju Prawnego Rolnictwa (vol. 6, 1988).

Social Consciousness in Transition: Toward a New Economic and Political System

Maria Borucka-Arctowa

[*Editors' Synopsis:* Social consciousness is a significant factor in determining the scope of the transformations and the effectiveness of the reforms that are now sweeping across Central and Eastern Europe. This is the consciousness of transition, when elements of the old system exist side by side with those of the new, often resulting in incoherent and contradictory opinions. These contradictions are linked not only to the clash between the new consciousness and residues of the old, but also to the confrontation between the ideals of the new system and the actual experiences of it.]

Introduction

While Poles and others throughout East and Central Europe agree on the desirability of privatization, that consensus does not itself indicate that they all share a common vision of what the new social and economic system should be. There are multiple models of private ownership and market economy that the postcommunist societies of East-Central Europe can follow in privatizing, including prewar and extant Western systems. However, the starting point for East-Central European societies is completely different from that of other countries that have experienced privatization, and this difference requires different approaches. Various possible privatization scenarios have been outlined, ranging from spontaneous to constructed privatization. If one accepts the principles of market economics, of course, constructed privatization should play only a secondary role.[1]

Reliance on these extant models must take into account the consequences of changes in the social consciousness that forty-five years of Communism effected. By "social consciousness," I mean the perceptions and knowledge of the world people live in and the world they would like to inhabit. As Professor Trubek has stated,

> The consciousness of any society rests on its set of world views, on basic (and sometimes implicit) notions about what is natural, necessary, just, and desirable. . . . The worlds of meaning that we construct in turn shape and channel what we do and do not do. In this view, social relations and world views become inseparable.[2]

Social, political, and legal development is not predetermined by social structures. As Toynbee's "challenge response" theory recognized, events challenge individuals and society to change but do not determine what the change will be.[3] Consciousness plays a crucial role in social, politicolegal, and economic change because societies have several available responses to events from which to choose.

Analyzing the problems of social consciousness in connection with privatization, we must bear in mind that legal and economic privatization is not a goal in itself, but only a means to another goal, that is, transformation of the whole social system and of citizens' consciousness. The challenge confronting the postcommunist countries is to pursue social justice and rapid political, social, and economic change within a democratic framework which respects the rule of law and guarantees legal security. The key to this challenge is to understand the degree to which conflicts and ambivalence in the postcommunist social consciousness affect the scope and efficacy of the reforms, and, conversely, the degree to which the reforms affect social consciousness.

During the current period of transition from the ideals of revolution to concrete reforms, attempts to establish a new system often conflict with residues of the old consciousness, at the same time that actual experiences of the new system are disappointing expectations. These tensions must be considered the dominant themes of the privatization process. We are now in the midst of a breakthrough period, when the emerging order must confront the residue of the old consciousness and the contradictory opinions that exist from individual to individual, and from social group to social group. The former political-economic regime has transformed social consciousness, and the vestiges of that change are a significant impediment to the privatization plan. Antipathy toward statism and the effort to minimize state intervention in the market economies coexist with the necessity of state involvement with privatization. The upshot is that society's need for legal security has taken on special psychological significance as part of a broader need for social stability.[4] Because the legislative consciousness[5] is also, to some extent, rooted in the past, the legal system very often reinforces state paternalism, rather than favoring the development of individual responsibility necessary for a successful market economy. How measures such as the Act on Privatization[6] will affect legal consciousness sheds light both on the stimulation of self-reliance through legal incentives and society's acquisition of democracy and economic initiative.

In the first part of this paper I briefly discuss the impact of socialism on the current social consciousness. The second part outlines the problems of state programs which reinforce the old consciousness, instead of encouraging a new social consciousness more suited to a market economy. The third part discusses the dualism between felt and accepted values in the social consciousness, and the lack of information as obstacles to privatization. The fourth part argues that current legislative efforts and political rhetoric are actually undermining the transformation process. Finally, I conclude with a brief but optimistic observation on the potential for future change.

I. The Legacy of the Socialist Past: Tradition and the Need for Legal Security

Social consciousness is largely shaped by tradition, and the craving for traditional ways, somewhat paradoxically, has reinforced the desire of post-communist societies for change.[7] However, the preference for the familiar may be so strong that it stifles legal innovation. In fact, most analyses underestimate the degree to which the consciousness of this transition period reflects society's fear of legal principles and policies which are extraneous to either the former legal system or the idealized Western Europe. Even when people prefer Western European models, they prefer those institutions that remind them of their own "traditions." By urging a return to the "good old traditional values," the events of East-Central Europe are unlike history's most recent bourgeois revolutions, the French and American revolutions, which sought to abolish an evil past and build the world anew.[8] Rather, what is occurring in the postsocialist countries more nearly resembles earlier, backward-looking, bourgeois revolutions such as in the Netherlands or the Glorious Revolution in England, which were also marked by a fear of innovation, and the desire to preserve or return to lost traditions.[9]

This does not mean that tradition rigidly determines social choices. What society claims as its tradition is a progressive notion, that is, adaptable to current social needs.[10] Recent research reveals that people not only select and construe their old ways according to their present needs, but they will even conjure up "traditions" that never existed in order to defend modern institutions and social policies.[11] Polish tradition includes attachment to values and institutions that evolved during important moments in Polish history, most significantly the period between the wars, and the more than forty years of "true socialism."

Much of this tradition is simply not compatible with the shift to a market economy, and must be discarded if the transformation is to be successful. A complete return to prewar legislation is equally impracticable. We need to construct a legal system that meets current needs, not those of the past. The greatest difficulties are those inherited from the former, rejected system. For example, the fact that the communist administration distributed goods on the basis of privileges, not economic need, in an environment of chronic shortages led to growing differences between social groups and dependence on privileges.[12] Despite the shift to a new system, formerly privileged groups are trying to maintain their status by appealing to tradition. They compare their privileges to the myriad obligations (which people now call rights) that the state assumed during the more than forty years of state socialism.

The problem, of course, is whether the decision to eliminate illegitimate privileges while protecting legitimate "acquired rights" will threaten society's sense of legal security. Despite the decisions of the Polish Constitutional Tribunal stating the need for legal security,[13] the tribunal has refused to recognize some rights, which the tribunal calls privileges, that the former regime granted to individuals. The principle that the tribunal followed is that, out of the large body of law inherited from the former regime, only those rights which are compatible with notions of social justice, particularly equality, should be retained. Current debate focuses on how to apply this principle in the context of shifting political and economic conditions, with demands for rapid reform conflicting with demands for a state based on the rule of law (that is, legal stability, defense of acquired rights, and no retroactive sanctions).[14] These incompatible demands extend beyond the views of lawyers and are part of a prominent dualism in society's legal consciousness.

The rejection of the socialist political and economic system did not create a pure, free-market, social consciousness, particularly with respect to specific social expectations (for example, notions of economic and social equality). The acceptance of the market economy and private ownership often rests on the idealistic assumption that it is a way for *everyone* to achieve a Western European standard of living; it does not mean people accept the inegalitarian differences which result from initiative, ability, diligence, and chance. Society's egalitarian tendencies have led to the implementation of "privileges" in the new system in the form of state subsidies for some social groups in branches of industry, services, and farming. Society favors this type of privilege at the same time that it resents and condemns state intervention for having led to the country's economic ruin. These coexisting, contradictory beliefs are an example of residues of the old system appearing in the social consciousness of the new system.

II. Breaking Old Habits, and Creating a New Citizenry

The shift to a market economy begins on a footing that is completely different from anything in the country's own past, or the experiences of modern capitalist countries which did not undergo a period of socialism. This situation demands new solutions. Although it is relatively easy to establish small, private enterprises based on individual capital, privatization of the state-owned sector is complicated due to a great number (eighty percent) of monopolist, state-owned enterprises. If the privatization of such enterprises is to follow normal market principles, it is going to be a relatively slow process. Many enterprises and sectors of the economy are burdened with liabilities left over from the socialist regime. Among these are very large, inefficient factories requiring extensive modernization, unemployment resulting from layoffs of excess workers, environmental pollution, an administrative structure that is unresponsive to a market economy, a bureaucratic system of nepotism and favoritism, and a destroyed entrepreneurial ethos. Who will assume the "burden of liabilities" is a difficult question. Despite a general desire to reduce the state's participation in the economy, the state cannot avoid playing a vital role in setting the economic policies of privatization, implementing the laws, and distributing the liabilities of state-owned firms. But there are significant dangers in the state's assuming too great a responsibility for the success or failure of privatization.

The right of property is often characterized by an extremely liberal approach toward the issue of responsibility. All too frequently the property owner's rights are defined in a way that neglects or downright rejects functional social utility and responsibility. Such an approach deviates from the social doctrine of the Catholic church, an institution that has otherwise greatly influenced Polish society.[15] This reflects the tension between competing visions in the reforms—on the one hand, the liberal ideals of individual autonomy and freedom from government controls, and on the other hand, a new form of state interventionism which sees the state intervening in market forces instead of centrally administering the economy. Poland has adopted the latter view of privatization, implementing changes in the structure of property through *institutionalization,* that is to say, the setting up of government bodies to direct and control changes in ownership.[16]

From a purely economic standpoint, this decision made sense, but from a sociological view of the law, the decision to pursue a policy of institutionalization was a controversial one. Privatization offers the possibility of spreading ownership across society (through shareholding) and creating economic self-reliance, not just the creation of a capital market and an efficient economy. Supporters of the neoliberal reforms argue that the emphasis placed on the state's protective role not only burdens the state budget, but also inhibits the development of a sense of individual responsibility for one's self, family, and community. They urge a form of social privatization, where the responsibility for helping those in need is shifted to nonstate institutions.

However, society's profound attachment to the protective role of the state should not be treated as a mere residue of the former system. The problem can be seen in terms of protecting the economic and social rights of men. Society has legitimate claims to economic and social rights which the state is obliged to protect. Once the state has guaranteed these rights, it may adopt a more liberal approach to the reforms by shifting responsibility for their success to individuals and market forces. However, the countries of Central Europe, particularly the Hungarian and Polish parliaments, have been reluctant to fully recognize the obligation of their governments to protect these rights.

The citizens of the postcommunist societies must learn to take initiative, engage in risky behavior, and accept responsibility over their lives; they must learn to function, in other words, in a world without a paternalistic state. The extent to which the state should be involved in the creation of this new type of citizen is itself the subject of some discussion.[17] Nearly everyone agrees that the state should be less involved in the country's economic and social life than it was in the past, but few agree on how the state should go about becoming less involved. The popular maxim, "to the state only what is necessary; to society as much as possible"[18] provides little guidance. On the one hand, the state cannot abandon its role in the transformation to a free-market economy, the creation of new property rights, and the process of privatization. On the other hand, many of the new laws and policies actually *discourage* the development of an innovative and economically self-reliant citizenry—for example, the high cost of credit, fluctuating regulations, unequal economic treatment of certain groups, and barriers to entrepreneurship.[19] The current trend is to extend the state's involvement in the economy far beyond merely setting fiscal policies.[20] By continually assuming economic responsibilities during the transformation process, the state is prolonging the paternalistic tendencies of socialism, when the state was ultimately responsible for the success or failure of each aspect of the economic process and the well-being of all citizens.[21]

III. Dualism and Lack of Information: Impediments to Privatization

Although few firms have so far been privatized, research indicates that positive attitudes towards the general concept of privatization very often become negative when the firm targeted for privatization is where the respondent works.[22] In other words, workers are likely to favor privatization generally, but oppose privatization when it ceases to be an abstract possibility.

Social psychology speaks of this phenomenon as the coexistence of accepted and felt value systems.[23] Accepted values are general ideals that are consistent over time. They are reflected in social beliefs, political programs, and statements by public officials, and are transmitted through social groups, organizations, or the mass media. Felt values, on the other hand, are stereotypes and emotional reactions to real situations that are transmitted through informal channels. Felt values are fluctuating, relative, and situation-conditioned. People are conscious of their felt values and rely on them when responding to common, everyday situations. According to S. Ossowski, the relation between accepted and felt value systems is a dynamic one, and it is possible for contradictory value systems to coexist.[24] Situations, however, can force individuals to choose one value system over the other, as when workers who claim to favor privatization actually oppose its implementation.

Differences in expectations, images, or fears over privatization also stem from a simplified understanding of privatization and insufficient knowledge of the different methods possible under the Privatization Act. For example, among the fallacies that many Polish workers currently believe are that possession of shares in a company will protect an employee from being dismissed, that privatization of a firm will automatically lead to higher wages, or that buying shares will lead to quick profits in the form of dividends. Fears of even partial privatization that might result in their being dismissed or the enterprise going bankrupt leads to antireform attitudes and alliances, particularly in the big, state-owned enterprises. Employees do not perceive that profits are connected to a company's long term goals and the operation of the enterprise as a whole, including the need for modernization and investments. This approach can create a conflict between managers and employees, but more often than not, particularly in large, state-owned enterprises, it results in a specific alliance that cannot adjust to changes being introduced. Because management is often not prepared to assert a leadership role, it will delay making needed changes, hoping that in the future changes will be easier to implement.[25] To overcome this obstacle, it is absolutely vital that employees, negotiation participants, and others be consulted and provided with information. Managers should present and explain the different possible ways of privatizing firms. Managers, moreover, must deal with participation by workers' councils, and must consider the range of opinions voiced by delegates to the workers' general assembly in considering proposals to transform state-owned enterprises into private companies or to liquidate them.[26]

People's feelings of competence play a very important role in this educational process. One's sense of competence can be weakened by the appearance of many concepts and words that are new to the average speaker, such as "company," "employee," "employee shareholding," "liquidation of enterprises," "joint venture," and "leasing." The process of learning these terms differs from the process of adopting terms that are common to legal and nonlegal language, such as "judge," "court," "contract," and the like. Everyday experience plays a significant role in the acquisition of the ability to use the law.[27]

IV. Legislative and Social Consciousness: The Current Dilemma

Disharmony in social consciousness results when experiences of implemented changes disappoint the public's expectations for the new system. Because the social consciousness is unavoidably affected by the fact that the free-market games of interests have been ushered in by a system of centralized control, many scholars call this a period of inevitable contradictions.[28] The public is beginning to feel frustrated, threatened, and disillusioned, as job security disappears and the standard of living of most people continues to decline after the collapse of Communism.[29] In this context, government calls for patience, belt-tightening, and even patriotism can only undermine citizens' faith in the free market. Furthermore, the defensive nonmarket rhetoric of politicians, who refer to the reforms as a "historical experiment" in an effort to excuse the lack of economic recovery, leads to an equally defensive social consciousness that is not conducive to the creation of a stable market economy. People are more inclined to wait and see if the experiment works before they invest their money or energy in efforts that depend on the certainty and long-term stability of the free-market economy.[30]

Furthermore, society's receptiveness to state involvement is a significant element in the efficacy of the transformations, and the social impact of changing property relations. The general resentment of the state, combined with a growing impatience with Parliament's handling of the transformation, poses a threat to the effectiveness of the reforms and the democratic legal process. Under mounting accusations that its observation of legal formalities is delaying needed reforms, the *sejm* (Parliament) is often pressured into hastily passing laws that may either be incomplete or contain serious flaws. Even when given proper consideration, many legislative acts are seen to be inadequate when their implementation falls short of actual needs, requiring revisions and corrective laws. Reconciling the demands of legal procedures and efficient legislative activity becomes all the more difficult as the backlog of government-sponsored bills increases. Because accusations of foot-dragging formality coexist in the social consciousness with the conviction that the entire system must be rebuilt on the rule of law, some have begun to call for a shift of power to the executive branch, or even the installment of an authoritarian regime during the transition period.

The Polish Parliament's efforts to overcome legislative delays have resulted in a lack of *vacatio legis,* the appropriate period of time between the enactment of a law and when the law takes effect.[31] With increasing frequency, new laws are legally binding from the day they are enacted. A problem with this form of legislative acceleration is that the function of *vacatio legis* is not only to allow those who are interested to become acquainted with the text of the new law, but also to allow society to brace itself and make the preparations necessary for the proper functioning of the law. In a democracy which respects the rule of law, acceleration of the legislative process cannot ignore the citizen's psychological need for a sense of legal security in a time of rapid change.[32] Elimination of *vacatio legis* should occur only in extraordinary circumstances. This disturbing phenomenon was frequently criticized (especially by the Polish Spokesman for Civil Rights) as being an obsolete and incoherent remnant of the old regime.[33] The Polish Constitutional Tribunal has recommended that Parliament change it as soon as possible. Parliament subsequently enacted a statute (1991) which provides that laws take effect fourteen days after their promulgation unless the law specifically states otherwise.

Paradoxically, legislation that is intended to expand democratic participation may actually have the opposite effect until people have had time to become familiar with the new system. Very important to the successful transformation of legal consciousness is the citizen's sense of competence in the new system, which to a large extent can only be obtained through experience. We deal here with the problem of communicative competence, the ability to engage in public discourse regarding the implemented reforms. To take advantage of the opportunities provided by the new democratic system, the individual must be aware of the rights he possesses.[34] The introduction of unfamiliar concepts weakens this sense of competence so long as they remain abstract ideas.

Conclusion

Sociolegal research and discussion cannot ignore the importance of the emerging social consciousness in this period of political and economic transition. New situations engender a temporary legal consciousness which can play a fundamental role in the introduction of new legislative solutions. Theoretical discussions point to the power of social consciousness to determine the scope and efficacy of reforms.

Although the coexistence of conflicting views in social consciousness has been a significant obstacle to reform, the forecast need not be a gloomy one. Despite residues of the old consciousness, postcommunist societies sooner or later will realize the impossibility of returning to past solutions. Given this environment, the success of reformers will ultimately depend on their ability to tap this cognitive dissonance in order to stimulate independent thinking, and develop new solutions to the problems of the market economy and private ownership at the grass-roots level. After all, the shaping of this new social order depends on the capacity of individuals to create their own realities, not on the state's capacity to create reality for them. However, state involvement can hasten or delay the transition of social consciousness to the new economic and political system.

Notes

This article is primarily based on Polish experiences, research, and legislative actions. However, its analysis is generally applicable to the transformations taking place throughout East-Central Europe.

1. Tomasz Gruszecki, "Możliwe Scenariusze Prywatyzacji" [Possible Designs of Privatization], unpublished paper presented at the Conference of the Polish

Sociological Association, "Ownership Transformation and Society," Kraków, May 1991.

2. See David M. Trubek, "Where the Action Is: Critical Legal Studies and Empiricism," *Stan. L. Rev.* 36:575, 592 (1984).
3. Arnold J. Toynbee, *Civilization on Trial* (New York: Oxford University Press 1949) p. 12.
4. Janina Czapska, "Potrzeba bezpieczeństwa a prawo (The Need for Security and Law," in *Prawo w Zmiejacym się Społeczeństwie* (*Law in the Changing Society*), eds. Grażyna Skąpska, et al., (Kraków: Uniwersytet Jagielloński Press, 1992) p. 105. See also G. Skąpska, *The Legacy of Anti-Legalism* (forthcoming).
5. By "legislative consciousness," I mean the consciousness of those who shape the law during this transition stage, as reflected in the laws themselves, in lawmakers' support for a particular economic program during parliamentary or government debates, and in discussions between academics and practitioners in the field.
6. Specifically Articles 5, 6, 37 and 38 of the Act on Privatization of State-Owned Enterprises, July 13, 1990.
7. Basic features of tradition include its connection with the past, the way it is passed from generation to generation, and its normative character (something that should be continued and preserved, something that can guide us in our behavior). Martin Krygier, *Law and Philosophy* (Reidel 1988) p. 240; Maria Borucka-Arctowa, "Innovation and Tradition against the Background of Revolutionary Changes of Law—a Conceptual and Functional Analysis," in *Revolutions in Law and Legal Thought,* ed. Zenon Bankowski (Aberdeen: Aberdeen University Press, 1991) p. 81–83.
8. What separated radical and moderate currents in the wake of the French Revolution, for example, was the dispute over the degree to which society should be liberated from its ties to the past. See Borucka-Arctowa, supra note 7; Jan Baszkiewicz, *Wolność, Równość, Własność. Rewolucje Burżuazyjne* (Liberty, Equality, Property: Bourgeois Revolutions, (Warsaw: Czytelnik Press, 1981) p. 212.
9. The excellent lawyers who led the parliamentary opposition in the English revolution appealed to the "good old" common law. These lawyers voiced their opposition to innovation by invoking to the inviolable principles of the Magna Carta. However, the elevation of Parliament's lawmaking power and the threat of civil war paved the way for revolutionary innovations. Borucka-Arctowa, supra note 7, p. 84; Baszkiewicz, supra note 8.
10. The term "progressive tradition," however, was frequently used and abused by the socialist system.
11. See Eric Hobsbawn and Terence Ranger, eds., *The Invention of Tradition* (New York: Cambridge University Press 1983).
12. See, e.g., Lena Kolarska-Bobińska and Andrzej Rychard, *Polityka i Gospodarka w Swiadomości Społecznej* (Politics and Economy in Social Consciousness),

(Warsaw: Uniwersytet Warszawa Press 1990); Edmund Mokrzycki, "Dziedzictwo Realengo Socjalizmu: Poszukiwanie Nowej Utopii" (The Legacy of Rural Socialism: The Search for a New Utopia), in *Przełom i Wyzwanie* (Breakthrough and Challenge—Materials of the VIII Polish Sociological Association), (Warsaw-Toruń: Uniwersytet Nikołaja Kopeŕnika Press, 1991) p. 53–59.

13. Decision of the Polish Constitutional Tribunal, case K 3(88): "The protection of acquired rights is the basis of the citizen's legal security. This protection has an important and multifunctional axiological justification. The credibility of the state and its institutions depends on the state's effective execution of its authority. Depriving a citizen of his recognized rights is highly detrimental to the citizen's legal consciousness. One who discovers that the law will not defend him when his rights have been violated, loses respect for the law."

14. Kazimierz Działocha, "Państwo Prawne w warunkach zasadniczych zmian systemu prawa" [The State of Law in Conditions of Fundamental Changes of the Legal System], *Państwo i Prawo* 1:19 (1992).

15. See Krystyna Daniel, "Private Farm Ownership in a Changing Poland: Myth and Reality," in this volume.

16. See Statute of July 13, 1990, on the Privatization of State-Owned Enterprises and on the Ministry of Ownership Transformations.

17. For example, opinions are divided regarding the desirability of a requirement that future applicants for membership in the European Community meet certain economic standards. On the one hand, such standards may provide countries with the incentive to complete economic reforms quickly and thoroughly; or, on the other hand, by preventing full participation in the Common Market, they may actually impair the shift to a market economy. Maria Borucka-Arctowa, "European Integration and National Identity," in *Zwischen den Zeiten,* eds. Peter Gerlich and Krzystof Glass, (Vienna: Österreiche Gesellschaft für Soziologie, 1992) p. 86.

18. Janina Zakrzewska, "Koncepcja Trysstej Konstytucji" (Conception of the Future Constitution), 1 *Biuro Prasowe* [Bulletin of the Constitutional Council] p. 8 (1990) (originally presented at the session of the Constitutional Commission, Kancelaria Sejmu).

19. Grażyna Skąpska, "Beyond Constructivism and the Rationality of Discovery: Tensions and Paradoxes of the Transition Period," p. 6, paper presented at the international conference, Law and Society in the Global Village, Amsterdam (June 26–29, 1991).

20. Lena Kolarska-Bobińska, "The Role of the State in the Transition Period," p. 4, paper presented at the Working Group on Privatization and Economic Transformation of New Democracies, at the international conference, Law and Society in the Global Village, Amsterdam (June 26–29, 1991). For example, the state has created the ministry responsible for privatizing, continuing or shutting down state industries, and it may freeze wages in order to contain inflation.

21. Anna Turska, "Dynamika Ładu Normatywnego w Społeczeństwie Postotalitarnym" (The Dynamics of the Normative Order in a Post-Totalitarian Society), in *Prawo w Zmieniającym się Społeczeństwie* (in *Law in a Changing Society*), supra note 4, p. 277.

22. See Lena Kolarska-Bobińska, "Privatization in Poland: The Evolution of Opinions and Interests, 1988 to 1992," in this volume.

23. Stanisław Ossowski, "Konflikty Niewspółmiernych Skal Wartości" (Conflicts of Immeasurable Scales of Values), in *Dziela t. III* (in *3 Collected Works*) (Warsaw: Państwowe Wydawnictwo Naukowe, 1987) p. 99; Florian Znaniecki, *Nauki o Kulturze* (*Cultural Sciences*) Warsaw: Państwowe Wydawnictwo Naukowe, 1971) p. 451.

24. Ossowski, supra note 23, p. 99.

25. These attitudes and policies began to develop in the last decade of real socialism, as the consequence of unstable laws and regulations which shifted according to the prevailing political-economic situation. Mirosława Marody, "Jednostka w systemie realnego socjalizmu" (Individual in the system of real socialism), in *Co nam zostało z tych lat. Społeczeństwo polskie u progu zmiany systemowej* (*What's Left of Those Years: Polish Society at the Threshold of a New Political System*), ed. Mirosława Marody (London: Aneks Publishing, 1991) p. 261.

26. See Art. 5, 6, 37, and 38 in the Act of July 15, 1990, on the Privatization of State-Owned Enterprises.

27. A broader theoretical analysis of the acquisition of legal notions used in everyday language (linked with the ability to use the law), based on empirical research on legal socialization conducted in Poland and France, is presented in the following articles: Chantal Kourilsky, Maria Borucka-Arctowa, Skąpsla Magoska, Urszula Moś, Grażyna Skąpska, "Les 11–17 ans face au droit en France et en Pologne. Une enquête comparative de socialisation juridique," 21 *Revues d'Études Comparatives Est-Quest* 85 (1990); Maria Borucka-Arctowa, "Le rôle de la competence à la communication l'expérience franco-polonaise de socialisation juridique," 19 *Droit et Societé* 277 (1991); Chartal Kourilsky, "Socialisation juridique et identité du sujet," id., p. 259.

28. Kolarska-Bobińska & Rychard, supra note 12; Piotr Sztompka, "Dilemmas of the Great Transition: A Tentative Catalogue," unpublished paper presented at the II International Seminar on Culture and Socio-Psychological Prerequisites for the Transition to the Free Market and Democracy, Kraków (December 1991); Jadwiga Staniszkis, "Dylematy okresu przejściowego: przypadek Polski, w Społeczeństwo wobec wyzwań gospadarki rynkowej" (Dilemmas of the Transition Period: the Polish Case), in *Society in the Face of Challenges of the Market Economy* (Warsaw: Wydawuictwo Uniwersytetu Warsawskiego 1990).

29. See Sztompka, supra note 28, p. 6–7. Ironically, those most severely threatened by the economic reforms are factory workers in the imperilled heavy industries who, as the core of Solidarity, pushed hardest for the shift to the new system. See Adam Michnik, "The Two Faces of Eastern Europe," *The New Republic* (November 12, 1990); Mokrzycki, supra note 12.

30. The current regime must tread lightly when it invokes an ideological basis for its reforms or the public may be suspicious and not support the reform. In other words, the government must appeal to pragmatic goals that the public accepts, not abstract ideals, in order for its reforms to gain legitimacy.

31. "When determining when a law should come into force, the legislator should take into consideration that each and every decision in this matter may either protect and strengthen a fundamental value which is the citizen's confidence in the law, or it may infringe upon it. . . . Every legislative action which in essence deprives those who are interested from becoming acquainted with newly passed laws infringes upon this value." Sławomira Wronkowska, "Publikacja Aktow Normatywnych—Przyczynek do Dyskusji o Państwie Prawnyn" (Publication of Normative Acts: A Contribution to the Discussion About the State of Law), in *Prawo w Zmiejącym się Społeczeńsstwie* (*Law in a Changing Society*), supra note 4, p. 335.

32. See, e.g., Czapska, supra note 4.

33. According to a December 30, 1952 statute, the presumption is that laws come into force on the same day they are passed, unless the law itself specifically states otherwise.

34. Jürgen Habermas, "Toward a Theory of Communicative Competence," in 2 *Recent Sociology; Patterns of Communicative Behavior* pp. 1, 24, 115–148 (1972), and Jürgen Habermas, *Communication and the Evolution of Society* (Boston: Boston University Press, 1979) p. 90.

Beyond Constructivism and Rationality of Discovery: Economic Transformation and Institution-Building Processes

Grażyna Skąpska

[*Editors' Synopsis:* Now that the countries of East-Central Europe are committed to a market economy, the issue has shifted to what methods of implementing this commitment are appropriate. Some urge an all-at-once strategy, while others advocate a planned, regulated transformation. Professor Skąpska, however, points out that the choice is not so simple. The immediate shift to a market creates problems such as the unfair acquisition of state property by the former elites, inefficient owners, and the rise of organized crime. At the same time, government regulation of the process of privatization risks centralizing matters in the old tradition of the command economy, the very concept that the new societies are attempting to overcome. Under either scenario, the resulting distribution of wealth would raise concerns of efficiency, fairness and legitimacy. Professor Skąpska suggests that, rather than concentrating on the proper theory or model for economic transformation, reformers should establish a democratic process for formulating, adopting, and implementing the economic changes.]

Introduction

What can the political and economic transformation presently taking place in East-Central Europe teach those who place great hope in democratic revolutions, free markets, and a more open society? An obvious reason for the interest in this transformation is the spectacular, rapid, and unprecedented collapse of a system based on the Marxist principles of nationalization of the means of production, subordination of the economy to political command and central planning, and replacement of the capitalist economy, motivated by the growth of profit, with the socialist economy, motivated by "equal" distribution of wealth. Economic transformation in the context of rapid and overwhelming disintegration of the communist system poses a daunting challenge to those responsible for changing the monetary system, reforming the banking system, and transforming basic institutions such as the law. As profound as this economic transformation is, though, it is an element of even deeper changes—political, social, and cultural.

As recently as 1985, one could still characterize a collection of political essays written by several highly prominent theorists in the former Czechoslovakia in the following way:

> None of these essays is explicitly unfriendly to the socialist idea or socialist principles. None advocates a return to capitalism or even liberal democracy; and none is touched by the various forms of free market ideology that has since become dominant in the Anglo-Saxon West. . . . The socialist tradition, in one form or another, still haunts these essays.[1]

Similarly, the Polish Round Table Agreements of 1989 presented an ambivalent view regarding market-oriented reconstruction of the Polish economy, expressing preference for social ownership and "democratic planning." However, from the very minute the former dissidents gained political power, the need for economic transformation and the growing apprehension of economic collapse captured the attention of the new political elites.

The economic transformation occurring in East-Central Europe represents only one aspect of the ongoing deep and radical transfiguration of the entire societies. It is an important part of the homogenized and "equalized" social structure, and also of the life-worlds of the people living in a system in which reason, dignity and liberty, self-rule and responsibility, representation and participation were either absent or feigned, along with efficiency, and individual merit and achievement.

The economic transformation, moreover, constitutes a crucial element of the process of further political change, leading to the reallocation of wealth and power. The success of the democratic transformation, then, is closely linked with the success of economic reform and the construction of an efficient economy, on the one hand, and the legitimation of the newly emerging power relations and allocation of wealth, on the other. The success of government in East-Central Europe, where the transformation was initiated by political and moral protest, then, does not rest only on economic performance. Quite the contrary, the economic success of the government rests on the fulfillment of claims to self-government, participation, and the rule of law that informed the goals of the democratic opposition and the goals of the anticommunist revolutions in the region. The objective of the ongoing changes is the reconstruction of individual rights as well as the normative structure of society. Such a reconstruction started from the very general consensus which provided the normative framework for the anticommunist revolutions. The consensus reflected a broad alliance of people across occupational, educational, and regional lines.

In view of this background, then, the economic transformation of postcommunist Europe can be explained only in light of the political and moral context of the process. In East-Central Europe, as probably nowhere else in the modern world, changes in the economic system, its rationalization, processes of privatization and reprivatization, were initiated by massive efforts to democratize the political system. They were informed by ideas of freedom and liberty, but they also have an important moral context: while the transformations purport to reject the old system of undifferentiated political-economic domination that generated corruption and waste, they do so on the basis of worldviews, values, and ideologies shaped by existence within that system. Such a general thesis is informed by the Durkheimian idea that social changes cannot be fully understood without taking into account the ways in which changes in both the normative and realistic conditions of action are usually the unintended consequences, or system effects, of the interrelations of economic, political, religious, and moral subsystems.

The first part of this paper describes the significance of the consensus that led to the peaceful revolutions of East-Central Europe, the importance of human agency in the process of transformation, and the relevance of ways of life formed under the rejected system. The second part details the conceptual frameworks that are competing for the front seat in the process of transformation: "organic" versus "at one stroke." The third part shows how these competing frameworks apply to the competing models of privatization, that is, "spontaneous" versus regulated, and discusses the problems and social tensions that arise under each model. The fourth part extends the conceptual frameworks to competing models of property rights, and rights of access to privatization, that is, employment-based versus citizenship-based rights, and suggests that support for each model depends on the strength of the group that is the primary beneficiary of those rights. Finally, the fifth part notes the transformative power of property rights and the importance of democratic process, that is, that tensions between emerging social groups, and support for competing models of transformation, can be resolved if property rights are established by democratic process.

I. The Human Agency: Political and Moral

The consensus that led to the peaceful revolutions is a crucial aspect of the transformations. It was marked by alliances that crossed the traditional boundaries of occupation, education, and region. This consensus combined the negative content of overthrowing the existing regimes with the positive content of ideals and ideas of a democratic society. Consequently, the revolutions were not only peaceful, they had an almost contractlike quality that led directly to the process of building new political, legal, and economic institutions. The transformations were based on a general consensus that was inspired by the efforts of the intellectual elites, but backed by mass movements. This consensus valued the ideals of democracy, freedom, and government accountability but opposed utopias imposed on society "from above." The existence of this consensus explains why certain changes are now occurring in East-Central Europe, why some reforms have failed while others have succeeded, and what sort of institutions are emerging from the process of transformation.[2]

The examples of peaceful transformation in East-Central Europe (primarily Poland, the former Czechoslovakia, Hungary, and the former East Germany) show the importance of "human agency" in transformation: profound social change informed by the aspirations, ideals, value systems, beliefs, and worldviews of social actors. The efforts of the former democratic opposition, dissidents, and intellectuals who sought to show the true meaning of the "really existing socialism," is what made these revolutions both possible and peaceful. These efforts were the aggregate individual actions of the members of *Solidarność* and the movements for human rights, civic rights, and ecological concerns. To the dismay of many observers, the "antitheoretical" goals of these groups have been disappointing: the negative awareness of what is no longer acceptable[3] and the rather general postulates of more freedom, a more liberal society, the rule of law, and the peaceful transformation to a nonutopian society.[4]

Curiously, the democratic revolutions in East-Central Europe were both idealistic and anti-utopian. The revolutions were informed by the ideals of an open-ended and participatory democracy, accountable government, and social participation. These ideals raised important questions of the institutional role of human agency. At the same time, however, the revolutions were deeply opposed to the construction of new utopias, especially if they came in the form of allegedly inevitable rules of history discovered by philosophers or sociologists. The leaders and participants of the peaceful revolutions invoked and relied on principles that contained a strong *moral* quality. Generally, these principles opposed the subordination of individual ways of life and value systems to models, imposed by a bureaucratic apparatus of the Communist party, aimed at the realization of the official utopia. Specifically, these principles were directed against the abuse of authority, the disintegration of civil society, the subordination of public and private life to the ideological utopia, social experimentation, and the corruption of public officials and politics.

The unusual context of the peaceful revolutions gives rise to three points regarding the significant political and economic features of the ensuing transformations. First, the state is the main actor in and agent of economic change. Second, the emerging institutional order is the result of political compromise. Third, the state is charged with reducing the tensions that arise as the result of emerging patterns of wealth distribution that conflict with the old ways of life.

Because the state not only continues to be the principle owner of the means of production and employer, but is also the main agent of economic transformation, the state's performance of the tasks of economic transformation through government agencies generates questions and debate over the political legitimacy of its methods. Consequently, claims of legitimacy tie the success of transformation to the values and expectations which inform social actions. As the main agent of economic transformation, the state must confront questions of the legitimacy of its methods to bring about the shift to a free market, that is, macroparameters aimed at economic stabilization. As the main owner of the nationalized property, the state must confront questions over the legitimacy of specific forms of denationalizing (privatizing) the economy. As the main employer, the state must confront questions over the legitimacy not only of the direct consequences of privatization for the employees of privatized firms (the risk of unemployment), but also over the participation of employees in the privatization process.

The institutional order that is emerging in East-Central Europe is the result of political compromise over the methods for achieving economic transformation, privatization, and property rights. These compromises will inevitably resolve the tension that exists between competing models of spontaneous versus controlled privatization, and employment-based versus citizenship-based property rights. Achieving such compromises will depend on the institutional framework that exists for resolving political conflicts[5] between interested parties.

If the transformation of the economy is to be successful, the government must play an active role in the process of compromise formation, that is, the democratic negotiation (and renegotiation) of the rules of the game that will lead to the establishment of a new institutional and social order, and a new dynamic of the social contract. However, one cannot ignore the moral context of the postcommunist transformation—the ways of life, value structures, and interests of peoples educated and socialized within the very system that generated their sense of demoralization, their opposition to the abuse of power, and democratic ideals. This is the moral legacy of the communist system.

As a number of commentators have observed, Marxist economies suffer from a decline in personal responsibility, the work ethic, attitudes toward the public good, and concepts of public interest.[6] It is no coincidence that the decline in national product parallels a concurrent decline in national morality. Therefore, in dealing with disputes over the legitimation of emerging institutions and the new distribution of power and wealth, the governments of East-Central Europe must resolve tensions that exist between efforts to rebuild the economy, and the introduction of an effective democracy. These tensions are expressed in the conflict between the declared ideals of the peaceful revolutions, and the concrete ways of life shaped within the social structure that led not only to the citizenry's demoralization, passivism and dependency, but also to the exploitation of state resources through privileges.

II. Organic Reform, or Transformation at One Stroke?

Two different theories surround the debate over economic transformation in East-Central Europe: the "organic" theory of neoclassical economics of the free market and systemic self-regulation, and the less popular theory of modernization that has its roots in a "constructivist" philosophy of the "revolution from above." As I have tried to show elsewhere, each of these competing approaches paradoxically generates internal inconsistencies under the prevailing conditions of East-Central Europe.[7]

Some neoclassical liberal economists have urged rapid, all-at-once privatization in East-Central Europe. This approach departs from the well-known assumption of "organic" economic processes which "naturally" lead to the self-developing and self-regulating characteristics of the system. The theory emphasizes the value of the "spontaneous order" that arises from rational discoveries made by participants in the economic game.[8] Accordingly, the legal system should be fully privatized so that private law is composed primarily of contractual arrangements.[9]

The simplest neoclassical models state that the only plausible role of government in East-Central Europe is the downsizing of the state by creating a legal framework for reducing taxes, eliminating customs duties and the privileges of domestic businessmen, limiting the power of centralized banks, and generally removing state interventionism in the market. In line with this model are proposals for across-the-board deregulation of business, labor, and financial relations.[10] Such an idealized free market, however, is overly simplistic (and probably exists only in the form of a computer game) because it fails to account for the importance of the economic, political, and social context of transformation.

The policy of "active withdrawal" and deregulation during the first two years of economic transformation in Poland gave rise to the uncontrolled plunder of state property, which in the social consciousness became "nobody's property." It also exposed the weak domestic economy to international competition with often heavily subsidized foreign products (such as, for example, the agricultural products of the European Community), and provoked a merciless fight for the preservation of state-granted privileges. In the end, the policy of "active withdrawal" has resulted in the public's disappointment with the transformation and with the concept of a free-market economy, and has led to popular calls for greater state involvement in the transformation, new industrial and fiscal policies, protective tariffs, new taxes, credit schemes, and interventionist regulation.

More realistic, "organic" proposals advocate a narrowed scope of state activities during an initial stage of transformation that will enable people to be self-sufficient, but at the same time emphasize the importance of the government's role in the formation of the necessary macroparameters to restore economic equilibrium. Called the "surgery of stabilization,"[11] this first stage is a form of radical anti-inflationary monetary reforms to contain government spending (and hence balance the budget), by reducing subsidies to state-owned enterprises and controlling wages. The obvious short-term result of this policy is a drastic decline in living standards, and growing unemployment. The consequences of this heavy burden on society are two-fold: the legitimation of both the deficit and the government's increasing involvement in social welfare.[12]

Calls for an increasingly active state, even under the "surgery of stabilization," is one reason to reject idealized free-market models in favor of the alternative philosophy of "modernization from above." This philosophy has its origins in the historical experiences of East-Central Europe, as in the Bismarkian model of government—which envisaged a "revolution from above" with a protective, social state—or the active role in both modernization and social protection played by the Polish government before World War II.[13]

Under this theory of "modernization from above," the more the modernizing elite assumes leadership, the more the modernization process itself will have an "intellectual revolutionary" character.[14] According to this theory, the process of modernization depends on the conscious operations of the new system, which in turn is dependent on the involvement of the political elites in initiating and performing the transformation.[15] These blueprints are implemented by "governmental" law, that is, rules (directives and instructions) issued by government agencies.[16]

The inconsistencies between the reformist policy of reconstruction (the "surgery of stabilization") and rapid transformation (the "active withdrawal" policy) affect the direction of social change that the state pursues.[17] Both policies take the form of designs implemented by a state that has active industrial and social programs, and that actively develops and protects new concepts of property rights. Acknowledging that the transition from state socialism to a free-market economy carries political risks, Kazimierz Poznanski argues that those risks are the product of the blueprint reforms formulated by the ruling elites,

> the product of poor judgment by decision-makers [rather] than by objective obstacles. The communist utopia was abandoned only to be replaced by great illusions, so that once again state bureaucracies are placing great trust in untested "projects" and making society believe in quick cures.[18]

According to Poznanski, the overly rapid dissolution of state structure paradoxically contributes to this problem:

> The paradox of transition to capitalism is that while it is aimed at an eventual reduction of state involvement, to succeed, the transition requires that the state be active during the initial stage of that process. While through most of the communist period the objective of the state was to facilitate a further expansion of its power, the transition should be viewed, above all, as a form of limitation imposed upon the state by the state. Thus, if the state apparatus is allowed to lose its influence instantly, let alone disintegrate, in all likelihood the transition to capitalism will degenerate into costly economic chaos.[19]

Like others, Poznanski advocates slower reform, that is, the gradual construction of market institutions and the controlled, organic growth of the private sector subordinated to a conscious industrial policy of withdrawing public sector involvement.[20] However, it is doubtful whether the surgery of stabilization could be implemented in a slow, "organic" manner because of the political and social components of economic transformation.

In the societies in which democratic political reforms initiated large-scale economic transformation, the results have turned against the interests of those who initiated the reforms: state employees (particularly workers in state-owned factories) who won their liberty lost their job security. As a consequence, rapid stabilization can win democratic support only if the painful part of the process, the recovery, is brief. Here the surgical metaphor is quite appropriate. The "at one stroke" strategy of creating the conditions necessary for a free market, as far as they are related to the stabilization policy, would seem to be better than a piecemeal approach.[21] The more general success of economic transformation will therefore depend on the methods of compensating the important agents of democratization (workers of state-owned factories and, more importantly, of state-owned enterprises) for the decline in their standard of living, status, and power.

The success of transformation depends, then, not only on innovative privatization programs, but also on programs concerning the fundamental values and interests of a democratic society. A successful transformation cannot exist without the liberation of "human capital." The failure of certain modernization efforts might well be due to the failure to address this important concern. It is necessary for the transformations to go beyond both constructivist and free-market ("rationality of discovery") models, and include in the process not only society's interests groups, conflicts, and the conflicting aims and goals motivating people to undertake actions, but also the sources of conflicts and challenges to further democratic development, social reconstruction, and economic success.

III. Spontaneous or Controlled Privatization?

Those who advocate organic economic reform would probably agree with Milton Friedman's analysis that the social characteristics of market agents are wholly irrelevant to the workings of the market.[22] But in a reality shaped by the legacy of nationalized property and Communism, the social characteristics of market agents are very important, at least during the *process* of privatization. During this process, the government's active distribution of wealth generates questions of legitimation.[23] These social characteristics concern phenomena such as the "enfranchisement of the *nomenklatura*," the rise of mafia-type normative structures, and the fear of opening weak domestic markets to powerful foreign capital. These characteristics concern the emerging social relations that are based on the distribution of power, wealth, rights, and responsibilities, and on the social characteristics of those who come up as "winners" and "losers" in the privatization process, that is, the emerging social order.

Under the Communist regime, of course, the real meaning of state ownership of the means of production was quite different from the nominal meaning. Nominally, it meant public ownership, where the state functioned as the owner on behalf of the citizenry. According to the official ideology, the public sector was the property of "the whole people," or "the whole society."[24] In reality, the party-state bureaucracy set economic parameters, retail prices, taxes, wages, prices of the means of production, and "dividends" which must be paid from them, as well as the rights to produce objects for purchase or sale, to control production and to make decisions. As János Kornai has observed, the party-state bureaucracy exercised the economic rights of the owner of a nationalized economy.[25]

However, the state was a very inept owner. The party-state bureaucracy did not exercise effective control of its "property," because it acted on too little information to accurately calculate production quotas; the state's commitment to full employment limited its range of action. This had three consequences. First, it led to employees holding considerable "negative control" of production in state enterprises, because their wages and job security did not depend on their performance. Simultaneously, it led management and workers, in reporting to the "commanding heights," to falsify information regarding enterprises' economic performances. Finally, because neither the individual nor firms operated under the threat of economic sanction (unemployment and bankruptcy were unknown to command economies) most individuals and firms sought to enrich themselves at the expense of the state.

The phenomenon of demoralization that is characteristic of command economies was the result of the lack of clearly defined ownership rights. In the language of public-choice economics, the lack of rights in ownership means that no individual has sufficient interest in the economy to give up illicit gains for betterment."[26] In reality, the command economy transformed national property into "nobody's property" and, during the last stages of the command economy, allowed the legal and illegal mass appropriation of national property by those with the ability to exploit information and their connections.

Economic transformation in East-Central Europe involves specific problems stemming from the normative structures of nationalized property. Next to questions of efficiency, the most important of these problems concern the fairness of the transformation and the allocation of power and wealth. These are crucial for deciding questions of legitimation, and confronting the tensions and contradictions that exist between the spontaneous, organic, "bottom-up," privatization processes and the controlled, centralized, privatization programs.

A. Spontaneous Privatization and Questions of Legitimacy, Fairness, and Efficiency

Proponents of the organic approach to economic transformation propose a relatively slow, spontaneous, privatization process based on already existing grass-roots mechanisms, experience, business culture, and capital. They point to the Hungarian and Polish processes of privatization that began long before the anticommunist revolutions. These processes granted partial private property rights to managers of state-owned firms and allowed quasi-private businesses to exist on a foundation of nationalized property. In Hungary these reforms were initiated in the late 1960s and early seventies, while in Poland such reforms were initiated by the so-called "dual track" program of 1985 to 1988.

The Hungarian and Polish programs operated on the rationale that private activities would make the state sector more efficient, and were supplemented by reforms calling for the systematic conversion of public enterprises into other forms of ownership.[27] However, many believe that the processes that resulted from the predemocratic, communist reforms were neither "spontaneous," nor a truly organic form of transformation to a free-market system.[28] The final reform enacted by the Communist regime in Poland was legislation in 1989 to convert failing enterprises into joint-stock companies, and to permit managers of state enterprises to engage in economic activities outside their primary duties.[29] This form of "spontaneous" privatization became known as "the enfranchisement of the *nomenklatura*"[30] because those who possessed the needed experience, information, connections, and financial resources to take advantage of these initial reforms were government bureaucrats, local and national Communist party functionaries, and managers of state-owned enterprises. Because of their positions, these groups were able to appropriate nationalized property by assuring themselves of the most valuable privatized state assets, often at undervalued prices.[31] Opponents claim that the enfranchisement of the *nomenklatura* is to blame for perpetuating the old structures of domination, an unfair distribution of the benefits and burdens of transformation, and the emerging, unfair structures of property relations.[32]

The sale of shares in privatized companies also presents a problem with the sources of capital that enable groups to participate in spontaneous privatization. Hungary and Poland present two different strategies for generating private capital in the initial period of spontaneous privatization. As the first stage of its spontaneous privatization, Hungary opened the door to quasi-private business within state-owned companies, leading to the creation of private capital. In Poland, initial privatization was strongly associated with the expansion of the shadow economy, that is, "black" currency transactions, "black" work abroad, and "black" foreign trade. The state's hunger for foreign currency, due to a growing public debt, led to the liberalization of foreign travel and the legalization of foreign deposits of undocumented origin in Polish banks.[33] There were several other significant consequences of the growing shadow economy: an enormous gap between public wages and nonlegal transactions, the corruption of state officials, and the rise of an underground, mafialike economy and legal order.[34] By definition, spontaneous, uncontrolled privatization means the tacit validation of this antilegal culture. Privatization on these terms would therefore depart from the establishment of an economic system based on the rule of law.

By contrast, privatization through liquidation is spontaneous but legal. Both solvent and insolvent enterprises are dissolved, and their assets leased or sold to their employees (managers and workers). In terms of the numbers of firms that have been privatized, liquidation has been the most successful form of privatizing state-owned enterprises in Poland.[35] However, this fairly organic, bottom-up process has provoked serious doubts over whether it is either an efficient or fair form of economic reconstruction.

First, given the limited financial ability to pay for shares, employers and managers may be reluctant to buy them. They may well be unwilling to take the risks necessary to make the company efficient. If their actions are motivated solely by a desire to preserve their jobs, rather than to make the firm efficient, then privatization through liquidation may lead to economic stagnation. If the political uproar that occurred following the efforts of Polish state banks to collect from indebted farmers and state-owned enterprises is an accurate indication of popular attitudes, such fears are quite justified. Second, liquidation may unfairly and inefficiently limit participation in privatization to the employees of privatized enterprises, denying others (including more efficient investors) the right to participate in a significant part of economic transformation. Third, there are understandable but irrational objections to spontaneous privatization through the sale of national assets to foreign investors, who have at their disposal immense resources compared with domestic capital.[36]

The growing criticism of spontaneous privatization in East-Central Europe stems from the disenchantment during the first years of economic reforms that is caused by all of the above-mentioned phenomena: declining living standards combined with the appropriation of national property by the previous communist officials, an increasing antilegal (mafia) culture, fear of foreign capital, and to a lesser degree, criticism that privatization through liquidation is unfair, for example, to public servants and nonemployees. These factors must be considered if further economic reforms are to be pursued and the institution-building process is to rely on spontaneous privatization.

B. Regulated Privatization and Questions of Efficiency, Fairness, and Legitimacy

The scenario of controlled and regulated mass privatization is one based on the principles of direct political control of the privatization processes, and the active economic involvement of the government as shareholder. Regulated and controlled privatization obviously tends to centralize the privatization process, regardless of whether it is in the "equivalent" form (sale of large amounts of cheap shares to small bidders at public auction), or "on equivalent"/very cheap form (as in the case of the Czechoslovakian large-scale voucher privatization plan). It also leads to the state creation of artificial economic agencies in blueprint mass privatization programs. This may involve the introduction of political criteria inconsistent with the philosophy of a free and open market, that is, preferences for small investors, state control of further circulation of shares or vouchers, and the exclusion of foreign investors.[37]

Even more important for the future development of property relations and social restructuring, centralized and regulated mass privatization leads to the emergence of large-scale passive ownership, and polarization between the uninformed and inexperienced mass shareholders, and specialists operating on behalf of institutional investors. This latter group determines not only where the bulk of investments go, but who controls the decision-making process within the privatized companies. In the absence of "strategic owners," that is, shareholders having a number of shares sufficient to affect decisions, the most important rights to make decisions regarding dividends, capital investments, prices, and wages are exercised by managers of mutual investment funds or supervisory boards. And this is the optimistic scenario.

The pessimistic scenario holds that the newly-born "capitalists," who have no understanding of the workings of the market, immediately attempt to sell their shares or vouchers, leading to speculation and quick personal profits at the expense of the legitimacy and political justification of the transformation.

Implementation of both spontaneous privatization and top-down blueprint projects raise serious doubts about, first, the role of the state in the processes of transformation and, second, the perpetuation of old patterns of wealth and power. One possible way of dealing with the dysfunctional effects of transformation, which threaten the success of economic reform, is to link privatization to social processes and goals, through reflective regulatory structures aimed at pluralistic privatization, in which all interested parties and groups are able to participate. Such open and pluralistic regulations require clearly defined property rights and rights of access to privatization, and clear rules for enforcing those rights. Although such rights must inevitably be the result of social compromise, they can fulfill some of the expectations of a democratic society. Clearly defined property rights and rules of participation in privatization would help establish the rule of law by subordinating all government activities to the protection of the rights of the citizenry.

IV. Employment-based or Citizenship-based Access to Privatization

The processes which accompany the formation of property rights and determine participation in privatization programs in East-Central Europe speak not only to questions of economic efficiency, or the "technicalities" of legal regulations, but go to the very basis of the new political and social order, and the axiological foundations of the emerging legal order. The competing models of transformation offer competing models of rights to participate in privatization: the spontaneous/organic approach offers employment-based rights, while the planned approach offers citizenship-based rights. Each of these models has strong support and opposition that varies according to the interests of the groups that dominate the process of economic transformation in the countries of East-Central Europe. In Poland, workers are among the primary beneficiaries of the privatization program despite their poor wages and growing unemployment.[38] In Hungary, managers play the most important role in economic reform. And in the former Czechoslovakia, the cornerstone of economic transformation is through large-scale privatization by vouchers sold to everyone, next to the very advanced and thorough process of reprivatization.[39]

In Poland's case, despite mass privatization efforts to create broad, citizenship-based property rights, and to formulate a concept of "civic property,"[40] those property rights that have so far evolved under the spontaneous/organic (bottom-up) process are generally related to employment, and specifically geared towards preserving one's workplace. This form of property rights legitimizes and privileges employee participation in privatization, and stands opposed to the spontaneous privatization of the former *nomenklatura,* which is popularly regarded as "theft."

In the former Czechoslovakia, on the other hand, there is much criticism of employment-based property rights or privileges related to the workplace. Analyzing the political pressures that materialized under the Czechoslovakian program of mass privatization through vouchers, one can say that:

> [p]olitical pressures had to be resisted to prepare for the voucher privatization. . . . For instance, a demand was put forward for the issue of a large quantity of employee shares and for their sale for perhaps as little as 80 percent of their nominal prices. The demand is antisocial because it discriminates against citizens whose employing organizations are not to be privatized (teachers, nurses, etc).[41]

From the point of view of economic, social, and political transformation, then, privatization means the restructuring of society. Therefore, it is vital that the criteria used to establish action-oriented, basic, economic rights aim not just at achieving an efficient economy and legitimizing the democratic government, but at justifying the new inequalities. From this point of view, the processes of compromise, the reflective structures of an open legal system, and the pluralistic character of privatization are again worth emphasizing.

V. Beyond Utilitarianism: The Regulatory but Transformative Power of Property Rights

Economic transformation in the face of rapid and overwhelming disintegration poses a challenge to all those who wish to reform institutional structures (especially the law) in order to create a rational and efficient economic system in East-Central Europe. The need for such profound economic transformation as an element of the broader change—political, social, and cultural—was not widely accepted at the outset of the peaceful revolutions.[42] Once the previous dissidents assumed power, however, the new political elites immediately focused their attention on the growing apprehension of economic collapse and the need for economic transformation.

The most important lesson to be learned from the anticommunist revolutions in East-Central Europe is, in my view, the problem of the relationship between economic transformation and the transformation of the emerging normative structures. Analyzing the tensions and contradictions of transformation, I have stressed the role of the state and its agencies as the main agents of economic reform, the problem of arbitrariness, and the implementation of blueprint projects "from above" by means of instrumental, bureaucratic laws. At the same time, I have emphasized the various spontaneous processes of privatization throughout East-Central Europe, indicating differences of social processes, of value structures, and of worldviews accompanying economic transformation.

Ultimately, in a democratic system, the emergence of spontaneous processes will determine the direction and outcome of reforms, even in a situation of profound, government-led transformation. Therefore, legitimate, clearly defined, property rights are crucial for resolving contradictions between organic and rapid reform, and between spontaneous and regulated privatization, for directing and controlling state activities, for invalidating illicit methods of appropriation of state-owned assets, and for eliminating the tension between competing desires for employment-based or citizenship-based privatization. In situations of conflicting claims concerning participation in privatization processes, all interested parties and groups must be able to participate in the process of defining property rights. Compromises in this process will have a great transformative power. If arrived at by democratic process, the new property rights will legitimate the transformation of economy and society and, most importantly, subordinate the entire process of transformation (as well as all government activity) to general, legitimized rules. They will provide evidence of the concept of an open, reflexive law, based on social compromise and clear rules of participation in privatization.

Notes

The first version of this article was written during my visit to the American Bar Foundation, Chicago, as a Visiting Research Fellow. It was prepared for the proceedings of the Joint Working Group on Privatization and New Democracies in Amsterdam during the Congress of the American Law and Society Association and the Research Committee on the Sociology of Law, ISA. It was also presented during a seminar held at the American Bar Foundation. Apart from the friendly and inspiring general discussion at the congress and at the seminar, I would like to thank the colleagues from the foundation, Bill Felstiner and Terry Halliday, for their helpful comments, and Greg Alexander from Cornell University for his generous help in preparing the final version of this article.

1. Steven Lukes, Introduction in Václav Havel, *The Power of the Powerless* (Armonk, NY: M. E. Sharpe, 1985), p. 7.
2. According to a recent book by Leszek Balcerowicz (the father of the Polish economic stabilization plan), work on an alternative economic system was conducted by a group of young economists in Poland in 1978 and continued during the 1980s with representatives of *Solidarność*. This project was premised

on two conditions: that the new system would be more efficient than its contemporary, and that the economic reforms would be based on social agreement over the nature of the reforms and their manner of realization. Leszek Balcerowicz, *800 dni—szok kontrolowany* (800 Days: A Controlled Shock) (Warszawa: Polska Oficyna Wydawnicza, 1992) p. 14. Employee participation was also a crucial element of the company law reform introduced in Poland in 1981. Kazimierz Strzyczkowski, "Przedsiebiorstwo panstwowe," in Ludwik Bar, ed., *Instytucje prawne w reformowanej gospodarce narodowej* (*Legal Institutions of the Reformed National Economy*) (Wroclaw-Warszawa-Krakow-Gdansk-Lodz: Ossolineum, 1989) p. 82–131. Quite different were the views of Vaclav Klaus, who expressed the need for a strictly market-oriented reform and a belief in *homo oeconomicus*. See John F. Fund, "Czechoslovakia's Free Market Minister," *Wall Street Journal* (March 2, 1992).

3. Piotr Sztompka, "The Intangibles and Imponderables in the Transition to Democracy" 24 *Studies in Comparative Communism* 296 (1991).
4. Samuel N. Eisenstadt, The Breakdown of Communist Regimes and the Vicissitudes of Modernity, *Daedalus* 25 (Spring 1992).
5. Grażyna Skąpska, *Prawo a dynamika spolecznych przemian* (Law and the dynamics of Social Change), (Krakow: Uniwersytet Jagiellonski Press, 1992), p. 5.
6. John Clark and Aaron Wildavsky, *The Moral Collapse of Communism* (San Francisco: Institute for Contemporary Studies, 1990), pp. 1–18, 303–346. By "Marxist economy" I intend centralized, command economies where the means of production have been nationalized, the economy has been subordinated to the political goals of the Communist party, one of the most important goals of which being the transformation of the economy into a "gigantic distributional coalition." Id. at 11.
7. Grażyna Skąpska, "Economic Reform in Poland: Liabilities of the Past and Paradoxes of the Present", mimeo (1992).
8. Robert Sugden, *The Economics of Rights, Co-operation, and Welfare* (Oxford: Basil Blackwell, 1986), p. 14.
9. Bruce L. Benson, *The Enterprise of Law* (San Francisco: Pacific Research Institute for Public Policy, 1990), p. 331.
10. Steve Hanke, interview published in Biuletyn Informacyjny Krakowskiego Towarzystwa Przemyslowego (Information Bulletin of Cracow's Industrial Society) Nr. 7–8 (1990).
11. János Kornai, *The Road to a Free Economy* (New York: Norton, 1990) pp. 102–178.
12. Jerzy Baczynski, "Zrobcie cos!" (Make Something!), *Polityka* (January 18, 1992).
13. Janusz Zarnowski, "Spoleczenstwo Drugiej Rzeczpospolitej" (Society of the Second Republic) (Warszawa: PWN, 1973) pp. 17–21; Winicjusz Narojek, "Socjalistyczne Welfare State" (Socialistic Welfare State) (Warszawa: PWN, 1991).

14. Gino Germani, *The Sociology of Modernization* (New Brunswick, NJ: Transaction Books, 1981 p. 46.
15. Anthony Giddens, *Central Problems of Social Theory: Action, Structure and Contradiction in Social Analysis* (London: Macmillan, 1979) pp. 122–171.
16. Grażyna Skąpska, "Economic Reform in Poland: Liabilities of the Past and Paradoxes of the Present," (1992), mimeo.
17. Jacek Kochanowicz, "Polska—bilans otwarcia" (Poland—the Opening Balance), in 1 *Przeglad* spoleczny 18, 19 (1992); Jacek Kochanowicz "Dilemmas of Transition from State Socialism in East Central Europe," mimeographed paper presented at Conference in the Center of European Studies, Harvard University (1991); Kazimierz Poznanski, "Market Alternative to State Activism in Restoring the Capitalist Economy," *Economics of Planning* 25: 56 (1992).
18. Poznanski, supra note 17, p. 55.
19. Kazimierz Poznanski, "Privatization of the Polish Economy: Problems of Transition," *Soviet Studies* 44: 653 (1992).
20. Id. at 61; Peter Murrell, "Evolution in Economics and in the Economic Reform of the Centrally Planned Economies," mimeographed paper, Department of Economics, University of Maryland (1991).
21. Jeffrey Sachs, "Accelerating Privatization in Eastern Europe: The Case of Poland," paper delivered at The World Bank, Washington, D.C. (April, 1991).
22. Milton Friedman, *Capitalism and Freedom* (Chicago: University of Chicago Press, 1976) p. 34.
23. John Vickers & George Yarrow, Economic Perspective on Privatization, *Journal of Economic Perspectives* 5: 89 (1991).
24. The share of the public sector in 1988 was as follows: Czechoslovakia: 99.3 percent; East Germany: 96.4 percent; Hungary: 92.9 percent; Poland: 81.2 percent (due to mostly private agriculture). János Kornai, *The Socialist System: The Political Economy of Communism* (Princeton, NJ: Princeton University Press, 1992) p. 72.
25. Id. at 62.
26. Clark and Wildavsky, supra note 6, p. 236.
27. Kalman Mizsei, Privatization in Eastern Europe: A Comparative Study of Poland and Hungary, *Soviet Studies* 44: 283 (1992); see also Poznanski, supra note 17, pp. 642, 643.
28. By "free market" I mean an economic system based on the formally fair and equal chance to participate in transactions, clearly defined property rights, and the rule of law.
29. By the end of 1989, the Communist government had established more than two thousand joint-stock companies, mostly small parts of large state-owned enterprises. The state owned the large joint-stock companies, and other companies were put in the hands of managers, with the participation of state enterprises. According to the official 1990 study of 152 joint-stock companies, about

half the directors of those enterprises had shares in or belonged to the boards. Poznanski, supra note 17, pp. 644, 660.

30. Michael Marrese, Rapporteur's Report of June 1990, ESD, World Bank Seminars on the Transformation of Planned Economies, mimeograph (1990).

31. This practice occurred both during the period of predemocratic reform, and even into the postcommunist phase of transformation (and was continued by some members of the new political elites). Jadwiga Staniszkis, "Political Capitalism in Poland," *Eastern European Politics and Society* 5: 1 (1990).

32. Jacek Tarkowski, Enfranchisement of Nomenklatura: From Feudalism to Capitalism, *Uncaptive Mind* 15 (November–December 1989); Jacek Tarkowski, Endowment of the Nomenklatura, or Apparatchiks Turned into Entrepreneurchiks, or From Communist Ranks to Capitalist Riches, *Innovation* 4: 89 (1990).

33. Mizsei, supra note 27, p. 285.

34. Maria Łos, From Underground to Legitimacy: The Normative Dilemmas of Post-communist Marketization, in ed. Maria Łos, *The Second Economy in Marxist States* (Hampshire: Macmillan, 1989) p. 4.

35. Such leveraged buy-outs reached a total of 659 enterprises in 1991 in Poland. Ministerstwo Przeksztalcen Wlasnosciowych (Ministry of Ownership Changes), Dynamika Prywatyzacji (Dynamics of Privatization), nr. 1 (1991).

36. The sale of cheap shares in the public privatization programs in Poland was made under the principle of initially selling shares to small bidders who, according to studies, invested only a small portion of their income in stocks. Investors were primarily rather young and well-off. Interestingly, the majority of these initial investors sought to invest in shares of companies that would be privatized in the future. 140 *Gazeta Wyborcza* 15 (czerwca 1992).

37. Foreign investors play an important role in the privatization of enterprises in Hungary and the former Czechoslovakia, and a very limited role in Poland. However, in Hungary, where foreign companies at the outset of privatization bought the best companies, measures have been proposed to control the domination of Western multinationals, and to stimulate domestic participation privatization programs through easy terms of payment and domestic preference over foreign investors where bids are similar. Nicolas Denton, "Privatization in Eastern Europe, *Financial Times*" (July 3, 1992) p. 8.

38. Even if Polish workers and independent labor unions are unsuccessful in achieving collective ownership of enterprises through ESOPs or employee stock (in which individual employees can own stock), the true power of this group is indicated by their successful resistance to attempts to subject to their enterprises to treasury control. Kazimierz Poznanski, supra note 17 at 651.

39. Mizsei supra note 27, p. 288; Martin Kupka, "Transformation of Ownership in Czechoslovakia," *Soviet Studies,* 44: 309 (1992).

40. Jan Szomburg, "Dilemmas of Privatization in Poland" mimeographed paper presented at conference, Transition in Eastern Europe Sudosteuropa Gesellschaft, Munich (1991).

41. Martin Kupka, "Transformation of Ownership in Czechoslovakia," *Soviet Studies* 44: 297 (1992), p. 309.
42. See, e.g., Lukes, supra note 1, p. 7. See also Marek Dabrowski, "Coraz dalej od normalnosci" (Ever Further from Normality), *Lad* Nr. 5 (1989).

New Forms of State Ownership in Poland: The Case of Commercialization

Dariusz Chelmiński
Andrzej A. Czynczyk
Henryk Sterniczuk

[*Editors' Synopsis:* Poland's drastic and rapid privatization plan worked initially; however, just months after the plan was enacted, the remaining state-owned monopolies drained society because the new tax base was not yet developed enough to support them. Political and practical problems have hampered effective privatization and the development of capitalism. Most of the firms to be privatized are still in a nominally transitional phase known as "commercialization," which perpetuates state control of the economy. Commercialized firms are subject to the disadvantages of the state's passive role as owner.]

Despite implementation of the Polish government's privatization program in 1990 and 1991, only a few dozen firms are now in private hands. Many of the eight thousand firms included in the program remain state property. Most large firms have been "commercialized," that is, transformed into nominally private entities, but with the whole of their stock owned by the treasury. There is good reason, therefore, to examine the state's performance as a continuing owner of firms.

The form of state ownership that has emerged in the course of privatization is quite different from state ownership as it existed during the forty-odd years of Communism in Poland. We will focus on what happens to a firm when it is commercialized, and how the state has comported itself as the firm's interim owner. Our thesis is that the state has failed in this role precisely because it has failed to act as an owner.

We first describe the economic and sociopolitical context of privatization in Poland, the legal framework of privatization (particularly the underlying assumptions of commercialization and its goals), and results to date. Using the results of an empirical study of commercialized firms,[1] we then examine the obstacles to commercialization, how the powers of government administrators compare with those of the firm's managers and supervisory board, who profits from or is benefitted by this kind of ownership, and who exercises political, economic, and social control over the commercialization process. We conclude that within commercialized firms, business has continued pretty much as it had when firms were directly controlled by the state, despite the apparently radical change of replacing employee self-management with autonomous management boards. Finally, we offer some observations on how the lack of an ownership interest in the development of the commercialized firms is responsible for many of the current failures of privatization.

I. The Economic and Political Context of Privatization in Poland

The core of Poland's radical privatization program is the restoration of private ownership rights. Previous attempts to revitalize the communist economy through the creation of a "socialist market" failed, due to the lack of private ownership of the means of production. This was true not only of past Polish reforms, but also of experiments in Hungary and even Yugoslavia, where communist politicians wanted a market to coexist with the communist structure of power and state ownership of assets Polish privatization is intended to avoid duplicating these failures, by restoring the institution of individual ownership to the Polish economy. Without these rights a market economy cannot be built in postcommunist countries.

The current transformation of the postcommunist economies is unprecedented in modern economic history, and gives new meaning to the word "privatization." In developed Western countries, privatization simply means the sale of state assets to private parties. These sales are motivated either by budgetary constraints or by a political ideology that presumes the economic superiority of private ownership. Developing economies have also used privatization to strengthen traditionally weak financial markets. In each of these cases, however, privatization simply enhances an already existing market.

Postcommunist privatization, on the other hand, involves not simply the divestment of state assets, nor just the sale of state firms. Rather, it is a process of transforming an entire economy and a society, both of which were weakened by years of Communist rule. If it succeeds, privatization will have three consequences that it has not had either in the West or in developing countries: first, it will create a new ratio of employees to owners of companies; second, it will contribute to the formation of a middle class; and third, it will transform social relations, enabling individuals in different social strata to appreciate each other's value. In the postcommunist world, then, the social meaning of privatization is as important as the economic meaning; privatization in this context means re-creating normal society.

The Polish economic adjustment plan, spearheaded by Deputy Prime Minister Balcerowicz, was designed to stabilize the national economy with a "shock therapy" of rapid, radical, systematic change to make the socially painful transition stage as short as possible. The plan, announced in October 1989 and implemented in early 1990, was welcomed by international financial organizations and world business leaders, and is now being recognized as the textbook example of a successful monetary policy for the postcommunist transformation. The country's extremely dire social and economic conditions necessitated the choice of this shock therapy. The economic institutions under state socialism simply failed to perform the requisite allocative functions of a minimally successful economy. Several developments are ample evidence of this failure: the environmental disaster; a housing crisis; the burden of foreign debts; soaring inflation caused by exorbitant wage increases; the depreciation of Polish currency; a mounting state deficit; a severe decline in the gross national product; and, perhaps more important, a total breakdown of the ability to maintain a centrally planned economy.

The Balcerowicz stabilization plan could hardly cope with *all* of the above destabilizing factors in addition to the mismanagement of public policy. The plan's first goal was to reign in both inflation and the imbalance of payments. Several measures were introduced to achieve this goal, including the lifting of virtually all price controls; rapid devaluation of the Polish Złoty to nearly the level of the uncontrolled black market rate; relaxation of restrictions on trade and payments; implementation of a fiscal policy aimed at reducing the public deficit and limiting the availability of credit; imposition of a tax on wage increases; monthly adjustable and positive real interest rates for the zloty.

Initially, the stabilization plan was a virtual economic miracle. Within the first two months of 1990, the country went from an economy of shortages to one of overabundance. Basic capitalist devices, such as interest rates, exchange rates and customs duties, changed daily life in just a few weeks. Inflation declined significantly, and the Polish Złoty was strengthened.

Serious problems, however, followed the initial successes. The country's economic policy created stagnation in the state-owned sector. This, in turn, resulted in a budget deficit. The reason is simple: state enterprises did not adapt to the new economic situation, and the dynamically expanding private sector was still too small and taxes from it too uncollectible to compensate for the state's loss of revenues. How could an economic plan so praised by international financial institutions and most of economic opinion lose its creative power after its initial success against inflation? The answer lies in the failure of the process of privatization to live up to its expectations.

The Balcerowicz plan was premised on two underlying assumptions. The first was that privatization would occur almost overnight, therefore making it realistic to expect a market-type reaction to the market instruments of the stabilization plan. Although this was an unreasonable assumption, the stabilization plan was not possible without it. One consequence of the assumption was that financial instruments designed for a market economy had to interact with state-owned monopolies that had neither a profit incentive nor an understanding of how to invest capital. The second assumption was that the new private incentives would overcome the problems inherent in running state firms and the national economy, that is, that privatized firms would immediately adopt market strategies and become the driving forces behind the national economy. This assumption oversimplified the process of strategy formation and implementation. According to the experiences of the first privatized firms, privatization of a firm neither yields immediate economic results nor leads automatically to successful management because it does not create the macroeconomic conditions favorable to profitability, nor provide managers with new skills or knowledge of international markets. Because the country's economic stagnation hurts privatization by reducing incentives for both domestic and foreign investment, Poland may have to risk amending its economic stabilization plan to create a business climate more compatible with privatization.

II. The Sociopolitical and Legal Framework of the Privatization Plan

A. The Sociopolitical Environment

Legality is one of the most important prerequisites of the privatization process in the postcommunist environment. In 1946, it was enough to send off a squad or two to nationalize private property. The same technique obviously cannot be used in a democratic system. Because privatization is a transfer of ownership rights from state to private hands, it is a highly sensitive political issue and requires political legitimacy achieved through consent. While in the long run privatization may gain social legitimacy, at the moment many blame legal and financial analyses for the slow pace of privatization, and continue to search for a procedure that could privatize the entire economy overnight.

From the very beginning, privatization has operated under heavy political and social pressure. Liberal economists and politicians demanded immediate implementation, while activists in workers' councils pushed for a form of privatization that would not impair their own control over the industrial system. As in the past, both of these interests shape discussion of privatization policies today.

B. The Legal Framework

All privatization of state and municipal firms is conducted on the basis of the Act on Privatization of State-Owned Enterprises of July 1990.[2] The Act provided two parallel methods of privatization. The "capital path" was a two-step procedure, used primarily for privatizing large firms. The first step, *commercialization,* involved the transformation of state firms into joint-stock or limited liability companies, in which the national treasury initially owned the whole of the stock. The second step involved the sale of the firm's stock to individual buyers, whose purchase of the firm would complete its privatization.

The other procedure that the Act provided was *liquidation*. This technique is available to privatize smaller companies. Liquidated state firms were either sold, included in the holdings of another company for sale, or leased out. This paper addresses only commercialization, because of its greater impact on the Polish economy, and the special role the state has played in this process.

The Minister of Privatization made the decision to commercialize a firm after the firm's managing board and workers council had approved the transformation of the firm. The newly commercialized company assumed all of the rights, obligations, and assets of the former state firm. Acting on behalf of the treasury, the Minister of Privatization appointed a supervisory board of six to nine members, and appointed the company's first managing board. While unions continued to exist in the new companies, workers' councils, a form of worker self-management, were abolished. To compensate employees for their loss of self-management, the Act gave them the right to appoint one third of the supervisory board, and the right to buy up to twenty percent of the company's stock (or the equivalent of their annual earnings, whichever was less) at half price.

The commercialization phase was expected to take a maximum of two years, the time necessary to sell most of the companies' stock. To facilitate this process, the Act gave foreign investors the right to buy up to ten percent of a commercialized company, but purchase of greater percentages was possible by consent of a government agency. The Act also provided for the issue of privatization coupons distributed free of charge to all citizens. These coupons could be redeemed for stock in the commercialized companies held by the Treasury. However, Parliament did not decide either the value of the coupons or their date of issue until the end of 1991.

The goal of commercialization was to create the legal, economic, and social conditions for a state firm's transformation into a private company. State firms generally suffered from being overly large, antiquated, poorly organized and incompetently managed by the powerful workers' councils, which had the right to dismiss the firm's managing director. Management was divided between the firm's managing director and its workers' council, but the lines of responsibility between these two institutions were quite unclear. Unions also played an important role, with union ambitions often reaching far into matters of management. The resulting arrangement, commonly referred to as the "triangle of power," frustrated effective management by restricting the managing board's ability to act. At the same time, responsibility for the firm's performance was also blurred. The special interests of individual groups typically prevailed over the interests of the firm as a whole, and conflicts hampered the development of a coherent strategy capable of responding to market demands. The new decisional structure attempted to avoid these problems by adopting a professional management model in which managers held considerable discretionary power.

Trying to assure workers that their new right to appoint a third of the supervisory board and their preferential stock options were adequate compensation for the abolished workers' councils, the government told employees that "the preferences granted by the Act to employees are relatively extensive. Apart from the considerable price reduction [of stock], the right to appoint a third of the supervisory board ensures that employees retain control over the company's development and its fate."[3] Critics of the Act, however, argued that a third of the board seats hardly guaranteed employee influence. Furthermore, critics pointed to the fact that employees would be able to buy only seven to nine percent of their company's stock at half price, due to a provision in the Act limiting an employee's purchase of preferential stock to the equivalent of her annual earnings.[4] Despite these objections, the Polish Parliament passed the Privatization Act of July 13, 1990 almost unanimously. Only two members voted against the Act.

III. Impediments to the Stabilization Plan

While the stabilization plan's primary objective was to stop hyperinflation, its measures have adversely affected the rate of privatization. By November 1991, the Minister of Privatization had approved 350 state-owned firms for liquidation. Eighty percent of these were for leasing firms to employee-owned companies.[5] Only 220 firms had reached the final stage of privatization, when the firm's name is deleted from the Register of State Enterprises. Yet most of these firms still lacked a private owner.

By September 1991, 214 state firms had been commercialized. However, as few as twenty of these companies were able to sell fifty one percent of their stock to become fully privatized. Moreover, while the Act required the sale of a company's stock within two years of its commercialization, it also allowed extensions of this period. Experience suggests that once a firm is commercialized, further privatization proceeds at a very slow pace. For many firms, commercialization may last much longer than the statutory two years.

Commercialized firms now occupy a dominant place in the Polish economy. Seventy-six percent of commercialized firms are large firms with over five hundred employees.[6] Under the Communist regime, huge firms were the foundation of the Polish economy; the two hundred largest firms yielded thirty seven percent of all industry sales.[7] As majority owner of the commercialized firms, the state still owns the economy's most important firms, and there is no prospect that these firms will be transferred to private owners anytime soon. It appears, then, that the most important effect of privatization so far has been the emergence of a new form of state ownership.

Two aspects of the plan are primarily responsible for the slow pace of privatization, and the resulting prominence of this new form of state ownership. First, its tight credit policy, by driving up interest rates, made savings deposits more attractive than investment in newly privatized firms. Second, its "excessive wages" tax, the main tool for restricting incomes, shrank the pool of potential investors in private firms. Together with still-persistent inflation, the existence of this painful wage tax remedy continues to lower Polish real wages and the standard of living. If this trend continues, it may block the development of a capital market in Poland, forcing policy-makers to pursue privatization through gratuitous transfers.

In addition to economic barriers, political impediments contribute to the low rate of privatization. The commercialization phenomenon also has a political cause. Workers in the great industrial plants—the ones most frequently commercialized—are one of the most influential groups in Polish society. The social importance of the "great industrial working classes" dates back to the 1950s, when Poland adopted the Soviet model of industrialization, privileging industries that manufactured the means of production. This, in turn, resulted in the rapid development of heavy industry. Production was concentrated in huge firms, in which workers had special bargaining powers for wages and social privileges. Those working in heavy industry and in huge plants soon became the best-paid group in society. Instead of being related to the plant's economic importance, wages strongly depended on the branch of industry and size of the firm. Struggling for privileges, workers in the huge plants helped shape the structure of the economy in the 1950s, a structure that survives today. Employees of the huge firms were also an important part of political opposition, having led the series of protests against the Communist rule in 1956, 1970, and 1976. Finally, in May 1980, the workers of the great industrial plants went on strike and forced the Communist authorities to legalize the independent trade union Solidarity. Later, in 1988, strikes in the great industries initiated the political crisis which led to the fall of Communism. Workers are a large and well-organized social group, and they are well aware of their interests. Just as the Communists could not afford to ignore this group, the current government cannot afford to ignore the working class if it is to pursue its plans of economic transition. The ownership transformation of huge firms is hardly conceivable without the support (or at least consent) of the workers.

IV. Commercialization as a New Form of State Ownership: Empirical Findings

The basic goal of commercialization is legally to transform state firms into commercial companies, so that their stock can be sold to private investors. A transition period between commercialization and the sale of stock was created to allow the "restructuring of the company, including discharge of its debts, replacement of management, sale of unnecessary or burdensome property,"[8] in order to enhance the efficiency of firms before they were fully privatized. Increased efficiency is to be achieved through radical changes in the commercialized firm's organizational structure.

The most significant change in how commercialized firms are run was the elimination of employee councils. This change shifts a company's internal power structure from the self-management model to that of professional management. "It is economically reasonable to rely on managers," Lewandowski (who subsequently became Minister of Privatization) and Szomburg stated in their 1990 monograph, *The Decalogue of Privatization.*[9]

Commercialization was designed to institutionalize this new structure of managerial power in the firm, by limiting employee influence over management and strengthening the managing board's power. Supervisory boards were created to inject economic rationality into commercialized firms. As opposed to the employee councils, whose interests were mainly directed at a level of wages satisfactory to the workers, the supervisory board was established to represent the financial interest of the owner in the profits of the firm. There was a strong belief that the external control would be more efficient and rational than the control exercised by the workers. Government supervision was to be limited to controlling the privatization process; the newly formed companies were granted considerable independence from government interference in management decisions.

It is far from clear how many of these expectations can be realized when commercialized firms remain state property. It is important to understand how the state has comported itself as owner of these firms, and how responsibilities are divided between the "owner" (government administration) and those charged with managing a firm. We intend to show why the state-owned commercialized companies have failed to adapt to the market.

The following analysis is based on the findings of an empirical study of 10 randomly selected commercialized firms, conducted in the first half of 1991. The study included firms of different sizes (the smallest having 290 employees and the largest 3025). The firms represented various branches of industry throughout Poland: food, electromechanical, glazing, paper, and shipbuilding. The study was qualitative in nature. In each of the examined firms a number of extended interviews were conducted with representatives of the main groups: the managing board, the unions, the former employee councils and the supervisory board. In addition, a series of "focus group" interviews were also conducted with employees of each firm. The methodology extended beyond mere description of respondents' attitudes and opinions. The study was an attempt to document the new structure of power in the firm by comprehensively analyzing the social situation, relations between groups, conflicts, and the valid rules of the game.

A. The Social Structure of Commercialized Firms

Commercialization openly changed the firm's power structure. By eliminating employee councils, the managing boards' power was considerably strengthened. The elimination of employee councils occurred without protest in all the firms; the majority of employees treated it as a natural consequence of the change, and did not regret the loss. Even council activists confessed that the council was a fading institution.

After commercialization, the importance of trade unions in the firms declined rapidly. Without the councils, the unions could not dismiss members of the managing board, as a consequence losing their most powerful weapon against management. Even the strike, once the most basic mechanism for pressuring management, was now more difficult to invoke. People increasingly realized that a strike might result in the firm's bankruptcy, or could scare off potential investors. Threatened with unemployment, employees were less inclined to strike.

The unions were hurt by their lack of a clear identity under the changed circumstances. Solidarity activists, in particular, did not wish to give up their formerly key positions in firms, and could not decide whether to back the managing board, or limit union activity to the complaints of individual workers. The lack of identity not only hurt the union's ability to deal with the managing board, it also generated negative feelings among its own members, frequently leading workers to conclude that trade unions should be removed from firms altogether. Since unions could not effectively represent worker interests, support for the unions declined rapidly.

Under the new organization, workers found that their status had radically changed. Workers' decisions were now determined by the fear of unemployment, the inaccessibility of information, the lack of effective representation of their interests, low wages, and progressive impoverishment. Despite earlier promises that wages would be higher in commercialized firms, wages did not increase; indeed, wages declined in several instances, though they generally approximated wages in uncommercialized state firms. Real employee earnings in the commercialized sector fell by more than thirty percent in 1990, and the downward trend continued in 1991. Combined with inflation, the decrease in wages induced a further decline in the standard of living of the vast majority of Polish households. There was a growing sense of helplessness, lack of control, and absence of any prospects whatever among workers. Workers' low material rewards and social status fueled their disappointment with commercialization. The lack of available political channels for workers to articulate their growing frustration led to an extremely tense situation, threatening uncontrolled outbursts both within individual firms, and on a national scale.

One effect of commercialization was to polarize society into two distinct groups: those who lost from commercialization versus those who clearly profited from it. The clear losers were workers and the firm's lower-level management. The gainers were the firm's managers, worker representatives on the supervisory council, and, in a sense, even union leaders. These two groups differed from each other mainly in their respective shares of the firm's profits: high or low wages. Other traits that distinguished the two groups were job security and access to information. Workers were the most threatened by layoffs, but they knew very little about what was going on in their firms, because only managers, and to some extent union leaders, had access to such information. As a consequence of this polarization, the two groups had opposing views of privatization. On the one hand, managers and union activists supported commercialization of the firms as the only chance for improving the economy. On the other hand, most workers felt that the changes in the structure of state companies made commercialization entirely unattractive.

A number of psychological factors helped make this social polarization relatively permanent. First, and most important, the fear of unemployment forced a worker to put up with these unfavorable circumstances out of a sense of helplessness and lack of control. Second, workers and others believed that commercialization was only a transition stage, and that full privatization would eventually improve things. Finally, there was the sense that privatization was a natural and inevitable process, which accounts for the government's and workers' inability even to conceive of alternative methods of reform.

B. Failure of Commercialized Firms to Adjust to Market Demand

Commercialization neither initiated any serious changes in the way firms are managed, nor made firms responsive to external economic realities. There are several reasons for this: the lack of an owner, official economic policies, persistence of old management styles, the futility of making changes an eventual private owner might undo, fear of provoking strikes, and the questionable legitimacy of the commercialized firm.

The commercialized firms earned the reputation of being "nobody's property" because there was no visible owner, no one possessing needed capital or, more importantly, an interest in the firm's development. The Ministry of Privatization was ill-prepared to play the part of the active owner, as were the supervisory boards, which in most firms were insufficiently empowered and rather passive. And in any case, no institutional mechanisms existed that would encourage the board to act like a real owner.

National economic policies contributed to the overall failure of commercialized firms to introduce change. The tax on wage increases successfully barred *all* raises, even those resulting from an increase in the firm's productivity or a reduction in the firm's work force. The tax made it virtually impossible to introduce wage incentives to motivate workers. Another problem was the fact that the government's tight credit policy had effectively blocked *all* investment, even those necessary if firms were to modify production to adjust to a market economy. Because of the profound recession, most firms had no capital to reinvest in themselves, and the price of credit prevented them from obtaining loans to make changes. Clearly, the failure of firms to adapt to a market economy was not entirely the fault of the process of commercialization.

Although the managing boards acquired autonomy and higher salaries, for several reasons they failed to become more effective, or really any different from before. The newly appointed presidents of the commercialized companies were the firm's former managing directors, and no incentives were provided to encourage these executives to radically change management styles. Their mostly fixed salaries bore a very weak relation to company performance. Company executives, therefore, made no extra effort, even when executive inaction incurred considerable social risk. As a result, management in most commercialized firms went on basically as it had in the old state firms, disappointing the high expectations placed in the managing boards.

The sense that the commercialized firm was in a transitional stage was unavoidable, particularly in those firms that could realistically expect to become fully private, and the knowledge that a new owner might reject changes made during the transitional stage kept firms from initiating *any* change. In those firms most likely to become private, the board aimed all its energy at issuing stock and selling the firm quickly, seeking to preserve the firm's good financial standing, if possible. Everything else, including any internal restructuring, was left for the future, to be settled once the firm was in private hands.

In all the examined firms, fear of worker unrest and strikes also hampered the introduction of change. Managing boards, in their day-to-day dealings with workers, sidestepped all conflict, often at the expense of the firm's financial interests, by not making needed layoffs and conceding wage disputes. Despite the elimination of the employee councils, workers retained real power (though they were often unaware of it) which largely limited the ability of the managing boards to act. Workers, because of their unfavored status in the commercialized firms, refused to act as management's ally in the effort to reform the firm. The managing boards' only reliable allies were those in the narrow circles of the factory elites. Because workers bore the greatest burdens of privatization (risk of unemployment and shrunken material rewards) yet derived no direct benefits, the boards faced the troublesome task of introducing painful changes without the support of workers. Consequently, management generally worried about the social consequences of their decisions more than the economic ones. This approach led management to guarantee workers job security and (at least) subsistence wages in commercialized firms.

The legitimacy of the commercialized firms also posed a barrier to economically efficient management. Employees recognized neither the treasury nor its representative, the supervisory boards, as legitimate owners. Workers questioned the treasury's right to the firm's property in many commercialized firms, particularly those firms which had received considerable investments over the past several years. Having been told that their low wages were necessary in order to pay off the firm's debts, workers felt very much like co-owners. They refused to recognize the legitimacy of the supervisory council's role in the firm, and were particularly disturbed by the salaries board members received, which workers considered exorbitant. The same was true of the managing boards; workers still felt fully authorized to interfere with management's work. Even though they found it increasingly difficult actually to *control* management, workers effectively thwarted management's ability to carry out practical changes, such as modifying the wage system, which some boards attempted. They did so by refusing to recognize the autonomy of the state's appointed owner of the firm, the supervisory council. The problem of legitimacy proved to be one of the most important reasons why the changes that were to occur during the period of commercialization never took place.

Commercialization is very likely the final stage of transformation for many firms which never stood a chance of actually becoming private. Although most of the studied firms have actively searched for potential investors, their chances for full privatization have usually been poor. The best solution would be to find a serious foreign partner, but this has been possible in only a very few cases.

V. The State as Passive Owner of "Private" Companies

While the state does perform active roles in the commercialized firms, it is nevertheless passive in its role as owner. The state does little more than decide, upon a firm's motion and the consent of its managing board and employees, to transform a state firm into a single-partner company of the treasury. Upon commercialization, the Ministry creates a supervisory board and appoints two-thirds of its members, with the remaining third appointed by the firm's employees. The Ministry rarely interferes with the fully autonomous supervisory councils; virtually all contacts between the Ministry and the board are severed. Initially there was the fear that commercialization would impose government supervision on the firms, preventing them from becoming efficient and eventually private, but such fears proved unfounded.

The legal "owner," in the form of the treasury, is an entirely abstract construction with no clear rights of ownership.

Government agencies did not directly perform any functions of ownership. A June 1991 review by the Main Board of Supervision of the privatization process stated that:

> the Minister of Privatization failed to secure a proper representation of the Treasury's interests in companies and in its holding of stock at shareholders assemblies. By the end of April 1991, the Department of Ownership Supervision and Training had yet to be organized, nor had any records been kept of the Treasury's stock in companies or its revenues from privatization. There is no organizational agency to analyze whether the Treasury is efficiently utilizing its property in these companies.[10]

Research indicates that the Ministry of Privatization exerted no influence whatsoever over the activities of the supervisory boards. Upon appointment, members of the boards were simply informed that their task was to oversee the firm's financial performance and bring about prompt privatization, but no incentives were created to motivate the boards to be active or efficient, or even to encourage them to complete privatization by selling the firm. Initially, it was even unclear how board members would be paid. "There has been no elaboration of policies concerning, among other things, the remuneration of members of the managing and supervisory boards and the division of the firm's profits."[11] Eventually, the Ministry of Privatization set the monthly remuneration of members of supervisory boards at somewhat higher than the national average. From that point on, all members of the boards have been paid fixed monthly salaries regardless of the firm's actual performance. In addition, the only incentive to privatize the firm was the vague promise of a bonus for completed privatization, which was not even officially confirmed until the end of 1991. The situation of managing boards of the commercialized companies was similar to that of the supervisory boards. Again, no incentives were created to motivate board members. Salaries were an automatic multiple of the national average (six hundred percent, as a rule) and were high enough to make the profit-conditioned bonuses relatively unimportant as motivating factors.

However, there was one advantageous aspect to the state's passivity in supervising its own property: appraisal of management's performance replaced bureaucratic supervision. The supervisory board prepared an assessment of the managing board's performance which, in turn, was reviewed by the Minister of Privatization, representing the owner (the treasury). The problem was that the owner was practically nonexistent, and no other government agency exercised the owner's powers. The Ministry of Privatization, with a statutory duty to represent the owner, focused on the privatization of the commercialized firms. Because, at least initially, the Ministry expected that privatization would occur quickly, the agency devoted insufficient attention to providing incentives to motivate company authorities to be economically efficient, probably the main reason why commercialized companies were much less efficient than had been expected. To date, there has been no significant change in how these companies operate. The state, the formerly inefficient owner of state firms, is now the inefficient owner of single-partner companies of the treasury. The dreams of privatization have been shattered; the change of the firm's legal structure and its transformation into a private company has not itself been sufficient to increase efficiency. Failing to perform its duties as owner, the state has instead continued to interfere with commercialized firms through its fiscal policy (tax collection), and it has chosen to influence the activities of companies through the exercise of its political powers.

The key issue is the incompatibility of the roles of different government agencies with respect to commercialized companies. The Ministry of Privatization represents both the interests of the owner and the interests of the privatization process; these interests are not always compatible with each other. Privatization requires commercialized companies to enhance the value of stock in order to attract buyers. This has been achieved through restrictive financial measures: avoiding debts and freezing wages. These measures have led to the economic stagnation of most of the firms, where cost-cutting keeps firms from investing and even prevents them from making necessary repairs. In the same situation, a real owner would have behaved very differently, for example, by restructuring the firm, altering production, and generally making the firm responsive to market demands. Instead, in commercialized firms what has prevailed is a short-term strategy aimed at privatization by cutting costs, and avoiding investment and development. While this strategy might have made sense had state companies been rapidly privatized, it is harmful to firms when full privatization is delayed.

The state finds itself in a dilemma where its interests as owner of commercialized firms clash with its fiscal policies. The Ministry of Finance, as the agency in charge of the economic stabilization program, adopted measures to control inflation and balance the budget. These measures affect the financial condition and efficiency of the commercialized companies. Besides a forty percent tax on revenues, the companies are also obliged to pay the state its share of the owner's dividends. The government exempted companies from paying these dividends during the first months of commercialization, substantially lightening the financial burden on commercialized firms, in particular those possessing durable property. However, the government revoked this exemption in the summer of 1991, and the resulting financial hardship has been so great that many firms are left without the means to make investments. In addition, the anti-inflationary tax on pay raises limited the ability of firms to create wage incentives. The Ministry of Finance's methods of taxation have become perhaps the state's most basic tools for controlling the companies; the function of the owner's role and profits has been negligible.

Ultimately, the state put political considerations over its ownership interests, especially in those situations where the potential for serious social conflict exists. Company boards never know until the last minute what decision its "owner" (represented by the Ministry for Privatization) will make, particularly if the decisions involve potential conflict with workers. Managers fear that, faced with the threat of a strike, the state will pursue the political objective of stability and avoidance of conflict. For example, in the spring of 1991, the union of Poland's largest tourist agency, Orbis, demanded the dismissal of the company's president and vice president. This kind of demand was beyond the union's authority. The company supervisory board found the union's claims to be unjustified, but after consulting the Ministry of Privatization, decided to dismiss the two presidents for their inability to exercise authority in the existing social situation. By not supporting the managers of its property, the state once again failed to act like an owner.

Privatization of the entire economy would overcome many of the abovementioned problems, though the government has hardly had a perfect record as a privatizing agency. Because the goal of privatization has been to transfer ownership to private investors with the resources to develop the firms, the state should not have attached great importance to the selling price of the firms. Instead, because of the potentially substantial contribution to needed state revenues, the Ministry of Finance has sought the highest possible returns from privatization. The desire to negotiate high prices has largely delayed the privatization process, and the goal of high returns has tended to limit much potential privatization by making firms too expensive for investors.

Conclusion

The state has played a variety of often conflicting roles in the commercialized firms—owner, tax collector, privatizing agency, and political authority—that have largely impaired the state's administration of those companies, in addition to impeding the progress of the privatization process itself, which was supposed to remove such friction between government agencies. On occasion, the same government agency has been in conflict with itself. The problem, from the point of view of the commercialized companies, stems from the failure of the treasury to create an institution which acts like an owner. What happens to the state sector of the economy is often not the result of planning, but the result of a game of interests between or within separate state agencies. In our view, the lack of an owner's interest in the commercialized firms seriously hampers the privatization of the Polish economy.

Notes

1. See D. Chelmiński and A. Czynczyk, "Social Barriers to Privatization: The Legality of Institutional Order in Commercialized Firms". Research Report (Warsaw, Aug. 1990) (This study was conducted in the early half of 1991 and examined ten single-partner companies of the treasury. It was commissioned by the Centre for Privatization, The International Foundation for Capital Market Development and Ownership Changes in Poland.).
2. Act of July 13, 1990 on privatization of state enterprises, in 51 *Dziennik Urzędony,* [Journal of Laws] item 298.
3. Dariusz Śniecinski, "Bony prywatyzacyjne i preferencje pracownicze" [Privatization coupons and employee preferences], in 2/90 *Prywatyzacja* [Privatization] (October 1990).
4. Tomasz Jeziorański, "Pulapki pelnomocnika" [The traps of a plenipotentiary], in 19 *Zycie Gospodarcze* [Economic Life] (May 13, 1990).
5. Most of the firms privatized through liquidation are small and medium-sized firms. Forty-five percent have fewer than two hundred employees; thirty-six percent have between 201 and five hundred employees. Nineteen percent of the firms have more than five hundred employees. See "Dynamika prywatyzacji" [The dynamics of privatization], *Bulletin of the Ministry of Privatization* 2: 3, Published by the Office for Privatization Analyses (Warsaw, Sept. 1991).
6. Id. at 2.
7. See Janusz Lewandowski, Jan Szomburg, "Dekalog prywatyzacji" [The Decalogue of privatization], Institute for Market Economy and Ownership Rights Research, *Tygodnik Solidarności* [Solidarity Weekly] 45: 112 (November 9, 1990).
8. "Założenia rządowego programu prywatyzacji przedsiębiorstw państwowych" [Assumptions of the Government program of privatization of state enterprises], Office of the Government Plenipotentiary for Ownership Transformations (duplicated typescript), p. 13.
9. Lewandowski, supra note 7, p. 13.
10. Main Board of Supervision, Systemic Analyses Department, *Informacja o wynikach kontroli procesów prywatyzacji przedsiębiorstw państwowych, część I* [Inspection of privatization processes in state enterprises: Information on results, part I] (Warsaw, June 1991) p. 43.
11. Id., p. 43.

Has State Ownership Truly Abandoned Socialism? The Survival of Socialist Economy and Law in Postcommunist Hungary

András Sajó

[*Editors' Synopsis:* socialism still lives in Hungary. Among the causes of its survival are the retention of old attitudes; dependence on a state-run agency for management of "privatized" firms; a judiciary rooted in the past; and still-dominant state control masquerading as "public interest." Politics and self-interest thwart changes in government policy and the establishment of definite, progressive legal rules for privatization.]

One gets the feeling that, despite differences in their approaches, all the postcommunist countries of Eastern and Central Europe are desperate to resist radical change to a private, property-based, market system and its unpleasant social consequences.[1] In Poland, Ukraine, and Russia, privatization has served to continue previous practices of government ownership.[2] Rumania's policy, although introducing vouchers that seemingly make citizens the direct owners of nationalized assets, has maintained government ownership.[3]

The same experience has occurred in Hungary,[4] often cited as the Eastern European country "most prepared" for privatization. This paper argues that privatization in Hungary to a great extent continues or reproduces the previous social and cultural patterns of communist and precommunist Hungary.[5] Although Hungarian society aspires to Western models, the emerging social, economic, political, and legal structures have strongly *etatist* features that are radically different from Western welfare states such as Sweden. What passes as the "public interest" is often nothing more than a reflection of the former ideology of favoring state interests over private concerns. The actions of Hungarian judges and political leaders have too broadly legitimated the government's bureaucratic power to intervene in the economy. Instead of streamlining the process of privatization, this power has become the tool of the incumbent political party to keep itself in power, often at the expense of an effective privatization.

I begin with a brief review of the historical antecedents of ownership in contemporary Hungary, followed by a relatively detailed presentation of the legal structure of privatization. Finally, in the third and fourth parts, I offer a sociolegal analysis of the emerging legal system. My analysis indicates that incomplete privatization is both a source and symptom of the emerging legal system.

I. Historical Background

A. Prewar Notions of Market Economy and Private Ownership

Prewar traditions of ownership and market economy set the stage for the postcommunist privatization. The great majority of the population in prewar Hungary, peasants in particular, did not own land. Romantic anticapitalism was a popular ideology. Furthermore, the legal system contained remnants of feudal ownership, especially in the law of inheritance. For example, under medieval rules, big estates were not governed by the laws of free estate planning; generally the firstborn male inherited the land.

Although state and municipal ownership of property was not particularly extensive in prewar Hungary, there was already a strong tradition of government intervention in the economy. The most significant form of government economic intervention was through public sector contracting. The government extended its economic powers during the Great Depression of 1929, and even more so during World War II. When the Communist government came to power, it incorporated the prewar economic tools into its powers of command economy.

While prewar Hungarian law allowed the government to interfere in the economy, the system also protected private property as an unlimited right in the Roman law tradition. Furthermore, market mechanisms existed in the form of dynamic, transaction-oriented, legal concepts and business practices in a small but important sector of the economy. Middle-class groups who believed in the principles of commodity ownership did exist, but if the group was not exterminated during the war, as was the case with many Jewish Hungarians, then its members attempted to emigrate when the communist aftermath made such ownership impossible. A short-lived land reform created a new, landed, peasant class that was able to enjoy land ownership only very briefly, before being forced into farming cooperatives. Many then had to leave their villages to take up industrial jobs in the cities. As a consequence, few people remained in Hungary after the war who had experienced private ownership or market mechanisms.

B. What Did the Postcommunist System Inherit?

Although there were only insufficient legal guarantees of commodity ownership under state socialism, some of the entrepreneurial tradition did survive, and even expanded within the tolerated private economy, particularly in both the small business sector and private agriculture. Still, entrepreneurial skills are not well developed in Hungary.

During its last two decades, the Communist regime granted limited economic reforms which gave socialist managers greater independence from the Communist party, resulting in a shift from centralized planning to a more market-oriented system.[6] New elites who were emerging from the communist *nomenklatura* were increasingly interested in assuming positions in private businesses. In fact, the collapse of the Communist regime was partly caused by this shift of the elites' interest.

The economic situation today is only slightly different from that during the last years of Communism. The domination of large enterprises and farms in the bankrupt state sector reflects the bureaucratic interests of socialist centralization, which permitted *de facto* monopolies to exist in many industries. The state continues to exercise its ownership rights through a financial bureaucracy, presently the State Assets Agency.[7] The credit system is underdeveloped, and banks do not offer special services for new ventures. Because the government owns the controlling majority in most commercial banks, the state is able to maintain and control a centralized system of banking which protects the financial interest of the banks and private companies by prohibiting firms from exiting the market or discharging their debts through bankruptcy.

II. The Legal Structure of Hungarian Privatization

A. The Privatization of Industries

The Transformation Act of 1989[8] established the rules for the transformation of state-owned enterprises into two forms of business corporations: stock corporations and limited liability companies. Ownership of stock corporations is generally through ordinary shareholding, although there are exceptions (such as for foreigners) where ownership is held through freely transferable "certified shares." The minimum share capital of the stock corporation must not be less than ten million forints (approximately $125,000), and limited liability companies must be capitalized with a minimum contribution of one million forints (approximately $12,500). These minimum capital requirements are not prohibitive by Hungarian standards.

Prior to their transformation into stock corporations, state-owned enterprises are managed either by enterprise councils or by administrative management.[9] Enterprise councils, which make only fundamental management decisions, are composed of employee-elected members and representatives of management, some of whom are appointed by a general manager. The general manager is appointed by the council. The most common transformation is that of firms managed by enterprise councils which initiate the transformation on their own.

Under administrative management, the enterprise's founding agency (typically a ministry or a municipality), which controls the firm, will appoint its general manager. However, the State Assets Agency (SAA),[10] may determine whether directly to transform one of these firms into a private enterprise. When the SAA makes this determination, the agency appoints a commissioner initially to manage the enterprise during its transformation. In preparation for its transformation to a private company, the enterprise prepares a balance sheet and transformation plan which contains the business purposes of the transformation, an inventory, a draft memorandum of association, and a letter of intent of the new members.

In implementing the Transformation Act, the leaders of the Communist transition government were accused of selling state property for their own benefit. Consequently, the government amended the privatization procedure to check the privatization process, by creating the SAA to oversee transformation activities. Initially, enterprises could transform themselves without the consent of the SAA, as long as external partners agreed to contribute an increase of twenty percent or one hundred million Hungarian forints (approximately $1,250,000) to the firm's initial capital.

Although all privatization decisions of the SAA were initially subject to judicial review, there was some resistance to the creation of this agency. The National Deregulation Board voted against the establishment of the agency, for fear that it would concentrate too much power in the hands of government, and slow down the process of privatization. The Board recommended that, were the agency to exist, it should be subjected to strict conflict-of-interest rules. The government rejected the Deregulation Board's recommendation, and Parliament failed to enact such legislation on its own.[11] Instead, the government has allowed for greater conflicts of interest by abolishing, in 1992, the rule that one person may not sit on more than two boards of directors (although at the same time, stricter rules were imposed on financial institutions). Both the rejection of the Board's recommendation and the elimination of this board of directors requirement had the goal of making it possible to reward government loyalists with new jobs.

There is no "intermediate" legal status of enterprises undergoing transformation, although in practice administrative management is an intermediary phase. In theory, enterprises maintain control of their assets during the transformation phase, and are liable for all debts and other liabilities incurred before, during, and after their transformation. This is called "total succession of rights and obligations." Under the emerging system the SAA sets the conditions of transformation (which may or may not involve external capital or participation) and retains possession of the nontransferred shares.

Following further allegations that it was selling out government property, the government amended the law on transformations in September 1990[12] to give the SAA still more power to control the privatization process.[13] Under the amended law, the SAA reviewed an enterprise's transformation plan, and established the terms of its transformation. The SAA took title to those shares not sold to private parties, and donated twenty percent of the revenue from the sale of the assets to the "new" corporation.[14] If the SAA were an autonomous entity pursuing the private interests of the firms, this scheme could be perceived to have merit. However, five months after the amendment was passed, the government assumed direct control of SAA, bypassing parliamentary supervision and abolishing judicial review. An increasing number of enterprises are submitted to the direct government control of administrative management, in which the SAA determines when and how to carry out privatization, based on the enterprises' transformation plans and balance sheets. However, the Council of Ministers must consent to the privatization of "trusts."[15]

Special schemes apply to municipal property. Act XXXIII of 1991, on the Transfer of State Property to Local Authorities, transfers complete control of ownership of state-owned residences and commercial properties (shops, and so on) to the local authority with jurisdiction over the property. Where plots of land larger than one thousand square meters are involved, the SAA must approve the transfer.

A special scheme establishes the procedure for privatizing lands managed by farmers' cooperatives: members of the cooperatives have a claim to some of the land, while former, prenationalization owners may use their compensation vouchers to reacquire land of the cooperative at forced auctions. Under the forced auction system, cooperatives offer part of their land to a restricted bidding, participation in which is restricted first to previous landowners, and second to cooperative members. A 1990 law created a special privatization scheme for small businesses in retail trade, catering, and services which employ fewer than ten persons (or fifteen in the case of catering and hotels).[16] These businesses were ordered to submit balance sheets to the SAA, which must determine by September 25, 1992, when and under what conditions the businesses will be privatized. Private purchase of these shops is possible only through public auction. The same is true of gas stations.[17] According to the Minister of Trade, about half of these small commercial entities (three thousand out of six thousand) had been privatized by Spring, 1992.[18]

The Hungarian banking situation reinforces the state's control over enterprises undergoing transformation, and provides private enterprises with few opportunities to achieve independence from the state. As a consequence of the conflict-of-interest rules of the Banking Act,[19] a number of progovernment members of Parliament were appointed to the board of directors of the major banks, and several general managers were replaced by new managers believed to be more loyal to the government. Although the law of financial institutions prevents banks from playing a direct role in the privatization process, banks do play important and sometimes crucial roles in transformation decisions and even in appointing management. Many state-owned enterprises are in debt to the banks. In the first years of privatization there was a considerable amount of debt-for-equity conversion. Banks subsequently became more cautious and less willing to provide loans in these transactions. The government currently owns a majority of the shares of most large commercial banks, and, beginning in 1992, has imposed new bank directors. However, under the 1991 Act on Financial Institutions, the government must give up its controlling majorities of banks beginning in 1995.

Companies are entitled to contract with the SAA for the right to manage government assets. The emerging system stresses reliance on "managing firms," which manage and sell assets on behalf of the SAA, providing the agency with revenues in the form of predetermined sales profits or dividends. In August 1991, the SAA developed a scheme enabling private consultants to oversee on the agency's behalf the privatization of smaller companies (less than three hundred employees, and assets of less than three hundred million Hungarian forints (approximately four million dollars).

Once this transformation has occurred (which may or may not involve the transfer of shares), the remaining options are:

(1) direct sale of the corporation to foreign or domestic entities, including the sale of shares to holders of compensation vouchers, if the SAA so decides;
(2) sale of assets (including liquidation);[20]
(3) sale or distribution of shares to employees.

Under all three of the above-listed scenarios, the assignment of the former state-owned firm's liabilities remains unchanged so long as the privatized firm is the same entity.

B. Privatization of Public Services and Agriculture

The government has allowed very little expansion of private initiative into the areas of education, health, welfare services, and the mass media, despite laws which accept the idea of a privatized public service (welfare) sector.[21] In response to diminishing state resources for higher education, the Ministry of Education prepared approximately eleven drafts for the establishment of private universities.[22] However, existing universities strongly oppose private competition, and the government wishes to avoid the creation of institutions that might deviate from the government views. Consequently, each of the eleven drafts imposed more rigid restrictions on the founding of private universities. Similar trends emerged in high schools, where, however, some privatization has occurred and is quite class-biased. Also, privately sponsored programs may operate within public schools.[23] But the only "private" education to receive the support of the central government is religious education, due to the fact that religious schools are considered more progovernment than public schools, which may preserve liberal or socialist values.

All efforts to privatize health and welfare services have been fruitless. The obstacles to privatization in this area stem not just from the government's organizational inertia, but also from the active opposition of the medical profession. Doctors seek to maintain their privileges under the state health system.

With respect to the media, the government has insisted on retaining control.[24] The reason is that private broadcasting would undermine a governmental privilege, which the government appears to have no genuine interest in allowing to occur.

In the area of nonindustrial privatization, progress has been made only in agriculture. Under the system of state socialism, agriculture was dominated by large cooperatives, which are now bankrupt and on the verge of dissolution. By using their compensation vouchers at forced auctions, precommunist landowners have the opportunity to partly repurchase their former lands.

III. Social and Political Interests in Maintaining the Socialist System of State Property Management

Privatization in Hungary is occurring slowly. The government halfheartedly (at best) supports measures that would accelerate the process, because managers, workers, and government leaders all have vested interests in government's retaining control of many of its industries and services.[25] Managers obviously wish to maintain their present positions. Workers and labor unions would prefer a subsidized state sector to ensure the security of their jobs. While leaders claim that state control of industries helps government to effectively implement economic policies during the transformation, privatization policies so far indicate that the government's interest in retaining state control of enterprises and the economy is in reality motivated by political concerns: the incumbent political party seeks to use state control of enterprises to secure political loyalties. Rather than providing people with incentives to develop the entrepreneurial skills necessary to compete in a market economy, current government policies encourage a system of reliance on favoritism, and development of political loyalties.

Privatization began in Hungary during the last two years of Communist rule, and the process that has since evolved retains many characteristics of society's economic dependency on the state. From a strictly legal point of view, the communist reforms transformed many state-owned enterprises into limited liability companies.[26] However, most of the stock in these companies was either owned by the state directly, or held by banks or other companies under the state's control. Managers of state-owned enterprises often formed their own limited liability companies and acquired ownership over the firm's most valuable assets. As of Spring 1992, total private investment in Hungarian state assets well exceeds a billion dollars. An estimated ten-billion-dollars-worth of state enterprises were scheduled to be privatized under the government's 1989 privatization program, which promised to privatize forty to fifty percent of state-owned enterprises within four years.[27] When privatization began in 1989 there were some seventeen hundred state-owned enterprises. According to government claims, about ten percent of state-owned assets in the industrial sector was privatized by March 1991. However, as of March 1992, private parties were the sole owners of more than 130 former state-owned companies and majority owners of another 150 companies in which the state had been reduced to a minority share (these figures include foreign owners). There were 1699 foreign and joint ventures in Hungary at the end of 1990, with a total capital of 44.6 billion forints ($628 million) with $180 million of foreign investment. One third of these companies ended 1990 with a loss. Today, the state-owned sector accounts for an estimated eighty percent of Hungary's industrial production. The data suggest that the original 1989 privatization plans will remain on paper, and that the economy will remain state property (although often bankrupt).

The government has officially pursued two conflicting methods of privatization. The first advocates a relatively fast process with limited government intervention; the second calls for a strictly interventionist policy. So far, this second policy has prevailed. Under the interventionist policy, the government's most important instrument is the State Assets Agency, which reviews virtually all privatization transactions. The agency has not issued any clear policy guidelines.[28] However, because the agency has limited resources, and is very vulnerable politically, its functionaries, who are mostly low-level bureaucrats of the previous regime and party apparatus, are extremely cautious and slow in arriving at their decisions. Often they choose to review deals struck between state enterprises and private investors. Unfortunately, the government often invokes direct control of the agency to satisfy the considerations of partisan politics. The government offers a number of excuses for this restrictive approach to privatization, the two most frequently used being the desire to avoid selling off too much state property (and thereby inducing an overwhelming foreign presence),[29] and the need to secure existing employment.

The government has resisted a policy of radical privatization mainly out of the fear of the unrest (and loss of votes) that would result from the increase in unemployment that radical privatization would surely spark. It is true that in the state sector, unemployment is on the rise, and state-owned companies face bankruptcy, while private-sector small businesses continue to grow and employ more people. However, because these small companies have a high tax-evasion rate, this fact has not resulted in any net revenue gains for the government.

Apart from government bureaucracy and government managers in Hungarian enterprises, the major actors in the privatization process are foreign investors (major multinationals, institutional investors), small foreign entrepreneurs (often of Hungarian descent), and, to a limited extent, the emerging Hungarian entrepreneurial class (coming partly from the previous communist management). It is practically impossible to evaluate the international political dimension of privatization, that is, the extent to which the government is prepared to grant concessions to foreign investors as a political favor. For example, in 1990, a Hungarian daily newspaper was sold to a French group connected with important French politicians who were close to Hungary's Prime Minister (which caused a major scandal in Hungary when this fact was revealed).

The most significant social relationship in the privatization process is that between the government and its political party supporters, on the one hand, and the managerial class employed in state-owned enterprises, on the other. The managers of these enterprises attained their positions thanks to their close ties to the previous regime's *nomenklatura*. However, once installed in their administrative positions, these managers had been able to acquire considerable managerial skills. The new government has nonetheless tried to eliminate these managers on several occasions, partly out of personal dislike of the former Communists, but mostly to create positions for members of the Hungarian Democratic Forum (MDF, the political party behind the new government) after the party came to power.

The government made several attempts to satisfy the expectations of MDF party loyalists by installing them in positions held by previous Communist party elites. In September 1990, a government decree ordered new management elections in state-owned, "self-governing," enterprises, in which worker-elected councils appoint the director. After eighty five percent of the directors were reelected, frustrating government intentions by giving the former Communists widespread local control, MDF leaders were forced to adopt a more careful, gradual process of changing management. The government now seeks to create new management positions for party loyalists through its control of the SAA.

The political approach to the management of firms undergoing transformation affects not only how the firms are internally managed, but what market strategies they adopt.[30] Because of the growing number of layoffs, employment relations increasingly depend on political loyalties under the current regime.

However, the present regime is less successful at enforcing its political interests than its predecessor, although this is not to imply that the previous regime was always able openly to exercise direct control over the economy or state enterprises, particularly during the waning years of socialism. In 1984, enterprise managers became formally independent of the government bureaucracy. The government consequently refrained from openly intervening in matters of enterprise management, and instead controlled state-owned enterprises through disguised economic means, such as setting prices, and providing subsidies and loans. Because the postcommunist government has lost its most direct means of economic *dirigisme*, political leaders have substituted the ability to exercise the state's rights as owner of private enterprises, in order to pursue political goals. At shareholders' meetings, government representatives now use their majority votes to discipline managers.

Continuity with the past exists even through those who are charged with overseeing the privatization process. Former political elites were able to exploit their positions in government to create opportunities for themselves in private ventures. However, those who are low in the economic and party bureaucracy were often unable to find coveted private-sector employment. Consequently, these former bureaucrats now hold key positions in the government's property management system.

The need of the governing coalition to maintain its political constituency is one reason the current government is reluctant to privatize quickly (and instead seeks to retain state control of the privatized sector). Recent polls indicate that, if an election were held today, the government would not get more than twenty-five percent of the vote.[31] Supporters of the current government feel that changes have been both inadequate and too extensive (in frustrating their interests). The government must offer rank-and-file MDF members some form of financial benefits to maintain their loyalty when these members do not directly benefit from a given program. By holding a command position in the nation's economy and social life (including the media), the government hopes to improve its chances of reelection. If the government retains its command of the state sector, it can privatize companies by installing a private management of its own manufacture and loyalties.

The government also uses its contracting power as a tool to maintain political loyalties. The largest purchasers in the economy are still the government itself, and industries and services controlled by the government. There are no rules of government procurement, or even a requirement of cost-efficient government contracting.[32] Instead, political loyalties and friendly political relations play a prominent role in securing government contracts.

IV. Privatization's Impact on the Legal System

Because elements of the current legal system deviate from the ideal of a system based on the rule of law, the legal ramifications of privatization have been controversial. The government eliminated judicial review of the SAA's privatization decisions, and it has systematically undermined parliamentary control of the SAA. Parliament is unwilling to impose detailed rules on the agency, and the agency is reluctant to invent itself.[33] Because the government has not filled this vacuum with detailed procedural rules, the SAA now operates essentially according to shifting and unclear government policies.

Throughout the reign of Communism, the legal system paid lip service to formal guarantees of private property. Although the Hungarian Constitution guaranteed private property (and even allowed for its limited acquisition) and the country's 1959 Civil Code expressed most of the key concepts of a market economy, such as freedom of contract, judges made excessive use of their power to interfere in market transactions. These judicial attitudes, which were formed under the communist system, are at the heart of current legal incompatibilities with a market system. Furthermore, current policies, which disguise the former state interest as "public interest," promote dependence on the state and the party in power, not individual autonomy more suited to a market economy. These characteristics of the new system undermine the hope of establishing a system based on the rule of law, which can only impede the progress of privatization. The success of privatization depends to a great extent on the confidence of private investors and legal predictability that the rule of law confers.

Hungarian judicial attitudes are ill suited to a market economy, rooted as they are in the socialist tradition of the primacy of public interest. Although the corporate law devised in the last year of socialism granted companies considerable autonomy from judicial interference, Hungarian judges received their legal training under a command economy (and we can rule out any chance that they will be replaced in the near future). In the law of contracts, for example, judges have little understanding or desire to protect either reliance or expectancy interests, and they sometimes balk at awarding monetary damages. The former judicial ideology of favoring state interests is now expressed as the "public interest," a term judges now invoke to legitimate government legal powers and regulatory intervention, and to discourage state-owned companies from going into bankruptcy or incurring financial losses, because they regard such losses, at least to an extent, as a loss in national wealth.[34] Courts sometimes use formalistic arguments to invalidate privatization deals, in order to protect government interests.

With the lack of clear administrative procedures or a clear separation of powers, legal uncertainty, once common under socialism, is reemerging, despite the state's commitment to the rule of law.[35] This may have seriously impaired privatization.[36] The present form of privatization is instrumental in creating the social basis of the emerging legal system. A system based on the rule of law presupposes that many individuals will not be dependent on the government. The present form of privatization does not promote such autonomy in society. Instead, Hungarian privatization has adopted old traditions of dependency on personal relationships, fostering networks of personal loyalties to political power-holders. The success of Western investors may even depend on their assumed loyalties, and the intentions and policies of the government at any given moment (for instance, government contracts, energy prices, and so on). In respect to the uses of government property, the Constitutional Court has ruled that government has discretion so long as the use does not arbitrarily discriminate against protected private rights. This reasoning gives leaders *carte blanche* to use privatization as a legal and political tool for maintaining society's dependence on the state, and on the small party currently in power.[37] Fortunately, because political conflicts are extremely legalistic, a number of the Constitutional Court's decisions (primarily regarding reprivatization) have strengthened the emerging system's sense of legalism, albeit somewhat superficially.

The present government is simply unable to reward loyalty with the same massive subsidies the Communists provided their supporters. Consequently, the loyalties of private owners extend only so far as their business interests will allow them, often bitterly disappointing leaders in government.

Lack of clear privatization rules not only undermines the willingness of people to trust or participate in the privatization process, but also furthers the public's disrespect for the law. Noncompliance with the law was an accepted social rule under Communism. Meeting a targeted goal, conducting business, or simply surviving often forced one to cheat around the letter of the law, or ignore the law entirely. The present system also encourages these tendencies. Because official privatization is slanted to maintain state control, illegal or "nonlegal" forms of privatization now occur outside the loose legal structures. The private sector enters into dubious contracts for state-owned companies, and for needed television equipment, research institutes, and public schoolrooms. The problem with "nonlegal" privatization is that the private sector is able to avoid paying taxes, social benefits, and spending money on things such as worker safety requirements.[38] Between December 1991 and March 1992, thirteen thousand limited liability companies were registered.

In a meaningful sociological sense, it is difficult to find a Western legal system which resembles the emerging Hungarian legal order.[39] Without a history of bargaining and cooperation, trust and negotiation are difficult. Social actors become conflict-oriented; contracts are often broken. Because the state plays a prominent role in society, one might be inclined to discuss the phenomena of privatization in terms of a welfare system. After all, the transformation of citizens' rights, and restrictions on clear (traditional, profit-maximizing, unlimited) property rights are characteristics of the welfare state.[40] And in some ways, privatization in postcommunist countries can actually expand the state's role into parts of society where before the state's influence was not felt. One cannot deny that, even in a successful private economy, there exist "intricate tangles of contractual arrangements"[41] between government agencies, local authorities, and private players, but in the postcommunist societies the state's role is determinative, not just supportive. Instead of enriching autonomous private parties, privatization in Hungary has made private parties more dependent upon the state.

However, bankrupt postcommunist governments have only superficial similarities to the welfare state. Substantively, they do not function as social welfare states. The postcommunist state seeks ways of curtailing welfare services instead of expanding them, depriving employees of benefits, extending working hours, and raising the age of retirement.[42] Ironically, the collapsed socialist welfare state has been replaced by a government with a functional and politico-cultural interest in maintaining the status quo of welfarism. The inherent contradictions of state-controlled privatization suggest that widespread unofficial laws adequately serve large groups and maintain important aspects of social life. However, this development of privatization is dysfunctional as law. The lack of a properly functioning legal system (and its colonization by other spheres of life) seriously threatens national goals of becoming a partner in international trade and encouraging foreign investment. European investors, for example, demand a predictable, formal legal structure. Hungary is a deeply divided society in transition, in which inherited, premodern, social structures may ultimately dominate formal law and other modern and postmodern institutions, harming most of those who must seek out their lives within those unwritten real or imagined structures.

A Tentative Conclusion

It is too early to evaluate the ultimate success or failure of privatization policies in Hungary, but the policies and practices so far contain a great deal of bad news, tempered with a small amount of good news. The bad news is that privatization is hampered by the uncertainties and constant changes of laws and practices which bear much in common with the late stages of socialism, both in the regulation of privatization itself, and the outcome it produces. Under Communism in Hungary, political concerns dominated economic policies, and today politics continues to overwhelm the state sector, and even the emerging para-private sector.[43] In this respect, socialism survives not only in the power of the previous elite,[44] but in the continuation of Hungarian socialist economic institutions. The good news is that it is too early to call the situation immutable.

Notes

1. András Sajó, "New Legalism in East Central Europe: Law as an Instrument of Social Transformation," *Journal of Law and Society* 17:329 (1990); András

Sajó, "The Struggle for Ownership Control: The New Content of State Ownership Forms in Eastern Europe," *International Journal of the Sociology of Law* 18:4 (1990).

2. The future of the Czech and Slovakian policies is unclear at this writing.
3. Rodica Seward, Steven Glick, and Jean-Yves Martin, "Romania Pursues Its Own Road To The Market Economy," *Financial Times* (October 17, 1991) p. 3.
4. Vouchers were distributed as part of the government compensation plan to former owners of property. The compensation vouchers, which represent a fraction of the nationalized property, can be used in public bids to purchase shares. There is no secondary market for these vouchers, as the government failed to proceed by public bids or auctions (there was only one company designated for this process in six months, and even that company was not an attractive investment opportunity).
5. This is not to deny that privatization in Eastern Europe serves a number of different official purposes and social functions. Privatization will have different social consequences in the different countries of the region.
6. András Sajó, "Diffuse Rights in Search of an Agent," *International Review of Law and Economics* 10:41 (June 1990).
7. See Section II, infra.
8. Act VII of 1990, törvény az Állami Vagyonügynökségröl és a hozzá tartozó vagyon keseléséröl és haznosításáról [Act VII of 1990 on the State Assets Agency and on the Assets Managed and Utilized by It], 3 *Hatályos Jogszabályok Gyüjteménye* 122, 143 (1990) (enacted as part of the implementation process of the 1989, amended in Act LIII of 1990); évi XIII, törvény a gazdálkodó szervezetek és a gazdasági társaságok átalakulásáról [Act XIII of 1989 on the Transformation of Economic (Business) Organizations and Economic Companies], id. at 8 (Amendments: 1990. XVIII. törvény a gazdálkodó szervezetek és gazdasági társaságok átalakulásáról szóló 1989); évi XIII, törvény módosításáról [On the Amendment of Act XIII of 1989 on the Transformation of Economic (Business) Organizations and Economic Companies], Id. at 170 évi LXXII, LXXXVI; törvény a tisztességtelen piaci magatartás tilalmáról [Act LXXXVI of 1990 on the Prohibition of Unfair Market Behavior], 3 *Hatályos Jogzabályok Gyüjteménye* 180 (1991); évi XVI, törvény Koncesszíoról [Act XVI of 1991 on Concessions], 3 Hatályos Jogszabályok Gyüjtemenye 318, and 1991. évi XXXIII. törvény egyes állami tulajdonban lévö vagyontárgyak önkormányzatok tulajdonába adásáról [Act XXXIII of 1991 on Transferring Property of Certain State Owned Objects to the Ownership of Local Self-Governments], Id. at 405; évi VIII, törvény az állam vállalatokra bízott vagyonának védelméröl [Act VIII of 1990 on the Protection of State Assets Entrusted to Enterprises], 3 *Hátályos Jogzabályok Gyüjteménye* 126 (1990) (this Act, amended in 1990, granted more extensive powers to the agency); évi LXXI, törvény az állami vállalatokra vonatkozo egyes jogszbályok módosításáról [Act LXXI of 1990 on Amendment of Certain Rules Concerning State Owned Enterprises], Id. at 170. State owned enterprises are governed by az állami

vállalatokról szóló 1977, évi VI, torveny [Act VI of 1977 on State Owned Enterprises], 2 *Hatályos Jogzabályok Gyüjteménye* 234. The transformation of state-owned enterprises into legal entities was established in 1988, évi VI, törvény a gazdasági társaságokról [Act VI of 1988 on Economic (Business) Associations].

9. A "trust" is a conglomerate of enterprises which exist as separate legal entities; the government (Council of Ministers) administers the rights of the founding organization.

10. Often translated as the "State Property Agency."

11. Initially, Parliament wished to appoint the SAA's board of directors, but in one of the first acts passed in the freely elected Parliament the Prime Minister retained this power. See Act LIII of 1990, supra note 8. Parliament raised no serious objections to this curtailment of its power.

12. See Act LXXII of 1990, supra note 8. This was the reason officially stated in the justification submitted with the Draft to Parliament.

13. A new privatization package was passed in the summer of 1992. The new law requires the SAA's consent for all transactions exceeding $250,000. Art. 20 of 1990: LIV tv. Az idölegesen állami tulajdonban levö vagyon értékesitéseröl, hasznositásáról és védelméröl (Act LIV of 1992 On Marketing, Utilizing and Protecting Assets in Temporary State Ownership), Magyar Közlöny, July 28, 1992. The Cabinet now determines which assets will remain state owned. Property thus designated is to be managed by a State Property Management Stock Corporation. Art 2, 1992: LIII. tv. A tartósan állami tulajdonban maradó vállalkozói vagyon kezeléséröl és hasznositásáról (Act LIII of 1992 On the Management and Utilization of Entrepreneurial Assets Remaining Permanently in State Ownership), Magyar Közlöny, July 28, 1992.

14. Art. 21, Act XIII of 1989.

15. For a review of privatization in the energy sector, see Richard O'Neill and Ashley Brown, "Privatization and Regulation of the Oil, Natural Gas, and Electric Industries in Hungary," *Energy Law Journal* 13:25 (1992).

16. Act LXXIV of 1990, supra note 8.

17. It is interesting to note that, given the notorious problem of contamination at underground storage tanks at gas stations, the SAA has directly assumed the environmental liabilities of gas corporations.

18. *Magyar Nemiet,* (August 10, 1992).

19. 1991 évi LXIX, törvény a pénzintézetekröl és a pénzintézeti tevékenységröl [Act LXIX of 1991 on the Activities of Financial Institutes], *Hatalyos Jogszabályok Gyüjteménye* vol. 3 (1991) p. 562.

20. Corporations that remain state-owned (with shares managed by the SAA) are governed by the general rules of bankruptcy and liquidation.

21. 1990, évi V, törvény az egyéni vállalkozásról (Act V of 1990 on individual entrepreneurship), *Hatályos Jogszabályok Gyüjteménye* vol. 3 (1990) p. 103.

22. The committee also submitted the drafts to existing public universities for comment.

23. On the other hand, municipalities, which for the most part the central government does not control, must provide buildings for vocational schools.

24. The government's *de facto* monopoly of the public media spurred several constitutional crises when the President of the Republic, instead of signing different government proposals, "defended" the opposition's views of freedom of the press by refusing to appoint deputy directors to the public broadcasting system, and refusing to fire the directors of the public radio and television systems. The Prime Minister successfully challenged the President's authority in the Constitutional Court, which issued a ruling restricting the President's powers. Judgment of June 10, 1992, Constitutional Court, 36/1992 (v. 10) AB h. (1992) [*Magyar Közlöny* (June 10, 1992) p. 2025].

25. The Office of Fair Competition successfully resisted attempts in 1989 to confer it with the power and obligation to dismantle government monopolies.

26. For a case study discussing investors' difficulties, see Martin S. Thaler, "The Privatization of Petofi Printing House: Joint Ventures and Other Financing Techniques in Poland, Hungary, Czechoslovakia, and Romania," *Practicing Law Institute* vol. 613 (1992).

27. Since 1991, however, the government has emphasized the need to maintain state ownership of industries of "strategic importance."

28. See discussion, Section III, infra.

29. This accounts for restrictions on the sale of mass media and real estate to foreigners.

30. For example, in 1990 the newly appointed director of the state-owned record company announced that he would produce records of previously unpopular composers and artists who represented "national ideals of music." However, the company has met with increasing financial difficulties in the last two years.

31. Sonda-Ipsos, *Neti Vildygazdeság* (March 26, 1992) p. 81.

32. Government-controlled contractors advertise only in progovernment newspapers. The results of any bidding, even when bidding exists, are not publicly disclosed.

33. Parliamentarians and administrators share the belief that parliamentary acts should set regulatory policy and leave details to administrators, who will put regulations into practice. Legislators consider new laws, particularly those regarding economic activities, part of an emerging framework.

34. On the other hand, to the Hungarian judiciary's credit, the courts found that the government-owned airline, Malev, liable for breach of contract with a major contractor, Pratt & Whitney. Jonathon Moses and Junda Woo, " 'Blacklist' Shield in Salomon Lawsuits," *Wall Street Journal* (May 7, 1992) p. B5.

35. For problems of uncertainty related to environmental laws, see *The New York Times* (May 13, 1992) pp. 1, 13.

36. As O'Neill and Brown point out, "It is very important that the rules of the transition of the government from owner to regulator be well planned and have a high degree of certainty. . . . [t]he multiple roles of government remain a problem. The government is simultaneously owner, regulator, and guardian of national security. These roles all pull it in different directions and threaten to lead to muddle." Supra note 15, p. 42.

37. The ruling Hungarian Democratic Forum (MDF) party has fewer than thirty thousand card carrying members, as opposed to the Communist regime, which boasted eight hundred thousand party members in a country of ten million inhabitants.

38. Shell corporations are also used to avoid the consequences of very arbitrary alien laws. For example, Chinese are subject to deportation, but executives of registered companies are exempt from this law. Chinese refugees use a small capital for registration purposes, then pass the money to newcomers, who set up their own companies in order to avoid deportation.

39. In a formal sense, the Hungarian legal system is very close to the German.

40. Vilhelm Aubert, "The Rule of Law and the Promotional Function of Law in the Welfare State," *Dilemmas of Law in The Welfare State,* ed. Gunther Teubner (New York: de Gruyter, 1986) pp. 32, 33: "It is customary to define the welfare state by reference to certain rights of the citizen and by the states' ability to meet the claims which flow from these rights. . . . [A]ll welfare states share the characteristic that the government disposes of a very large share of the wealth of the nation, possibly close to half of the national product. . . . The government is distributing much more wealth, in absolute as well as in relative terms, than it did in the period of the *Rechtsstaat.* Some of this power to distribute is used to reward, and the withholding of resources from people who feel that they have a claim may be subjectively experienced as a punishment."

41. Ibid.

42. Interestingly, similar events are presently occurring in Western welfare states such as Sweden, and privatization efforts in Great Britain and the U.S. have similarly sought to reign in welfare services.

43. By "para-private sector," I mean formally privatized companies and sectors in the economy where the government and its bureaucracies exert more or less direct control.

44. This power still exists, but is exercised in a very different manner from in the past, and shared with the new emerging political forces.

PRIVATIZATION AS A GENDER ISSUE

Joan C. Williams

[*Editors' Synopsis:* Under state socialism, many parental benefits, such as child care, were provided by the state, with substantial state subsidies. One of the consequences of privatization in the new democracies has been elimination of these benefits. Professor Williams argues that the effect of shifting the cost of familial benefits from the state to the individual is gender-specific. Wholesale privatization of this sector of the economy seriously risks leaving women and children as disproportionately impoverished in East-Central Europe as they are in the United States. This gender difference has long been apparent in the U.S. and is becoming so in postcommunist Europe as well.]

> Women consistently proved the most politically conservative and change-resistant group in every nation in Eastern Europe and in the Soviet Union surveyed in a Times Mirror poll. . . . Women profess consistently less democratic values and appear to have absorbed more socialist thinking than have men. . . . The reasons for women's conservatism are elusive: The researchers speculate that it may rise from the extreme difficulties of women's daily life, or [from] their role as nurturers.[1]

Privatization has not often been analyzed as a gender issue.[2] This quote suggests it is one. Why are women as a group more apprehensive than men about the value of "liberty" and economic "freedom" in East-Central Europe? An answer to this question requires not only more information about East-Central Europe; it can also be informed by an understanding of the interaction between gender and privatization in the United States. In this essay, I begin that process.

In the United States, as in other industrialized countries, employers assume an ideal worker without child care (or other caretaking)[3] responsibilities.[4] And yet, of course, children have daily, and very time-consuming, needs. This creates a conflict between work and family—not for fathers, who generally are free to perform as ideal workers to the extent that class, race, and personality constraints allow them to do so—but for mothers.[5] In the East-Central European countries under Communism, the costs of childrearing were socialized to a significant extent, through subsidized child care, paid childrearing leaves of up to three years, and a range of other family benefits.[6] These programs buffered the individual mother, to some extent, from the full marginalizing impact of the conflict between work and family.[7]

In sharp contrast, the U.S. provides few buffers against marginalized motherhood, in part because of the national reluctance to socialize "welfare" costs for activities conceived of as inherently private.[8] The individual mother trying to perform both as an ideal worker and an ideal mother typically has no guarantee of reinstatement after childbirth,[9] no leave to allow her to care for a sick or very young child, no access to subsidized child care.[10] She is left, in fact, with fewer social supports than in virtually any other industrialized nation.[11]

In short, work and caregiving are structured to be incompatible; the costs of childrearing are then privatized onto U.S. women and the children dependent upon them. As the new democracies of East-Central Europe privatize, they appear to be following this pattern. Day-care centers are being shut down at a dizzying rate;[12] childrearing leaves and other parental benefits are being rapidly eliminated.[13] In this context, the new democracies need to focus on a striking characteristic of privatization, U.S. style: roughly 20% of all U.S. children,[14] and fully half of African-American children[15] live in poverty. Women in East-Central Europe have begun to experience the forces that produce these statistics[16]: their uneasiness about the march to Western-style democracy is "elusive" only to the extent the gender dimension of privatization remains invisible.

This essay is designed to challenge that invisibility. It begins with a brief description of the extent to which women's domestic burdens were socialized in the formerly communist countries, and a brief exploration of the gender dynamics of privatization in those countries. It then explores U.S. women's experience in ways that may offer guidance for the process of privatization in Europe. The first step is to understand how the current sex/gender system in the U.S. privatizes childrearing costs onto women. One way it does so is by refusing to socialize any significant part of those costs; another is by defining human capital—the chief form of family property in the U.S.[17]—as the personal property of the husband. When the family unit is intact, this definition of property rights presents some problems,[18] but these problems magnify considerably upon divorce. As the new democracies shift the costs of childrearing from the state back to the family, they should decide who should own the family wage as a fundamental issue of social entitlements, rather than leaving the issue to be decided in the divorce courts.

I. Socializing Mothers' Burdens

Progress toward gender equality under Communism generally involved socializing mothers' burdens. One can explain why by comparing conditions in Europe with those in the U.S. The strong ideology of gender equality in the U.S. has largely removed the stigma from male contributions to household work, at least among the professional middle class.[19] Sociologist Arlie Hochschild describes Seth, a successful lawyer: "If he'd had the time, he could have done the laundry or sewing without a bit of shame."[20] Of course, he in fact did little child care and less housework[21]; yet the sense that men are "just about to begin" sharing in domestic work pervades the U.S. scene.

In East-Central Europe, by contrast, male contributions to domestic work are often perceived as demeaning to the manliness of the male,[22] if not to the womanliness of the female as well.[23] And yet many formerly communist countries needed women workers and remained committed to a formal ideology of equality.[24] The obvious solution was to socialize childrearing costs, rather than changing the gendered allocation of work within the family. Individual countries differed substantially in the extent to which such costs were socialized,[25] and individual women still performed virtually all of the shopping, cooking, and housework.[26] But, women often received subsidies and time off to perform "their" duties, and were supported by subsidized child care as well.

The most dramatic illustration is the former German Democratic Republic (GDR). In the GDR, about ninety-two percent of working-age women worked outside the home, supported by what one knowledgeable commentator has called "an exemplary program of maternal and child-care support"[27] that included maternity leave with guaranteed reemployment, sick leave, paid time off for child care and housework, mandatory affirmative action plans, enforcement of equal pay for equal work, and a consistent propaganda effort that encouraged gender integration of the skilled trades and professions.[28] When Germany was unified in 1990, many of these programs were cancelled.[29]

Reports from other East-Central European countries appear to confirm this picture. The Commonwealth of Independent States (C.I.S.) offers one example. The Soviet Union never offered as substantial a support system as did the GDR, but the once-elaborate system of child care is being dismantled.[30] Moreover, in Russia and elsewhere, traditional restrictions on women are emerging in full force. News media contain many reports of employers refusing to hire younger women on the grounds that their maternal responsibilities make them unreliable workers.[31] Proposed legislation in Russia bars women from the most desirable jobs by banning mothers of children under fourteen from working more than a limited number of hours per week.[32] Moreover, women in East-Central Europe are being brought face to face with the fact that "free expression" in a patriarchal society often means sexual exploitation. For example, in Moscow an advertising firm recently asked applicants for a receptionist position to submit a full-sized photo, preferably in a bikini, to display their "full super-attractiveness"; applicants for a secretarial position in a new brokerage house were told to come to the interview in a miniskirt.[33] In this atmosphere, age discrimination against women is flourishing: many employers (in addition to refusing to hire women of childbearing age) refuse to hire women over forty because they are too old.[34] Finally, the collapse of distribution systems in Russia has a gender dimension. Shopping for food and clothing are normally the responsibility of women, who must spend many hours in lines that grow longer as supplies become more scarce.[35]

Russian women's lives show them the links between economic vulnerability and privatization. In Moscow, over seventy percent of the newly unemployed are women between the ages of forty-five and fifty-five; the overwhelming number of peddlers are older women and young mothers.[36] In other countries, as well, women are swelling the ranks of the unemployed in record numbers.[37] In this context, the question is not why women favor privatization less than men, but why newspaper reporters consider the reasons for their disfavor "elusive."

As the new democracies privatize, the remainder of this essay will argue, they can learn from the example of the United States. Perhaps the most important lesson is an obvious one: that in societies where socialism is taboo, programs that socialize childrearing costs are difficult to achieve. The U.S. lags far behind most other industrialized countries in maternity benefits, parental leaves, and child care.[38] These data have ominous implications for women living in East-Central European societies in which men often contribute little to domestic work.

In the United States, the traditional feminist focus is not the allocation of childrearing costs between women and the state, but rather the allocation between men and women. In this sense, Western feminism is structured by the privatized society from which it emerged in ways American feminists have rarely recognized. Perhaps feminism in the new democracies should be more focused on the socialization of childrearing costs; though the contraction of the public sphere and the fervor against socialism may be such that this formulation will prove as doomed in East-Central Europe as it has been in the U.S.[39]

But if American feminists can gain insights into Western feminism from the experience of East-Central European women,[40] the new democracies can learn from the experience of American women as well. One would assume that the new democracies would not include among their goals a society in which one in five of their children live in poverty. If this assumption is true, they need to understand the forces that make children the poorest group in the U.S.[41]

II. Gender, Poverty, and Private Property in the U.S.

Data indicate that the property system in the U.S. enriches men at the expense of women and children. Most dramatic are the shockingly high levels of childhood poverty, which contrast sharply with the comparatively low childhood poverty statistics of other industrialized nations.[42] The links between childhood poverty and gender emerge in sharp relief with the figure that three-fourths of children in female-headed households will experience childhood poverty.[43] Children are poor in significant part because they are dependent upon women, who themselves experience disproportionate poverty. Sixty percent of all people in poverty are women;[44] two-thirds of the elderly poor are women.[45] Much more dramatic are the poverty levels of women who lack a family claim on resources owned by men. Female-headed households are five times more likely to be poor[46] and up to ten times more likely to stay poor than are households with a male present.[47] Rising rates of female and childhood poverty reflect the fact that woman-headed households are increasing; nineteen percent of all families and fully fifty percent of African-American families are headed by women.[48]

Particularly given the very high rates of single motherhood and the rising divorce rates in East-Central European countries,[49] these statistics should give pause to the architects of privatization in the new democracies. It is worth understanding how these poverty rates emerge from the current gendered property system in the United States. To do so requires a rewriting of U.S. legal history, for the accepted wisdom is that the property system *used* to block women from property ownership, but that the problem was solved in the mid-nineteenth-century. In fact, the contemporary statistics on the impoverishment of women and children suggest that the property system continues to block disproportionate numbers of U.S. women from property ownership to this day. But it has done so in different ways at different periods, as the following description shows.

At common law, women's legal status was governed by the law of "coverture." To quote William Blackstone, "the husband and the wife are one person in law, that is, the very being or legal existence of woman is suspended during marriage."[50] Coverture was the legal expression of the view that women were intellectually and spiritually weaker than men, and in need of their guidance.[51]

The common law gave husbands extensive authority over the property of their wives. Wives' personal property was fully owned by the husband.[52] Husbands also were entitled to possession, use, and income from wives' real estate; their interest could be mortgaged by the husband and seized by his creditors.[53] In unsettled economic times, wives' property often was seized for husbands' debts.[54] One commentator summarized coverture as follows: Although a man was morally obligated to cherish and support his wife, the common law permitted him to squander her property with impunity, to deprive her at will of creature comforts, and if she complained to "chastise her roundly"[55] (but with a stick no thicker than his thumb).[56]

The accepted wisdom[57] is that the mid-nineteenth-century Married Women's Property Acts ended women's blocked access to property by abolishing coverture in favor of a more enlightened embrace of equality for women.[58] Recent work has substantially undermined this interpretation. Many Married Women's Property Acts, passed simultaneously with other debtor relief statutes, were designed not to achieve gender equality but to protect family property from husbands' creditors in uncertain economic times.[59] Equality for women was not an invariable, or perhaps even a frequent, goal or effect of Married Women's Property Acts.[60] Instead, supporters called upon imagery drawn from the ideology of domesticity, the ideology that allocated market activities to men, while women were allocated the newly isolated "separate sphere" of domesticity, to which they were uniquely suited by their natural bent towards nurture and self-sacrifice. Supporters of the Married Women's Property Acts called on imagery of virtuous wives victimized by unscrupulous, fortune-seeking husbands,[61] and often focused on mothers' need for control over property so they could protect and nurture in the domestic sphere.[62]

Once Married Women's Property Acts are viewed as expressions more of domesticity than of equality, it also becomes easier to explain their slow progress in granting women anything approaching full relief from the strictures of coverture.[63] Many of the acts only allowed women to control property they brought into marriages, not the right to contract or to their wages.[64] In Georgia, for example, wives gained ownership of their wages only in 1943.[65]

This revisionist interpretation of the Married Women's Property Acts generally only defers, for a period, the triumphal vision of equality for women. If equality was in fact achieved, how do we explain the contemporary impoverishment of U.S. women?

This impoverishment is rarely recognized for what it is: an integral part of the sex/gender system that has succeeded domesticity. The most overt characteristic of this system is the shift from domestic ideology to the ideology of gender equality. This shift was accompanied by key changes in the institution of marriage. Whereas marriage traditionally involved an irreversible commitment, as emotional gratification and personal fulfillment "became the *sine qua non* of marriage, divorce became an indispensable element in the institution of matrimony."[66] The divorce rate in the U.S. skyrocketed: only eight percent of marriages ended in divorce in 1870; today nearly fifty percent do.[67]

The divorce rate and the ideology of gender equality are widely recognized as important phenomena; less well understood is that they are integral parts of a larger family ecology. A central tension in that ecology is the coexistence of the ideology of equality with sharply differentiated gender patterns within marriage. In the contemporary United States, wives ordinarily subordinate their careers to their husbands', even in the absence of children—perhaps the single most continuous aspect of wives' traditional subordinate status.[68] Moreover, once children are born, wives do eighty percent[69] of the housework and a highly disproportionate share of the child care: one study estimated that fathers spend an average of only twelve minutes a day on solo child care.[70] Fathers' lack of family contributions means that employed mothers bear a "double burden" of market and domestic labor, which translates into less sleep,[71] less leisure,[72] less time at meals,[73] and much longer hours than either their husbands[74] or traditional housewives.[75] Wives' "second shift" combines with sex discrimination, sex segregation, and the pattern of subordinated careers to bar women disproportionately from desirable jobs: the result is that labor market participation differs dramatically between men and women. Fully forty percent of mothers with children under six do not work outside the home;[76] roughly one third of women who do, usually work part-time.[77]

The contemporary sex/gender system, therefore, combines three basic elements: the ideology of equality, sharply differentiated gender patterns within marriage, and marital instability. The key gender shift between the domesticity/wage labor gender system and the contemporary system is *not*—as is often believed—a shift from dependent to independent wives. Instead, the key shift is from wives totally cut off from market resources to wives who are secondary workers with careers subordinated to both their husbands' and their children's (socially constructed) needs.[78] Wives' "double burden" means that men's market participation is relatively unaffected by fatherhood: men of all classes feel they should be entitled to perform as ideal workers to the extent they choose to do so.

The final element of the contemporary sex-gender system is the least well-recognized of all: a shift in the nature of wealth. In an insightful article, John Langbein has documented a key shift in the nature of wealth in the twentieth century.[79] Whereas, as of the beginning of the nineteenth century, wealth was held primarily in the form of real estate, by the end of the twentieth century one primary form of wealth was human capital.[80] Langbein notes that, although traditionally:

> wealth transmission from parents to children tended to center upon major items of patrimony such as the family farm or the family firm, today for the broad middle classes, wealth transmission centers on a radically different kind of asset: *the investment in skills*.[81]

During the period when physical assets were the key to economic power, women were barred from ownership and control. Now that women can own physical assets, such assets no longer constitute the crucial component of economic power. In most families, human capital is the major form of family wealth.[82] Just how unimportant physical assets have become is suggested by data on divorcing couples. Study after study has documented that most divorcing couples own little or no property apart from household possessions. In 1956, a study of divorcing families in Detroit found that forty percent owned no property beyond household posssessions, and only eighteen percent had property worth more than $4000;[83] a 1978 study of California found that fewer than half of divorcing couples had any major assets such as a house, business, or pension, and the median family could earn the median amount of assets in merely six months;[84] a 1991 study of New York found that even relatively wealthy families had accumulated wealth worth less than a year's family income.[85]

Family law scholars have long recognized that the primary asset of most American families is not physical property but the human capital of individual family members.[86] Langbein's focus on intergenerational transfers means he misses the single most important mechanism for family wealth transmission: the gender roles that systematically diminish wives' and enhance husbands' human capital.

Feminists have long noted that marriage hurts women's and helps men's careers.[87] The key mechanism here is men's sense of entitlement to performing as a "responsible worker," related to the linkage of virility to employability.[88] Because the "ideal" worker is one without daytime child care responsibilities, even men who believe in gender equality end up tapping a flow of domestic services from their wives: that they have to, in order to meet their employees' expectations— and their own.

Although men of all classes feel entitled to be ideal workers,[89] significant class differences emerge in the mechanisms of disinvestment in women. In the middle and upper classes, where the ideology of gender equality is strong, gender is less likely to determine career choice. Instead, disinvestment occurs within marriage. After the birth of children, the wife becomes "more realistic" and "chooses" career marginalization so that her children can receive care according to middle-class standards without affecting her husband's ability to perform as an ideal worker: the chief mechanism of disinvestment is the "mommy track."[90] Among the working class, where the ideology of gender equality has less strong a hold, and rigorous sex segregation of the work force persists, the chief mechanism of disinvestment is job "choice."[91]

Together, these two mechanisms are remarkably effective in concentrating human capital ownership in men. Yet women, upon divorce, remain responsible not only for the care, but for the lion's share of the financial support of children.[92] Studies document that treating fathers' human capital as their personal property not only impoverishes women, but also results in systematic disinvestment in children.[93] Children of divorce, as compared to children in intact families, are less likely to equal or surpass their parents' social and economic status, or obtain a college education.[94] One study found that well over half of divorced parents' children were downwardly mobile: they were less likely to go to college, more likely to drop out of college because of financial difficulties, and only about half as likely to enter professions, as their fathers.[95] Thus the legal rules defining fathers' human capital as their personal property cuts off not only women, but also children, from human capital accumulation.

To summarize: three systems of property law have been integral parts of three gender systems in different eras of American history. Coverture expressed the pre-nineteenth-century view that women's inferiority required their welfare (and their assets) to be entrusted to men. In the nineteenth century, the predominant thrust behind the Married Women's Property Acts was the view that men belonged in the competitive market sphere, while women needed enough—but no more— control over family property than was necessary to protect their separate, domestic sphere. Today, the ideology of equality ensures that women have the formal right to own property, but the law defines property in a way that excludes human capital—leaving women with disproportionately little property to own.

How much of this history is relevant to the new democracies of Eastern Europe and the former Soviet Union? Two basic continuities are the construction of wage labor in a way that creates a conflict between work life and caregiving, and the persistence of traditional gender patterns that allocate caregiving to women. These patterns set up the central dynamic in which adults who care for children (or the elderly, the sick, or anyone else) typically do so at the cost of economic marginalization. Assuming for the moment that the state stops socializing childrearing costs, the allocation of childrearing costs among men and women takes on a new importance, particularly after divorce, which is a key context in which women and children are cut off from fathers' human capital.[96] The issue of who owns the human capital of the principal wage earner involves fundamental questions about how to allocate entitlements. Yet in the U.S., this issue has never been addressed as a question involving the definition of property rights; instead, it arises only in divorce courts, framed as a clash between men's right to self-fulfillment and women's right to continued dependence. The following section examines how this formulation contributes to the impoverishment of women and children by framing mothers' claims to economic resources in ways that make them seem inherently unappealing and unconvincing.

III. Divorce Law

Coverture at least was open in debarring women from ownership of economic resources, and arguments for or against coverture rested on substantive reasons for allocating entitlements. By contrast, divorce courts are the chief mechanism for allocating entitlement to human capital, in a legal context that focuses not on the relative merits of different systems of entitlement, but on a particular marriage and a series of three boxes: child support, alimony, and property division. Both the boxes and the context disadvantage women in significant ways.

The divorce context means that mothers' claims to family resources are decided in the framework of a particular marital failure, where the key issue from the husband's viewpoint is whether his freedom is going to be significantly eroded by obligations to his former family.[97] This means that wives' claims to human capital are decided by courts and legislatures (predominantly male in the U.S., and even more so in East-Central Europe),[98] in a context in which husbands' and wives' interests sharply diverge. Moreover, husbands' interests are easy to frame in the language of liberty and personal self-fulfillment, which has always been strong in contemporary North America,[99] and which the fall of Communism has strengthened in Europe.

In sharp contrast, the wife making a claim on family resources has to contend with powerful societal messages about the undesirability of dependence. Americans' distrust of dependence,[100] fed by feminists,[101] dates back much earlier, to the association of dependence and corruption in the republican tradition.[102] Europeans' distrust of dependence presumably has been reinforced by their experience with Communism. While powerful rhetorics enhance husbands' position in the divorce cases, then, equally powerful rhetorics undermine the position of the wife.

In at least some East-Central European countries, divorced mothers received a stipend from the states.[103] This system presumably will end, and mothers will be left depending on the fathers of their children for resources, in a context where mothers almost invariably have custody, rarely make as much as men,[104] and receive no government help to finance child care. They will be left, in short, much in the circumstances that have combined to impoverish American women and their children upon divorce.

In this context, the postdivorce allocation of resources between mothers and fathers takes on pressing importance. The new democracies may well benefit from an understanding of the U.S. experience.[105] U.S. family law's three little boxes disadvantage women in many ways. An obvious one is that the key box for granting wives access to husbands' human capital is the dismal little box of alimony. Under the traditional fault system, alimony was awarded only in contexts where the husband had defaulted on his marital obligations. Nonetheless, it became associated with stereotypes traditionally used to control, discredit and disempower women. "Alimony drones" were (and continue to be) associated in the popular imagination with scheming, manipulative women cheating men out of their fruits of their hard work.[106] Alimony, in other words, is a concept rendered improbable by misogyny, yet we inherit it as the only family law box available in which to place wives' claims for access to the family wage.

Alimony's off-putting emotional tone means that it starts off as a disempowered concept. In fact, few women have ever been awarded alimony.[107] Moreover, alimony's image problem—combined, one suspects, with the self-interest of predominantly male legislatures—led legislatures to eviscerate alimony during the no-fault "divorce revolution." Common legislative changes restricted alimony to situations where the wife could not support herself[108] and, even then, to limited time periods for "rehabilitation"[109]—as if raising children were some unmentionable disease. The erosion of permanent alimony fundamentally changed property rights by eliminating wives' traditional entitlement to the family wage even for women who had been outside the labor market for decades. The elimination of alimony to women who could "support themselves" eliminated even temporary alimony for a majority of women in a system where the paradigm couple consisted of an idea-worker husband and a marginalized-worker wife.

The precariousness of women's claims to husbands' human capital within the framework of alimony is dramatized in the 1980 Indiana case of *In Re McManama*,[110] which involved a wife who had done all the housework as well as put her husband through law school. She had earned roughly fifteen thousand dollars to her husband's one thousand, two hundred and fifty dollars; they had exhausted six thousand dollars of joint savings as well.[111] When the trial court awarded a mere three thousand, six hundred dollars to the wife in hundred-dollar-a-month installments, its decision was overturned by the state Supreme Court.[112] The Supreme Court interpreted a statute allowing for "equitable" distribution of marital property to bar recovery for the wife. The trial court, it held, had really awarded *income* (alimony) to the wife, to which she was not entitled, because she could support herself.[113]

Again the disempowered family-law context: because the majority treats the case as a matter of statutory interpretation, it never even articulates reasons why the statutory term "property" should be interpreted to preclude human capital. Yet one may be able to guess some of its rationale from the *McManama* dissent, which responds to the argument (heard in conference?) that the husband's degree lack the characteristics of traditional, fully commodified property. The dissent stated:

> It is true that a professional degree lacks many of the attributes of tangible property. It does not have an exchange value on the open market, and since it is personal to the holder, it cannot be inherited, assigned, sold, transferred, or conveyed.[114]

The degree should be considered as property nonetheless, the dissent argued, citing the "new property" case *Arnett v. Kennedy*[115] to the effect that "[a] profession or job is frequently far more valuable than a house or bank account."[116]

The *McManama* dissent's citation of *Arnett* dramatizes, first, the lack of property-law language available even to sympathetic courts for arguing that human capital constitutes property. Charles Reich's focus, after all, in his analysis of the "new property,"[117] was on governmental benefits and "the troubled boundary between the state and the individual."[118] Contemporary courts should not—and after Langbein's article perhaps will not—have to turn to new property cases to explain the central role of human capital in family wealth.[119]

McManama also dramatizes the costs of framing claims to postdivorce income in family law's three-boxes-and-you're-out format. This rigid formalism allows courts to evade the fact that, by denying recovery for the wife, they are creating property rights for the husband. Note the circularity of the *McManama* court's argument: the wife has no property because the court holds she has no legally recognizable claim. Yet the only reason she has no legally recognizable claim is because the court holds she has no property.

Outside of family law's three-box approach, the fact that human capital does not fit the definition of traditional property rights could just as easily be mobilized to support an award to the wife as to the husband, on the grounds that human capital within the family has unique properties that make it unsuitable for the traditional on-off model of ownership. In the divorce context, however, the holding that the degree is "not property" cuts solely against the wife, because if the award does not fit the property box the only box left is the despised and eviscerated box of alimony. The three-box approach thus allows the court to evade the fact that the law degree is the husband's "sole, exclusive, and despotic" property only because it so holds: with a difference holding the court could avoid the despotism.

McManama also dramatizes a drawback of making wives' claims to human capital dependent upon judicial discretion in the highly charged war-of-the-sexes atmosphere of the divorce courtroom. Feminists have long recognized that discretion presents a severe problem in family law, but they need to be a lot more direct about why judicial discretion has proved so deterimental to women.[120] Not only are the overwhelming majority of judges men;[121] in the United States, they are successful members of a (legal) profession characterized by high investments in human capital, combined with long working hours fundamentally incompatible with childrearing.[122] Judges, therefore, are likely to be the direct beneficiaries of precisely those flows of domestic services they so consistently hold are "not property." This conclusion may well seem logical to them because judges also are likely to adhere to the ideology of gender equality,[123] and so to have substantial personal investment in the view that their success results not from a system of gender privilege within the family, but simply from "choices" different from their wives'.[124] It is a short step from many judges' personal experience to the view—which emerges clearly in divorce cases—that the integrity of wives would be insulted by an acknowledgement that they sacrificed so their husbands could be both a father and an ideal worker.

Even in the relatively rare instances in which judges are women, they are by definition successful women who are likely to fall into one of two groups. By far the larger one consists of women who never married, assuming we can generalize from the statistics that nearly two-thirds of executive women are childless.[125] The smaller group are women who have managed to build up their own human capital despite their participation in traditionally female roles. Both groups of women may well identify more with high-human-capital men than with mothers marginalized by motherhood.[126]

The entrenched assumptions of family law have affected not only divorce law, but also the proposals for its reform.[127] A brief commentary on these proposals may help suggest directions for East-Central Europe in its path to privatization.

At the most basic level, family law has influenced many commentators to translate the problem of postdivorce impoverishment into a call for a new theory for alimony.[128] This formulation greatly understates the importance of what is at issue. What's at stake is not merely a new rationale for an unattractive concept that has never helped most women. The issue instead is whether to stop allocating property rights in ways that cut most women and children off from the chief form of family wealth upon divorce.

Commentators' tight focus on alimony has also deflected attention from the ways alimony and child support work in concert to systematically exclude on-going family claims to fathers' human capital. The economic studies underlying child support guidelines rigorously preclude consideration of any needs beyond "current consumption." Thus, child support, calculated according to the guidelines, excludes the portion of mortgage payments allocated to repayment of principal, and children lose access to family savings that in two-parent families are used to cover such expenses as medical emergencies or college tuition.[129] The way the child-support system cuts children off from their fathers' ability to accumulate wealth is integral to any consideration of fathers' postdivorce obligations.[130]

Both in the U.S. and in East-Central Europe, post-divorce obligations need to be conceptualized, not solely as matters of divorce law, but as part of a broad inquiry about entitlements to family wealth. A potentially useful resource in framing that inquiry is the historical notion of the family wage. In the nineteenth century, men mobilized the ideology of domesticity—the notion that women "ought naturally" to be in the home—to support their claims to wages high enough to support a family.[131] While husbands made this argument to their employers, one suspects they less often made it to their wives. And yet the phrase did reflect popular notions of intrafamilial property ownership quite different from those prevalent today. Many husbands in working-class communities handed over their paychecks to their wives, and received in return only an allowance for their personal discretionary spending.[132] Postdivorce claims to income should be seen in this light. Recent scholars, obsessed with fault or its absence, sometimes lose sight of the fact that traditional alimony expressed a different notion of family entitlement from what exists today. The underlying message was that wives had a permanent entitlement to the family wage.[133] The question is how to return to that prior understanding.

A threshold issue is whether the "family wage" concept is applicable in contemporary life, given the truism that today wives as well as husbands work. The description of family ecology offered above is helpful in this context. The family ecology in the U.S. is one in which wives marginalize their market participation so their children can have parental care while their husbands perform as ideal workers, earning the bulk of the family income.[134] The same gender system may well emerge if childrearing costs are privatized back onto women in the formerly communist countries.

This description allows us to reframe the basic unfairness of the current system: at divorce, the family wage is abruptly redefined as the personal property of the husband. This process strikes not only divorced women[135] and their children,[136] but also an extraordinary range of political forces in the U.S. as outrageous.[137] The question is how to design political rhetoric to tap that sense of outrage; the answer may have important implications for East-Central Europe.

U.S. commentators are sharply divided. Those scholars exploring new rationales for alimony, virtually without exception, assume the undesirability of a standard based on need.[138] Their sharp dismissal of need—the current test for alimony[139]—stands in sharp contrast to the work of others, who have argued that family law should abandon its current fixation on equality, and focus instead on a standard of property division based on womens' needs.[140] At first glance, a focus on divorced women's needs seems not only unobjectionable, but highly desirable. Who could object to a system designed to meet women's needs? Yet the issue is not whether women's needs should be met, but whether arguments framed in terms of need are the best way to accomplish that goal. Past experience suggests they are not. Although need has always been the traditional standard, alimony (as I have noted) never has been awarded to more than a small minority of women[141]—despite the fact that divorce typically has left women in need. Moreover, a recent study of property division statutes found judges reluctant to base property allocations on need, even where statutes explicitly authorized them to do so.[142] Judges instead had a strong tendency to allocate property in "equal" shares.[143] Even where judges awarded the wife, as the economically weaker spouse, a greater than "equal" share of the property, they tended to rationalize their decision not on grounds of need, but on the grounds of her greater contribution.[144]

Why is "needs" rhetoric so unappealing? The answer emerges in clear relief if we consider divorce law in the context of the larger realm of political discourse in the U.S. To return to the property division study, note how judges were attracted to the idea of equality. In fact, of course, the "equal" division they effected was not truly equal.[145] But that is not the point. The point is that judges are strongly attracted to the notion of "equal" treatment—thereby making it a powerful framework in which to articulate family claims to the family wage. United States legal historians have documented that "rights talk" is a key resource for articulating moral claims in legal language.[146] This is not to say that rights talk always works; only that it frames moral claims in the way most easily heard in the United States.

People in the United States—and perhaps increasingly in East-Central Europe as well—are more receptive to arguments based on claims of *entitlement* than to claims based on *need.* "From each according to his ability, to each according to his need"[147]: if any principle is discredited in the U.S., this is it.[148] To say "you must give women postdivorce income because they need it" sounds less like demanding justice than like asking for charity in a peculiarly unpersuasive tone of voice.

The question is how all this will play out in the postcommunist countries. Will the abandonment of state socialism make it difficult for women to articulate their claims to the family wage in terms of needs? If so, what alternatives do women have? This question can only be answered in the context of a background knowledge of political discourse in each country.

A final comment can be brief. Sociological data document a number of assumptions underlying judges' tendency to allocate the family wage lopsidedly to the father,[149] and commentators have been effective in challenging most of these assumptions.[150] They have been less forceful in responding to judges' often unarticulated belief that the husband needs "his" salary because he will remarry and support a second family.[151]

This needs to be challenged head on: why *should* husbands have that right? Despite the underlying ideology that all adults are entitled to pursue self-expression,[152] the idea that a *mother* should be entitled to ignore her existing children's emotional and financial needs because she wants to remarry and have new children strikes one as bizarre. Mothers always have had children for life.[153] If that restricts their life options—indeed, if it drives them into poverty—so be it: into poverty they go.

Fathers' relationship to children should be similarly immutable. If that restricts fathers' ability to "start afresh"; indeed, if that impedes their ability to establish new, more fulfilling emotional relationships—then that is a price of fatherhood.[154] It always has been a price of motherhood. As mothers know only too well, the decision to have a child significantly restricts future freedom. Preserving fathers' freedom at the expense of children's poverty not only disadvantages women to benefit men, it is profoundly irresponsible to children.[155]

People concerned with the impact of privatization and Westernization on the new democracies may be well advised to raise this question early and often in the months and years to come. Particularly in Russia, a disturbing dynamic can easily be imagined. If, as some Western commentators have claimed, the bond between mother and child has long taken precedence over the bond between husband and wife,[156] one can easily imagine a system in which mothers, but not fathers, are expected to retain long-term, unconditional responsibility for children. If this cultural sense is combined on the one hand with a refusal to socialize the costs of motherhood, and on the other with the contemporary Western commitment to allowing men self-fulfillment in the form of a new relationship with a new (typically younger) woman, the prospects of privatization for Russian women and children may be grim indeed.

Conclusion

In the new European democracies, as in all industrialized countries, work is structured in a way that imposes costs on adults involved with child-rearing or other caregiving. One key element of socialism in the formerly communist countries was the socialization of some of the costs of child-rearing. One result of the "growth of democracy" is that these costs are being reprivatized onto individual women. This is, I argue, a key reason why women support the transition to democracy in lower numbers than men.

The privatization of childrearing costs could well lead, in East-Central Europe, as it has in the United States, to dramatic rates of impoverishment among children. This essay suggests two complementary approaches by which the new democracies can avoid family privatization, U.S. style. First, they can maintain subsidized childcare programs and other childrearing benefits to the maximum extent possible. Second, to the extent that divorced mothers are forced to rely for financial support on their ex-husbands, the new democracies can treat the issues of family entitlements to the family wage as a fundamental issue of entitlements rather than as a discretionary issue of divorce law. If the issue is framed as one of how to define property rights, it is hard to imagine that women and children will be left as disproportionately impoverished as they are in the U.S.

Notes

Many thanks to Gregory S. Alexander, June R. Carbone, Richard H. Chused, Karen Czapanskiy, Lorna Martens, Milton C. Regan, Jr., Reva Siegel, and Barbara Bennett Woodhouse for thoughtful comments on prior drafts, to Lorna Martens for guidance in European sources, and to Megan Mahony and Lisa Tittemore for expert research assistance.

1. "Eastern Women Most Conservative, Poll Shows," *Vancouver Sun* (September 16, 1991) Monday 1st Edition, pp. A1, A11. The "difficulties of women's daily lives" section of quote refers to the Soviet Union, but women's lives are also difficult in other East-Central European countries. *See, e.g.*, "German Women Struggle for Rights," *Calgary Herald* (May 7, 1992) p. A20 (stating that ten percent unemployment rate for East German women under Communism has risen to sixty-seven percent since reunification); Tamara Jones, "Walls for Women in Germany," *Los Angeles Times* (August 6, 1991) p. A1 (reporting that female workers in East Germany now find it harder to get jobs, child care, abortions, and divorces, and that some believe democracy has set them back forty years); Gail Schmoller, "Novelist Strives for Total Democracy in Yugoslavia," *Chicago Tribune*, (December 15, 1991) p. 1 (describing problems for women in East-Central European Countries, such as lack of representation in new governments in Poland, Czechoslovakia, Hungary, Bulgaria, Romania, Croatia, and Slovenia, being fired first in unemployment layoffs, and loss of child-care subsidies; also cites problems specific to the former Yugoslavia, including dirty, low-paid jobs, a pay rate equal to sixty-five percent of men's earnings, lack of contraceptive alternatives, and poor child care); Petra Weber, "Women: Underpaid and Overburdened," *The Hungarian Observer* (May 1990) (women earn on average 20-30% less than men); Leslie Nabors, "The Fair Sex," *The Hungarian Observer* (June, 1991) (explaining that women in Hungary are not given equal pay for equal work, and jobs with high concentration of women are belittled; also noting increase in pornography as function of increase in freedom of expression); Jonathan Kaufman, "Women Find Freedom Doesn't Mean Liberation," *Boston Globe* (December 27, 1990) p. 1 (finding increase in pornography and cuts in child care in Poland; also increases in violence against women in Hungary, Poland, Czechoslovakia, and former East Germany); Slawomir Majman, "A Return to the Kitchen," *The Warsaw Voice* (March 22, 1992) (concluding that women are the "losers" in the Polish transformation process); Celestine Bohlen, "East Europe's Women Struggle With New Rules, and Old Ones," *New York Times* (November 25, 1990) § 4, p. 1 (stating that as East-Central European countries make conversion to market economies, women face danger of losing jobs, maternity benefits, and other social guarantees).
2. A notable exception is the recent forum in *Signs*, "Forum," *Signs* 17:112 (1991). See also Marilyn Rueschemeyer and Hanna Schissler, "Women in the Two Germanys," in *German Studies Review* (1990) 71; Hildegard Maria Nickel, "Women in the GDR: Will Renewal Pass Them By?" 6 *Women in*

German Yearbook 99 (1991). See also Inga Markovits, "Last Days," *Calif. L. Rev.* 80:55 (1992) (description of GDR legal system in the final days before unification).

3. *See* Nadine Taub, "From Parental Leaves to Nurturing Leaves," *Rev. of Law and Social Change* 13:381 (1984–85) (stressing need for work leaves for a wide range of caregiving responsibilities).
4. *See* Joan C. Williams, "Deconstructing Gender," *Mich. L. Rev.* 87:797 (1989).
5. *See* Joan C. Williams, "Gender Wars," *N.Y.U. L. Rev.* 66:1559, 1596–1608 (1991) [hereinafter "Gender Wars"].
6. See Dorothy J. Rosenberg, "Shock Therapy: GDR Women in Transition from a Socialist Welfare State to a Social Market Economy," *Signs* 129, 17:129, 137, 148 (1991); Julia Szalai, "Some Aspects of the Changing Situation of Women in Hungary," *Signs* (1991) 17:152, 163; G. Schmoller, supra note 1; Blain Harden, "Study Sees Setbacks for Polish Women," *Washington Post* (March 14, 1992) p. A24; Patricia Clough, "Dreaming of a Return to the Kitchen Sink," *The Independent* (July 2, 1990) p. 14; Bohlen, supra note 1; Jones, supra note 1; Kirsten Gallagher, "Democracy Denies Women Certain Freedoms," *Calgary Herald* (October 3, 1991) p. A5. Mary Ann Glendon's extensive writings explore the Western European approaches to socializing childrearing costs. See Mary Ann Glendon, *The New Family and the New Property* (Toronto: Butterworth & Co., 1981) [hereinafter *New Family and New Property]*; Mary Ann Glendon, *Abortion and Divorce in Western Law: American Failures, European Challenges* (Cambridge, MA: Harvard University Press, 1987); Mary Ann Glendon, *The Transformation of Family Law: State, Law, and Family in the United States and Western Europe* (Chicago, University of Chicago Press, 1989) [hereinafter *Transformation of Family Law*].
7. See Alfred Kahn and Sheila Kamerman, *Child Care: Facing the Hard Choices* (Dover, MA: Auburn House, 1987) p. 265 (discussing differences in parental leave policies in United States and European countries).
8. "Part of the background for this has always been that family issues are outside of the government domain. As a family member, it's your responsibility to work that out on your own. That's made it more difficult in terms of mobilizing action on this issue." Felicity Barringer, "In Family-Leave Debate, A Profound Ambivalence," *New York Times* (October 6, 1992) p. A1 (quoting Barbara Willer, Public Affairs Director of the National Association for the Education of Young Children).
9. Some states give mothers the right to reinstatement, such as the California statute at issue in the *Calfed* case. See *California Federal Sav. & Loan Ass'n v. Guerra*, 479 U.S. 272 (1987); 1978 Cal. Stat. 4320 (1980) (codified as part of California Fair Employment and Housing Act at Cal. Gov't Code § 12945 (West 1980)).
10. *See* Kahn and Kamerman, supra note 7, pp. 112–14.
11. Id., p. 265. See also Barringer, supra note 8; Nabors, supra note 1.

12. See Rosenberg, supra note 6, pp. 132, 144; Gallagher, supra note 6; Jones, supra note 1; Nabors, supra note 1; Kaufman, supra note 1; Schmoller, supra note 1.
13. See Gallagher, supra note 6; Jones, supra note 1; Nabors, supra note 1; Kaufman, supra note 1; Schmoller, supra note 1.
14. See National Commission on Children, *Speaking of Kids: A National Survey of Children and Parents* (Report of the National Opinion Research Project 1 (1991).
15. Ibid.
16. Perhaps the most dramatic and visible of these forces is women's disproportionate representation among the unemployed. See Schmoller, supra note 1; Gallagher, supra note 6; Jones, supra note 1; Bohlen, supra note 1. In the GDR, although women constituted only just over half of the thirty-seven percent unemployment, only one quarter of those who found new jobs were women. Rosenberg, supra note 6, p. 132. The irony of this situation in the former GDR is that, "an overwhelming plurality" of women voted for the conservative Christian Democrats, "believing that their brand of free-market capitalism would bring prosperity" that would benefit everyone. Kaufman, supra note 1.
17. See Lenore Weitzman, *The Divorce Revolution* (Glencoe, IL: Free Press, 1985), pp. 52–69; Marsha Garrison, "Good Intentions Gone Awry: The Impact of New York's Equitable Distribution Law on Divorce Outcomes," *Brooklyn L. Rev.* 57:621, 729–730 (1991).
18. See "Gender Wars," supra note 5, p. 1603 n.57:248 (citing studies that compare relation between economic independence and power in the home). See also *Transformation of Family Law*, supra note 6, p. 307 (wage-earning spouse controls the family assets).
19. The term "professional middle class" is from Lillian Rubin, *Worlds of Pain* (New York: Basic Books, 1976), pp. 9–10. Arlie Hochschild, in her justly famous study, does not add an explicit class dimension to her analysis of the Holts, although the refusal of Evan Holt to contribute to housework and child care may well have been related to class issues of the sort discussed by Lillian Rubin. See Arlie Hochschild, *The Second Shift* (New York: Viking Press, 1989), pp. 33–58. Nancy Holt held a professional job, and her ideology of equality conformed to the pattern dominant in the professional middle class; Evan did not hold a professional job, and his more traditional gender attitudes may well reflect a blue-collar upbringing. See id., p. 189 (concluding that working class tended toward traditional ideal whereas middle class tended toward egalitarian one; but noting that "the tug between the traditional and egalitarian models of marriage runs from top to bottom of the class ladder."); Rubin, supra, pp. 96–103 (discussing differences in gender ideology in middle- and working-class families).
20. Hochschild, supra note 19, p. 112.
21. Hochschild, supra note 19, pp. 112–115.
22. Cf. Catherine Dunphy, "Men Rule Despite "Equality" in the U.S.S.R.," *Toronto Star* (November 18, 1990), p. A1 (" 'My husband cook?' laughs a Le-

ningrad official. 'You must be joking. I have never seen him wash a cup. Sometimes I come home and I am so-o-o tired, but I must cook a three-course meal for him' "; Bohlen, supra note 1 (relating situation of Rozse Hodson, a member of the Hungarian Parliament, where "while her husband has been supportive of her political career, there are times when even he turns to her with complaints about an empty refrigerator or an untidy apartment" and quoting Hodson explaining that " '[t]his was a macho society and it still is. . . .' "); Kaufman, supra note 1 (quoting Johanna Kurz, of the Center for Women's Studies at the Free University in Berlin that " '[t]here was always a base of traditional thinking in these countries, like the belief that women should raise the children.' ").

23. See Clough, supra note 6 (quoting Professor Eniko Bollabas of Szeged University in Hungary who explained that single women, career women, women scholars and scientists are "a constant target of cabaret jokes on the assumption that they are deviant and unfeminine" and finding that in Poland, Hungary, and Czechoslovakia, "[t]he idea that parenting and housework could be joint responsibilities appears to be unknown. . . ."); Dunphy, supra note 22 (discussing a Georgian woman's sense of the importance of cooking from scratch: "She does not shirk; she takes no short cuts. Even if fast food were available, it is unlikely she would buy it. She believes this makes her better than the Western working wife and mother."); "Conference on Equality of the Sexes," *Polish News Bulletin*, available in LEXIS, Nexis Library, Omni File (April 1, 1992) (reporting that, in opinion of spokesperson of Polish political group, Communists destroyed image of maternity for propaganda purposes which then "turned against women themselves. . . . Now we want a return to the maternity ethos because nature created women so they would bear children."); Krystyna Lubelska, *Polish Women Still Wait in Line—For Their Rights*, *Los Angeles Times* (May 26, 1991) (quoting Eva Kazimierska, a Polish genetics professor who asked whether "in emphasizing the woman's right to self-realization, pleasure and comfort, we do not prejudice the children's right to normal development?" and stating that during Polish Youth Pastoral Conference "many people stated that women should go back to their 'natural functions' " and "that relegating women to the kitchen and the bedroom would be the panacea for Poland's economic troubles.").

24. See Rosenberg, supra note 6, p. 137 (noting ideological commitment of communist party in GDR to the emancipation of woman and the economic necessity of drawing women into the work force); Szalai, supra note 1, p. 157 (explaining rapid extension of employment in Hungary in last decades based mainly on increasing involvement of women); Kaufman, supra note 1 (citing Johanna Kurz, of the Center for Women's Studies at the Free University in Berlin that " '[t]he social control' of Communism 'had a great impact on the behavior of men in regard to women. . . . The women in East Germany worked. They were part of the party. There was a special concept of emancipation. This is now seen as old-fashioned.' "); Schmoller, supra note 1 (quoting Creation feminist Slavenka Krakulic that while there was ideology of equality for women in Eastern Europe after WWII, it was equality in name only); Bohlen, supra note

1 (finding that in Eastern Europe equal rights for women written into laws did not translate into a change in thinking about women in society).

25. GDR had a comprehensive program. See Rosenberg, supra note 6, p. 129 (listing "array of economic rights" found in GDR, including guarantees of employment, affordable housing, free medical care and education, paid parental leave and day care and "a variety of other benefits, transfer payments, and subsidized services."). Scattered reports suggest that other formerly communist countries offered some but not all of the services and benefits available in the GDR. See, e.g., Kaufman, supra note 1 (reporting cuts in subsidies for children's clothing in the former Czechoslovakia); Bohlen, supra note 1 (concerning danger of women losing job security, generous maternity benefits including twenty-four week maternity leave at full pay and three-year leave at partial salary with a promise of job security, and other social guarantees in Hungary); Schmoller, supra note 1 ("child care translated into crowded, poorly staffed centers" and "government-supported maternity leave for six months to a year might cover the cost of a train ticket after inflation" in the former Yugoslavia).

26. See Schmoller, supra note 1 (noting that in the former Yugoslavia "[w]ithout their husbands sharing in the work or the help of modern appliances such as washing machines . . . 'women worked triple shifts.' "); Kaufman, supra note 1 (quoting Lech Wałesa: "tomorrow I will be at work at 9:30 like always . . . [a]nd my wife will cook breakfast and lunch."); Bohlen, supra note 1 (explaining that failure of equal rights in law to be accompanied by change in assumptions about division of gender roles in society left women in Eastern Europe "with two jobs, one at work and the other at home, and that led to the kind of bone-tiredness that afflicts women of all ages. Household chores and childrearing are still seen as women's work"); Clough, supra note 6 (citing Czech journalist who reports "The division of labor at home is still a traditional one. . . . Women do the cooking, men do the repairs. In most cases the shopping is done by the women."); Ben Kubasik, "Sex and the Soviet Union," *Newsday* (December 19, 1990) (stating that while eighty-six percent of Soviet women work outside home, "[w]omen do almost all the shopping, waiting in line three hours for a loaf of bread, if it can be found.").

27. Rosenberg, supra note 6, p. 138. See also Nickel, supra note 2, pp. 99–103 (GDR policies intent on reconciling motherhood (rather than parenthood) with employment); Rueschemeyer & Schissler, supra note 2, pp. 73–76 (historical background on development of GDR policies), and 76–81 (drawing somewhat less sharp distinctions between the two Germanys than does Rosenberg). Another study that stresses the similarities between the two Germanys is Christiane Lemke, "Beyond the Ideological Stalemate: Women and Politics in the FRG and the GDR in Comparison," 1990 *German Studies Review* (DAAD Special Issue) 87. Lemke highlights the different kinds of gender equality achieved in each context. While GDR went much further in socializing the costs of gender roles within the family, women gained relatively little political power. Id. at 88. While the FDR gave women relatively few childrearing supports, its women did gain significant political power. Id. 88, 91–92.

28. Rosenberg, supra note 6, pp. 137–39.

29. Rosenberg, supra note 6, p. 129. Moreover, GDR women are faced with incorporation into a society that retains very traditional attitudes towards women. The Federal Republic of Germany's famously restrictive abortion policy is matched by the low percentage of women employed (fifty-five percent). Its tax policies strongly favor "housewife marriage"; its family policies that encourage mothers to leave the work force; its labor, education, and childcare policies discourage their return. See also Rosenberg, supra note 6, pp. 133–34 (calling West Germany "an essentially conservative society, which is especially evident in gender issues."); Robert Ampuero Espinoza, "German Unification Seen Prejudicial to Women in Ex-GDR," *Inter Press Service*, available in LEXIS, Nexis Library, Omni File (May 10, 1991) (quoting German parliamentarian that "Western Germany is a developing country as far as its policy towards women"); Jones, *supra* note 1.

30. See Katrina Vanden Heuvel, "*Women of Russia, Unite!*," *New York Times* (September 12, 1992) p. 21.

31. See Gallagher, supra note 6 ("Single mothers in particular are viewed as less desirable employees because of their domestic responsibilities. . . ." according to Berlin women's rights activist Christine Schindler); Jones, supra note 1 ("I fear many employers believe that men are more reliable workers," commented Peter Hintz, parliamentary state secretary of the Women and Youth Ministry in Bonn); Drusilla Menaker, "In Poland, Job Market is Down, Discrimination Up," *Chicago Tribune*, (July 5, 1992) (citing Helsinki Watch report that women are being denied employment in Poland and "[t]he reasons are often given openly: women get pregnant, have children, use maternity leaves and sick leaves to care for children, and thus it is economically advantageous to hire men."); Vanden Heuvel, supra note 34 (explaining women have been turned away from jobs because of they were too old or because their maternal responsibilities "made them unreliable workers."); Francine Du Plessix Gray, "Reflections: Soviet Women," *The New Yorker* (February 19, 1990) p. 58 (women viewed as unstable workforce because of high rate of absenteeism because of childbearing and need to care for children when they are ill).

32. See Vanden Heuvel, supra note 34.

33. See Vanden Heuvel, supra note 34. Marcel Garces, "Russia: Women Getting Bitter End of the Stick in Market Economy," *Inter Press Service*, available in LEXIS, Nexis Library, Omni File, May 10, 1991 (sexual discrimination and harassment increasing). The increased emphasis on individual rights in the GDR translates into increased rights for fathers upon divorce. See Markovits, supra note 2, at 11–13.

34. See Gallagher, supra note 6; Yelena Khanga, "No Matryoshkas Need Apply," *New York Times*, (November 25, 1991) ("If you're female, over thirty or overweight . . . you can just forget it."); cf. Vanden Heuvel, supra note 34 (reporting that seventy percent of newly unemployed in Moscow are women between ages of forty-five and fifty-five).

35. See Dunphy, supra note 22 ("I hate shopping, I hate it. My husband–men–they will only line up for things they want–cigarettes, vodka," said a woman

dentist in former Soviet Union.); Clough, supra note 6 ("In most cases the shopping is done by the women" in the former Czechoslovakia).

36. See Vanden Heuvel, supra note 34.
37. See, e.g., "German Women Struggle for Rights," supra note 1 (stating that ten percent unemployment rate for women under communism in East Germany has risen to sixty-seven percent since reunification); Schmoller, supra note 1 (asserting that women are being fired first in unemployment layoffs in Poland, the former Czechoslovakia, Hungary, Bulgaria, Romania, Croatia and Slovenia); Brandon Mitchener, "East German Women Miss Working," *International Herald Tribune* (November 4, 1992) ("Women bear the brunt of layoffs in Eastern Germany, and afterwards have a harder time than men finding new jobs; sixty-five percent of unemployed are women); Patricia Clough, "Poland: Time Warp for Women," *The Ottawa Citizen*, April 14, 1992, at A7 (Polish women are being fired faster than men; chances of women getting work again are slender); Elaine Carey, "Educated, Middle-Aged, Out-of-Work; Most of Moscow's Jobless are Women," *The Gazette* (Montreal), February 27, 1992, at B7; Garces, supra note 37 ("Women make up the highest percentage of people out of in Russia.").
38. See Kahn and Kamerman, supra note 7, p. 265 (discussing differences in parental leave policies in United States and European countries).
39. President Bush has twice vetoed a national family leave act. See Renee Tawa, "Taking Time," *Chicago Tribune* (October 25, 1992) p. 5 (reporting Congress failed to override President Bush's veto of national family leave bill); Richard Whitmire, "State of American Family at Heart of Campaign Debate," Gannett News Service, available in, LEXIS, Nexis Library, Omni File (August 20, 1992) (noting Bush vetoed family leave act that had been passed by Congress); Barringer, supra note 1 (citing Bush veto of family leave bill).

Another problem in East-Central Europe is the failure of women to mobilize around these issues. Despite the existence of some courageous and eloquent voices, See, e.g., Peter Edwards, "Glastnost Not All Roses, Conference Told," *Toronto Star* (February 22, 1991) p. F1 (Olga Lipovskaya); Schmoller, supra note 1 (Slavenka Drakulic); Kaufman supra note 16 (Johanna Kurz); Bohlen, supra note 1 (Sonja Licht); Petra Weber, "Women: Underpaid and Overburdened," *The Hungarian Observer* (May, 1990) available in LEXIS, Nexis Library, Omni File (Eniko Bollobas), most women are not working actively to protect the programs that have socialized childrearing costs. See Edwards, supra; Bohlen, supra note 1; Nabors, supra note 1; Dunphy, supra note 22; Khanga, supra note 38. The reasons are complex: exhaustion, fear of ridicule, and hopefulness that a rising (economic) tide will raise all ships, probably play a role. See Bohlen, supra note 1 (describing "bone-tiredness" that affects women of all ages and discourages political activism); Clough, supra note 6 (finding in Poland, for example, the "word feminism means a crazy, old, ambitious, ugly, lonely woman"); Kaufman, supra note 16 ("Over the long run, many women agree, the economic changes transforming their countries will make their lives easier"); Rosenberg, supra note 6, at 148 (explaining that women voting for conservative alliance were not voting against their own perceived interests but rather were placing broad category of economic gain ahead of what they saw as narrower "women's interests").

40. For Western feminists who have discussed the relationship between the impoverishment of divorced women in the U.S. and the constricted scope of the public sphere, see Martha Minow and Deborah Rhode, "Reforming the Questions, Questioning the reforms: Feminist Perspectives on Divorce Law," in *Divorce Reform at the Crossroads* eds. Stephen D. Sugarman and Herma Hill Kay (New Haven, CT: Yale University Press, 1990), p. 191 [hereinafter Sugarman & Kay].

41. See National Commission on Children, supra note 14, at 1.

42. *National Commission on Children, Beyond Rhetoric—A New American Agenda for Children and Families* 15 (1991). One study of six industrial countries found that the "United States, which is the wealthiest country of the six studied, had the highest poverty rate among children and the second highest among families with children." See also Timothy M. Smeeding and Barbara Boyld Torrey, " 'Poor' Children in Rich Countries," *Science* 242:873 (1988).

43. See Gender Wars, supra note 5, p. 1604 (citing Sara E. Rix, "The American Women" 1990–91" (New York: Norton, 1990), p. 5).

44. Zillah R. Eisenstein, "The Sexist Politics of the New Right: Understanding the 'Crisis of Liberalism' for the 1980s," in *Feminist Theory*, editors Nannerl O. Keohane, Michelle Z. Rosaldo and Barbara C. Gelpi (Chicago: University of Chicago Press, 1982), p. 91.

45. Id.

46. R. Sidel, supra note 45, p. 3.

47. Diane Pearce, "Welfare is Not for Women: Why the War on Poverty Cannot Conquer the Feminization of Poverty," in *Women, The State and Welfare*, edited by Linda Gordon (Madison, WI: University of Wisconsin Press, 1990), p. 266. This statement is an accurate comparison between men and women as groups, but does not rule out income and wealth variations among men. In 1988 African-American male, full-time workers earned only seventy-five percent of what white, male, full-time workers earned per week. U.S. *Bureau of the Census, Statistical Abstract of the U.S.* (1990) p. 409. Furthermore, working-class white men have seen their relative position erode in the past twenty years. See Frank Levy and Richard Michel, *The Economic Future of American Families: Income and Wealth Trends* (Washington, D.C.: Urban Institute Press, 1991), pp. 28–32.

48. Irwin Garfinkel, Sara McLanahan and Dorothy Watson, "Divorce, Female Headship and Child Support," in *Women's Life Cycle and Economic Insecurity*, edited by Martha H. Ozawa (New York: Praeger, 1989), p. 101. Estimates are that forty-five percent of white children and eighty-four percent of African-American children born in the late 1970s will live with a single mother at some time before they reach the age of eighteen. Id. p. 102. See also R. Sidel, supra

note 4, p. 18; F. Levy and R. Michel, supra note 52, p. 38. (noting a " 'swap' in which elderly families moved from the bottom of the income distribution to the lower middle, while their 'vacated places' at the bottom were fallen by new female-headed families with children."); Jason DeParle, "Child Poverty Twice as Likely After the Family Split, Study Says," *New York Times* (March 2, 1991), p. 8.

49. See, e.g., Dunphy, supra note 22 (one third of all marriages in USSR end in divorce); Jones, supra note 1 ("One third of the east's [GDR] children were born out of wedlock."); Susan Poizner, "The Sorrowing Mother and Child," *Jerusalem Post* (September 4, 1992) (citing Barbara Heldt, Professor of Russian at University of British Columbia, referring to sacred icon of Russian Orthodoxy which depicts mother and child and explaining "single mother is almost an inevitability in Russia. . . . Long before the revolution, Russians were keyed into this icon figure of the sorrowing mother, and by the time socialism came along they just gave her a bit more economic support so that the sorrowing mother can just go on sorrowing"); John Eisenhammer, "Sisters Are Sent Back to the Kitchen after Unification," *The Independent* (May 21, 1991), p. 8 (reporting one third of mothers in East Germany live alone, and that worst hit by unification are those single mothers who have their lost child care support systems); Bohlen, supra note 1 (noting that financial autonomy is especially important in countries like Hungary, and former Soviet Union and East Germany, where divorce rate is high).

50. Peggy A. Rabkin, *Fathers to Daughters* (Westport, CT: Greenwood Press, 1980), p. 121.

51. For a study that stresses regional variations in coverture, see Marylynn Salmon, *Women and the Law of Property in Early America* (Chapel Hill, NC: University of North Carolina Press, 1986,) pp. 14–16. For a capsule description of the ideology of female inferiority that contrasts it with the domestic ideology that came later, see Joan C. Williams, "Deconstructing Gender," *Mich. L. Rev.* 87:797, 803–04, 806–09 (1989) [hereinafter "Deconstructing Gender"].

52. See Salmon, supra note 55, p. 15. Wives retained ownership only of their beds, clothing, "ornaments and trinkets." See Tapping Reeve, *The Law of Baron and Feme, of Parent and Child, of Guardian and Ward, of Master and Servant, and of the Powers of Courts of Chancery* 98 (1816), *quoted in* Marlene Stein Wortman, *Women in American Law*, Vol. 1, (New York: Holmes and Meier, 1985) p. 38.

53. Husbands received an "estate jure uxoris," which left legal title with the wife, but gave the husband the right to possession, rents, and profits to all lands, whether her interest arose before or during the marriage. The husband could sell and mortgage his estate in the land, and it could be seized by his creditors. See David H. Bromfield, *Book Review*, *Mich. L. Rev.* 85:1109, 1111 (1987); Rabkin, supra note 50, at 20. In other words, the wife could regain access to her real property if she outlived her husband. Husbands could not alienate wives' land outright without their "free" consent through the practice of "private examination." See Salmon, supra note 55, p. 15.

54. See Richard H. Chused, "Married Women's Property Law: 1800–1850," *Geo. L.J.* 71:1359, 1400–1404 (1983) (noting "widespread economic problems" and linking them to the first wave of Married Women's Property Acts).

55. Max Bloomfield, *American Lawyers in a Changing Society, 1776–1876*, (Cambridge MA: Harvard University Press, 1976), p. 95, quoted in Isabel Marcus, "Locked In and Locked Out: Reflections on The History of Divorce Law Reform in New York State," *Buff. L. Rev.* 37:375, 396 (1988/89) [hereinafter Marcus, "Locked Out"]. During certain periods in certain jurisdictions, a minority of well-to-do women could escape some of the strictures of coverture by setting up (or, more typically, if their fathers set up for them) "separate estates" in equity that limited the husband's control. The influential historian Mary Ritter Beard asserted in 1946 that equity effectively mitigated the harshness of the common-law doctrine and gave women substantial control over property. See Mary Ritter Beard, *Women as Force in History: A Study in Traditions and Realities* (New York: Macmillan, 1946), pp. 131–33. The current consensus is that equity only helped a small number of well-to-do women. See, e.g., Suzanne Lebsock, "Radical Reconstruction and the Property Rights of Southern Women," *J. Southern Hist.*, 53:195, 199, n.12 (1977) (early critique of Beard); M. Salmon, supra note 55, at 31 (stating and documenting current consensus that separate estates "remained inaccessible to the majority of women.") Salmon explores in depth the point that separate estates did *not* always give control over property to women themselves; instead, control often was given to male trustees,. See id., pp. 100–18. This was, in theory (and sometimes in fact) to protect wives from coercion by their husbands. Id, pp. 104–08.

56. This is the origin of the phrase "rule of thumb." Caitlin Borgmann, "Note: Battered Women's Substantive Due Process Rights: Can Orders of Protection Deflect Deshaney?" *N.Y.U. L. Rev.* 65:1280, n.3 (1990).

57. See, e.g., *Sawada v. Endo*, 57 Haw. 608, 612; 561 P.2d 1291, 1295 (1977) ("The effect of the Married Women's Property Acts was to abrogate the husband's common law dominance over the marital estate and to place the wife on a level of equality with him as regards the exercise of ownership over the whole estate.").

58. Cf. Lawrence M. Friedman, *A History of American Law* (New York: Simon & Schuster, 1973), p. 362. Friedman restates the traditional view that the Acts "released women from bondage," id. p. 362, but argues that the Acts in fact ratified changes that had already occurred in women's status, id. pp. 362–363, an interpretation that has not been confirmed by subsequent historians. See, e.g., Salmon, supra note 56, pp. 14–57, 81–140.

59. See Richard H. Chused, "Late-Nineteenth Century Married Women's Property Law: Reception of the Early Married Women's Property Acts by Courts and Legislatures," *J. Am. L. Hist.* 29:3, 4, n.3 (1985) ("It is now generally agreed that the first wave of married women's acts were adopted in part because of the dislocations caused by the Panic of 1837"); Lebsock, supra note 59, pp. 201–02.

60. See Lebsock, supra note 59, pp. 197, 209; (southern Acts not linked with feminism); Richard H. Chused, "Married Women's Property Law: 1800–1850," *Geo. L.J.* 71:1359, 1361 (1983); (some Acts not precipitated by desire for equal rights for women); Norma Basch, "The Emerging Legal History of Women in the United States," *Signs* (1986) 12:99 (discussing shifting coalition of advocates for debtor relief, more legislative and less judicial control, and those concerned with the status of women); Marcus, *Locked Out*, supra note 59, pp. 401–2, 399 (Acts "not intended to degender access to property"); James W. Ely, Jr., *Book Review, UCLA L. Rev.* 31:294, 298 (1983)(legislators who passed the New York Act "never intended to alter traditional marriage patterns or produce a major shift in the social role of the sexes").
61. See Lebsock, supra note 59, pp. 200–201.
62. See Chused, supra note 63, pp. 1409–12; Ely, supra note 64, pp. 58–59.
63. This slow progress has been noted by many authors, notably Chused, supra note 63, pp. 1409–12.
64. See Chused, supra note 63, pp. 1397–1412; Lebsock, supra note 59, pp. 196, 201, 209, 214.
65. See Lebsock, supra note 59, p. 209.
66. Frank Furstenberg, "Divorce and the American Family," *Ann Rev. Soc.* 16:379, 380 (1990), quoted in Barbara Bennett Woodhouse, Book Review: "Towards a Revitalization of Family Law," *Tex. L. Rev.* 69:148 (1990).
67. See "Deconstructing Gender," supra note 4, p. 824.
68. *See* Norma Heckman, Rebecca Bryson and Jeff Bryson, "Problems of Professional Couples: A Content Analysis," *J. Marriage and Fam.* 39:323 (1977) (finding that women are expected to place their careers secondary to the needs of their families and the needs of their husband's careers); Jeylan Mortimer, Richard Hall and Reuben Hill, "Husbands' Occupational Attributes as Constraints on Wives' Employment," *Soc. Work and Occupations* 5:285 (1978) (suggesting that attributes of husband's work limit sharing of family work and put pressure on wife to support husband's career to the detriment of her own work participation and attainment).
69. See Donna H. Berardo, et al., "A Residue of Tradition: Jobs Careers and Spouses' Time in Housework," *J. Mar. and Fam.* 49:391, 388 (1987). Another study showed that husbands barely contribute enough to domestic labor to make up for the additional work their presence in the household creates. See Judith A. Heath and David H. Cicel, "Patriarchy, Family Structure, and the Exploitation of Women's Labor," *J. Econ. Issues* 22:781, 788 (1988).
70. See Graeme Russell and Norma Radin, "Increased Paternal Participation: The Fathers Perspective," in *Fatherhood and Family Policy*, editors Michael Lamb & Abraham Sagi (Hillsdale, NJ: Lawrence Erlbaum Associates, 1983), pp. 139, 142 (reporting on studies that found fathers in typical families average twelve to twenty-four minutes a day in solo child care). For other studies that report fathers spending more time on child care, see Nijole Benokraitis, "Fathers in the Dual Earner Family," in *Dimensions of Fatherhood*, editors Shirley

Hanson and Frederick Borett (Beverly Hills, CA: Sage Publications, 1985), p. 254; Frances Grossman, William Pollack and Ellen Golding, "Fathers and Children: Predicting the Quality and Quantity of Fathering," *Dev. Psychology* 24:82, 84 (1988), quoted in Woodhouse, supra note 70, p. 284.

71. See Hochschild, supra note 19, pp. 3, 279, n. 2, quoting Shelley Coverman, "Gender, Domestic Labor Time, and Wage Inequality," *Am. Soc. Rev.* 48:626 (1983).

72. See Hochschild, supra note 19, pp. 271–73 ("leisure gap" of eleven to nineteen hours per week).

73. Id., p. 279.

74. Id, p. 3 (employed mothers work roughly fifteen hours longer than employed fathers each week).

75. See Health and Cicel, supra note 73, p. 787 (employed wives work 144 percent of total time of traditional homemaker).

76. See "Gender Wars," supra note 28, p. 1600.

77. Id.

78. For an analysis of the social construction of children's needs, see id., pp. 1622–24.

79. See John H. Langbein, "The Twentieth-Century Revolution in Family Wealth Transmission," *Mich. L. Rev.* 86:722, 723 (1988).

80. See Langbein, supra note 83, p. 723. The other primary form of twentieth-century wealth is financial assets. Id.

81. See Langbein, supra note 83, p. 723.

82. In fact, one law-and-economics scholar has estimated that human capital constitutes roughly seventy-five percent of wealth in the contemporary United States. Robert C. Ellickson, Exemplars of Empirical Research, Panel on Research Agendas in Property Law, Association of American Law School's Conference on Property Law, Spokane, Washington (June 10, 1992). For the statistics underlying this calculation, see Robert C. Ellickson, "The Untenable Case for an Unconditional Right to Shelter," *Harv. J. Law and Pub. Pol.* 15:17 (1992).

83. Garrison, supra note 17, at 728 (citing William J. Goode, *After Divorce* 217 (1956); cf. Susan Klebanoff, "To Love and Obey 'Til Graduation Day—The Professional Degree in Light of the Uniform Marital Property Act," *Am. U. L. Rev.* 34:839, 840 and nn.3, 4 (citing cases showing couples typically accumulate "few tangible assets because they funneled all their resources into one spouse's education").

84. Weitzman, supra note 17, pp. 57–60.

85. See Garrison, supra note 17, p. 728.

86. For a pioneering study, see *New Family and New Property*, supra note 6, pp. 91–96.

87. See, e.g., Margaret Poloma, Brian Pendleton, and T. Neal Garland, "Reconsidering the Dual Career Marriage: A Longitudinal Approach," in *Two Paychecks:*

Life in Dual-Earner Families, Joan Aldous, ed. (Beverly Hills, CA: Sage Publications, 1982).

88. See e.g., David Fletcher, "Recession Adds to Marriage Failures," Press Association Newsfile, (October 13, 1992) available in LEXIS, Nexis Library, Omni File (stating that men are particularly hit by unemployment, which affects self-confidence and self-esteem); Miles Socha, "Support Group Aims to Help Couples Coping with Joblessness," *Toronto Star* (May 23, 1992) p. J16 (explaining that men's identities are particularly tied to their occupations); Gilbert A. Lewthwaite, "Does a Bad Economy Mean More Suicides?," *Star Tribune* (November 13, 1991), p. 4A (describing depression, low self-esteem of jobless men); "Is Work an Antidote to Depression," *Chicago Tribune* (November 25 1990) p. 6 (relating results of study finding unemployed men showed higher levels of depression than women, working or not, and speculating that because men's self-esteem is tied up with how they perform on the job, work and work-related problems more likely to cause depression in men).

89. Variation by race may be significant. The history of African-American men's blocked access to good jobs may mean they have developed a self-image that ties virility less to employment status. See J.L. Gwaltney, *Drylongso: A Self-Portrait of Black America* (New York: Random House, 1981), pp. 173–74 ("One very important difference between white people and black people is that white people think that you *are* your work. . . . Now, a black person has more sense than that because he knows that what I am doing doesn't have anything to do with what I do when I am doing for myself."); Jacqueline Jones, *Labor of Love, Labor of Sorrow* (New York: Basic Books, 1985), p. 326 (explaining that young black men affirm their masculinity through sexuality as possibilities for educational and economic advancement decrease due to increase in unemployment). But cf. Diane E. Lewis, "Job Situation Worsening for Blacks and Latinos," *Boston Globe* (August 18, 1991) p. A35 (reporting that recession and cuts in training programs result in higher unemployment among Black and Latino men, along with lower self-esteem and destabilization within families).

90. See, e.g., Felice N. Schwartz, "Management Women and the New Facts of Life," *Harv. Bus. Rev.* (January-February 1989) p. 65; Elizabeth Ehrlich, "The Mommy Track," *Business Week* (March 20, 1989) p. 126; Meredith Chen, "Women at Work: A New Debate," *Los Angeles Times* (March 3, 1989) p. 3; Audrey Freedman, "Those Costly 'Good Old Boys,' " *New York Times* (July 12, 1989) p. A23. For a comprehensive listing of articles related to the mommy track debate, See Gender Wars, supra note 5, p. 1601–1602 note 242. Rosenberg's study of the GDR suggests that some of the forces that lead to the "mommy track" in the United States are also at work in the GDR. See Rosenberg, supra note 6, p. 139 (explaining that despite extensive framework created to support women, women tended more often than men to take part-time work because of family responsibilities, accept jobs beneth their qualifications to be near home, or to postpone career advancement because of small children).

91. See Hochschild, supra note 19, pp. 60–62 (gender ideology has less strong hold in working-class families); Vicki Schultz, "Telling Stories About Women

and Work: Judicial Interpretation of Sex Segregation in the Workplace in Title VII Cases Raising the Lack of Interest Argument," *Harv. L. Rev.* 103:1749 (1990) (stressing role of employers in shaping women's "choice" of jobs); Vicki Schultz & Stephen Petterson, "Race, Gender, Work, and Choice: An Empirical Study of the Lack of Interest Defense in Title VII Cases Challenging Job Segregation," *U. Chi. L. Rev.* 59:1073 (1992). See also Rosenberg, supra note 6, p. 139 ("The result [of integrating women into work force without revaluating traditionally 'female' industries or introducing women into skilled trades] was a high degree of female representation in professions alongside continuing gender segregation of the rest of the labor force.").

92. L. Weitzman, supra note 17, pp. 352–356; Hochschild, supra note 19, pp. 249–53; Heather Ruth Wishik, "Economics of Divorce," *Fam. L. Q.* 20:79, 93–98 (1986).

93. The literature on the impoverishment of women and children upon divorce is extensive. For a recent comprehensive listing, see Milton C. Regan, Jr., "Divorce Reform and the Legacy of Gender" (Book Review) *Mich. L. Rev.* 90:1453 (1992). For the notion of systematic disinvestment, see June Carbone, "Equality and Difference: Reclaiming Motherhood as a Central Focus of Family Law," *Law and Soc. Inq.* 17:471 (1992).

94. See Judith S. Wallerstein and Shauna B. Corbin, "Father-Child Relationships After Divorce: Child Supporting and Educated Opportunity," *Fam. L. Q.* (1986) pp. 109, 122–123 (quoted in Barbara Bennett Woodhouse, "Toward a Revitalization of Family Law," *Tex. L. Rev.* 69:245, 269) (1990). Woodhouse stresses the importance to generation-to-generation human capital transfers. Id., pp. 69:269–271.

95. Wallerstein & Corbin, supra note 98, pp. 122–123.

96. Another key context is single motherhood. For discussions of the prevalence of divorce and single motherhood in East-Central Europe, see Eisenhammer, supra note 54, p. 8 (reporting one third of mothers in East Germany live alone); Dunphy, supra note 22 (one third of all marriages in USSR end in divorce); Jones, supra note 1 ("One third of the east's [German] children were born out of wedlock."); Poizner, supra note 54 (citing Barbara Heldt, Professor of Russian at University of British Columbia, explaining "the single mother is almost an inevitability in Russia").

97. Often husbands' freedom involves the freedom to attract a new (and normally younger) wife: fifty-five percent of divorced men are married within three years of their divorce and twenty-one percent more had "cohabitors." Sugarman and Kay, supra note 44, p. 246, n.2 (citing "Parenting in the Binuclear Family: Relationships between Biological and Stepparents," in *Remarriage and Stepparenting: Current Research and Theory* (New York: Guilford Press, 1987), pp. 185–86).

98. See Schmoller, supra note 1 (finding "women have less representation in the new governments in Poland, Czechoslovakia, Hungary, Bulgaria, Romania, Croatia, and Slovenia, dropping from an average of thirty-three percent to less

than ten percent); Ellen Hume, "The Sex that Perestroika Has Forgotten," *Los Angeles Times* (December 23, 1990), p. 1 (describing Congress of People's Deputies in Soviet Union as "a sea of male faces" and finding that although women are fifty-three percent of population they are only five percent of the newly elected Congress).

99. See Robert Bellah, et al., *Habits of the Heart* (New York: Harper & Row, 1985) p. 142–47 (discussing the central role of therapeutic notions of emotional self-fulfillment in contemporary American life). One expression of the therapeutic ideal is the elevation of individual emotional gratification above stability in marriage. See Woodhouse, supra, note 70, p. 181 and sources cited therein.

100. Lenore Weitzman's famous study of California suggests that judges are more up-front about their distrust of dependence than they are about their solicitude for men's freedom. L. Weitzman, supra, note 17, pp. 188, 194–98.

101. See, e.g., Betty Friedan, *The Feminine Mystique* (New York: Norton, 1963), pp. 47, 344 (stating that women must have independence and creative paid work that lets them develop interests and goals of their own).

102. See Stanley N. Katz, "Thomas Jefferson and the Right to Property in Revolutionary America," *J.L. & Econ.* 19:467 (1976) ("Dependence begets subservience and venality, suffocates the germ of virtue, and prepares fit tools for the designs of ambition."); J.G.A. Pocock, *The Machivellian Moment* (Princeton, NJ: Princeton University Press, 1975), p. 75 (stating that, to Renaissance civic humanists, "[t]o become dependent on another was as great a crime as to reduce another to dependence on oneself.").

103. In the GDR, divorced mothers received the state stipends allocable to single mothers. These stipends are being eliminated. See Jones supra note 1 ("It [divorce] also becomes a financial question for women now . . . because you have to hire a lawyer, and you have to worry about alimony and child support too. The state took care of you in the east."); Eisenhammer, supra note 54 (reporting on loss of automatic child benefit and child care for single women); Gallagher, supra note 6 (describing situation of single woman in East Germany after cuts in prenatal, medical, and child care services). They, too, presumably will need to turn to their children's fathers for funds.

104. In Hungary women earn twenty to thirty percent less than men. See Weber, supra note 43 (explaining that this occurs despite official equal-pay policy because jobs tend to be segregated, and jobs where women predominate are worse paid and have lower prestige); Majman, supra note 1 (stating that thirty to forty thousand people get divorced in Poland each year and that Alimony Fund set up to help families without fathers turned out to be completely inefficient). In the former Yugoslavia women earn a pay rate equal to sixty-five percent of men's earnings. See Schmoller, supra note 1 (describing problems for women in the former Yugoslavia).

105. Note that, in theory, courts in most American jurisdictions make an "equitable" distribution of marital assets. See *Transformation of Family Law*, supra note 6 pp. 227–28. The problem is with what judges perceive to be "equitable." Despite the statutory redefinition of "contribution" to include the provi-

sion of homemaking services in many states, the invisibility of women's work has meant that the husband's contribution typically is valued much more. See Maryland Special Joint Committee, *Gender Bias in the Courts* (1989), pp. 65–66 and n.33; Weitzman, supra note 17, pp. 106–08.

106. See, e.g., Jane Rutherford, "Duty in Divorce: Shared Income as a Path to Equality," *Fordham L. Rev.* (1990) 58:539, 563, quoting *Newsweek* (July 17, 1989) p. 6 (divorce lawyers call financially dependent women with no personal income "shoppers," as in, "she'll need a ton of alimony. She's a shopper.") The undervaluation of women's domestic labor—to the point where homemakers themselves at times apologize that they "don't work"—also fuels the fire against alimony. For a quote from a judge that has undertones both of republican distrust of dependence and puritan commitment to the virtues of hard work, see L. Weitzman, supra note 17, p. 144 ("Alimony was never intended to assure a perpetual state of assured indolence. It should not be allowed to convert a host of physically and mentally competent young women into an army of alimony drones who neither toil nor spin and become a drain on society and a menace to themselves.")

107. Mary C. O'Connell, "Alimony After No-Fault: A Practice in Search of a Theory," *N. Eng. L. Rev.* 23:437 (1988) (reviewing various studies documenting alimony available in from 9.3% to 18.8% of divorces); Jana B. Singer, "Divorce Reform and Gender Justice," *N. C. L. Rev.* 69:103, 1106–07 (1989).

108. See Weitzman, supra note 17, p. 148.

109. See id., pp. 149–150.

110. 272 Ind. 483, 399 N.E.2d 371 (1980). The "degree cases" are a rare context in which wives' contributions to husbands' careers have been conceptualized in terms of property. Significantly, these cases typically involve not only homemaking services but also "real" (that is, financial) support by wives, which fits more readily into the rubric of traditional property. Moreover, only one jurisdiction (New York) has found for the wife on a property theory in a way that creates a significant claim on future income. *O'Brien v. O'Brien*, 489 N.E.2d 712 (N.Y. 1985). Most states have balked at holding "income" as "property." See Milton C. Regan, Jr., *Family Law and the Pursuit of Intimacy*, p. 145 (New York: New York University Press, 1993) [hereinafter *Pursuit of Intimacy*].

111. 399, N.E. 2d at 371.

112. Id., p. 373.

113. Id.

114. Id., pp. 373–74 (Hunter, J., dissenting).

115. 416 U.S. 134 (1974).

116. 416 U.S. at 207.

117. Charles Reich, "The New Property," *Yale L.J.* (1964) 73:733.

118. 399 N.E.2d at 374 (quoting Arnett v. Kennedy, 416 U.S. 134, 207, n.2 (1974)).

119. Even before *McManama* was decided in 1980, some scholars had begun to apply the human capital analysis to family law. See, e.g., Elizabeth Landes, "Economics of Alimony," *J. Leg. Studies*, 7:35 (1978); Combs, "The Human Capital Concept as a Basis for Property Settlement at Divorce: Theory and Implementation," *J. Divorce* 2:329 (1979). See also Joan Krauskopf, "Recompense for Financing Spouse's Education: Legal Protection for the Marital Investor in Human Capital," *U. Kan. L. Rev.* 28:379 (1980); Elizabeth Smith Beninger and Jeanne Wiedage Smith, "Career Opportunity Cost: A Factor in Spousal Support Determination," *Fam. L.Q.* 16:201 (1982).

120. See Mary Ann Glendon, "Fixed Rules and Discretion in Contemporary Family Law and Succession Law," 60 *Tul L. Rev.* (1986) p. 1165; Jane Murphy, "Eroding the Myth of Discretionary Justice in Family Law: The Child Support Experiment," *N.C.L. Rev.* 70:209, 229 (1991); Karen Czapanskiy, "Gender Bias in the Courts: Social Change Strategies," *Geo. J. Legal Ethics* 4:1, 8 (1990). The most sustained attempt to limit judicial discretion was the Child Support Enforcement Amendments of 1984, Pub. L. No. 90-378, § 18(a) (codified at 42 U.S.C. § 667 (West Supp. 1992)) which mandate states to generate guidelines for awards of child support.

121. In state courts or last resort, 35 judges are women and 356 are men; in state intermediate courts, 81 judges are women and 833 men. Two hundred sixteen federal court judges are women; 2618 are men. Telephone Interview with Rae Lovko, Staff Associate, National Center for State Courts (August 27, 1992).

122. See Joan C. Williams, "Sameness Feminism and the Work/Family Conflict," *N.Y. L. School Rev.* (1990) 35:347 (analyzing elite law firm practice as based on a system of gender privilege); "Gender Wars," supra note 5, p. 1619 (documenting widespread incidence of long hours in American legal profession).

123. Even if this is only in words, not deeds. See L. Rubin, supra note 19, pp. 96–98; A. Hochschild, supra note 19, pp. 189–93.

124. For further discussion of this issue, see "Gender Wars," supra note 5, pp. 1594–96, 1629–32.

125. See Felice N. Schwartz, "Management Women and the New Facts of Life," *Harv. Bus. Rev.* (January-February 1989), pp. 65, 69. Another study reported that ninety-seven percent of male corporate leaders but only thirty-nine percent of women at equivalent levels of management have children. See Felice Schwartz, *Breaking With Tradition* (New York: Warner Books, 1992), p. 106. Women lawyers are also much more likely to be childless than male lawyers. American Bar Association Commission on Women in the Profession, *Lawyers and Balanced Lives* (1990), p. 4.

126. This is an example of a "gender war." of the type that characterizes the current gender system. *See Gender Wars, supra* note 5, pp. 1561, 1601 note 242, 1624–29.

127. An extraordinary outpouring of creative scholarship addresses U.S. women and impoverishment upon divorce. See, e.g., Margaret F. Brinig & June

Carbone, "The Reliance Interest in Marriage and Divorce," *Tul. L. Rev.* 62:855 (1988); June Carbone, "Economics, Feminism and the Reinvention of Alimony: A Reply to Ira Ellman," *Vand. L. Rev.* 43:1463 (1990); John Andrew Chandler, "A Property Theory of Future Earning Potential in Dissolution Proceedings," *Wash. L. Rev. J.* 56:277 (1981). Jane W. Ellis, "Surveying the Terrain: A Review Essay of Divorce Reform at the Crossroads," *Stan. L. Rev.* 44:471 (1992); Ira Mark Ellman, "The Theory of Alimony," *Calif. L. Rev.* p.44:3 (1989); Garrison, supra note 17; Sally F. Goldfarb, "Marital Partnership and the Case for Permanent Alimony," *J. Fam. L.* 27:151 (1988–89) Krauskopf, supra note 123; O'Connell, supra note 111; Regan, supra note 97, p. 1471; *Pursuit of Intimacy*, supra note 114; Rutherford, supra note 110; Carl E. Schneider, "Rethinking Alimony," *B.Y.U.L. Rev.* 197 (1991); Singer, supra note 111, at 1103 (1989); Sugarman & Kay, supra note 44; L. Weitzman, supra note 17; Woodhouse, supra note 70.

128. See, e.g., Ellman, supra note 131; O'Connell, supra note 111; Rutherford, supra note 110; Schneider, supra note 131; Singer, supra note 131. But see Woodhouse, supra note 70; Regan, supra note 97.

129. See Nancy D. Polikoff, "Looking for the Policy Choices Within An Economic Methodology: A Critique of the Income Shares Model," p. 27, 33, *in Essentials of Child Support Guidelines Development: Economic Issues and Policy Considerations*, proceedings of the Women's Legal Defense Fund's National Conference on the Development of Child Support Guidelines (1986) pp. 30–31; Karen Czapanskiy, Foreword, in *Essentials of Child Support Guidelines Development: Economic Issues and Policy Considerations*, pp. 5, 12. Proceedings of the Women's Legal Defense Fund's National Conference on the Development of Child Support Guidelines (1986).

130. My thanks to Karen Czapanskiy for bringing this point to my attention, and to Ann Shalleck and Nancy Polikoff for helping me develop it.

131. For a recent addition to the literature on the family wage, see Maurine Weiner Greenwald, "Working-Class Feminism and the Family Wage Ideal: The Seattle Debate on Married Women's Right to Work, 1914–1920," *J. Am. Hist.* 76:118 (1989).

132. Ellen Ross's studies show that working-class families in late 19th and early 20th century London had a very different sense of property entitlements within the family than we have today. See Ellen Ross, "Survival Networks: Women's Neighbourhood Sharing in London Before World War I," 15 History Workshop 4 (1983); (husbands handed over the larges part of their weekly earnings to their wives; this "wage" was seen as her property). See also Ellen Ross, " 'Fierce Questions and Taunts:' Married Life in Working-Class London, 1870–1914," Feminist Stud. 81:575, 580–85 (1982).

133. In the absence of fault, of course: at-fault wives whose husbands were awarded divorces were not entitle to alimony. See Weitzman, supra note 17, p. 12.

134. "Gender Wars," supra note 5, pp. 1596–1608.

135. Many divorced wives clearly think of their husbands' career as a joint enterprise, and his wage as a family wage. See Weitzman, supra note 17, pp. 138, 155, 158.

136. I base this on the reaction of students in my Property classes over the past five years, as they express outrage at their fathers' failure to provide support to their (divorced) mothers. See also Weitzman, supra note 17, p. 353 ("Not surprisingly, the children of divorce often express anger and resentment when their standard of living is significantly less than that in their father's household.").

137. An example is the proposal being developed by Democrat Thomas Downey and Republican Henry Hyde for a four billion dollar public works program for parents who cannot meet their child support payments. For reports on this unusual alliance between a liberal and a conservative, see William Raspberry, "The Welfare-Work Dilemma," *The Washington Post* (May 15, 1992); "Making Delinquent Parents Pay," *Hartford Courant* (May 16, 1992). See also Tom Downey, Henry Hyde, and John Lewis, Geraldine Jensen (Association for Children for Enforcement of Support), Nancy Ebb (Children's Defense Fund), and Harry Wiggins (State of Virginia), Press Conference, (May 12, 1992).

138. See supra note 132.

139. See Weitzman, supra note 17, p. 148 (explaining that no-fault divorce statutes reject traditional rationales for alimony and now based alimony on need).

140. Fineman, supra note 134. For critiques of Fineman's focus on asset division, see Note, "Divorced from Reality," (Book Review), *Harv. L. Rev.* 105:2110 (1992), 2114; Regan, supra note 96, p. 1471.

141. See supra note 111.

142. See Suzanne Reynolds, "The Relationship of Property Division and Alimony: The Division of Property to Address Need," *Fordham L. Rev.* 56:827 (1988), 844–49, 864–65 ("courts are not relying on the discretionary factors relating to need in making property dispositions"), id., 866.

143. Id., pp. 866–71.

144. Id., pp. 857–59, 871–77.

145. The notion that an award of fifty percent of family assets to an ideal-worker husband with no resident children and fifty percent to a marginalized mother with custody of one or more children is "equal" is evidence of divorce courts' peculiar aphasia that children also are individuals who need income and assets (notably housing) in order to thrive. *See* Weitzman, supra note 17, at 104. ("Under the equal division rule, 'equality' means that three people (the wife and, on average, two children) share one half of the marital assets while one person (the husband) is entitled to the other half for himself.").

146. See Thomas L. Haskell, "The Curious Persistence of Rights Talk in the 'Age of Interpretation,' " *J. Am. Hist.* 74:984 (1987); Symposium, "The Constitution and American Life—A Special Issue," *J. Am. Hist.* 74:656–1034 (1987).

147. Karl Marx, "Critique of the Gotha Program," in *The Marx-Engels Reader*, editor Robert C. Tucker, 2d ed. (New York: Norton, 1978), p. 531.

148. For a similar argument, see Patricia A. Cain, "In Search of a Normative Principle for Property Division at Divorce" (Book Review), *Tex. J. Women and Law* 1:249 (1992). An exception is for children's needs; hence, the importance of framing postdivorce obligations in terms of children's needs wherever possible. See Letter from Barbara Bennett Woodhouse to Joan C. Williams, August 24, 1992; Barbara Bennett Woodhouse, "Hatching the Egg: A Child-Centered Perspective on Parents' Rights," *Cardozo L. Rev.* 14: (1993) (forthcoming).

149. See Weitzman, supra note 17, pp. 110–13.

150. See, e.g., the use of the term "new property" to challenge the traditional notion that "he who earns it, owns it," by Mary Ann Glendon and Lenore Weitzman. See *New Family and New Property*, supra note 6, pp. 91–96; Weitzman, supra note 17, pp. 110–42.

151. See, e.g., Ricki Lewis Tannen, "Report of the Florida Supreme Court Gender Bias Study Commission," *U. Fla. L. Rev.* 42:825–28 (1990) (lax judicial attitudes towards child support enforcement; "I've remarried," one of the excuses offered as reasons why a father cannot support his children.)

152. *Gender Wars*, supra note 5, pp. 1562–64 (discussing ideology of self-interest, especially in context of motherhood).

153. For a fascinating study of the imagery surrounding mothers who abandon their children, see Carol Sanger, *Separating from Children* (Ann Arbor, MI: Univ. of Michigan Press, forthcoming 1994).

154. Immutable financial arrangements between fathers and children may help prevent the emotional disinvestment so common among divorced fathers in American families. Only about one-sixth of children see their fathers as often as once a week even relatively soon after divorce; after ten years, almost two-thirds have almost no contact at all. See William A. Galston, "When the Bough Breaks: The Costs of Neglecting Our Children," *The New Republic*, (December 2, 1991) p. 6.

155. See supra notes 14-15 and accompanying text (providing statistics on children living in poverty in United States); Woodhouse, supra note 70, pp. 268–70 (describing impact of divorce on children, including increased likelihood of poverty and limited educational opportunity); Weitzman, *supra* note 17, pp. 352–53 (considering effects of divorce on children, particularly middle-class children).

156. See Du Plessix Gray, supra note 35, pp. 48–49 (discussing matriarchal patterns in Russia).

IV

Toward A Fourth Way— Programmatic Statements

Neither the Market Nor the State: Housing Privatization Issues

Duncan Kennedy

Editors' Synopsis: We say market, we say reprivatization. But that market has many names. If, after the dogmatic faith in the benefits of the planned economy, there comes an equally dogmatic faith in the benefits of the market, then we are in trouble. Because the market is to the economy what freedom is to democracy: a primary condition. But the market is not a self-activated mechanism that can replace the economic policy of the state and the economic activity of the people. The market has several names. We know the difference between the market as it is seen by Milton Friedman and the market with a human face as it is perceived by, say, the leaders of Swedish social democracy.

The cult of the market will lead to the great triumph of Friedmanism. But what does it mean to be Chicago Boys in a post-Communist country? It can mean a certain particular economic practice—that is, the determination to pursue a reform of relations of ownership. But it also can mean a glorification of egoism, a contempt for the weak and the poor, a disrespect for Christian options in defense of the most disadvantaged. In this, by the way, lies the paradox of the Solidarity movement. On the one hand, we opt for the market and for reprivatization. On the other, the upheaval in Poland was the creation of striking workers of precisely the huge industrial enterprises that are the least profitable, the ones that will have to be closed down.[1]

This paper makes a tentative, preliminary proposal of a housing privatization policy for a district of a large city in which most of the residential housing stock has been publicly owned and maintained, and operated with subsidized rent levels. The proposal is animated by the ideals of solidarity and participation. Its form contrasts not only with state ownership but also with the more familiar forms of classically liberal privatization in which solidarity and participation play little or no role.

The discussion proceeds from the general to the concrete. Part I identifies as a crucial issue in privatization the choice between regulatory and structural approaches to realizing solidarity and participation. Part II summarizes "institutionalist" thinking about the dynamics of an urban residential housing market following a conventional privatization of the publicly owned stock. Part III outlines the range of structural and regulatory policies currently pursued in Western housing economies. Part IV proposes a specific, eclectic mix of these policies as an alternative to an unrestricted distribution of public housing units to their occupants.

This is not a "practical" proposal because it is not based on a careful study of a particular post-communist urban housing situation. I produced it as a way of thinking about what I observed during two visits to Hungary in 1990 and 1991, but I am not an expert on the situation in that country, nor even on housing. The proposal represents an attempt to develop the conceptual vocabulary for talking concretely, even technically about a "third way" between the extremes of state socialism and liberal capitalism, rather than a solution to the actual housing privatization dilemma of a particular city.

I. Structural vs. Regulatory Solidarity and Participation

The proposal has three important characteristics. First, the policy is a specific combination of the whole range of different kinds of initiatives that have characterized social democratic and democratic socialist housing policy in Western Europe and the United States. It combines a market sector based on absolute ownership, a small fully public sector, a variety of types of restricted private ownership, and housing allowances. It also proposes to "steer" the evolution of public, restricted and private sectors through a particular mix of the regulatory regimes and institutions current in the West.

Second, the core of the policy is the creation of a limited equity cooperative sector within which residents hold inalienable rights to participate in building management, and an alienable but narrowly defined interest in the building's market value. Third, the policy takes advantage of the transitional regimes' ownership of the great majority of all residential and commercial property. It proposes to set up the limited equity sector through privatization to sitting tenants, and to finance the improvement of the housing situation of the poorest part of the population through the proceeds of sale of market rate units and through the profits from the state's commercial real estate.

The proposal quite obviously belongs to the general category of "third way" social thinking. It rejects, both in practice and as an ideal, the full "decommodification" of housing through collective ownership or through the establishment of an inalienable, state-backed housing entitlement. It equally rejects, both in practice and as an ideal, the assimilation of property in residential housing to the model of the abstract commodity subject to the classical rules of contract and tort.

However, the proposal does not claim or aspire to "transcend" this traditional duality through a new synthesis. It is rather an example of third-way thinking toward the eclectic, opportunistic adaption of all available social forms for the achievement of a balance, and toward the disintegration and colonization of the commodity form rather than toward its abolition. In this it is strongly influenced by socialist housing policy in Sweden, and analogous to the development of worker ownership schemes based on the restricted definition of shareholder rights.

The proposal is eclectic in that it attempts to "unleash" market forces while at the same time channeling them through a combination of "regulatory" and "structural" solidarity and participation. Both aim to prevent the evil of the modern slum, an area of exclusively low income residence characterized by physically and morally degrading housing conditions and neighborhood social pathology.

By regulatory solidarity and participation, I mean legal regimes that are understood as public interventions, generally through administrative agencies such as planning boards, rent control authorities and building inspectorates, that limit the exercise of otherwise absolute ownership rights, with the goal of protecting weak parties and the common interest. In this proposal, the main function of regulatory intervention is the preservation of neighborhood stability, and thereby the prevention of the polarization of the residential stock into high and low-income sectors. The goal is both to preserve class diversity for its own sake and to prevent alternation between downward cycles of disinvestment and upward cycles of gentrification for vulnerable groups.

By structural solidarity and participation, I mean the distribution among the variety of actors affected by housing decisions of "sculpted" property rights ("sticks" from the "bundle" that makes up absolute ownership), carefully designed so as to induce solidarity and participation through private action backed by private law remedies. The prime example of the structural approach is the definition of a resident's interest in a limited equity cooperative. The interest is private property, includes full possessory and succession rights, and is freely alienable. The participation rights attached to the unit are inalienable, as are the obligations to other building occupants. The property interest is limited to the right to recoup initial investment and improvements, but only a small fraction of any "speculative" or "urbanistically created" surplus. The remainder of the surplus belongs to other actors, which may include the cooperative, a community bank of some kind, the locality and the state. In "Limited Equity Housing Cooperatives as a Mode of Housing Privatization," which appears later in this volume, we develop the details of an institution of this kind, and describe how they might effect housing policy objectives.

A system in which most of the residential housing stock is held under such a regime is conceptually one of private property. There is no forced conversion of units from "full" to limited equity, no requirement that new construction be organized in that form, no legal obligation to buy a cooperative as opposed to an absolutely owned unit, and owners are free to sell *what they own* at any time. Yet it is also clear that this is a more "social," less individualist version of a private property system than one in which absolute ownership is the norm. It is a structural solution because the values of solidarity and participation are enhanced through the internal definition of the commodity of residential housing, rather than through a regulatory overlay on an individualist private law regime. Its great potential virtues are to prevent the "normal" tendency of even a regulated market to force the poor into slums, and to extend the possible sphere of democracy to include building self-management.

II. A Nightmare Privatization Scenario: The Institutionalist View

No developed Western economy in fact relies primarily on either the market or on state ownership to house the lower-income segment of its population. Throughout the West, both center-right and center-left governments have had extensive housing policies since World War II. This is a striking phenomenon, given the ideological commitment of these countries to the market.

As an explanation of the regulatory commitments of Western housing economies, imagine the following model housing situation. It is an ideal-type reconstruction of late nineteenth- and early twentieth-century European and American experience, and also, very significantly, of the current experience of those parts of Western markets that are unregulated or weakly regulated. Its relevance to postcommunist Eastern Europe is speculative.

Imagine that eight hundred thousand of a city's one million residents are housed in two hundred thousand very similar state-owned units, with more or less equal density (persons per square foot) and amenities. Commercial and recreational facilities are minimal. These units are relatively modern, are deteriorating quite rapidly, and are viewed as unappealing by traditional cultural standards. Their occupants have incomes varying from extremely low to quite high, and the differences in income are likely to increase through time.

Another hundred thousand residents of varied income levels live in twenty-five thousand "traditional" (late nineteenth- and early twentieth-century) state-owned units close to the city center. These are either in bad condition or are deteriorating rapidly. One hundred thousand high-income residents are housed in fifty thousand very high quality private units that have never been part of the state sector.

The government charges rents significantly below operating costs, based on the number of rooms in the unit. A state agency, known for its inefficiency, manages the whole stock, maintaining it in a more or less uniformly deteriorating condition. The housing deficit is made up out of the proceeds of progressive income taxation of the population as a whole. Tenant selection procedures have produced a random distribution of units among people of different income levels.

Now imagine that the state transfers all its units to their occupants for nothing. Further imagine that there are no restrictions on resale, on the form of tenure (rental, cooperative, condominium), rents, demolition, change of use, or structural modification of units. The state housing management enterprise is privatized. All subsidies end. The institutionalist view is that there are likely to be several dynamic tendencies.

A. Upper-income Housing Consumption

Upper-income households will sharply increase their consumption of housing and housing services and create homogeneous upper-income neighborhoods. These households (including some of those now in the private stock) will purchase new space, consolidate units, upgrade and rehabilitate, and attract private investment in new amenities and new services. They will use their higher incomes to bid space away from low-income households, and their high incomes will make the development of their neighborhoods attractive to private investment.

Since there are significant neighborhood effects of development, and great commercial advantage in investing in consolidated upper-income areas, there will be pressure to displace low-income families from any area that begins an "upward development spiral." These spirals are processes of cumulative change, based on "feedback effects," in which a given housing improvement increases the profitability of making a further improvement, and so on. They will produce income homogeneity in improving neighborhoods.

Some upper-income families will be able to afford the high cost of new construction. This will occur partly in existing upper-income areas, partly on undeveloped suburban land, and partly through the demolition of low- and middle-income units near the city center. High-income development will not produce enough new housing for "trickle down" (low-income families move into stock vacated by new upper-income construction) to ease the emerging shortage of low-income housing. (If new construction is truly unregulated, private developers and squatters will build very low quality housing, new slums, on the far outskirts of the city.)

Upper-income people will be better off in this situation for three reasons. First, they no longer subsidize the housing of lower-income groups. Second, the market offers them many new, affordable alternative uses for the part of their income they want to devote to housing. Third, there are now many homogeneous upper-income neighborhoods, rather than only a few.

B. Middle- and Lower-income Housing Consumption

Middle- and lower-income households will reduce their consumption of housing, relocate in poor neighborhoods, and suffer a general loss of wealth.

When the state distributes all units, at the same time terminating subsidized maintenance, it enriches one part of the population and impoverishes another. Every household now finds itself with a new asset, an apartment. But every household now faces either an immediate increase in living expenses, to sustain the old level of maintenance, or a decline in housing amenity.

For upper-income households, as pointed out above, this is probably a desirable situation: they prefer to spend a higher part of their incomes than they do on housing, in exchange for a higher level of amenity. Privatization increases the supply for them, so that they can make these expenditures at prices lower than those previously prevailing in the small private stock.

For a second, middle group, the benefits of ownership in a free market more or less balance the loss of the subsidy. This group may increase, reduce, or just maintain the current level of operating expenditures, but whatever that decision, it sees itself as benefitting from proprietary rights, including succession, ownership of improvements, and appreciation of asset value. These households would pay something to become owners, or at least not object to transfer.

For a third, low-income group, having to accept unsubsidized ownership is a financial disaster. For this group, the immediate increase in outlay necessary to keep up maintenance will require a reduction in other necessities, such as food, clothing, and health care. The decline in housing amenity, or in other consumption of necessities, means that the benefits of equity ownership are less than its liabilities. These households would not agree to become owners if given a choice.[2]

Many low- and middle-income tenants will sell their units for prices well below present market rates, and purchase less desirable units with lower operating costs, or rent similar lower-cost units, in newly homogeneous poor neighborhoods. Low-income owners, who face either sharply reduced consumption of necessities, or sharply reduced housing amenity, are under great pressure to sell. Their goal will be to move to smaller, less desirable quarters with lower operating costs. Where there is an upward spiral of neighborhood improvement, upper-income buyers will offer low- and middle-income owners prices for their units that exceed their use value in their existing condition. Low- and middle-income owners will sell, using the proceeds to buy or rent in less expensive neighborhoods.

The prices will be low for a number of reasons. First, the supply of market rate housing has increased enormously with privatization, but the demand, at least in the short run, should be basically the same. Second, low-income owners who cannot afford unsubsidized operating costs will have to sell. Third, there will be a significant number of unsophisticated low- and middle-income owners who will choose quick sale at a low price to "speculators," and other incompetent sellers who will be defrauded.

We would expect little long-run increase in the wealth of low-income people because they are likely to spend the proceeds of sale on new housing, or to meet their current expenses, or to cope with emergencies. This means that privatization is unlikely to modify the basic class and income hierarchy of the society.

Areas that do not experience an upward spiral will lose most of their upper-income residents to the improving areas, receive large numbers of displaced low-income renters, and become higher in density and economically homogeneous. There will be little or no reconfiguration or commercial development of low-income neighborhoods. Social problems will concentrate geographically, further reenforcing the tendency to polarization.

C. Characteristics of the Low-income Rental Sector

In this scenario, a low-income rental sector should emerge, characterized by several features. First, the sector will include a professional large landlord class and a petty bourgeois amateur group using ownership of a building or two as a way to begin family wealth accumulation. They will sometimes be excellent service providers, and sometimes incompetent or abusive. Second, lower-income tenants will pay higher absolute rents than at present, and receive in return a smaller proportion of the total stock (with more people to each room). Third, low-income apartments will deteriorate and have a very low "floor," meaning that conditions in the worst-maintained units will be likely to violate cultural norms about squalid living conditions. Fourth, there will be no substantial participation of low-income renters in building management.

To summarize, there will be a reduction in the actual housing consumption of the lower income half of the population, increasing density, a steady increase in the private market rents for low-income units, and physical deterioration of the low-income stock by comparison with the period before privatization. Low-income households will suffer three distinct wealth effects: first, the removal of government subsidy of operating expenses of their units with no concomitant tax reduction; second, upward pressure on rents based on market power of upper-income groups that want more space; and, third, concentration in low-income neighborhoods with accompanying downward spirals of social pathology. The wealth effects will increase low-income malnutrition, poor clothing, homelessness, and so forth. These negative effects are likely to be far greater than the positive wealth effect of acquisition of an apartment.

D. Low-income Market Instability

It is likely that the low-income neighborhood markets will be continuously unstable. Upgrading spirals in particular parts of the large uniform stock will be initiated by differences in amenities, such as distance from the center or from employment, public transportation, attractiveness of terrain, and so forth. The decisions of large investors to reconfigure whole areas, and the random effects of small improvements that bring a rush of followers, will also be important. The residential area of the central city is likely to "gentrify," meaning that all low-income residents will be bought or forced out, as upper-income households bid up prices beyond their ability to pay.

Whatever the pattern established in the first postprivatization period, it is unlikely to be stable over the long run. The reason for this is that the housing situation of the lower-income half of the population is dominated or driven by their relative position in the income distribution, rather than by their absolute or real income level.

The distribution of income is likely to become more unequal, after privatization of the economy. If growth is irregular, with fluctuations in the relative employment and income levels of social groups, or if there is significant migration between country and city, each change will set off dramatic new cycles of instability in the private residential stock.

It is important to see that these do not conform to the typical neoclassical liberal image of a system in stable equilibrium which responds to a changed input by the minimal adjustment needed to return to stability. In modern housing markets, small changes often produce cumulative feedback effects that leave the system quite far from where it started. For this reason, there are always likely to be significant masses of the lower-income population that are experiencing either displacement through eviction, or rapidly increasing rents as upper-income households bid for their space. Other significant parts of the population are likely to be experiencing neighborhood decline, with low rents, but significant social distress and unrest.

E. Political Polarization

The period of intense housing reconfiguration following privatization is likely to generate two groups with a deep interest in the continuation of an unregulated market regime. The first group consists of developers, land speculators, the luxury unit construction industry, the small entrepreneurs who convert and upgrade units, and landlords. The second group consists of that part of the upper-income group that hopes to use the monetary fruit of its labor (or its accumulated communist wealth) to dramatically improve its housing situation (at the expense of the lower-income group). In a democratic political system on the model of the West, the free-market groups will have large financial resources to invest in media, policy formulation, the corruption of public officials, and political campaigns. They will exercise an influence altogether disproportionate to their numbers.

Privatization on this model will generate a third group, low-income tenants, likely to be permanently opposed to the free-market housing policy. This group will have been impoverished by the transition process, and will have continuing grievances caused by the instability of the market in poor neighborhoods. Equally important, it will be a group accustomed to the social condition of private-market tenant, in which there is no incentive to invest in the unit, no practical power to influence what happens to other units in the neighborhood, and a relationship of class and social antagonism with a large bureaucratic or petty bourgeois landlord. The combination of impoverishment, disempowerment, and neighborhood instability often produces antidemocratic politics. A policy of "radical" privatization of this kind, with these results, is likely to alienate most of the bottom half of the income distribution from whatever political party puts it into effect.

III. Structural and Regulatory Alternatives

There are four basic domains of government housing policy in the West. These are:

(1) macropolicy to encourage new construction and control it through regional planning;
(2) housing allowances based on income and family size;
(3) regulation of the landlord-tenant relationship; and
(4) private and public law regulation of tenure (the legal form of ownership).

A. Macropolicy

The most basic policy of Western governments since World War II has been to encourage the construction of large quantities of housing. The second, equally basic policy has been regional planning, intended to control urban growth and to assure that the siting of new industry takes housing needs into account.

An important development in macropolicy has been the development of so-called "exactions." These are requirements that developers include in their costs a provision to offset the costs they will impose on the housing environment by their activities. At one level, this means requirements that they build roads or schools or day-care centers in their projects. Another important type of exaction is one that requires developers whose projects increase pressure on the low-income stock to include new low-income units.

B. Housing Allowances

Housing allowances are state grants to households designed to increase their ability to buy housing in the private market. The state can base them on income, family size, disability, or any other criterion. They increase the bargaining power of recipients *vis-à-vis* unassisted groups, and in the process enrich the owners of the existing housing stock, who can charge more than before because of increased demand. They allow recipients to choose how to spend their housing budget, rather than concentrating them in state-owned units. But they are open to their own variety of corruptions and abuses.

C. Legal Regulation of the Landlord-Tenant Relationship

Regulation of the landlord-tenant relationship includes various kinds of policies. One type of regulatory policy is a nonwaivable provision in residential leases requiring the landlord to invest enough in maintenance to keep the unit up to a minimum standard of "habitability." This type of provision is enforceable both through a public regulatory process (including criminal sanctions), and through private actions that tenants or tenant organizations bring against landlords.

A second form of regulatory policy is eviction control. This means that landlords may not terminate residential leases "at will," that is, at the landlord's discretion. The tenant has a nonwaivable continuing right of occupancy except where the tenant fails to pay the rent or behaves in an antisocial manner. A goal here is to encourage tenant investment in rental units.

A third form of regulation is rent control. Applied selectively, the purpose of rent control laws is not to redistribute income from landlords to tenants, but to prevent low-income tenants from being displaced when a change in upper-income demand threatens to price them out of their homes.

An additional form of regulation guarantees tenants participatory rights. Tenants may hold nonwaivable rights to participate in building organizations and local tenant unions. They also may hold nonwaivable rights to comanage various aspects of building life, and a right to good-faith collective bargaining over lease terms, including rents.

D. Regulation of Tenure

Policies aimed at the form of tenure, or legal ownership, have three objectives. The first is to encourage equity ownership (property rights) and discourage rental. The second is to develop forms of collective equity ownership rather than individual ownership. The third is to develop forms of ownership that discourage the neighborhood instability caused by "upward spirals" resulting from upper-income groups's demands for space that lower-income groups presently occupy.

Nonwaivable regulation of the landlord-tenant relationship will encourage ownership at the expense of tenancy. But there are further possibilities, ranging from subsidies, to owner-occupants (to prevent them from becoming renters), to flat legal prohibition of rental occupancy.

Where the state gives or sells a building (or part of it) to tenants, the deed might require that that the owner-occupants retain *nonwaivable* collective rights. The group controls building maintenance, rules for conduct, and selection of new occupants. A basic choice here is whether to allow decision-making by majorities, or to require supermajority or unanimous decisions. Contracts between collectives and building maintenance organizations are regulated by the state.

A basic social-democratic policy goal pursued in the West is to prevent changes in income distribution and business cycle shifts from progressively shrinking the part of the total housing stock that is available to the bottom half of the population. With respect to the rental stock, tenants' rights are partly designed to slow or prevent the displacement of low-income tenants when their units become desirable to higher income groups. But insofar as the state succeeds in promoting ownership rather than tenancy, the low-income stock becomes vulnerable to "buy-out." In periods of instability (gentrification), low-income owners sell their units to high-income buyers and use the proceeds to displace other low-income people.

To prevent this, the state can organize new low-income owners in limited equity cooperatives (LECs). LECs provide security of tenure, the right to inherit, full managerial power, and the right to recoup some portion of individual investment in units. But the right to appropriate "speculative" increases in equity, that is, to capture the market premium offered in periods of gentrification, is retained either by a nonprofit organization, the state, or a community land trust established for this purpose.

IV. An Alternative Policy

Through a variety of policy tools, the state can pursue a very different version of privatization. The aim of this privatization policy is to achieve a mix of goals, including the following:

(1) redistribution of income between richer and poorer halves of the population, so that the rich pay for some part of the housing of the poor;
(2) moderating or at least reducing market instability, the quick and wide swings in housing conditions that accompany the restructuring that is continuous within capitalism;
(3) moderating or at least reducing the class polarization of the housing stock, with its concomitant class segregation, impover-

ishment of the already poor, and social disintegration of poor neighborhoods;

(4) empowering low-income groups by giving them responsibility for the management of their buildings and neighborhoods.

What follows is an outline of a four-point alternative policy aimed to have an effect with respect to all four goals.

A. Sale of Units at Market Rates to Finance the Policy

Any sitting tenant should be allowed to buy his unit with no restrictions other than those existing in the currently private stock. These sales should be priced at *private market rates*, based on comparison with units now in the private stock, without state loans or interest subsidy. There should be restrictions on quick resale to deter speculation. The proceeds from these sales should be used to finance the rest of the program. Some of the desirable units occupied by poor tenants should be auctioned to the highest bidder without restrictions or subsidies, guaranteeing relocation of occupants. Again, the proceeds should be used to finance the rest of the program.

B. Sale of Units as Limited Equity Cooperatives

Some middle- and low-income units should be given or sold at below-market prices to tenants, with state financing at low interest rates, but with substantial deed restrictions. The first purpose of deed restrictions is to make sure that this part of the stock will continue to be available at low rents or finance charges to middle-income people. The restrictions should also organize apartment owners into cooperatives, with substantial control of building management and new owner selection.

Other units should be sold, at below-market rates, to large professional landlords with restrictions designed to assure the rights of present tenants, continuing middle-income affordability, and tenant participation in management. Substantial preferences, including price and interest rate concessions, should be given to nonprofit private housing organizations (for instance, trade unions). Such organizations should receive state-financed assistance in their formation and in training their personnel.

The proceeds of market-price sales should be allocated to the limited equity and rental sectors, for two purposes: to create a program of housing allowances for low-income households (for instance, pensioners, very low-wage workers), designed to allow them to own or rent restricted units, and to finance low interest rehabilitation loans.

C. Continued City Ownership of Low-income Units

Cities should continue to own and maintain subsidies for some presently city-owned units, but these should be restricted to low-income households unable to function effectively in the private or restricted markets (for instance, the disabled, the elderly, people of diminished competence, socially disorganized families). The proper balance between this policy and that of housing allowances can be determined only by experiment over time.

City-owned units should be geographically dispersed in upper- and middle-income buildings, except where it is desirable to operate "sheltered environments" (for instance, for the mentally ill). City tenants should have participation rights in their buildings, whether the other units are cooperative or landlord-owned. Dilapidated city-owned units should be rehabilitated using proceeds of private market sale.

D. Strategic State Presence in Housing Markets

The state should strategically retain buildings in neighborhoods likely to increase rapidly in market value, in architecturally significant areas, and in areas important for access to center-city culture. These buildings should be leased for terms of years to private entrepreneurs, who then release them at market rates.

The state should create a building-management enterprise, operated for profit as a public utility. It should be required to take all offers, from the limited equity and restricted rental sectors, as a competitor for the private sector. The state should also set up housing court, an inspectional agency, a legal services tenant-advocacy organization, and a planning administration, each legally independent. The role of these agencies is to enforce tenant rights against private landlord, state, and tenant-collective abuse, and to combat neighborhood instability, using zoning, rent control, and "linkage" programs in upgrading neighborhoods, and code enforcement and subsidies in deteriorating neighborhoods. The agencies should also regulate new development according to a regional plan.

Conclusion

Supposing that one arrives at conclusions about which goals to pursue and what tools to employ, a crucial question is that of the competence and size of the administrative apparatuses that will carry out the various policies. If the free market produces corruption by producing great fortunes, the regulated market produces corruption through thousands of small-scale incentives to evasion. The desire of the rich to increase their housing consumption puts them deeply at odds with the poor, and the desire is strong enough to motivate widespread lawlessness. Each regulatory policy calls on a different apparatus (whether the civil courts, building inspectorates, planners in the Ministry of Finance, and so on). The ideal policy mix will take full account of administrative possibilities and impossibilities.

Notes

1. Adam Michnik, "The Two Faces of Eastern Europe," *The New Republic* (November 12, 1990).
2. The beneficiaries of the wealth effects are likely to be old communist elites, prewar elites, new entrepreneurs, and the intelligentsia. The victims of privatization will be the lowest-paid members of the working class, and entitlement-holder groups such as pensioners and the disabled. Equity owners in the old private stock are likely to experience a long-term wealth loss as their units have to compete with newly privatized ones.

Limited Equity Housing Cooperatives As A Mode of Privatization

Duncan Kennedy
Leopold Specht

[*Editors' Synopsis:* Building on the analysis in Kennedy's previous paper, "Neither the Market Nor the State: Housing Privatization Issues," the authors detail a concrete method for privatizing formerly public housing in cooperative form.]

This paper instantiates some of the ideas briefly developed in "Neither the Market Nor the State: Housing Privatization Issues," in this volume. We describe a proposal that we made in 1990 to create housing cooperatives in one district in Budapest (District XIII). This proposal represents no more than a tentative suggestion. We both lack the specific technical and the local knowledge that would be necessary to write as experts. Further, we discuss only issues that seem likely to have a significant effect on the viability of the overall model of limited equity cooperatives. Actually implementing the model in a community that wished to privatize its public housing stock would, of course, require close attention to local laws and customary practices. Leopold Specht was the primary author of section II, Duncan Kennedy of sections I and III.

The goals of the proposal are:

(1) to secure ownership rights of the current occupants of public housing;
(2) to rehabilitate the existing housing stock;
(3) to promote self-management by occupants, rather than state management;
(4) to prevent the polarization of the stock into luxury, middle-, and low-income tiers; and
(5) to promote neighborhood stability by stemming spirals of rapid gentrification or deterioration.

The proposal is liberal, or free-market in character; that is, it is an authentic form of privatization. It is liberal in several senses. First, it respects the property rights of current occupants of public housing. Second, the transition to a private housing market would be entirely voluntary and based on the rights of joint-tenancy shareholders, rather than on public ownership. Third, the new system would respect freedom of contract, private property rights, and profit maximization. Finally, the state's participation in the new system would be minimal.

Although liberal, the proposed model seeks to retain a social interest in the urbanistically created surplus from future growth. Three aspects of the model reflect this goal: creation of a profit-oriented local development bank to make loans for rehabilitation, improvement, and expansion of the local residential housing stock; retention by the bank of an interest in the urbanistically created surplus; and use of the surplus to promote the housing goals of the locality.

I. The Proposal

The proposal is to privatize the District's publicly owned residential housing stock by giving the units to their occupants, organized in limited-interest joint tenancies.[2] The District will transfer publicly owned units to the District Development Bank, and the Bank will in turn transfer them to the joint tenancies, with the limitation described below.

A. Organization in Joint Tenancies

Each joint tenancy will consist of a number of units, and will correspond to a single building, to a part of a large building, or to several small buildings sharing common facilities. Each current occupant will become the owner of one share in the joint tenancy, which will be governed by its shareholders.

The joint tenancy will own the building. It will receive title from the District Development Bank free of charge, in exchange only for entering into the limited-interest contract. The joint tenancy will pay neither rent, nor any kind of purchase price to the District. Every joint tenancy is entitled to a rehabilitation and improvement loan from the Bank. Ownership of a share entitles the owner to occupy the unit, to modify it, to lease it, to transfer it to children at death, and to sell his interest in it at any time, all subject to the regulations adopted by the joint tenancy.

The functions of the joint tenancy are:

(1) to maintain and improve the common areas;
(2) to adopt and enforce regulations governing the exercise of owner rights;
(3) to represent the owners in their dealings with other private parties, the District and the District Development Bank, and the organization of joint tenancies.

All joint tenancies will be members of an organization of joint tenancies. It will be governed by majority vote of its members. Each member will pay a small annual fee for its support. The functions of the organization are to gather information, provide technical assistance, and represent the interests of the joint tenancies.

B. Self-management

The owners of the units in the joint tenancy are responsible for deciding how much maintenance, rehabilitation, and improvement to do, and who will do it. They are also jointly responsible for allocating the costs of maintenance, rehabilitation, and improvement among themselves, and for collecting and actually paying all expenses. The goal of the legal rules for organizing joint tenancy[3] should be to give the joint tenancy power to decide by majority vote how to manage the building, with relatively little power of individual shareholders to require or prevent joint tenancy action. A joint tenancy that enters into a rehabilitation or improvement loan contract with the District Development Bank is obliged to adopt this internal organization, until the full repayment of the loan. A joint tenancy that chooses not to participate in the loan program can adopt any internal governance system it wishes.

C. Individual and Bank Interests in the Joint Tenancy

1. Sale of Units

The owner of a share in a joint tenancy is free to sell at any time. On sale of the unit, the owner is entitled to recoup from the market sale price the investment he has made in the unit. The owner's investment includes several components. The owner's *initial* investment is the gray market value of the unit at the time of entering into the joint tenancy (that is, the price that could be obtained from a successor tenant under the public housing regime), or the actual price paid if the tenant has bought the unit from the State.[4] In addition to the initial investment, the owner's investment includes two other components: the cost of all improvements made to the property after the initial investment, and a return or profit on the sum of the initial investment plus the cost of improvements. This profit would be equal to the interest rate on savings deposited in a bank during the same period, or to the rate of inflation, whichever is greater. Thus, if the return on savings had been five percent throughout the period of investment, but the rate of inflation had been ten percent, the owner would receive his initial investment and improvements plus ten percent interest.

If the market sale price is less than the owner's investment, defined as the sum of the three items above, the owner is entitled to the full proceeds of sale. But if the market sale price is greater than the owner's investment, the owner is entitled only to recoup his investment, and to ten percent of the excess of the market sale price over that investment. Thus, if the owner's investment were one million forints, and the market sale price were two million forints, the owner would receive one million one hundred thousand forints.

Turning to the joint tenancy's interest, if the market sale price is less than the owner's investment, the joint tenancy receives nothing from the sale. If the market sale price is greater than the owner's investment, the joint tenancy receives ten percent of the excess. Thus, in the example above, the joint tenancy would receive one hundred thousand forints.

The joint tenancy should be obliged to deposit this money in the District Development Bank, and to spend it only for rehabilitation or improvement of the joint tenancy common areas, or to retire existing debt to the Bank (thereby reducing monthly payments for all shareholders).

Finally, concerning the District Development Bank's interest, if the market sale price is less than the owner's investment, the Bank receives nothing from the sale. If the market sale price is greater than the owner's investment, the District Development Bank is entitled to eighty percent of the excess. Thus, in the example above, with an owner investment of one million forints and a market sale price of two million forints, the District Development Bank would be entitled to eight hundred thousand forints.

If the District Development Bank agrees to a sale at the market price, it has no right to determine who the buyer shall be. If a sale occurs, the Bank must devote its share of the proceeds to its program of loans for rehabilitation, improvement, and expansion of the District's residential housing stock.

The District Development Bank will also retain, in the contract establishing the joint tenancy, a right of first refusal for all units in the joint tenancy. If the Bank decides to exercise its right of first refusal, it has two possible courses of action. First, it could decide that the unit should be sold below the market price, as part of the Bank's program to provide housing in this neighborhood for people who cannot afford to pay the full market price. The price to such a person would have to amount at least to the owner's investment, his share of the surplus, and the joint tenancy's share of the surplus. In the example above, the District Development Bank could not sell the unit for less than one million two hundred thousand forints.

Alternatively, the Bank has the right to purchase the unit itself, at a price covering the interests of the owner and of the joint tenancy, in order to incorporate it into the limited social housing sector described below.[6] Note that this right, like the right to sell the unit at less than the market sale price, arises only *when the owner has decided to sell.* The Bank has no right to force a sale.

2. Leasing of Units

Some limitation on the owner's right to lease his unit is necessary to prevent unit owners from appropriating the urbanistically created part of the market value of the unit. On the other hand, limitations on the owner's right to lease may produce a black market in leased apartments. In practical terms, the compromise chosen for this point will probably have important consequences for the long run viability of the scheme as a whole. The compromise must fit the particular "housing culture" of the District. For example, a scheme that depends on the members of the joint tenancy to police illegal leases will work or not work according to the attitudes and practices that neighbors customarily adopt toward one another.

Here is a possibility: The leasing of units is permitted, subject to approval of the lessee through the same procedure that governs approval of new unit owners, but the leasing owner must share the rent with the joint tenancy and with the Bank, according to a formula that grants the owner a fair return on his investment in the unit, but reserves the bulk of the surplus over that amount to the other parties.

D. Protection of Gray Market Rights and Elimination of the Gray Market

The interest of an occupant of a unit who acquired it from the previous occupant by paying a gray market price is protected in two ways. First, his occupancy right is protected through ownership of a share in the joint tenancy. Second, his interest in the joint tenancy includes the gray market value of the unit as of the time of the establishment of the joint tenancy, or includes the value as determined according to one of the alternative formulae.

On sale of the unit, the share owner can recoup his investment, so long as the market sale price of the unit is greater than his interest. However, it is a crucial part of the proposal to halt all future gray market sales. The District should proceed immediately to register the current occupants of all units, thereby conclusively establishing who has occupancy rights.

In the future, the owner of a share can sell his unit only through the procedures established here. A private sale, at the market rate or at a gray market percentage of market, would defraud the joint tenancy of its ten percent share of the excess of the market price over the owner's investment, and would defraud the District Development Bank of its eighty percent share of that surplus. Moreover, the joint tenancy has a right to approve or disapprove potential buyers (subject to rules against discrimination, described below). For this reason, a purported sale by a share owner to a private party in violation of the shareholder's contractual agreement with the joint tenancy must be legally void. Such a sale should be subject to being set aside whenever it comes to the attention of the authorities, regardless of how much time has passed. The unit sold fraudulently reverts to the ownership of the joint tenancy, subject to the rights of the District Development Bank.

An occupant of a publicly owned unit, who does not either buy the unit from the District under existing law, *or* join a joint tenancy, loses the right to resell the unit to another private party on the gray market. In the future, when a public housing tenant vacates his unit, it reverts to the District. Illegal occupants of public units should be evicted.

E. Loans to Joint Tenancies for Rehabilitation and Improvement

Every joint tenancy is entitled to receive a rehabilitation or improvement loan from the District Development Bank. In exchange, the joint tenancy must agree to the form of organization that we discuss below.[8] The purpose of this form of organization is to promote joint tenancy self-management, and to assure the best possible use of the loaned funds.

The timing, the amount, and the repayment and interest conditions of the loan depend on two factors: the availability of funds to the Bank, and the condition of the units in the joint tenancy, with respect to the degree of deterioration and the level of comfort. Ideally, the Bank would make larger loans on more favorable terms to joint tenancies in more deteriorated buildings, and to joint tenancies in buildings with "no comfort" or "half comfort" (that is, buildings lacking all or some standard amenities such as indoor plumbing and central heating).

The joint tenancy is legally responsible for the repayment of the loan and interest. The security for the loan is the building. The loan would be in the form of a line of credit with the Bank.

The joint tenancy decides how to spend the rehabilitation and improvement loan, and how to supervise the work. Both the District Development Bank and the organization of joint tenancies will provide technical assistance in undertaking these tasks if requested. The Bank enforces the requirement that all loan funds be spent on rehabilitation or improvement of the property.

The sources of funds are foreign capital invested directly in rehabilitation and improvement loans through the Bank; foreign capital raised through the mortgage or sale of the District's commercial property and development sites; and capital raised by the sale of residential units at market, including the Bank's eighty percent share in the surplus over investment generated by the sale of joint-tenancy units, or the sale at market of units whose occupants have not joined joint tenancies or become owners under existing law.

F. Housing Allowances for the Poorest Families

The District should provide a housing allowance to families whose incomes are so low that they cannot afford the maintenance and loan repayment costs of living in a joint tenancy.[9] The source of funds for the allowance should be the surplus of commercial rents over the District's cost in maintaining publicly owned commercial property. This source of revenue should be strictly tied to providing housing allowances, and not be incorporated in the general District budget.

G. Retention of a Limited Social Housing Sector

The District should retain a certain number of units in joint tenancies, and perhaps a small number of whole buildings. The units the District retains should be managed by the District as a fully public "social housing sector." These units should be reserved for individuals or families that are unable to manage their own housing affairs, including disabled, elderly, mentally ill, and socially disorganized households.

Through the Bank, the District may purchase units in joint tenancies, offered for sale voluntarily by their owners, at a price representing the cost to the Bank of exercising its right of first refusal. The joint tenancy in which such a unit is located has no right to prevent such a sale.

II. The District Development Bank

The District Development Bank would be created as a private financial institution, with majority control by the District, operating for profit with the goal of developing the District's residential housing stock through the system of limited-interest joint tenancies.

A. Goals and Activities

The Bank's goals are:

(1) to amass and allocate capital for the development of the residential housing stock;
(2) to create incentives for the creation and operation of limited-interest joint tenancies;
(3) to recover and allocate the urbanistically created surplus from the growth of the District in such a way as to increase the residential housing stock, prevent the polarization of the stock between rich and poor, and preserve neighborhood stability.

The Bank has two primary activities. The first is to establish joint tenancies by transferring previously publicly owned buildings to their occupants, reserving an interest in the surplus of the future market sale price over the investment and interests of the unit owner and joint tenancy, and a right of first refusal. The Bank's second primary activity is making loans to joint tenancies for rehabilitation and improvement, and financing new construction in the joint-tenancy form. In addition, the Bank would perform several subsidiary functions, including providing a variety of financial and commercial services to joint tenancies in competition with private entities, or contracting for these services on behalf of joint tenancies (thereby increasing their bargaining power). These services would include insurance and real estate brokerage, and building operation.

The Bank's profit orientation means that its activities must be commercially sound in each area, and not based on state subsidies. The Bank is not an administrative agency, and has no regulatory power. Nor is it part of the state or municipal bureaucracy. It will make financial and other services available to the joint tenancies and others, at prices that allow it to cover its costs fully over time. More generally, it would influence the joint tenancies and the general development of the locality's housing stock through its choices in allocating capital and by providing incentives.

B. The Bank's Structure, Management, and Dividend Policy

The founders of the Bank would be the District government and (preferably) a foreign partner. After the Bank's establishment, the two founders would sell part of their shares so that there would be four types of shareholders:

(1) the District's government;
(2) the foreign partner (either a commercial bank or a foreign insurance company);
(3) joint tenancies that wish to invest in the Bank's shares; and
(4) individual owners of joint-tenancy units who wish to invest in the Bank's shares.

The District government would hold more than fifty percent of the shares. It would contribute occupied publicly owned units, for conversion to limited-equity joint tenancies, and would also contribute vacant publicly owned units, for conversion or sale at the market price. The foreign partner would hold approximately twenty percent of the shares, and would contribute money capital in hard currency. Joint tenancies would hold approximately twenty percent of the shares, and would contribute either in the form of money capital, or in kind (turning over the ownership of the building to the Bank). Individual joint-tenancy unit owners would hold approximately ten percent of the shares, and would contribute either in the form of money capital or in kind.

There should be provision for change with respect to the participation of joint tenancies and individual owners. During the initial period after the founding of the Bank (for instance, for the first ten years), the system of participation should be fixed. But at a later point it might be desirable to increase the basic capital of the Bank by increasing the contribution of joint tenancies and individual owners. It should be possible to change the structure to accommodate this increase, and, if advisable, an eventual shift in majority control from the District to joint tenancies and individual unit owners.

Individual owners of units in joint tenancies would have the minority control rights that the Company Law allocates to a block of ten percent of the total shares. These rights would be granted even if all individual shareholders taken together do not represent ten percent of the shares of the Bank.

The District government and the foreign partner would have the right to representation on the Board of Directors and the Board of Supervisors. However, their representatives would not have a majority of the votes in either body.

If dividends are paid to shareholders, linear (pro rata) distribution would be the rule. The articles of association should contain a provision stating a preference for the reinvestment of profits in the development of the residential housing stock. It should require a qualified majority of the General Meeting to decide to pay a dividend to shareholders.

III. The Bank's Loan Program

Crucial to the success of our proposal is that it include a formula for allocating the Bank's residential housing development capital among buildings that consent to become joint tenancies. This formula should make sense on the assumptions that there is little or much capital available, and few or many buildings that are willing to become coops. The amount of capital available and the number of buildings that will convert are unknown, and will depend in part on the design and success of the program over time. Therefore, this initial formula should be regarded as decidedly provisional. As conditions change, the formula will have to change also.

The formula needs two components: one setting amounts of loans for different kinds of buildings, and a second setting an order of allocation of available funds. We assume that, other things being equal, the Bank will make a larger loan to a building of lower comfort level than to one of higher comfort level, and a larger loan to a building in a more deteriorated condition.

One approach would be to distribute the loans according to the time of application. But it might be much more useful to set up a determinate sequence of buildings or neighborhoods, and require their occupants to choose their form of organization according to the Bank's timetable, rather than their own. The reason for this is that the loan program has two goals. The first is to bring about the improvement of the stock from the bottom, that is, beginning with the units that are in the worst condition and have the lowest level of comfort. The second goal is to induce occupants of buildings with presently or potentially high market value to enter the joint-tenancy program, thereby securing the urbanistically created surplus to the Bank.

Both of these goals are necessary for the equitable distribution of the benefits of privatization. Specifically, both are necessary to prevent privatization of publicly owned housing from randomly distributing the windfall of a very valuable apartment to those families that happen to occupy units that have a good location, or are on the path of future development. These occupants are no more entitled to a sharp, unearned increase in their wealth than are occupants of units that are farther from the city center and structurally less desirable. Indeed, those who live in the less desirable units arguably have a greater claim to gain some benefit from privatization than those who are already well provided for.

The goals are to some extent in conflict. We can illustrate the conflict by looking at two extreme cases. At the upper extreme, there are buildings that are upper-income, in good condition, and have a high market value. At the other extreme, there are buildings that are in poor condition, are low-income, and have low market value. At the upper end, it will take a very large loan, but one that is not socially desirable, to induce the upper-income building occupants to enter a limited-interest joint tenancy. At the bottom end, incomes are low enough that the loss of the current maintenance subsidy, when moving from a low rent to a joint-tenancy regime, will make conversion unattractive. Adding the costs of a rehabilitation loan just makes the situation worse. For the upper group, it makes sense to go for the most extreme market solution; for the lower group, any amount of market system is more than they can afford.

If we allocate the loans building by building, adjusting the amount in each case to induce every unit to enter a joint tenancy, we would end up allocating most of the loan funds to a small number of upper-income families that already occupy excellent housing. The rest of the total loan funds would go to the great majority of middle-income occupants in middle-condition buildings. The low-income group would not participate at all.

On the other hand, if we adopt a single formula based on the condition and quality of the building, the number of buildings that convert to joint tenancy will depend on how high the loan is. The best buildings with the highest value are likely to stay outside the system, unless it is possible to raise an unrealistically large amount of capital, and no amount of loans will make conversion attractive to low-income buildings. The conflict will be less extreme to the extent that some high-value buildings close to the center are in very bad condition and/or occupied by lower-income families, and some low-value buildings far from the center are occupied by middle- or upper-income families.

The District should take action to make the conflict less extreme by increasing the incentive for occupants of high-value buildings to convert to joint tenancies. The obvious way to do this is to eliminate or modify the present practice of selling units to occupants at fifteen percent of market (or less). The reason for doing this is that it is immoral for the State to distribute a large, unearned, wealth increase on the basis of the random fact of occupying a publicly owned unit with a high market value.

The fact that many of these occupants purchased their units on the gray market does not support giving them full ownership of their units for a fraction of market value. The reason for this is that the District's joint tenancy scheme guarantees them the present value of their gray market investment, as well as perpetual occupancy rights. There is no valid reason to give them more than this.

If it is not possible to eliminate the fifteen percent sales, it should be possible to slow them down, by administrative measures, or to modify the procedure by insisting on the full observance of all substantive and technical requirements of the law. To the extent such a policy of full enforcement of all the provisions of the law makes it much more difficult to buy at fifteen percent, occupants should be more willing to enter joint tenancies in exchange for reasonable development loans (plus protection of gray market investments and occupancy rights).

Another possibility is a compromise between the goals. This would require reestablishing two different loan formulae, one for low-market-value buildings and another for high-value buildings. But, the high-value formula should be less than necessary to induce all high-value buildings to enter the coop system, and the low-value formula should be more than is likely necessary to induce these buildings into the coop system.

It may be politically impossible to implement a proposal of this kind. The reason would be that it openly discriminates between buildings according to their market value, giving a larger loan to a higher-market-value building, even when it is in exactly the same condition as a low-market-value building. All the same, it would be desirable to effect such a discrimination, because it would increase the ability of the Bank to provide development loans in the future for low-market-value buildings. It would do this because it would increase the number of high-value buildings in which the Bank holds an interest (eighty percent of the surplus of market value over occupant investment).

When units in these buildings are sold, the proceeds that go to the Bank become available for further development loans that would be targeted to low-value buildings. Moreover, this Bank interest will capture increases in urbanistically created value over the indefinite future, providing a perpetual fund for improvement of the housing stock.

Yet another compromise solution would be to begin with a single formula, granting relatively large loans for conversion, and to target these loans administratively to high-value buildings. When this targeted program has led to the conversion of many high-value units, the Bank would change the formula, reducing the amount of loans. It would then use these smaller loans to induce the lower-value buildings to convert to joint tenancies.

The procedure would be for the District to adopt a privatization program that proceeds, building by building, under a single formula. When a building is selected for privatization, the occupants have three choices:

(1) enter the coop system in exchange for a loan determined according to the formula;
(2) all occupants buy their units at fifteen percent, or whatever the existing law allows; or
(3) give up their units to the Bank possibly in exchange for equivalent housing elsewhere.

Here it would be necessary to adopt some set of regulations governing how the occupants of the building vote in deciding which course to follow. It would be important to structure the regulation to give a preference for a joint-tenancy outcome. One way to do this would be to convert the building automatically to a joint tenancy (with a loan according to the formula) unless eighty percent of the occupants wished to purchase the building under the existing fifteen percent law. This would allow low-income occupants, who have no desire to move, and no funds available to pay for both higher maintenance costs and purchase-loan costs, to block the sale—as long as they make up more than twenty percent of tenancy. They would have a preference for the joint tenancy because of the absence of any initial cost of purchase, and the availability of a low-cost development loan. The joint-tenancy organization suggested in the Appendix would also give them some protection from a later decision by an upper-income building majority to greatly increase monthly charges in order to upgrade the building.

None of these proposals (eliminating or restricting sales at fifteen percent; adopting two formulas instead of one; implementing two formulas over time) will help draw the lowest-income occupants into the joint-tenancy system. They can barely afford their current low rent; they could not afford the actual maintenance done on their units; they could not afford the carrying charges on anything but very small rehabilitation loans. To deal with this problem, we propose a combination of a housing allowances program, and retention of fully public housing units. The initiation of the joint-tenancy conversion program does not require the District to change its administration of units that remain public. But as the District's total expenditures for maintenance are reduced by the conversion process, the cross-subsidy, from the excess of commercial rents over maintenance costs, will become available for concentration on low-income occupants and units.[10]

The joint tenancy program may be worth pursuing to the extent of available loan capital, even if the relevant calculations[11] show that relatively few high-value buildings can be converted. The reason for this is that future urban growth will cause large, unpredictable increases in value. If the District converts most of the currently low-value stock to limited-interest joint tenancies now, it will be able to direct the use of these certain, but spatially unpredictable, value increases when they occur. In other words, there is probably no "threshold" loan amount, or a threshold number of convertible buildings, below which the program is impractical or useless. Even a small program would be worthwhile, and a small program should not be much more expensive per building than a large one. Before extending this analysis to deal with the issues of housing allowances and the retention of a fully public "social housing sector," we need some reaction to what has been done so far, and some idea of the feasibility of the different options we have outlined.

IV. The Internal Organization of the Joint Tenancies

This section discusses, although only in a very preliminary way, the important legal question of the internal organization of the limited-interest joint tenancies. When the occupants of a building decide they want to participate in the District's program, they form a joint tenancy. If they wish to receive a rehabilitation loan from the District Development Bank, they have to agree to a particular organizational form. What should that form be?

In a general way, there are three very different models for the internal organization. The first model is based on maximum protection for the rights of individual unit owners at the expense of all other objectives. In this model, a single unit owner would be allowed power to require the joint tenancy to achieve a prescribed level of maintenance of common areas, to prevent the building from exceeding that level, to modify, lease, divide, or deteriorate his own unit without interference from the joint tenancy, and to take advantage of rigorous procedures, including judicial review, before the joint tenancy could evict him for nonpayment of charges or misconduct. Moreover, there would be sharp limits on the extent to which the joint tenancy could regulate the behavior of its members with respect to the use of the apartment and common areas.

The second model is just the inverse of the first, locating much power in the joint tenancy over all these matters, so that a majority of the unit owners have a maximum ability to actually undertake self-management.

The third model locates the power neither in the individual unit owner nor in the majority of shareholders of the joint tenancy, but in an executive or management body. The virtue of this third model is that it retains the power of the joint tenancy, but relieves the unit owners from having to participate directly in decisions, like that to evict for nonpayment, that are likely to be controversial and unpleasant.

We do not believe that there is any form of internal organization that will eliminate all problems. Each form has its own serious weakness and vulnerability to abuse. Any practical form of organization must be a compromise between the three models. The compromise should be drawn with great attention to the particular characteristics of the group that will be bound by it. The Draft Charter of a Limited Equity Cooperative that we have included as an Appendix to this paper sets out one possible resolution of these issues, but as a starting point for discussion rather than a firm proposal.

Appendix

Draft Charter of a Limited-Equity Cooperative

A. The Association

1. *The Association has legal personality:*
    a. the Association owns the building or buildings;
    b. the Association consists of the shareholders:
        i. every unit owner, with one share apiece,
        ii. the District Development Bank, with one share;
    c. except for the DDB itself, no owner or lessee of a unit in another limited-equity cooperative established by the DDB can own a share representing a unit in this Association;
    d. the Association can be dissolved only by unanimous vote of the Association, including the DDB;
    e. except as specified in A(3)(i) below, this Character can be modified only by unanimous vote of the shareholders, including the DDB.
2. *The governing body:*
    a. composed of one vote per unit (the DDB is not part of and has no vote in the governing body);

   b. decision by majority vote of unit owners present except in the cases indicated below;
   c. notice, quorum, and procedural requirements as specified in [the Act governing Cooperative Associations].
3. *Powers and rights of the governing body:*
   a. determination of expenditures for maintenance, rehabilitation, and renovation;
   b. power to borrow money for maintenance, rehabilitation, and renovation;
   c. determination of fees, charges, and assessments to unit owners to cover the obligations of the Association;
   d. right to ten percent of the excess of market price over investment on the sale of any unit;
   e. right to sell any unit that has no owner entitled to occupancy (for instance, as a result of foreclosure of the interest, death without succession by a "member of the immediate family" [see below], and so forth);
   f. approval of transfer of whole or part of unit ownership:
      i. approval of new unit owners,
      ii. approval of sublessees of a whole unit,
      iii. approval of rent-paying co-occupants,
      iv. approval of use of unit as security for loans;
   g. regulation of unit condition:
      i. required minimum maintenance by unit owner when it affects other units,
      ii. regulation of physical modification of units, as by internal subdivision, addition or modification of windows, enclosure of balconies, and so forth;
   h. regulation of conditions of occupancy, including:
      i. commercial or other nonresidential use,
      ii. number of occupants, unrelated occupants, children, pets, and so forth;

[Alternative: At the time of adoption of the Charter, the Association adopts a set of regulations with respect to the matters in §§ (f), (g) and (h) above. Because the unit owners have entered the Association in reliance on these regulations, there should be a further Charter provision:]

   i. when they are incorporated into the Charter, the governing body can modify regulations under headings (f), (g) and (h) above only by a two-thirds vote of unit owners.
4. *The building committee:*
   a. the governing body shall elect a building committee for a fixed term, subject to removal at any time by the governing body;
   b. the building committee has legal power to act on behalf of the associa-

tion (make contracts, and so forth) in relation to legal entities external to the Association, but cannot bind the Association to anything but a "routine maintenance expense" without a prior vote of the governing body;

c. the building committee is responsible for the collection and payments of fees, charges, and assessments to unit owners to cover the obligations of the Association;

d. the building committee has power to enforce the regulations of the governing body against unit owners, subject to the specific provisions defining the rights of unit owners.

5. *Limitations on the powers of the Association, the governing body and the building committee:*

   a. no action shall be taken that is inconsistent with the rights of unit owners as specified below;

   b. no action shall be taken that is inconsistent with the rights of the District Development Bank as specified below.

B. The Rights of Unit Owners

1. The unit owner has the property rights over his unit specified in the [Act Governing Jointly Owned Apartment Buildings] except as expanded or limited by this Charter.
2. The financial interest of the unit owner consists of his investment, defined as initial valuation plus improvements, plus ten percent of market value in excess of investment.
3. The unit owner has the right at death to devise the unit to a member or members of his "immediate family," [as this term is defined. . . .] and such a devise is not subject to disapproval by the Association. The owner can devise his financial interest in any way consistent with the [Statute of Wills]. In the case of a devise to a person not a member of the "immediate family," the occupancy right and the right of sale pass to the Association. In the case of intestacy, the members of the "immediate family" inherit full ownership in the order specified in the [Act on Intestate Succession]. If there is no member of the "immediate family" entitled to the property, the financial interest passes according to the [Act on Intestate Succession], but the occupancy right and the right of sale pass to the Association.
4. The unit owner has the right to sell his unit at any time for any price, subject to the rights of the Association and of the District Development Bank as specified in this Charter.
5. The unit owner has the right to sublease his unit, to subdivide it, or to rent an undivided portion, in accordance with the following rules: [*this EXTREMELY IMPORTANT provision needs to be worked out so as*

not to defeat the whole scheme by the creation of a class of landlords of cooperative units].

6. With respect to the imposition of any sanction against him by the governing body or the building committee, a unit owner has the procedural rights specified in the [Act Governing Cooperative Associations].
7. After a decision by the governing body or building committee to impose a sanction on him, a unit owner has the right to [review by the Dispute Resolution Body of the District Development Bank]. That body shall resolve the dispute consistently with the mandate of the DDB to promote housing affordability and neighborhood stability.
8. In the event the governing body decides on expenditures above and beyond "normal maintenance" requiring an increase in fees, charges, and/or assessments that would "significantly reduce the affordability of the building," any unit owner can appeal the decision to the [Dispute Resolution Body of the DDB]. That body shall resolve the dispute consistently with the mandate of the DDB to promote housing affordability and neighborhood stability.
9. In the event the governing body chooses a level of maintenance that threatens "to significantly reduce the quality of the building," any unit owner can appeal to the [Dispute Resolution Body of the DDB]. That body shall resolve the dispute consistently with the mandate of the DDB to promote housing affordability and neighborhood stability.
10. Any unit owner can challenge any regulation or by-law (not part of this Charter) of the Association before the [Dispute Resolution Body of the DDB], which shall invalidate it if it is "unreasonable," having due regard to the mandate of the DDB to promote housing affordability and neighborhood stability.

C. *Rights of the District Development Bank*

1. The DDB has the right to apply to court to place the Association "in receivership" in the event of mismanagement or abuse by the governing body or building committee.
2. The DDB has the right, on sale of a unit at the market price, to eighty percent of the excess of the market price over the investment of the unit owner.
3. The DDB has a right of first refusal of any unit offered for sale by the owner or by the Association.
4. The DDB has the right, if it chooses to purchase a unit from the owner or from the Association, to sell the unit below market price, and the governing body has no right of approval of the buyer.
5. The DDB has the right to lease any unit it owns at a rent of its choosing, and the governing body has no right of approval of the lessee; provided

that: if the DDB chooses to rent a unit that it owns, the tenant, and not the DDB, shall exercise the rights of a unit owner in the governing body.

D. General Clauses

1. In the event of any dispute arising about the interpretation of this Charter, the body adjudicating the dispute shall interpret this document so as to protect and further the rights of the individual unit owners, the rights of the Association as a whole, and the public interest, represented by the DDB, in development of the housing stock, housing affordability, and neighborhood stability.
2. Neither the Association, the governing body, nor the building committee shall, by any act or omission, discriminate against a unit owner, or an applicant for any form of occupancy of a unit, on the basis of race, ethnicity, religion, gender, sexual orientation, physical disability, marital status, or income.
3. Each signatory of this Charter agrees to abide by its provisions in good faith. In the event of any dispute arising about the interpretation of this Charter, the body adjudicating the dispute shall interpret the document so as to prevent any party from acting otherwise than in good faith with respect to its particular provisions and general spirit.

Notes

1. We are not using the term joint tenancy in any technical legal sense. We discuss the possible legal forms of the joint tenancy below. See Section I. C., infra.
2. We discuss some of the important questions relating to the internal organization of the joint tenancy in Section IV infra.
3. Another possibility would be to determine the gray market value as of a specified date. Yet another would be to set the investment as key money paid to the state, or a *verifiable* gray market payment to a private party, and allow for improvements and interest from the date of first occupancy. We do not have enough information to make a recommendation on this point.
4. See Section I. G. infra.
5. The Bank's interest is as described above.
6. See Section IV. infra.
7. For the mechanics of such an allowance, see Raymond J. Struyk and Jozsef Hegedüs. *Integrating State Rental Housing with the Private Market: Designing Housing Allowances for Hungary* (Washington, D.C.: Urban Institute Press, 1991).
8. Further analysis of the design of the loan program requires information about the actual composition of the stock, the quantity of loan capital that might be

available, and the political preferences and constraints under which the program will be carried out. The main questions to be answered or estimated would seem to be: (1) How are the existing buildings distributed according to market value? (2) For loans of different amounts, what proportion of buildings of different value would convert to joint tenancies? (3) Assuming either a single formula for all buildings, or different formulas for high- and low-value buildings, what would be the total cost of the whole loan program for different levels of conversion of the whole stock?

In addition to these matters, we need to have an idea of the distributive consequences of making large loans to induce high-value buildings to convert. Specifically, we need to know the correlation between market value and income of occupants, the correlation between market value and comfort level/deterioration, and the correlation between comfort level/deterioration and income. On the basis of this information, it should be possible to estimate roughly the trade-off between, on the one hand, inducing more high-value buildings to convert, and, on the other, distributing the loans equitably in terms of comfort level, building deterioration, and income level.

9. See note 8 supra.

Republicanism, Market Socialism, and the Third Way

William H. Simon

[*Editors' Synopsis:* The idea of a "third way" (or "fourth way," as we have called it) is not a mere fantasy. Various economic and legal arrangements in the U.S. and other capitalist societies have embodied the values of such an alternative approach. Even today in the West economic institutions exist that reflect aspects of classical republicanism and market socialism. This paper surveys these practices, analyzes their formal characteristics, and evaluates criticisms of them.]

Is there a "third way" of economic reform between capitalism (in both its laissez-faire and social-democratic variants) and socialism? The most frequently given answer to this question is no. It is widely asserted throughout the world that the relative success of capitalist economies, the failure of communist experiments at decentralizing reform, and the absence of any empirical examples of successful, alternative, economic systems concludes the case against the notion of the third way, or any similar alternative to capitalism.

A more sophisticated response holds that the question is confused. The question assumes that the notion of capitalism entails a limited, determinate set of institutions, when in fact capitalism is compatible with—and has spawned—myriad institutional forms. The bare idea of the market means little more than economic decentralization. The idea of private property can also be implemented in a variety of ways. Capitalism, moreover, empirically has extensively accommodated not only regulatory and tax constraints on private property, but also many forms of nonprivate property, including government property, commons, and charitable trusts. Actual capitalist economies are a hodgepodge of institutional forms that could be infinitely modified and rearranged without causing the society to cease being capitalist. Thus, the argument goes, since the commitment to capitalism in the abstract precludes so few concrete institutional options, it's pointless to talk about whether there's some third way.

This essay is a partial dissent from these responses. I argue that there is a vision of economic reform that can be usefully distinguished from capitalism (in both its laissez-faire and social-democratic variants) and socialism, and whose promise (while admittedly speculative) has not been discredited by recent history.

I. The Social-Republican Model

This alternative can be found in converging elements of the traditions of economic republicanism and market socialism. Like the social-democratic variant of capitalism, the alternative rejects both socialist state property and capitalist unlimited private accumulation. However, to a greater extent than social democracy, it pursues its concerns by encouraging a politically desirable *primary* distribution of income and wealth.

There are myriad versions of republicanism and market socialism. The ones of concern here share a commitment to participation and equality in the economic sphere, and a sympathetic focus on small-scale, locally rooted enterprise. It would be a difficult task to disentangle republican from socialist rhetoric in the many political movements that invoked these themes in mid- and late-nineteenth-century America and Europe. The themes were expressed in terms that mixed republican and socialist rhetoric in the labor radicalism of this period, for example, in the programs associated in America with the Knights of Labor, in France with Pierre-Joseph Proudhon, and in Germany with Ferdinand Lassalle, as well as in the agrarian counterparts of these movements.[1] Social-republican themes appear in more distinctly republican rhetoric in the tradition of political thought that J. G. A. Pocock has traced to James Harrington, and that influenced the Jeffersonian agrarian republicanism and the petty bourgeois strands of Jacksonian democracy, Whig political economy, and the radical republicanism of the Civil War era.[2] One can also find overlapping themes in the more distinctly socialist rhetoric of the market socialist theories and programs developed since the 1950s in East-Central Europe, especially in the former Yugoslavia.[3]

Perhaps the most revealing feature of the social-republican vision is a distinctive notion of property. Social-republican property affords the possessor far more autonomy than state socialist property, but subjects her to two types of restraints alien to conventional capitalist property: transfer or alienation restraints that confine control of the property to active or potentially active participants in a community constituted by the property, and accumulation restraints designed to limit inequality among members of such a community. These core features of social-republican property operate as restraints on the commodification and capitalization of relationships. They restrict the ability of the owner/citizen fully to monetize or liquidate her interest, or to convert anticipated future benefits into present lump sums. They thus encourage the owner to view her interest as a stake in a particular, long-term relation.

While social-republican property norms are most readily associated with fairly radical projects of broad-scale economic reform, there are important discrete examples of this type of property in contemporary American society. Social-republican norms tend to be routinely imputed to a narrow set of political or citizenship entitlements, such as voting rights. Although social republican property is rarer in the private economic sphere, there are some interesting examples of it there, such as limited equity housing and production cooperatives.[4] Moreover, a variety of regulatory and welfare policies, such as certain forms of tax relief and rent control, create interests that resemble social-republican property, and may in fact be inspired by social-republican principles.

The social-republican political vision sees property ownership as a safeguard of citizen independence and a check on the abuse of state power. At the same time it seeks to check both the abuse of property rights that threaten community, and property accumulations that threaten equality. Historically, large-scale creations of social-republican property have typically followed wars and revolutions, and have usually been financed with resources confiscated from conquered peoples or the losing sides in civil wars—the land-redistribution programs associated with the American Homestead Act, and the agrarian law of ancient Rome are famous examples. In stable, contemporary societies, social-republican property typically emerges on a smaller scale, usually induced through conditions on government loans or grants, or regulatory or tax exemptions. From a social-republican point of view, the current large-scale privatization projects in East-Central Europe present an opportunity for large-scale creation of social-republican property, without the violent or coercive confiscation that has attended such efforts in the past.

II. Citizenship Rights as Social-Republican

Contemporary American legal and political culture is neither socialist nor republican. The more prominent conceptions of property in the culture are classical liberal or social-democratic, rather than social-republican. There is, however, an important core of rights where liberal culture tends both to impose alienation and accumulation restraints, and to justify these restraints in the same political terms as republicanism and market socialism. These are the rights associated with "citizenship," understood in its popular rather than its technical legal meaning to denote the minimal rights of membership in the community. These rights at least include the right to remain in the country, the right to the protection of the laws, and the right to vote in elections to public office.[5]

It is uncontroversial that these core citizenship rights are constituted with strong alienation and accumulation restraints. Although the right to remain in the United States is notably scarce in the economic sense and would undoubtedly command a substantial price were it marketable, holders of the right cannot transfer it. (They can renounce or forfeit it, though this is not easy to do for citizen holders.) There is no way to acquire more than one American citizenship. And with a few exceptions, American citizenship requires foregoing citizenship rights in other nations.[6] The right of legal protection is also nontransferable, and is defined in terms of equality; it is a right to legal treatment on terms comparable to those on which other citizens are treated.[7]

Voting rights associated with citizenship are also strongly nontransferable (though not nonforfeitable). In general, voting rights must be exercised by the holder herself in person; proxies are precluded.[8] The purchase and sale of votes is typically defined as criminal, often in distinctively republican rhetoric as "corruption of voters."[9] And of course, voting rights typically must be allocated on the basis of "one man [sic], one vote," a principle that requires, within limits, that the electoral process be structured so that voters have equal influence.[10]

Citizenship rights are allocated through a political/legal process that emphasizes criteria of familial and geographical proximity. People can acquire citizenship automatically by being born within the territory of the country regardless of their family relationships, or by being born to citizen parents regardless of where. The naturalization criteria are more complex, but they too emphasize kinship and geographical proximity (prolonged residence).

That mainstream liberal society defines the core of the citizenship rights it recognizes in terms identical to the social-republican approach shows that the social-republican perspective differs less over the nature, than over the scope, of citizenship rights. The social-republican perspective is more prone to treat economic interests as matters of citizenship.

III. Property and Residence

Political communities are defined geographically in terms of residence. However, in a liberal polity, residence does not connote property ownership, even for citizens; legal residence has come to mean largely a state of mind, an "intention to remain" within the jurisdiction. This much is enough to entitle the citizen to exercise narrowly defined political rights of citizenship, but citizenship entitles the citizen to not much more than these rights.

Nevertheless, the social-republican argument that political participation without property cannot be fully meaningful to the individual retains some strength. People still require property as a practical means both of effective participation, and of enjoyment of the fruits of participation. Consider an argument that Robert Ellickson has made recently in the very unsocial-republican language of public choice theory.[11] If people succeed through political action in improving their communities, then to the extent outsiders share their values, much of the value of the improvements will be capitalized into higher real estate prices. The housing market translates public success into private wealth.

From a social-republican perspective, this is troubling for several reasons. One concern is that private gains may divert citizens' attention from the common good in political decision-making. Another concern is that inequality will be exacerbated. Ellickson, however, focuses on a more central concern. To the extent that the market capitalizes civic improvements in real estate values, only owners will typically benefit from them in the long run. In particular, tenants will find that their rents increase by an amount representing some or all of the market value of their shares of civic improvements. They may in fact lose their membership in the community entirely, because they can no longer pay the increased rents. At best, they will find themselves paying their landlords for improvements that represent the fruits of their own political participation. On the other hand, since tenants have only minimal economic investments in their communities, a decline in the quality of community life affects them differently from owners. They are more likely to have the option of moving without suffering great loss.

The important implication is that citizens who lack the kind of long-term property right associated with ownership may not need to participate politically to protect their interests, and may not be able to benefit from such participation. Thus, arguably they lack strong incentive to participate responsibly or at all. Even on its own narrowly economic terms, the argument requires many qualifications,[12] but it contains an important measure of truth, as any long-standing tenant in a neighborhood undergoing gentrification knows.

Although there is ample republican precedent for the idea of restricting franchise to the propertied, there is an alternative republican response to this tension—extending property to the enfranchised. Universalizing housing ownership interests gives people security against inflation, and channels economic incentives into the political process by making the entire class of citizens the "residual claimants" on communal wealth.[13]

The idea that citizens should have a property interest that gives them a secure and substantial stake in the community plays some role in mainstream American legal and political culture. The "homestead" provisions of laws governing the enforcement of creditors' rights connote republicanism by both their names and their substance. These laws exempt from execution by creditors some portion of the value of the debtors' home. Such laws typically have a built-in transfer and accumulation restraint, in the requirement that the home be used as the debtor's primary residence to qualify for the exemption. Where the exemption cannot be waived, it acts as a transfer restraint by precluding the debtor/home owner from putting his property at risk as security for credit. And the exemption is sometimes limited to a maximum amount to prevent it from shielding great wealth.[14]

Social-republican notions may also play some role in the advantages conferred on ownership, as opposed to tenancy, by the income tax exemptions for interest payments and in-kind housing income to owner-occupiers.[15] It also appears pertinent to property tax provisions that wholly or partially immunize home owners from increases based on rises in market value since the time of purchase.[16] Such provisions protect citizens from having their welfare reduced or from being pushed out of the community because of real estate inflation.

However, these forms of property only weakly manifest the defining features of social-republican property: alienation and accumulation restraints. The property tax regimes contain an implicit alienation restraint. The incumbent owner cannot transfer her advantageous assessment; a sale triggers reassessment at the market value. To the extent tax advantages are conditioned on owner occupancy, they involve a weak accumulation restraint. Although they are often available for multiple homes, they often are not available for investment property.[17]

The two types of property interests in residence that best approximate the social-republican ideal occupy a more marginal place than the tax subsidies. They are, first, tenant interests under rent control regimes, and second, limited-equity ownership interests, especially those organized as housing cooperatives. Very few American jurisdictions have rent control, and only a tiny fraction of owner-occupied housing is subject to equity limitations, but both rent control and limited-equity ownership have grown in recent years, and there has been increasing interest in both as possible responses to the low-income housing crisis of the past two decades. Outside the United States there are countries in which large sectors of the housing stock have been subject to such regimes.[18]

Since the republican tradition has often equated the ownership necessary to political autonomy with freehold interests, rent-controlled tenancies may seem a poor approximation. However, rent control potentially gives tenants property interests that are nearly as adequate as the freehold for the purposes of security and political motivation, and contain built-in alienation and accumulation restraints.

Typically, rent control statutes give the tenant security of tenure at a controlled rent.[19] The tenant cannot be evicted except for "cause," which of course includes nonpayment of the lawful rent. The rent usually is fixed in terms of a base rent negotiated in the past, which is then adjusted periodically to reflect increases in the landlord's costs. The regime is designed to allow the landlord to recover his costs plus a "fair" return on his capital, but to exclude producer surplus and return to the scarcity value of the site (economic "rents"). Thus, the regime provides some of the same security as ownership against dispossession due either to landlord whim, or to rising real estate values.

Still, the security of the rent-controlled tenancy is in some respects weaker and in some respects stronger than the social-republican ideal. It is weaker because tenants can be evicted for disturbing or injurious conduct that owners might get away with, and for reasons that have no analogy in the ownership situation; for example, when the landlord wants to recover the premises for her own use or that of a relative. It is stronger because, since the tenant is protected against losses in market value, she has a lesser stake in her residence than the prototypical owner.

However, in other respects, the rent-controlled tenancy satisfies social-republican norms better than ownership: it is subject to strong explicit alienation and accumulation restraints. The requirement that the benefitted tenant be a resident (and sometimes that the premises be her primary residence) functions as both types of restraint: it precludes accumulation of protected occupancy rights, and precludes transfer to nonresidents. Moreover, a further common restriction specifically precludes the tenant from transferring any of her rights for value, even to a successor resident. This means that the tenant cannot capitalize her rights as the "residual claimant" of the housing. She can enjoy without cost increases in the value of the premises due, for example, to improvements in the community, but she can enjoy them only in kind, and must remain in place to do so. These property rights thus give her a positive inducement to work for the improvement of the community through political means, and impose costs on withdrawing from the community.[20]

Another form of social-republican property in housing is limited-equity ownership. A movement for "social ownership" of housing has urged freehold owners to voluntarily adopt equity limitations on their homes, by alienating a portion of the equity to land or home trusts responsible to the community.[21] However, the most common source of equity limitations is through conditions on grants or loans by governments or nonprofit institutions, or on permits or tax dispensations by governments.

Various government and nonprofit agencies subsidize housing to low- and moderate-income people. One approach is for the agency to become the owner of the housing, and to rent it at subsidized rates to qualified low-income people; when done by governments, this is the standard "public housing" approach. Another approach is to give the subsidy to a private landlord in return for an agreement to rent to low-income people at stipulated rents. A third approach is for the agency to subsidize the construction, rehabilitation, and/or purchase of a dwelling, and then to confer ownership on the occupant, subject to equity limitations. This approach has been tried, for instance, in connection with programs that rehabilitate dilapidated properties acquired by municipalities through condemnation or the enforcement of tax liens.

Limited-equity ownership interests are defined by at least one or the other of—and typically both—a transfer restraint and an accumulation restraint.[22] If the dwelling is part of a cooperative association, the restraints will be enforceable by the cooperative. Whether or not a cooperative is involved, ultimate enforcement authority will be lodged in some governmental or nonprofit entity, perhaps the one funding the subsidy, perhaps some other one, such as a land bank or community development corporation created for this purpose.

The transfer constraint, in addition to conditioning ownership on continued occupancy as a primary residence, will give the cooperative and/or enforcement authority control over the transfer of the equity interest. It may require resale to the cooperative or enforcement authority (which can then decide on its own who to retransfer it to), or give it a right of first refusal, or require its consent to sale, or require that the buyer satisfy stipulated conditions, especially with regard to income.

The principal accumulation restraint concerns the resale price of the interest. One sort of restraint merely requires sharing of gains with the subsidizer or enforcement authority. The more exacting restraints limit the sale price to the amount of the purchase price, plus any capital improvements paid for by the owner, plus interest on these amounts, perhaps at the home mortgage rates prevailing at the time of the purchase or improvements. A variety of intermediate standards have been used or proposed.

The more restrictive standards seem most consistent with social-republican principles. They provide security of tenure, enable the owner to recover his investment when he needs to leave, but deny him the opportunity to capitalize his surplus in the home or the scarcity value of the site. Critics have argued for more generous standards, on the ground that the departing owner may need more money to purchase on the market in the area to which he moves.[23] But this seems dubious. A market-level sales price may remove the home from the low-income housing stock (or require the diversion of subsidies that would have been available for other units to keep it there). It also enables the departing owner to take some of the subsidy out of the community. Moreover, it is an overly-broad way of dealing with the hypothesized problem, since the departing owner will not necessarily have a low income when he leaves, and may not encounter high housing prices in the area to which he moves.[24]

A further objection to strict price restraints is that they seem inconsistent with the idea of "ownership." This is true if the reference is to the classical liberal conception of ownership, but it seems doubtful that the subsidy program itself is justifiable in classical liberal terms. The restraints seem quite consistent with social-republican ownership notions. There, home ownership means a secure physical place in the community, not control of a commodity whose value is defined in an impersonal market.

IV. Property at Work

The American economy has generated a variety of enterprises designed along social-republican lines. Such enterprises have often been termed "cooperatives," though the term is both over-and underinclusive. It is overinclusive because many nominal cooperatives lack the strong alienation and accumulation restraints entailed by the social-republican vision. It is underinclusive because some variations of enterprises with other designations—mutual companies, partnerships, corporations with employee stock ownership plans—do have such characteristics.

Cooperative enterprise in the social-republican sense was at the core of some of the more important nineteenth-century radical movements. Such radical programs failed politically, but the social-republican vision has always had some power, and even today a variety of laws and programs give symbolic and—typically small—material support for cooperatives.[25]

Since producer cooperatives are most often portrayed as the paradigmatic social-republican institutions, I will focus on them. American statutes dealing with cooperatives typically reflect a fairly loose conception of such organizations, but most require, or at least imply, distinctive procedures concerning at least either control or the distribution of residual returns. The Capper-Volstead Act exemption for agricultural cooperatives, for example, requires that organizations either allocate voting control on a one-vote-per-member basis or that it allocate residual returns on the basis of patronage (work performed or goods sold through or bought from the cooperative), rather than financial investment.[26]

State cooperative corporation statutes are typically enabling legislation, designed to make clear that the corporate form is available to organizations that separate voting rights from capital contributions, and distribute net returns to patrons. They rarely strongly require such features as a condition of organizing under the statute, though they sometimes prescribe them in the absence of a decision by the corporation to opt for a different arrangement.[27]

Although the mandatory statutory conditions are weak, all cooperatives have transfer restraints, and many have substantial accumulation constraints. Since ownership shares in producer cooperatives confer worker-member status, they are nearly always subject to transfer restraints that mandate resale to the enterprise (which can then make its own decisions about who to admit), or give the enterprise options, rights of refusal, or rights of approval with respect to the transfer of rights by departing members. Such provisions, however, are not radically different from those commonly found in conventional small business arrangements.

The nature and extent of accumulation constraints vary more widely. Some cooperatives (or more generally, producer-owned enterprises) defy social-republican ideals by allocating voting or control rights on a basis other than one-person-one-vote. The departures that are most easily reconciled with social-republican principles allocate voting on the basis of "patronage" (in a worker cooperative, the amount of work performed). Those least reconcilable allocate rights in proportion to capital contributions.[28]

Perhaps the most revealing accumulation issue concerns the economic rights of members on departure. Here we can distinguish three general approaches, only the last of which seems fully consistent with social-republican principle. The least consistent approach is that of what might be called the *unlimited equity* cooperative. Here there are no limitations on the amount for which the departing members may sell (to a permissible buyer). The member sells her interest for its market value. This is true of most of the older contemporary American cooperatives.[29]

Where the departing member can sell for market value, one might say that her interest in the firm is not social-republican property, since it represents an interest in the future earnings of the firm that can be realized without remaining a member. Moreover, if the cooperative has been successful, the need of the new entrant to make a large payment will introduce inequality between the old and new members, and if the cooperative finances the purchase with a loan to the new member, this inequality will be reflected in lower current net payments to that member.

Nevertheless, two factors mitigate the tendency of unlimited equity provisions to dissolve social-republican property. First, most cooperatives are small businesses and, because of the high relative costs of disseminating and acquiring reliable information about such business, the market value of ownership interests in small businesses may reflect a greater discount of future earnings than that of large businesses. Second, since the memberships can only be sold to people who are acceptable to the existing work force as peers (and who either have the sufficient cash, or seem creditworthy), the pool of buyers will be limited, and this will impose a further discount. The interests reflected by these discounts—interests in future earnings that can only be appropriated by remaining with the enterprise—are kinds of social-republican property, though they are common features of small business generally, not just those styled explicitly in social-republican terms.

The second approach to capital appropriation can be called the *no-equity* cooperative. It is exemplified by the model of the self-managed firm espoused by Jaroslav Vanek, based in part on a critique of the Yugoslav experiments.[30] In this model, the enterprise must be financed entirely by debt. Not only is outside equity prohibited, but so is inside equity, or self-financing through retained earnings. The Vanek firm does not accumulate capital; its net worth is always zero, and workers benefit only through current distributions of residual earnings. The zero-net-worth norm would require not only that earnings be paid out as earned, but that increases in firm goodwill or going-concern value be immediately cashed out with borrowed funds.

If the unlimited equity cooperative lacks social-republican property because all its capital is subject to individual appropriation, the no-equity firm lacks social-republican property because it cannot accumulate capital at all. Vanek's approach is designed to avoid inefficiencies attributed by neoclassical economists to the labor-managed firm, but from a social-republican point of view, it creates new problems. Labor and product markets are competitive in the Vanek model. Though the compensation workers receive is variable, since it depends on enterprise performance, prospectively workers anticipate no more from association with their firm than the market rate for their services, which presumably they could get from other firms as well. If the enterprise is successful, workers will benefit, but they will be able to capitalize the success immediately. While workers get no additional payment when they leave, they have no strong economic interest in remaining either.

Thus, the centrifugal pull of market forces is likely to lead to high turnover that will jeopardize the identity of the enterprise as an enduring community. Changing market signals will constantly be inducing members to leave, or requiring the quick assimilation of outsiders. These pressures may be weaker than the corresponding ones in the economy envisioned by neoclassical economics, but they will remain substantial, and Vanek's model has no strong economic force countering them. In the social-republican view, an important reason for the creation and persistence of firms, especially ones that can be most plausibly viewed as political communities, is the productivity of a kind of goodwill capital or going-concern value that is necessarily illiquid. But Vanek's requirement that such capital be cashed out to maintain net worth at zero precludes this critical economic solvent. From a social-republican point of view, the fact that most successful firms necessarily acquire capital is a virtue, not as it appears in the Vanek analysis, a defect.

The form most consistent with social-republican principle is the *limited-equity* firm. The version with the most severe equity limitations is probably that prescribed in Yugoslav market socialism. Prior to the 1988 reforms, Yugoslavia broadly prohibited both employment and private ownership of capital. Where these prohibitions applied, all workers over the age of eighteen were members of the firm, or collective, entitled to equal votes in the selection of management (directly or through representative councils) and on a wide range of policy decisions (subject, however, to a variety of severe extra-enterprise constraints and pressures). The collectives received capital from banks or state agencies, subject to the duty to maintain its value through a depreciation reserve, to pay interest on it, and to pay taxes on net earnings. (For some enterprises these duties were lightened by the failure of the system to take account of inflation in setting either depreciation requirements or interest rates.) The members were the residual claimants on the firm's earnings. They decided, within significant limits, on the distribution of the net earnings after taxes among wages, reinvestment, and collective consumption. (The scope of this discretion varied broadly over time; it appears to have been widest from 1965 to the early 1970s.)[31] The workers, of course, could not alienate their rights of membership or capitalize their claims on earnings. They could benefit from their rights only to the extent they remain active members.

A version with less severe limitations is the one associated with the network of cooperatives at Mondragon, Spain. With over twenty thousand members, Mondragon is probably the largest producer cooperative institution in the capitalist countries, and it has had a remarkably successful track record over four decades. Its approach to organization has been popularized in the United States by several economic development consultants, notably the Industrial Cooperative Association, and it has been adopted here by a few cooperatives. Mondragon adheres to the one-person-one-vote principle, and limits income differentials between the lowest and highest paid members to a ratio of 1 to 3 (or 4.5 in exceptional cases). Members are paid weekly "advances" (as opposed to wages) at a fixed rate, and then twice a year are paid or credited with a distribution of net earnings or losses. A portion of the net earnings is retained as internal equity finance.[32]

In the Mondragon model,[33] as in conventional cooperatives and partnerships, each member has an individual account ("internal capital account"). The account reflects whatever the member paid upon admission, and the members' accumulated shares of retained earnings and losses. (Distribution of earnings and losses is calculated with a formula that weights each member's "patronage"—hours worked—and the size of her capital account.) These amounts are adjusted annually to reflect increases in the value of the firm, based on appraisals of its assets. Interest is allocated annually to the accounts based on the amounts in them. The accounts, and other rights in the firm, are not transferable by the members, but on departure the firm pays the member the amount in her account (though payment may stretch out over some years).

In contrast to the Yugoslav model, Mondragon permits members to capitalize a portion of their economic claims on the firm, but this portion is smaller than in the unlimited equity model, for at least two reasons. The stipulated price for the redemption of membership shares includes some allowance for inflation of individual assets, but not for goodwill or going concern value. Moreover, thirty percent of the firm's income is allocated to collective rather than individual accounts, which fund insurance and collective consumption activities such as education and recreation and, apparently, the subsidization of new entrants, who are charged far less as entry fees than any market measure of the value of the rights they receive.

Finally, we should consider some recent interpretations that suggest that the employment relation may be susceptible to reform along social-republican lines. Nineteenth-century social-republicans saw the wage-earner status as irreconcilable with social-republican values of independence. However, in recent decades reformers have proposed measures, such as "just cause" termination rules, that constrain the ability of the employer to use powers of discharge and discipline to subordinate employees in ways that are not reasonably required by the production process. The social-republican associations of such doctrines are reflected in the suggestion that they imply a vision of "the job as property."[34]

At the same time, some of the more adventurous experiments in work organization recently initiated by employers, and sometimes by unions, have extended some of the characteristics associated with ownership to workers. Profit-sharing and bonus compensation plans give workers a partial residual claim on enterprise earnings. Other reforms extend some incidents of control. "Team concept" production systems give workers some shop-floor control over the implementation of production procedures; and joint labor-management committees sometimes give employees information and opportunities to address production design, and even strategic business decisions over matters such as product development, subcontracting, and investment. Such opportunities are rarely extended as a matter of legally enforceable right, but in a few unionized plants they are guaranteed in collective bargaining agreements. Representation and voting rights on the boards of directors of public corporations is legally mandated in some European countries and has been collectively bargained in a few American ones. The more radical of these experiments seem to erode the line between ownership and employment.[35]

More than these organizational experiments, economic developments over the course of the century have given substance to the idea of property rights in the job. In recent decades, a large fraction of American workers have developed long-term associations with a single employer.[36] In the more stable, and often less competitive, "primary" sector of the labor market, long-term employment is the norm. A striking fact associated with this system is that, once an employee embarks on a career with a long-term employer, her compensation will often exceed that available to her in alternative jobs. In some industries, this phenomenon is a consequence of personnel systems that restrict hiring to "ports of entry" at the lower tiers of job hierarchies, and fill higher positions by internal promotion; thus, comparable jobs at other enterprises for a mid-career worker may be closed to outsiders. The fact that mid-career employees may have difficulty finding comparably paid jobs is also a function of compensation structures that reward long-term tenure. And these features in turn reflect the fact that the value of many employees is in large part a function of on-the-job training, and socialization in skills and attitudes that, because they involve idiosyncratic aspects of the production process, or the ability to collaborate effectively with a unique set of co-workers, are peculiar to the enterprise.[37]

Such developments might seem capable of providing an infrastructure for a regime of social-republican property. The worker in a long-term employment relation that pays more than she could get in the external labor market has an economic stake in the enterprise. This stake is nontransferable. It binds her to the enterprise in a way analogous to a nontransferable cooperative ownership interest. Of course, to play a meaningful social-republican role, such an interest would have to be legally secured, whether by strong collective bargaining guarantees, or by individual protections, such as "just cause" termination standards. Moreover, it would have to be complemented by accumulation constraints that permit workers to participate in control, and limit inequality in control and reward. Strong unions sometimes perform that role; some new experiments in work reorganization also take steps in this direction.

V. Efficiency and Exclusion

Two criticisms are most commonly made of the social-republican program. The first is that it sacrifices productive efficiency to equality. The second is that it achieves internal institutional equality only at the cost of making its institutions more exclusive than comparable liberal institutions. My view is that the first criticism is mistaken, or at least inconsistent with some plausible interpretations of contemporary economic trends, but that the second points to a real systemic problem, though hopefully a remediable one.

The efficiency argument focuses mainly on social-republican production institutions. The reply calls attention to the fact that a broad range of important types of production require illiquid, long-term investments. From the social-republican perspective, the most pertinent of such investments are those that resist commodification because they are embedded in particular relationships. One investment of this kind is individual education in knowledge or skills that are distinctively useful within the enterprise, venture, or bounded economic community. Another is education about the particular characteristics of another participant or potential participant in a common endeavor. Employers make such investments in recruiting and screening new employees; old employees make such investments when they train new employees; and we might consider this process an investment by the new employees as well. Enterprises make such investments in learning about their customers, suppliers, and trading partners. This type of learning might focus on both the reliability of the prospective collaborator, and the taste and technical characteristics that define her needs (as a customer) or capabilities (as a supplier).

The basic mechanisms of coordination associated with the market often seem inadequate for coordinating such investments in "firm specific capital." Spot markets are inadequate because firm-specific, human, capital investments require long-term coordination. Elaborately specified contracts are ineffective because the relevant contingencies are unforeseeable, and contractual specification inefficiently rigidifies the relation.

Yet, without specified contractual safeguards, collaborative behavior may make cooperators vulnerable in ways that deter people from engaging in it. Participants who invest in firm-specific assets risk that the others on whom the value of the assets depend will defect from the relation when it is individually advantageous for them to do so. Employers who invest in employees risk that the employees will leave; workers who invest in firm-specific skills risk that the employers will discharge them; workers who help other workers acquire skills risk that those they help will displace them. Firms face similar risks in imparting valuable information to potential collaborators (who may also be potential competitors), or in undertaking efforts to learn about or develop relations with them; the value of such investments depends on the willingness of the others to continue collaboration, even in situations where short-term individual interests might discourage it.

From this perspective, the incomplete commodification or liquidity of firm-specific human capital may be a redeeming virtue. Legal and economic arrangements that make it more difficult or costly for parties to withdraw from the relation may serve as safeguards that induce firm-specific, human, capital investments by reducing the risk of subsequent opportunistic withdrawal. For example, long-term employment guarantees may induce employee investments; deferred compensation arrangements may induce employer investments in employees. They do so, not by comprehensively specifying contingent obligations, but by locking the parties into a relationship in which each has an incentive to cooperate with the other, but in which the specific contours of the collaboration remain undetermined.

Thus, both the transfer and the accumulation constraints associated with social-republican property seem consistent with the development of firm-specific human capital. In areas of enterprise where the prospects for such investments are good, social-republican institutions may be conducive to, or at least compatible with, productive efficiency.

The other critique of social-republican property is that it achieves equality only at the cost of exclusiveness. Any community is potentially exclusive, but communities founded on social-republican property may have a tendency toward greater exclusiveness than those founded on classical liberal property. Social-republican property gives people an economic stake that tends to bind them to the community, but it also creates disincentives to the admission of new members on terms that preserve equality with existing members.[38]

Liberals have often argued that consent to the norms and practice of the nation should be sufficient to entitle outsiders to admission and citizenship.[39] However, the more admission and citizenship entitle entrants to economic equality with their fellow citizens, the more liberal admission policies entail drastic redistribution from old to new citizens. Social-republicans unprepared to accept this consequence—and traditionally few have been—must then choose between sacrificing their commitment to equality by admitting new members without the economic prerequisites of citizenship, or restricting membership to those who can bring with them sufficient wealth to secure their own economic independence.

Today one can see, in several countries on the receiving end of immigration streams, some association between tolerance for inequality and relatively open immigration policies. The relative liberality of the United States in immigration matters seems to be a result of its relatively great tolerance of inequality among citizens. American citizenship can be dispensed with some generosity in part because it entails relatively little in terms of economic rights. (And notably, immigrants are screened to minimize the likelihood that they will take great advantage of some of the economic rights that are provided; reliance on public assistance is often disqualifying.[40]) On the other hand, countries like Sweden or Canada, where citizenship entails relatively strong economic claims, have more restrictive immigration policies.[41]

Now consider the limited-equity interests in real estate created by rent-control regimes. One of the political functions of these interests is to anchor the citizen in the community, by protecting her from displacement due to property appreciation. But property appreciation typically reflects the desires of outsiders to enter the community. Applying controls universally would choke off new construction, and limit places for new entrants. Thus, the laws typically exempt new units, and allow them to rent at market rates. This, however, introduces an inequality between new arrivals and old-timers. New renters, for example, will pay vastly more for their units than older renters protected by rent control. The same dilemma attends property tax schemes that permit full reassessment only when the property is sold. This approach protects older residents from the pressures of property appreciation, but only at the cost of introducing a severe inequality between such residents and newcomers, who must pay higher taxes on comparable properties.

The problem also arises in the context of the social-republican business enterprise. Imagine an egalitarian enterprise composed of nontransferable individual claims on collectively held capital. The enterprise is successful; its value increases, and it can increase its profits by expansion. In these circumstances, the members face a dilemma. If they bring in new members on terms that preserve equality, they redistribute away from themselves, since they must then allow new members to share in returns from capital they now control.[42] They will thus be tempted to accomplish the expansion in ways that preserve for themselves the returns from the firm's capital, but subvert the social-republican character of the enterprise.

There are several ways of doing this. They can charge new entrants a large admission fee (or sell them shares at market value), as do most successful American producer cooperatives.[43] Or they can give lower patronage returns to new entrants than to old ones.[44] Or they can forego internal expansion and spin off a separate firm to produce supplies for them on terms that will involve lower returns to workers in the spun-off enterprise.[45] Or the members can reconstitute themselves as capitalist employers and bring in the new entrants as employees, a practice of some American producer cooperatives as well as cooperatives organized on more strictly social-republican lines in postrevolutionary Mexico, Peru under the Velasco regime, and Chile under the Allende regime.[46] The most extreme response, of which there are many examples in Europe and America, is for the members to sell the enterprise to an outside invester, pocket the proceeds, and themselves become, along with the new entrants, employees.[47]

An ambitious social-republican regime will respond to these threats of corruption, as Yugoslavia did, by prohibiting unequal treatment of new members. But the result of such a prohibition is likely to be exclusion: the incumbents can simply limit or forgo expansion in order to preserve for themselves the returns from their capital.

When the group does admit new members, how will it decide which members to take? Since membership in the successful social-republican institution typically will carry rewards with an economic value greater than the entry price, there will be a surplus of prospective entrants. One would expect that the members, if permitted, would rank prospective entrants in terms of personal qualities valued by the membership. It is troubling that ethnic homogeneity and even overt racism is a common characteristic of some of the more successful social-republican institutions, including many housing cooperatives and craft labor unions.

Of course, the cruder forms of ethnic, race, and gender discrimination are forbidden in America by the civil rights laws. But even to the extent such laws are enforced, they leave a broad range of latitude for discrimination based on ascriptive qualities that some find troubling. One response to such concerns would be to apply tight constraints on discrimination in entry decisions. The most extreme and effective way to preclude discrimination would be to have new entrants determined by queuing or lottery.[48] The composition of the queue or the lottery pool could be determined by some independent state agency, in accordance with a limited set of criteria of minimum suitability for membership in the institution in question (for instance, evidence of responsible prior conduct and, in the case of productive enterprises, relevant skills). Then when openings occurred, the agency could allocate them within the class so determined to those who had waited the longest, or by lot. Such procedures are commonly used to allocate publicly subsidized housing units. Although they are not currently used in connection with rent-controlled housing or subsidized enterprises, they probably could be.

Arguably, there is a case for social control, not only of the designation of new members, but of the size of the enterprise. One example of an effort in this spirit is the New Jersey Supreme Court's *Mount Laurel* decision holding unconstitutional various "exclusionary zoning" practices and requiring the accommodation of low-income housing construction.[49]

Another approach to the problem of interenterprise inequality that is at least superficially more consistent with enterprise autonomy is free or subsidized entry of new enterprises to compete with the more successful older ones.[50]

Yet, carried far enough to resolve the problem of exclusion, either forced admission or subsidized entry would amount to a repudiation of the social-republican ideal. As membership in the institution were forcibly expanded, the value of social-republican claims would decline and ultimately disappear. And while some degree of competitive entry is needed to spur efficiency and level large rents, too much competitive entry will threaten the organizational capital that sustains flexible cooperation and long-term investments.

In some respects, the dialectic of internal and external equality is inherent in any democratic vision that makes room for decentralized, collective self-organization. Recognizing the difficulty common to social-republican and more mainstream institutional arrangements might lead one to conclude that the problem of internal versus external inequality is not distinctive to the social-republican view, but represents a pervasive "dilemma of industrial democracy."[51] Nevertheless, the dilemma seems especially salient for the social-republican view, because of its relatively central commitment to equality and decentralized organization. The plausible argument of recent social-democratic literature that issues of interenterprise equity require centralized organization should be distinctively troubling for social-republicans. Certainly, the failure to elaborate responses to these issues is a central failing of much social-republican literature.

Conclusion

Social-republican property is neither as anomalous nor as implausible as the dominant mainstream conceptions of property often suggest. In a variety of contexts, it probably has a valuable role to play in connection with public subsidies for housing and business development. This role is to encourage enterprise democracy and to prevent the private appropriation of the subsidies.

But vindicating the democratic aspirations associated with this type of property will require attention to the problem of exclusion. Resolution of that problem, however, could threaten the vitality of social-republican institutions. The critical task is to design constraints on exclusion without excessively impairing the autonomy and security necessary for such institutions to flourish.

Notes

1. See Bruce Laurie, *Artisans Into Workers: Labor in Nineteenth Century America* (New York: Hill & Wang, 1989), pp. 141–75; James Joll, *The Anarchists* (New York: Grosset & Dunlap, 1964), pp. 61–83; Lawrence Goodwyn, *The Populist Moment: A Short History of the Agrarian Revolt in America* (New York: Oxford University Press, 1978).
2. For a survey of American developments, see Laurie, supra note 2, pp. 47–140.
3. Mihailo Markovic, *Democratic Socialism: Theory and Practice* (New York: St. Martins Press, 1982); Branko Horvat, *The Political Economy of Socialism* (Armonk, NY: M.E. Sharpe, 1982); Harold Lydall, *Yugoslav Socialism: Theory and Practice* (New York: Oxford University Press, 1984).
4. There recently has been a variety of proposals that would increase the importance of this type of economic interest there. Most notable among these are the views on economic reform presented in Roberto Mangabeira Unger, *False Necessity* (Cambridge: Cambridge University Press, 1987), which is market-socialist in tone, and Michael Piore and Charles Sabel, *The Second Industrial Divide: Possibilities for Prosperity* (New York: Basic Books, 1985), which appeals to republicanism. However, the idea of social-republican property is only implicit in Piore and Sabel, and is in some tension with parts of Unger's argument.
5. Only the latter right is uniquely associated with the technical definition of citizenship; residence is accorded to lawful "permanent residents," and most of the elements of legal protection are accorded to even visiting aliens, but the lay and legal definition of citizenship connotes at least these three rights (plus some additional elements, such as jury service and opportunities to hold public office). See Peter Schuck, "Membership in the Liberal Polity: The Devaluation of American Citizenship." *Georgetown Immigration L.J.* 3: 1, 2–9 (1989).
6. 8 U.S.C. § 1448 (naturalization requires renunciation of foreign citizenship); 8 U.S.C. § 1481 (citizenship forfeited by, *inter alia*, foreign naturalization).
7. Shuck, supra note 5, pp. 2–9.
8. Am. Jur. 2d, "Elections", 235. See also *Lucas v. Forty-Fourth General Assembly of Colorado*, 377 U.S. 713 (1964) (suggesting that rights to a fairly apportioned legislature are inalienable by holding unconstitutional a malapportioned legislature, despite approval by majority of the disadvantaged voters).

9. See, e.g., Cal. Elections Code § 29620.
10. *Baker v. Carr*, 369 U.S. 186 (1962). Citizenship also entails duties, notably of military service, that are typically defined as nontransferable and with a concern for equality of sacrifice. Social-republican concerns were prominent in the critique, during the Civil War era, of the provision allowing conscripts to pay a "substitute," and in the contemporary critique of the volunteer army. At least in wartime, the idea of a nontransferable duty of military service seems to command broad consensus. For an excellent discussion of this and related issues concerning inalienability, see Susan Rose-Ackerman, "Inalienability and the Theory of Property Rights," *Colum. L. Rev.* 85:931, 961–68 (1985).
11. "Cities and Homeowners' Associations," *U. Pa. L. Rev.* 130: 1581 (1982).
12. See Frank I. Michelman, "Universal Resident Suffrage: A Liberal Defense," *U. Pa. L. Rev.* 130: 1581 (1981).
13. Timothy Brennan, "Rights, Market Failure, and Rent Control," *Phil. & Public Affairs* 17: 66, 77 (1988).
14. See, e.g., California Code of Civil Procedure §§ 704.730, et seq., §§ 704.910, et seq., which creates an automatic homestead exemption to $30,000 that can be extended by recording a declaration to the full value. Homestead interests can generally be waived only to secure purchase money debts. See Bankruptcy Code § 522(f).

    The home owner-mortgagor's typically nonwaivable "equity of redemption," which gives him the opportunity after default to redeem his home until late in the foreclosure process, plays an analogous role. See, e.g., Grant S. Nelson and Dale A. Whitman, *Real Estate Finance Law*, 2d ed. (St. Paul, MN: West Publishing Co., 1985), § 1.1–1.4.

    For a discussion of several of the residence-related property interests mentioned here from a different perspective, see Joseph Singer, "The Reliance Interest in Property," *Stan. L. Rev.* 40: 611 (1988).
15. See Richard Goode, "Imputed Rent of Owner-Occupied Dwelling Under the Income Tax," *J. Finance* 15: 504, 518–19 (1960).
16. See, e.g., Cal. Const. Art. XIIIA, § 2 (codifying "Proposition 13"); see also *Allegheny Pittsburgh Coal Co. v. County Commission*, 109 S.Ct. 633, 638 n.4 (reserving the question of the constitutionality of such provisions).
17. Property tax *deferral* procedures that, instead of lowering taxes, postpone payment until the sale of the home or the death of the owner, have stronger accumulation constraints, both because they recapture the tax subsidy, and because they are typically conditioned on a showing of economic hardship or some status, typically old age, associated with economic hardship. See, e.g., California Tax and Revenue Code §§ 20503–04, 205082–5.
18. For example, in Sweden rents are typically controlled, and the "cooperative sector" has produced a substantial portion of the postwar Swedish housing stock, though the social-republican features of this sector have been diluted by recent reforms. John Gilderbloom and Richard Appelbaum, *Rethinking Rental Housing* (Philadelphia, Temple University Press, 1988), pp. 163–80.

On other European countries, see id., pp. 150–63; *Housing Co-operatives* (Geneva: International Labour Office, 1964).

19. See generally Kenneth Baar, "Guidelines for Drafting Rent Control Laws: Lessons of a Decade," *Rutgers L. Rev.* 35: 723 (1983).

20. Rent control is often accused of reducing housing supply by precluding price increases that would induce new investment. There is good reason to think that this effect may be quite small in many markets where tenants are most threatened by housing price inflation. See Note, "Reassessing Rent Control: Its Economic Impact in a Gentrifying Housing Market," *Harv. L. Rev.* 101:1835 (1988). The ideal rent control program transfers the surplus above costs (including "reasonable" return on investment) of low-cost landlords to tenants, without reducing maintenance incentives or precluding high-cost landlords from recovering their costs. It operates on the same principle as Henry George's social-republican land tax.

21. The City of Berkeley, California, was asked recently to consider regulating the resale of homes to impose equity limitations.

22. See, generally, Massachusetts Government Land Bank, *Building for the Commonwealth: Materials on Limited Equity Housing Cooperatives* (Boston, 1987); David Kirkpatrick, *Legal Issues in the Development of Housing Cooperatives* (National Development and Law Center 1981).

23. See Kirkpatrick, supra note 22, pp. 77, 82 (describing the argument referred to in the text).

24. Reliable enforcement of equity limitations probably requires that the owner be obliged to resell to a public or nonprofit entity at a controlled price. Alternatively, they should at least prescribe both income limitations on purchasers and price controls.

    Several limited equity programs in American municipalities appear to have quite weak equity limitations. This may be due to a lack of sympathy among administrators for social-republican property notions, and perhaps to a tendency to view housing subsidies as a short-term patronage resource.

    Resale controls were abolished in 1969 on a substantial segment of the Swedish cooperative housing stock, and there has been extensive debate over their desirability since then. Gilderbloom and Appelbaum, supra note 18, pp. 175–77.

25. To cite only three examples, the Capper-Volstead Act exempts cooperatives from many strictures of the antitrust laws. 7 U.S.C. §§ 291–92. Second, Subchapter T of the Internal Revenue Code gives preferential tax treatment to cooperatives. Internal Revenue Code §§ 1381–88. Third, Congress has created a network of "Banks for Cooperatives" to afford credit to agricultural and rural utility cooperatives. 12 U.S.C. §§ 2121, et seq.

26. 7 U.S.C. § 291. Similarly, the Internal Revenue Code exemption for cooperative income applies only to "patronage dividends," and not to residual returns on capital contributions. Internal Revenue Code § 1382 (b) (1). A separate exemption for agricultural cooperatives exempts dividends on capital stock if

they do not exceed eight percent, and all the stock is owned by the patrons. Internal Revenue Code § 521.

Capper-Volstead requires that the enterprise be operated "for the mutual benefit of the members," and Subchapter T requires that it be operated "on a cooperative basis"; both standards limit the use of outside equity. The extent of these limits is unclear, however. See Revenue Ruling 82–51, 1982–1 C.B. 117. Capper-Volstead requires that agricultural cooperatives that do not limit voting power to one vote per member may not pay dividends on stock in excess of eight percent, but provides no explicit limit for cooperatives with egalitarian voting rules. 7 U.S.C. § 291.

The principle that dividends on capital stock be "limited" (that is, capped at moderate rates) is prescribed in the rules of the Rochdale Cooperative Society that influenced nineteenth-century British and American cooperatives, and those of the International Cooperative Alliance that influence contemporary European ones. John Bonsin and Louis Putterman, *Economics of Cooperation and the Labor-Managed Economy* (New York: Harwood Academic Publishers, 1987), pp. 145–47.

27. See e.g., Mass. G.L. c. 157A, §§ 6, 7 (members must have equal voting rights; voting rights to nonmembers requires member authorization); Cal. Corporations Code § 12410 (cooperative membership shares nontransferable in absence of by-law to the contrary).

    Some American cooperatives are organized under general incorporation acts. Modern corporation statutes are generally flexible enough to accommodate worker cooperatives, and many state cooperative statutes have not been recently revised and were designed with consumer or marketing, rather than producer, cooperatives in mind.

28. Mutual water companies and public irrigation districts often allocate voting rights (and assessments) in proportion to acreage or land values.

29. For example, the plywood companies of the Pacific Northwest, cooperative taxicab companies in several American cities, and the cooperative garbage companies in the San Francisco Bay area. Katrina Berman, *Worker-Owned Plywood Companies* (Pullman, WA: Washington State University Press, 1967), pp. 194–96.

30. "Some Fundamental Considerations on Financing and the Form of Ownership Under Labor Management," in Jaroslav Janek, *The Labor Managed Economy* (Ithaca, NY: Cornell University Press, 1977), pp. 171–85.

31. See generally, Lydall, supra note 3, pp. 82–88.

    A distinctive arrangement with some kinship to the Yugoslav firm is that of Bewley's Cafes, a four hundred-worker restaurant chain in Ireland, that was transferred by its founder to a trust "for all those working for the firm, past, present and future." Robert Oakeshott, *The Case for Workers' Co-ops* (London: Routledge & Kegan Paul, 1978), pp. 79. The situation of the Bewley workers resembles that of the Yugoslavs, in that each participates in the current profits of the firm but has no capital stake that she can appropriate on departure. But, while in both situations the firm capital is subject to a trust for future workers, in the Bewley firm it is under the direct control of nonworker trustees, while in the Yugoslav firm it is under the direct control of the workers.

Arrangements of this kind are facilitated in Britain by the Industrial Common Ownership Act, Public General Acts and Measures of 1976 (E II, Pt. II, ch. 78); see Oakeshott, pp. 74–107.

32. The description of Mondragon in this and the following paragraphs is based on David Ellerman, "The Mondragon Cooperative Experiment," Harvard Business School, n.d. For a description of an American cooperative based on the Mondragon model, see the description of the O & O supermarket chain in Philadelphia, in Sherman Kreiner, "Worker Ownership as the Basis for an Integrated Proactive Development Model," *N.Y.U. Journal of Law and Social Change* 15: 227 (1987).

33. Some features of the Mondragon model are mandated by Spanish law on cooperatives. France and Italy, which with Scandinavia, have the most extensive cooperative movements, have statutes requiring the maintenance of collective reserves that cannot be individually appropriated on departure. See Commission of the European Communities, III *Prospects for Workers' Cooperative In Europe* (Luxembourg: Office for Official Publication of the European Communities, 1984). The chapter on France says of the collective reserve that it belongs "to the co-operative as a unit and is no sense the property of the workers—the latter merely have the right to enjoy the benefits deriving from its use." French cooperative law provides for the redemption of shares at book value with no adjustment for appreciation; according to the commentators, the "major difference between a worker cooperative and a conventional company is that there is no possibility of appreciation in the capital of the business" of the former. Hughes Sybille and Jean-Louis Ruatti, "Perspectives from France," in id., pp. F13–F14.

34. William Gould, "The Idea of the Job as Property in Contemporary America: The Legal and Collective Bargaining Framework," *B.Y.U. L. Rev.* 1986: 885.

35. See, generally, Thomas Kochan, Harry Katz, and Robert McKersie, *The Transformation of American Industrial Relations* (New York: Basic Books, 1986); William H. Simon, "The Politics of 'Cooperation' at the Workplace," *Reconstruction* 1: 18 (Winter 1990).

36. Robert Hall, "The Importance of Lifetime Jobs in the U.S. Economy," *Am. Econ. Rev.* (1982) 72: 716.

37. Peter Doeringer and Michael Piore, *Internal Labor Markets and Manpower Analysis* (Lexington, MA: Heath, 1971), pp. 64–90.

38. Although formulated in my own terms, this critique draws on (1) the neoclassical economic critique of the producer cooperative or "Illyrian firm"; see Bonsin and Putterman, supra note 26, pp. 13–79; and (2) recent social democratic critiques of what one might call the cultural republicanism inspired by Pocock. See Derrick Bell and Preeta Bansal, "The Republican Revival and Racial Politics," *Yale L.J.* (1988) 97: 1609 (1988).

39. See e.g., Bruce A. Ackerman, *Social Justice in the Liberal State* (New Haven: Yale University Press, 1980), pp. 80–95.

40. 8 U.S.C. § 1182 (a) (8), (15).

41. See Comptroller General of the United States, *Information on Immigration in 17 Countries* (January 12, 1979), pp. 14–28, 84–89.

42. In neoclassical theory, the egalitarian cooperative will expand only as long as a new worker generates income above the pre-existing average income per worker. On the other hand, the capitalist firm will expand as long as a new worker generates income above the marginal cost of employing her. Given declining marginal labor products, the cooperative will stop hiring at an earlier point than the comparable capitalist firm. See, e.g., Bonsin and Putterman, supra note 26, pp. 13–18.

43. Berman, supra note 29, pp. 194–96 (Pacific Northwest plywood cooperatives).

44. This would most likely take the form of an agreement by which the new worker purchased a membership share from the firm on an installment basis (or the firm loaned the worker the money to purchase the share), with the firm deducting the payments from the workers' current compensation. This is the procedure at Mondragon, Ellerman, supra note 32, p. ; at some law firms, though in the former and often the latter cases, the purchase price is subsidized at a rate below the market value of the share.

45. See Robert H. Frank, "Are Workers Paid Their Marginal Products?" *Am. Econ. Rev.* 74: 549, 567–68 (1984) (speculating that mainstream enterprises use this procedure to constrain intrafirm wage inequality).

46. Edward Greenberg, *Workplace Democracy: The Political Effects of Participation* (Ithaca, NY: Cornell University Press, 1986), p. 15 (sixteen to thirty-six percent of workers at Pacific Northwest plywood cooperatives studied in late 1960s were employees); Cynthia McClintock, *Peasant Cooperatives and Political Change in Peru* (Princeton, NJ: Princeton University Press, 1980), pp. 319–51 (examples from Mexico, Peru, and Chile).

47. Berman, supra note 29, pp. 85–92, 93–98 (plywood cooperatives). Sidney and Beatrice Webb argued that successful cooperatives would inevitably self-destruct either by selling out to outsiders or by bringing in new members as employees. For their argument, with numerous European examples, see "Special Supplement on Cooperative Production and Profit-Sharing," II *The New Statesman* (February 14, 1914), p. 1.

48. See Henry Greely, The Equality of Allocation by Lot, *Harv. Civ. Rts.-Civ. Lib. L. Rev.* 12: 113 (1977).

49. *Southern Burlington County NAACP v. Township of Mount Laurel*, 92 N.J. 158, 456 A. 2d 390 (1983).

50. This approach is prominent in the market socialist literature. See Jaroslav Vanek, *The General Theory of Labor-Managed Market Economies* (Ithaca, NY: Cornell University Press, 1970).

51. Masahiko Aoki, *The Cooperative Game Theory of the Firm* (New York: Oxford University Press, 1984), p. 54.

Legal Theory and Democratic Reconstruction: Reflections on 1989

Karl E. Klare

[*Editors' Synopsis:* Professor Klare describes the institutional structure of what he calls a "postliberal" form of democracy. Such a conception of democracy seeks to extend the idea of participation beyond the narrow boundaries of politics, strictly so called, to areas of nominally private activity, such as the workplace. Law, conceived of as inextricably connected with politics, plays a crucial role in the process of creating this form of democracy.]

Pundits to the contrary notwithstanding, the 1989 democratic revolution in Central and Eastern Europe did not signal an end to political evolution. Rather, it reopened many enduring questions about the meaning and institutional structure of democracy. Eastern Europe is living through what David Trubek has referred to in lectures as a "metaconstitutional moment," a period when it is possible to imagine that everything can be changed, that political, social, and economic institutions can be fundamentally transformed, a moment in which democracy can be "reinvented."[1] There is a chance to imagine and put in place a new, postliberal form of democracy, one that is more egalitarian, participatory, and environmentally sensitive; a type of democracy that is feminist in inspiration and design, and committed to ending racial hierarchy and injustice. Postliberal democracy would aim to multiply and enrich the opportunities for participation, extending them beyond the electoral arena to the administrative process, and to "private spheres" such as the workplace and the family. New linkages could be configured between social, economic, and political life—for example, between work and family—allowing more diverse possibilities for human self-realization and, in particular, allowing new roles and possibilities for women. The economic order could be made more solidaristic and participatory. New, nonhierarchical relationships between ethnic, racial, and religious groups could be fashioned, building a celebration of cultural diversity into social and political institutions.

The hopes underlying this essay may prove unfounded; to some extent they already have. The aspirations expressed may be difficult to sustain in light of the slow pace and conservative drift of economic reform throughout much of Central and Eastern Europe. Most tragic is the outbreak of national and ethnic violence: the catastrophe and shame of the killing and "ethnic cleansing" in the former Yugoslavia; the continuing fighting in the Caucasus; and the racist attacks on immigrants in Germany. Yet I remain hopeful that the receptive moment for ideas such as those expressed here has not passed. The work of reconstruction is the task of a generation or longer. The challenge of placing a democratic and egalitarian imprint on the legal order, and the opportunities to do so, will be constantly present as this work proceeds.

This article concerns the future of democracy in North America as well as in Central and Eastern Europe. The achievements and transformative possibilities of 1989 should also induce North Americans to reexamine and revise our own institutions, to rethink what democracy could mean for us. Lawyers and legal scholars in particular will want to consider what all this means for the role of law in the democratic transformation of societies. They can and should assist in the gradual diffusion and deepening of a transnational civic culture committed to democracy, equality, social justice, and nonviolent dispute resolution. This paper is conceived as a very modest contribution to that dialogue, from a perspective supportive of postliberal conceptions of democracy.

I. The Legal Infrastructure of Democratic Reconstruction

For most commentators, postcommunist democracy has an obvious institutional structure consisting of four basic components: representative political institutions, free markets, and human rights guarantees, all in turn founded upon the autonomous rule of law. Of course, many legal details need to be worked out. Wholly new codes across the range of public and private law fields will be required. But in the prevailing view, postcommunist legal reconstruction involves mostly technical or specialist work.

The implicit premise of this technical approach to legal reconstruction is that free markets and human rights codes each possess more or less determinate or canonical forms. The concepts of the "free market" and "fundamental human rights" are assumed to entail certain basic principles or guidelines of social organization, from which lawyers can deduce the array of rules that together make up and implement the legal structure of the market, and of human rights guarantees. With due regard for local refinements and subtleties, and for the choice of political structure (for instance, whether unitary or federal, parliamentary or presidential, and so on), the prevailing view is that the foundational choice of political and economic constitution—the choice for political representation plus free markets plus human rights, based on the rule of law—has built-in consequences for legal order, indeed, that this foundational choice largely *defines* the legal order. It follows that the task of lawyers is simply to work out the built-in rules and doctrines that correspond to this constitutional form. Once the foundational choice of regime has been made, the choice of rendering the legal order in detail is guided by the law's technical logic. In short, the role of law and lawyers in democratic reconstruction is largely *apolitical.*[2]

This technical conception of the role of law and of lawyers in democratic reconstruction is highly problematic. There are at least four basic reasons to question this technically oriented vision of legal reconstruction:

(1) In fact, the model of political representation plus free markets plus human rights guarantees plus the rule of law does not exhaust the meaning of democracy.
(2) The foundational choice of political/economic regime cannot determine the structure of a legal order, except in very general, albeit quite important, ways. A wide array of legal structures is compatible with the basic choice for a liberal, democratic, market-based system, and the variations between these legal structures have highly significant consequences for power relations within society.
(3) Therefore, the very process of articulating new legal orders will continuously reopen foundational questions regarding the character of the democracy under construction. As decision-makers go about giving legal content to the foundational ideals of representation, markets, and rights, they will be permanently and inescapably engaged in making significant political choices. Law and politics are not identical, to be sure. Legal argument and practice have their own specialized content and concerns, accumulated traditions, and constraining conventions. But neither are law and politics radically distinct; they are inextricably linked.
(4) It follows that the ideal of a neutral and depoliticized ("autonomous") rule of law is misconceived, and cannot supply an adequate jurisprudential underpinning for postcommunist transition, at least in the way the rule-of-law ideal has traditionally been understood in North America.[3]

The remainder of this article elaborates and defends these propositions.[4]

II. Law and Market Structure

A widespread consensus exists in Central and Eastern Europe to replace centralized state planning with a system of free markets. Centralized planning is rejected for both economic and political reasons. State economic control, with its accompanying "soft-budget constraints,"[5] produced endemic shortages, underutilization of labor, and slow and uneven rates of technological advance and economic growth, as well as tragic environmental damage. State control, at least on the Soviet model, also centralized political power, and foreclosed popular participation in economic and social planning.

As compared to a system of state planning, the market mechanism offers considerable institutional advantages as a way of making decisions about how to allocate society's resources. Properly designed markets provide economic actors with incentive structures oriented toward initiative, and with budget and price constraints that signal the consequences of action. Using markets to register consumer preferences and to allocate resources is a means of decentralizing social decision-making and, thus, of dispersing political power. This not only lends a welcome flexibility to economic processes, but markets can be designed to encourage grass-roots participation, as in the example of democratic collective bargaining. For these and other reasons, the consensus is that democratic reconstruction should be market-based.

This is not to say that market systems have no defects.[6] Extremes of inequality persist in advanced capitalist societies, where conspicuous accumulations of wealth coexist with the shame of homelessness. For all its economic achievements, the United States allows millions of people to live in cruel conditions of poverty and deprivation. As John Kenneth Galbraith has said, "no one in search of a better life would wisely move from East Berlin to the South Bronx."[7] The most thoughtful leaders of the effort to construct postcommunist futures are aware of the seamy side of market economics. For example, Adam Michnik has said "[t]he road to the market must lead through poverty and unemployment."[8] Markets are not seen as central to democratic renewal because they are flawless, but because overall the social benefits of markets seem to outweigh the harms of rigid central planning.

Let us therefore take the consensus in favor of the market as a starting point. It is often assumed that the idea of the free market connotes a fixed set of institutional and legal arrangements, and relatively sharp and precise criteria for distinguishing "market" from "nonmarket" institutions. These arrangements and decisional criteria, supposedly implicit in the concept of the free market, are thought to be given by its two most powerful organizing ideas: private property and freedom of contract.[9]

Now, obviously, the foundational choice to abandon central planning and opt for a market allocation has important ramifications for the content of legal order. This proposition is only true, however, at a fairly high level of generality. *The choice for markets over state planning does not foreclose a wide range of political decisions that must be made and can only be made in the course of defining and elaborating market structures in legal detail.* The free market does not possess a built-in legal structure, and therefore the process of specifying the law that constructs markets is eminently and inescapably a political project.

I will discuss two sources of indeterminacy in the legal construction of markets: indeterminacy in the conceptual underpinnings, and a set of second-order problems having to do with market nonparticipation and market failure.

A. *The "Logic" of the Free Market*[10]

A market is a set of norms, practices, and institutional arrangements for regularized and voluntary exchange. There must exist—whether explicitly or implicitly, formally or informally—rules or understandings that determine five things:

(1) the identity of eligible economic actors (which people and what artificial entities have the legal capacity to trade);
(2) the types and distribution of property entitlements (who initially owns what, and what can lawfully be done with property);
(3) the methods by which exchange can be effected and ownership transferred;
(4) how the product of joint efforts is to be divided; and
(5) the criteria for distinguishing "voluntary" from "coerced" exchanges.

These ground rules can be wholly or largely embedded in religious or customary norms, but I will take the typical modern case, in which the market-structuring rules are embodied in laws. The point may then be restated as follows: for a market to exist, at least over any long term, the state must at a minimum enact a law of property, contracts and torts.[11] Clearly this is an implicit assumption of free-market theory, and careful neoclassical economists make note that the concept of an allocatively efficient outcome is relative to the prevailing structure of legal rules and entitlements (among other background factors). At least until recently, however, economists and social theorists have tended to treat the question of precisely how the ground rules are defined as a technical matter for the attention of lawyers.

However, more than technical problems are involved. Legal capacity has always been a highly politicized issue, linked to such great historical questions as slavery, the decline of feudalism and the creation of labor markets, women's struggle for emancipation, and so on. Even supposedly "hard" concepts, like private ownership and voluntary exchange, are simply not self-defining. Most contemporary lawyers are skeptical that such concepts have an intrinsic meaning or that their meaning can be logically derived from the idea of free markets or from a general theory of human nature. Giving legal content to concepts such as ownership and voluntary exchange requires making political choices and value judgments within a particular historical and normative context.

The problem of indeterminacy arises not just because of the elastic character of basic concepts such as private property and free contract, but also because these concepts embody contradictory meanings, as the Realists showed. For example, private property implies freedom to use what one owns as one pleases (even at the expense of others' interests). But it *also* implies legal protection of one's property from harms caused by others, including harms caused by other peoples' use of their property. Thus, the concept of private property simultaneously implies both freedom from state regulation *and* regulatory controls on property use. This inner tension in the idea of private property gives rise to considerable leeway in specifying and applying property rules. And this is discretion with political spin: in the very act of setting the ground rules of a private property system, of defining exactly what private property *means* in legal terms, decision-makers are constantly engaged in determining the character and intensity of controls on property use.

Similarly, the idea of free contract connotes both the right to act in a self-interested manner, and also the obligation not to invade the justifiable expectations of others. Voluntary exchange signifies the parties' liberty to arrange their affairs as they see fit without governmental supervision, but also the need for government to police bargaining behavior in order to assure that contract obligations have been freely assumed. Contract law, like property and torts, embodies a permanent tension between the goal of promoting freedom of action and the goal of protecting interests in security.

All of this implies that the project of giving legal definition to market structures involves making an endless series of socially significant choices. The background legal rules for markets have distributive consequences. The rules affect power relations between employers and employees, large and small businesses, property owners, neighbors, and non-owners, creditors and debtors, and so on. That is, the new legal rules which concretize the idea of markets will to some extent distribute power within postcommunist society.

Legal learning surely can shed light on the process of defining market structuring rules, but, just as surely, legal discourse contains no neutral logic capable of resolving contested questions or determining choices about market structure. As Oliver Wendell Holmes pointed out long ago, to use a famous example, legal logic by itself cannot tell us whether or not peaceful picketing is coercive.[12] The answers to such questions turn ultimately on moral and political judgments, that is to say, on competing visions of the good society. A particular specification of property entitlements can emphasize the exclusive dominion of the owner, or the interests of the neighbors. A particular legal definition of free exchange can ratify the power of the already powerful, or enhance protections for dominated groups. The background rules can privilege a wide range of self-interested behaviors, or impose duties to respect the justifiable expectations and vulnerabilities of others.

If a society's economic life is predominantly organized through markets, then the precise legal structure of markets will have a profound impact on the degree to which the society's members can experience autonomy and self-realization, and on the extent of social equality. Whether the market structures chosen are more or less communitarian, more or less egalitarian, will depend on the social vision brought to the enterprise of giving markets their legal definition.

It follows that the idea of a "free" or "self-regulating" market is an illusion. To have a market at all assumes the existence of a background regime of legal rules and entitlements. It assumes, at a minimum, that the coercive power of the state can be invoked to protect property and enforce contracts. The state can withdraw from central planning, but it cannot withdraw from its role in defining market structures and property entitlements.[13] And, for the reasons outlined above, the background rules are not socially neutral; they distribute power and frame the possibilities of human fulfillment.[14] The choice of a particular market structure is therefore the implementation of a distinct regulatory strategy. It is a political choice, for which state actors—including judges—bear responsibility.

B. *Inequality, Nonparticipation, and Market Failure*

Democratic reconstruction should disperse decision-making by establishing governmental and nongovernmental processes that invite and encourage popular participation. Allocating resources based on consumer preferences as registered in market transactions is one obvious way of doing this. But there are risks to this approach. Market mechanisms take an aggregation of consumer preferences as a surrogate for the general welfare. A substantial danger that market outcomes will depart from the general welfare arises when property ownership is concentrated, income is unequally distributed, large numbers of people exercise little effective demand, and significant market imperfections exist. This point implicates a series of important questions for democratic legal reconstruction.[15]

The most basic problem is that market results will likely depart significantly from socially optimal outcomes in the presence of sharply unequal property ownership and income distribution. If the law effectuates consumer preferences in such a context, it ratifies a decision-making process based on unequal power. Moreover, the prevailing distribution of wealth and income is itself influenced by the existing structure of legal entitlements. The manner in which property, contract, and tort rights are defined affects the distribution of wealth and net income.[16] Thus, the law of property, contracts, and torts partly determines which members of a society will be able to participate effectively in resource allocation decisions, and what relative degrees of influence they will bring to market.

Law simply cannot be neutral in these matters. The values of autonomy and self-determination may or may not be served by effectuating consumer choices and private agreements. It all depends on the circumstances and context, including the way in which the applicable legal rules impact on and steer peoples' choices. Because market-structuring rules of law bear some responsibility for the substantive content of the choices people make and the contracts they choose to enter, it is necessary and appropriate in fashioning background rules of law to pay attention to the likely impact of proposed rules on human self-determination and equality.

Legal questions of political and social consequence are also raised by problems of market imperfection or market failure. Economic activities frequently have involuntary consequences, often quite negative, for persons who are not parties to the relevant transactions, or who do not even participate in the relevant markets. A consequence of this kind is called an "externality," and is recognized as an "imperfection" or "failure" in markets. The existence of market imperfections that block optimizing outcomes is generally thought to be a valid basis for government "intervention" in the market. Even the staunchest defenders of free markets acknowledge this point in principle, although they tend to view market failure as the exception rather than the norm.

Thus the very idea of the free market implies the use of governmental power to correct for market failure. Sometimes the appropriate corrective measures are made at the highest level, as in the case of environmental protection statutes and international environmental regulation. But it is also possible to correct for market failure by altering background legal entitlements. In the classic example, a liability rule is entrenched allowing victims to recover from polluters. The threat of liability should force polluters to "internalize" the costs of environmental damage into their budget calculations, and therefore into the price of their products, so that competitive considerations will create incentives to abate the harm.[17]

Those entrusted with the responsibility of giving legal content to postcommunist market structures must inevitably engage these questions of wealth inequality, market nonparticipation, and market imperfection. They should consider the implications of property, contract, and tort rules for the distribution of wealth, and how the structure of background rules will affect the interests of market nonparticipants and those whose market participation is limited by low income. They should design legal entitlements to eliminate negative external effects and other forms of imperfection that prevent markets from producing socially desirable results. To summarize, the task of postcommunist lawyers is not simply to put in place the technical legal underpinnings of the free market. The challenge and the promise of democratic legal reconstruction is to envision and specify market structures that, insofar as possible, reflect egalitarian, solidaristic, and participatory values. The struggle is not for the "free" market, but for *democratic* market structures.

III. Criteria for Democratic Market Construction

I propose the following criteria for democratic market construction that might inform the processes of legal change now unfolding in Central and Eastern Europe.

A. Property entitlements should be designed to foster the widest possible array of participation rights.

The Blackstonian image of property—as a relationship of absolute and exclusive dominion exercised by a unitary owner over an item of wealth—exercises such power in our legal culture that it is often difficult to imagine other conceptions of property that might be more desirable.[18] But the effort must be made. All people significantly affected by major business decisions deserve some consultation and voice in those decisions. It is undemocratic to deny such participation, and serious inefficiencies necessarily arise when resource allocation is based only on signals from the market, without additional institutional mechanisms for people to express their needs.[19] Postcommunist legal reconstruction should therefore be premised on the notion that all influential economic units and processes must be made responsive to democratic input. Participation opportunities should run in favor of people employed by or dependent upon large enterprises, and to communities whose vital interests an enterprise affects, or onto which the firm off-loads external costs.[20]

Due to wealth inequality and market failure, market transactions may not provide a viable mechanism for affected individuals to make themselves heard. Business corporations in the West regularly make investment decisions that profoundly affect employee interests but as to which the employees, particularly if nonunionized, have little or no say. This state of affairs is simplistically justified on the grounds that the company "owns" the business. Nothing in the idea of private ownership precludes us from deeming employees part owners of the business by virtue of their investment of human capital, with corresponding entitlements to participate in, or at least be consulted regarding, governance matters. Likewise, the idea of private ownership is consistent with an assignment of governance rights, consultation opportunities, or other entitlements to communities that provide businesses with access to labor, waste-absorption capacity (in the form of environmental despoliation), and other infrastructural resources.

B. Property ownership should be widely dispersed, and entitlements should be designed to inhibit wealth concentration.

Egalitarian as well as participatory values should guide the design of market structures and legal entitlements. Among other techniques, postcommunist legal reconstruction should vitalize previously marginalized property forms (for example, cooperative and municipal ownership) that will implement the equality goal.[21]

The ongoing privatization of state-owned enterprises in Central and Eastern Europe offers an extraordinary and historically unprecedented opportunity to redefine and disperse property ownership. Perceptive observers have understood that privatization in the postcommunist context involves the very creation of a legal and institutional infrastructure of property rights.[22] But the postcommunist nations are not limited to existing legal forms.

Hopefully a considerable portion of the newly privatized assets will eventually come into the possession of the citizenry on an egalitarian basis. But an egalitarian privatization program may lead quickly to a skewed distribution of wealth unless controls on concentration are enacted. The trick is to make such controls consistent with an incentive structure that promotes productive and allocative efficiency. From that point of view, creative design of market structuring rules might become as important as more conventional regulatory instruments such as taxation, antitrust policies, and fiduciary obligations.

Some observations and proposals on privatization appeared in the original, 1990 version of this paper, and were quickly outpaced by events in Central and Eastern Europe. Privatization and voucher programs have already been launched in several postcommunist nations, the Czechoslovakian program being perhaps the most ambitious and comprehensive to date. Policy-makers have tackled a host of complex conceptual and technical problems involved in large-scale privatization, including how to structure the transfer process (vouchers, auctions, valuation problems, and so on), how to guard against giveaways to former *nomenklatura* and foreign investors, how to structure the newly privatized enterprises, what mix of private and public ownership to aim for, and so on. Each of these questions implicates egalitarian and democratic concerns, and considerable commitment and creativity will be needed to carry those values forward as the process of institutional innovation evolves.

Detailed examination of these questions is beyond the scope of this paper.

Here I will briefly consider one particularly interesting approach that has been proposed.[23] This is the idea of focusing the privatization process on the creation of mutual funds or public holding corporations. In this model, the state transfers some or most of the ownership shares in operating enterprises to mutual funds, of which the citizenry at large are, in turn, made the beneficial owners or shareholders. The idea is to serve two goals simultaneously: to achieve the asserted efficiency advantages of concentrated, external, nonemployee control over enterprise management; and to promote the egalitarian objective of widespread ownership.[24]

From a democratic standpoint, the mutual fund approach has some serious limitations. By definition, it envisions the creation of new, highly concentrated centers of economic power which, it may be assumed, will be hierarchically organized and only minimally accountable, if at all, to democratic input from the beneficial owners. The danger of economic concentration is likely to become all the greater when stock markets and securities trading flourish. Moreover, even if the mutual funds build in some mechanisms of shareholder participation, it is unlikely that these devices will be more successful than their Western counterparts have been in overcoming the problems of agent self-dealing and shareholder coordination.[25] Endemic problems of this kind will limit both the efficiency and the egalitarian contributions of the mutual funds.

Second, the mutual fund approach to privatization amounts to a kind of pension or social security system based on general market outcomes (rather than on social guarantees). Whatever its other strengths and weaknesses, such a scheme is unlikely to create incentives for ordinary citizens to work at their regular jobs with greater diligence and creativity. What the proposal offers in the way of enhancing productivity (external controls on enterprise management) may well be outweighed by forgoing the productivity advantages of linking worker performance to profit-sharing incentives.

Finally, while the proposal contemplates that the operating enterprises will be restructured, the changes envisioned concern product lines, technology, and working methods. There has been little attention to changes in the organizational and operating format of firms. Rather, it is generally contemplated that the conventional, hierarchical model will be retained. That is, this approach to privatization makes no effort to democratize work or enterprise governance.

Postcommunist policy-makers and activists should experiment with a much wider array of legal and organizational alternatives for institutionalizing economic democracy. These might include worker ownership schemes and housing cooperatives, employee participation in firm decisions at both the strategic and operational levels, and the extension of collective bargaining. The privatization process offers a unique environment in which to launch and capitalize social innovations of this kind.

A model worth studying in this regard is a proven and efficient form of worker ownership adopted by a network of cooperative enterprises in Mondragon, Spain.[26] As many commentators have noted, the Mondragon form of worker ownership has not resulted in a significant democratization of firm decision-making or operations. The cooperatives' members annually elect representatives to the board of directors, but managerial power remains largely intact and is structured on a traditional, hierarchical model. There are significant constraints on employee control over the disposition of earnings. Moreover, members typically invest human capital for a very long term, trading off mobility for security. This feature is unattractive to many people, and to some extent conflicts with the dynamism and flexibility sought in the postcommunist world.

For these and other reasons, it may seem ironic to raise the Mondragon example in this context. Surely no suggestion is intended that the precise model should or could be exported wholesale to the East, although I do believe that some forms of cooperative ownership of enterprises, even relatively large enterprises, might be highly appropriate in some Central and Eastern European contexts.[27] The hierarchical organization of management and operations in Mondragon is not an inherent characteristic of the model.

In any event, my thought here is that the greatest relevance of Mondragon to postcommunist privatization may turn out to be in suggesting tools for democratizing citizen investment funds (as distinct from the question of democratizing work operations). In this regard, the Mondragon model has several intriguing features. Ownership shares cannot be purchased or sold in ordinary capital markets or private transactions. Purchase of a share is legally tied to admission to membership in a "political community" (the firm), which is in turn tied to performance of the functional role of working in the firm. All members have equal voting and governance rights within the firm, regardless of the economic value of their respective shares. Members are entitled to a current income stream (the equivalent of wages), but the appreciation value of their shares is retained in an "internal capital account." These accounts are "internal" or "noncommodified," in the sense that they have no market value because they cannot be bought or sold. They can be cashed out at the appreciated value, but only upon departure from membership (typically upon retirement). Newly admitted members buy in at an entry-level, preappreciation value; they do not have to (indeed, they cannot) purchase a share from a retiring member at the fully appreciated price. The fact that shares cannot be acquired on the market, and the relative affordability of the buy-in price, are egalitarian features designed to inhibit wealth concentration. But the egalitarian features are linked to appreciation and profit-sharing features that created incentives toward diligent and creative effort on behalf of the enterprise, toward a long-term perspective, and toward reinvestment rather than premature distribution of earnings.

These aspects of the Mondragon system might be carried over to the design of citizen investment funds created in the postcommunist privatization process. As at Mondragon, ownership of shares in the mutual funds could be linked to membership in a political community, providing opportunities for governance participation. There is no reason, in principle, why such membership needs to involve a lifetime commitment to a job. "Portability" devices (similar to the concept of pension portability in the West) could make cooperative or fund membership more fluid and transitory, and therefore open to linkage with a variety of statuses and roles (for example, membership in an industry, as distinct from possession of a job; residence in a locality; a philosophical commitment, such as environmentalism; or perhaps one's being a regular consumer of certain goods). The requirement of a membership of *some* kind would act as a brake on wealth concentration, and would provide some cohesion as a basis of shareholder coordination. To be sure, there should also be an array of diversified, general purpose funds, in which entitlement to membership involves little more than, say, being a citizen or permanent resident. Some small shareholders will prefer to trade off the benefits of governance participation for the convenience and security of conventional investment. The "socially linked" funds themselves ought to be afforded some opportunities to diversify risk by investing reserves in general funds or other opportunities.

The ownership entitlement in the mutual funds should include an array of governance rights. In the more conventional funds, this might involve periodic election of management, votes on major policies, and information access. These rights should be more refined than the familiar mechanisms of "shareholder democracy" in the West, but they may not be all that different in form, except in the crucial respect that voting would be on an egalitarian basis.[28] In the socially linked funds, governance rights should be more extensive, and should involve a wide range of roles, committees, and participation opportunities. Certainly, having relatively small, decentralized, and somewhat politically cohesive funds will not automatically solve the problem of devising effective instruments of shareholder coordination and control. But giving up the search for these mechanisms by eliminating shareholder participation altogether is hardly a solution either. The answers must be sought in the invention and development of novel forms of education and data dissemination, and in the creation of new forms of institutional and administrative democracy.[29]

The funds should also incorporate the idea of the internal capital account. In the course of large-scale privatization, the state should create a new type of property in the form of citizen investment vouchers, which would be distributed to the populace as partial reparation for the sacrifices they were forced to make during the Stalinist era. In future years, every citizen, upon reaching adulthood, would be offered an opportunity to purchase a voucher at an affordable price (and perhaps with subsidized loans). The voucher would entitle the holder to invest in any of the newly created public investment funds, and to have a social investment account established in his or her name. Entry into one of the socially linked funds, such as a regional development authority, might require the voucherholder to meet eligibility requirements such as residency, but it might also be that a mere interest in that fund's goals would suffice (if the fund were anxious to attract members). The voucher would only be valid in one fund at a time (or perhaps a small number of funds, in order to permit some diversification), but could be withdrawn and reinvested elsewhere. The investment accounts would have to be fully portable for life, so that vouchers could be reinvested at their appreciated values. However, by analogy to the internal capital account, the voucherholder would be permitted to cash out the account only on the happening of specified circumstances (such as retirement), and ordinarily cashing out the voucher would mean cancelling it, and giving up one's opportunity to invest through the voucher system. (Some early or partial cash-out possibilities, for instance, to assist in the purchase of a home, should be devised to add greater flexibility.) Most important, the property entitlements represented by the voucher would be personal to the holder. Thus, sale of vouchers in private transactions would not be possible. The wealthy would therefore be unable to purchase other people's economic governance rights, at least with respect to this form of capital.[30]

C. Legal entitlements should be structured so as to take account of and minimize the negative external effects of enterprise activity, capital accumulation, and economic modernization.

A tragic lesson of the postwar era in Central and Eastern Europe is that central planning offers no guarantee against environmental damage. But experience in the West teaches that market systems are also quite capable of generating unacceptable levels of environmental damage. Reversing the present drift toward planetary self-destruction will require regulatory solutions at both the national and international levels, and a sea change in cultural attitudes. While I do not suggest that private law remedies can provide adequate protection against environmental harms, nonetheless, the process of legal reconstruction should at a minimum not ignored, and indeed, it should seek out and embrace opportunities to entrench liability rules that deter environmental misconduct.

More generally, postcommunist law should seek to deter and to fairly distribute the costs of other negative external effects, including the costs occasioned by capital mobility and economic restructuring. Policy-makers traditionally look to systems of fines and levies in order to deter unacceptably risky conduct, and to transfer payments in order to socialize the costs of harms the community accepts as reasonable or inevitable. This mind-set overlooks another possibility, namely that the price system can perform deterrence and cost-spreading functions. To accomplish this, market-structuring entitlement rules must be designed to induce actors to internalize the costs of harms properly attributable to their activities.

The community as a whole benefits over the long run from market flexibility and economic modernization, but in the short term modernization and restructuring can visit exceptional harms on individuals who happen to work in declining industries, or to live in economically troubled communities. Enterprise liability is a method of using the price system to spread these costs, so that they are shared by the community at large, or at least by the consuming public. Enterprise liability inhibits firms that enjoy the profit-seeking opportunities created by market flexibility from externalizing the inevitable costs of economic adjustment onto others.

As with the case of environmental harms, I am doubtful that tort law is the optimal tool for coping with the social problems caused by economic restructuring. Administrative, nonlitigation-based programs, such as national health, retraining, and income maintenance schemes, are usually more efficient and more equitable policy instruments, particularly if bureaucratic ossification can be counteracted by new forms of client and community participation. My point is the more modest one, that tort approaches have certain advantages that should not be overlooked. These include the decentralizing, antibureaucratic potential of party-controlled litigation; the potential of party-initiated discovery techniques to enforce government and enterprise accountability; and the availability of exemplary awards to punish and deter egregious misconduct.

D. Democratic market construction should attempt to achieve the highest level of guaranteed social benefits and economic due process consistent with available resources.

The minimum social benefits package should include both substantive entitlements (for example, to income maintenance, health, shelter, education, child care, and the like), as well as economic due process rights (for example, protections against unjust eviction, unjust discharge from employment, or denial of government benefit, and protections against discrimination on account of gender, race, religion, sexual identity, handicap, or other invidious grounds).

This point primarily concerns statutory and administrative programs, and perhaps constitutional guarantees, as distinct from private law entitlements enforced by civil action. Social and economic guarantees are mentioned here for two reasons. First, such guarantees have an obvious market structuring role in the sense that they set a floor underneath market transactions, thereby adjusting power relations in the market. Celebrants of the free market often suggest that, as a matter of definition, a free market has no regulatory floor. But this view is mistaken for the reasons already canvassed. All markets rest on a regulatory floor established by the background legal rules specifying property entitlements and monitoring bargaining conduct. The real issue for debate is at what level the floor should be positioned. From that point of view, the difference between a background rule of law and a complex regulatory statute is unimportant.

From other perspectives, of course, the difference can be very significant, both in legal process terms and in socioeconomic impact. Well-defined administrative schemes may provide more certainty and predictability than litigation about the meaning of general norms. On the other hand, familiar problems like bureaucratic inertia and nonaccountability may vitiate the most well-intended administrative programs. This is a second reason to connect the question of market construction to basic social rights. A party-controlled litigation system, if properly constructed with an eye toward equal and relatively inexpensive access to the courts, might provide a basis for grass-roots legal action to define and expand social entitlements, and for interventions in the bureaucratic administration of entitlement programs. At the least, this possibility should not be overlooked in structuring rights and entitlements as between market participants (for instance, between landlord and tenant, or between employer and employee).

I am mindful of the debate regarding whether the economically devastated societies of Central and Eastern Europe can afford to promulgate high social and economic guarantees. Many people believe that a generous benefits floor is simply out of reach for the foreseeable future. Some people who are sympathetic in principle to high welfare guarantees have reluctantly concluded that it would be a mistake for postcommunist law to make such guarantees now. They point out that the Stalinist constitutions were replete with wonderful but hypocritical and unfulfilled promises of rights and entitlements. The fear is that more unfulfilled promises, even in the entirely different moral climate of democratic reconstruction, would breed cynicism and disrespect for law and rights.

A more austere view opposes generous social guarantees on principle. From this perspective, the highest priority is rapid economic development, and this is said to require harsh labor discipline and forced savings (that is, limitations of consumption) to promote productivity and capital accumulation. Central to this mind-set is the idea of a trade-off between efficiency and equity, between growth and equality. The belief is that inequality necessarily accompanies efforts to foster rapid economic growth by rewarding entrepreneurial activity, and that therefore only a "self-regulating" market can be a true engine of modernization.

This debate points out the deep connection between the question of legal rights and entitlements, and strategies for economic growth. The following are some possible lines of response to the view that welfare rights are either unaffordable or undesirable for postcommunist society in transition.

First, it is not obvious as a historical matter that a formula of harsh discipline, low consumption, and steep inequality is either necessary to or particularly helpful in promoting rapid economic growth. The contrary case can be made, that accumulation and market discipline, moderated by social and egalitarian concerns, is at least as productive a model over the long run, quite apart from humanitarian considerations. Inequality and unrestrained business power have economic costs, particularly in the long term, which might outweigh the advantages and even spectacular achievements of the inequality model of growth. Repressive growth policies may result in a deskilled working class robbed of productive potential and initiative; irreversible environmental damage; and wasteful and highly uneven investment patterns.[31]

Second, strategies that may have succeeded during nineteenth-century industrialization are unlikely to be well-suited for the postindustrial era.[32] Poland, for example, is unlikely to build an economic miracle on a platform of coal extraction and low-skilled, mass manufacture of cheap goods. An alternative, postindustrial development strategy is needed that builds upon the extraordinary organizational skills and creativity exhibited by Polish workers in creating and sustaining Solidarity during martial law, and in bringing down the Communist regime. Such a strategy implies high levels of participation and of social investment in human capital.

Third, beyond a certain point, a zero-sum fixation on the efficiency/equity trade-off is just mistaken. Joint gains occur. Equity can enhance efficiency. Entrenched workers' organizations are apt to respond more flexibly to economic restructuring and technological change when a baseline of financial security is assured. In the right atmosphere, worker participation can involve knowledge-sharing conducive to productivity advances. The experience of many successful postwar economies has been that granting generous welfare rights is a prudent and profitable investment in human capital.[33]

Finally, economic strategy has implications for political modernization. It is possible, but unlikely, that the postcommunist societies can combine exploitative economics with democratic politics. The creation of stable, democratic, political cultures in Central and Eastern Europe requires an economic strategy aimed steadily, if gradually, to improve conditions for the mass of farmers and workers, and to link them in a broad social grouping with the middle class.[34] Conversely, repressive economic measures seem likely to ignite retrograde political tendencies, such as anti-Semitism and authoritarian populism. While a case can be made that high levels of welfare rights will inhibit postcommunist economic modernization, the dilemma is that Eastern Europe probably cannot achieve democratic *political* modernization without egalitarian and solidaristic *economic* policies. The goal, then, must be to find an economic development strategy that is based upon, and makes a virtue of, an actively participating working class, a working class that is secure, highly trained, and as well provided for as economic circumstances permit. The design of legal entitlements and market structures should comport with this approach to development.

IV. Conclusion

This article has argued that the foundational choice for a representative, market- and rights-based system does not foreclose fundamental political controversy about the meaning, nature, and institutional structure of democracy. It surely does not foreclose fundamental political controversy about the content of legal order. While the foundational choice for representation, markets, rights, and the rule of law provides a general direction and orientation for postcommunist law, it leaves a vast range of politically and socially significant questions unresolved.

Will the people who brought down the Stalinist system seek to create a form of empowered, postliberal democracy? A more solidaristic version of democratic institutions and culture that embraces a positive conception of communal responsibility to provide decent living conditions and self-realization opportunities to all? Will they seek to take democracy into the private sphere, so as to unfreeze and erode all forms of illegitimate hierarchy, whether based on race, gender, ethnic group, religion, sexual identity, or other forms of illicit domination? Will they aim for a "greener," more ecologically sensitive democracy, and one that invites grass-roots citizen engagement, rather than encouraging political passivity? Or has the moment of democratic and egalitarian innovation already passed?

While no one knows the answers to these questions as yet, I am convinced that lawyers and others who are involved in or who study the legal system can play an important role in determining the future of the postcommunist society: a creative, politically and morally engaged role, not just a technical one. To meet the challenge, postcommunist lawyers—and lawyers in the West who wish to extend the democratization of social life here—must be sensitive to, and accept responsibility for, the socially constitutive and distributive significance of legal practices.

This may sound like a call for the politicization of law. I prefer to think of it as an appeal that we recognize the inevitably political character of legal practices, and develop an understanding of our work that links that recognition to democratic commitments. Even put this way, I can understand the discomfort and impatience of postcommunist lawyers for this sort of talk. After all, Central and Eastern Europeans heard about "politicized law" for forty-five years, and neither they nor I want any part of *that* conception of legality. Unfortunately, postcommunist lawyers will not find all they are looking for in traditional, formalist conceptions of legality either, and they will perforce have need of a revised jurisprudence in order to tackle the problems of democratic reconstruction. One can only hope that the enormity of the tasks they face will give rise to an imagination, ingenuity, and good spirit in legal reconstruction, equal to that with which the peoples of Central and Eastern Europe brought down the old regime.

Notes

This is a condensed version of an article originally appearing in *U. Brit. Colum. L. Rev.* 25:69 (1991) and based on my Douglas McK. Brown Lecture delivered on November 27, 1990. I am exceedingly grateful to Dean Peter Burns, the Faculty of Law, and the benefactors of the Douglas McK. Brown chair for the invitation to present this lecture. Appreciation is also owed to the John D. and Catherine T. MacArthur Foundation, the John Merck Fund, and to Northeastern University for generously funding an academic delegation I led to Poland and Czechoslovakia in the Winter, 1990. My understanding of the problems of democratic legal reconstruction was greatly enriched by our dialogue with legal scholars, government lawyers, and human rights activists. Many of the ideas discussed here were developed by and/or in collaboration with colleagues in the critical legal theory movement. I have relied particularly on the cited articles by Duncan Kennedy and Joseph Singer. I take sole responsibility for the views and formulations expressed herein.

Mary Joe Frug, Professor of Law, New England School of Law, a member of our delegation, died tragically on April 4, 1991. Mary Joe was a gifted feminist legal scholar and creative law teacher who cared passionately about social justice. She was an incomparable friend who brought warmth, joy, and wisdom into my life. This article is dedicated to her memory, a small tribute to her commitment, courage, and love.

1. Here the phrase is from Roberto Unger, "The Critical Legal Studies Movement," *Harv. L. Rev.* 96:561, 588 (1983).
2. These assumptions correspond to and reflect the basic premises of postrealist thought in North America: that the interdependence of contemporary life gives rise to discoverable principles of social organization in which all people share a common interest; and that an objective method of legal reasoning exists with which determinate, particularized conclusions about legal order can be derived from the general, shared principles of social organization. A classic postrealist text exemplifying these assumptions is Henry Hart & Albert Sacks, *The Legal Process* (tent. ed. 1958) (unpublished). For a critical view, see Unger, supra note 1.
3. Professor Singer defines "traditional legal theory" as approaches that "seek to maintain the separation of law and politics by describing decision procedures based on rational consensus that purport to generate [determinate] answers to legal questions." Joseph Singer, "The Reliance Interest in Property," *Stan. L. Rev.* 40:611, 624 n. 39 (1987).

4. I note, without further elaboration, a parallel between the dilemmas of postcommunist legal reconstruction and the difficulties of contemporary legal theory in North America. My argument here is that the foundational choice for representation plus free markets plus human rights plus the rule of law cannot, by itself, determine the structure of postcommunist legal orders.

   Similarly, the main currents of postwar North American legal thought—legal process and institutional competence theory, efficiency analysis, and rights theory—fail to provide a determinate method for resolving legal problems. See generally, Joseph Singer, "Legal Realism Now," *Calif. L. Rev.* 76:465 (1988).

   In this condensed version, I focus on the legal construction of markets. I discuss the legal construction of human rights guarantees in the original version of this article, pp. 95–102. Similar issues are posed by the question of how to structure political representation. See, e.g., Richard Parker, "The Past of Constitutional Theory—And Its Future," *Ohio St. L. J.* 42:223 (1981).

5. See János Kornai, "Resource-Constrained versus Demand-Constrained Systems," *Econometrica* 47:801 (1979).

6. Nor is it to say that a viable economic system can be constructed entirely through markets, with no element of centralized planning by the state (and with no planning by nominally private bureaucratic entities such as business corporations). As Robert Heilbroner pithily notes: "[N]o capitalism has ever made its way by relying on the energies of its private realm alone. . . . The market-driven sector, to which we genuflect, is the main source of energy, but the public realm, which we ignore or decry, is the guardian of the whole. . . . Capitalism is thus as intimately entangled with planning as it is with the market." Robert Heilbroner, "After Communism," *The New Yorker* (September 10, 1990) pp. 91, 97–98.

   For a classic statement of the point, see, generally, Karl Polanyi, *The Great Transformation* (1944; reprint Boston: Beacon Press, 1957).

7. John Kenneth Galbraith, "The Rush to Capitalism," *New York Rev. of Books* (October 25, 1990) p. 51.

8. Adam Michnik, "How Can They Stir the Soup in Poland?" *The Globe and Mail* (November 23, 1990).

9. Thus, even so perceptive an economist as János Kornai holds that "[t]he notion of a free economy . . . implies a certain configuration of property rights and a certain institutional and political structure," János Kornai, *The Road to a Free Economy* (New York: Norton, 1990) p. 22, and he treats the ideas of private property and free contract as having a relatively fixed, determinate content. See, e.g., id., pp. 39–40, 45–50.

10. This discussion draws upon some valuable but largely forgotten teachings of the American Legal Realist school from the period of the 1920s and 1930s. The best treatment of this aspect of Legal Realism is Joseph Singer's superb articles, from which I have freely borrowed. See supra notes 3 and 4. For other articles reviving and extending the Realists' arguments, see Duncan Kennedy, "The Role of Law in Economic Thought: Essays on the Fetishism of Commodi-

ties," *Am. Univ. L. Rev.* 34:939 (1985); Karl Klare, "Workplace Democracy & Market Reconstruction: An Agenda For Legal Reform," 38 *Catholic Univ. L. Rev.* (1988) p. 1; and Frances Olsen, "The Myth of State Intervention in the Family," *U. Mich. J.L. Ref.* 18:835 (1984).

The focus here is on indeterminacy in the basic organizing principles or "master concepts" of the free market. Mainstream theorists have attempted to overcome the problem of indeterminacy in the concept of the free market by elaborating rights and welfare maximization arguments in favor of private property and free contact. See Duncan Kennedy, "Neither the Market nor the State: Housing Privatization Issues," in this volume. How rights discourse reproduces the indeterminacy problem is discussed in the original version of this article. Critical legal theorists also argue that utilitarian approaches cannot resolve the indeterminacy problem, but discussion of that point is beyond the scope of this paper.

11. Of course, other foundational branches of law, for example the law of business organization and human rights law, may play a role in determining the identity and legal capacity of economic actors and other aspects of market structure.

12. See Vegelahn v. Guntner, 167 Mass. 92, 104, 44 N.E. 1077, 1079 (1896)(Holmes, J., dissenting).

13. David Stark and Victor Nee, "Toward An Institutional Analysis of State Socialism," in *Remaking the Economic Institutions of Socialism: China and Eastern Europe* eds. Victor Nee and David Stark, (Stanford, CA: Stanford Univ. Press, 1989), pp. 20–21. See also Victor Nee, "Peasant Entrepreneurship and the Politics of Regulation in China," in id., pp. 169, 172–73.

14. As Gerald Frug has written "[t]here is no such thing as the 'free market.' There are only alternative possible markets, each of which restrains as well as enhances human freedom." Gerald Frug, "The Ideology of Bureaucracy in American Law," *Harv. L. Rev.* 97:1276, 1365 (1984).

15. Numerous reasons why market outcomes cannot automatically be taken as a surrogate for the arrangements that maximize welfare are catalogued in Singer, supra note 3, pp. 703–05, 707–11, and 726–32.

16. See, generally, Morris Cohen, "Property and Sovereignty," *Cornell L. Q.* 13:8 (1927); Morris Cohen, "The Basis of Contract," *Harv. L. Rev.* 46:553 (1933); Robert Hale, "Bargaining, Duress, and Economic Liberty" *Colum. L. Rev.* 43:603 (1943); Robert Hale, "Coercion and Distribution in a Supposedly Non-Coercive State," *Pol. Sci. Q.* 38:470 (1923). See also Duncan Kennedy, "The Stakes of Law, or Hale and Foucault!" *Leg. Stud. Forum* 15:327 (1991).

17. Opponents of tort reform condemn expansive private remedies as a form of regulatory interference with the free market. If damage remedies are carefully designed to compel actors to internalize the costs of involuntary harms they cause, under circumstances such that bargaining processes will not produce the efficient or socially desirable result, then tort entitlements are fully consistent with the idea of a free market. The real objection is not to the *regulatory* character of expansive entitlement rules—all entitlement rules, even immunities

from liability—are regulatory. The true objection is to their *redistributive* potential.

It is not my claim that market deterrence through tort is the optimal solution to all or most problems of accidental injury or environmental harm. Tort processes have well-known limitations and defects. My more modest point is that this policy instrument should not be overlooked.

18. See, generally, Singer, supra note 3.
19. For a classic discussion of the point, see Albert Hirschman, *Exit, Voice, and Loyalty: Responses to Decline in Firms, Organizations, and State* (Cambridge, MA: Harvard Univ. Press, 1970).
20. This theme has inspired a growing body of legal scholarship in the United States proposing reforms in business and employment law designed to enhance worker and community participation. See, e.g., Alan Hyde, "In Defense of Employee Ownership," *Chicago-Kent L. Rev.* 67:159 (1992); Alan Hyde and Craig Livingston, "Employee Takeovers," *Rutgers L. Rev.* 41:1131 (1989); Karl Klare, supra note 10; Marleen O'Connor, "Restructuring the Corporation's Nexus of Contracts: Recognizing A Fiduciary Duty to Protect Displaced Workers," *No. Car. L. Rev.* 69:1189 (1991); William Simon, "Social-Republican Property," *U.C.L.A. L. Rev.* 38:1335 (1991); Joseph Singer, supra note 3; Katherine Stone, "Employees as Stakeholders Under State Nonshareholder Constituency Statutes," *Stetson L. Rev.* 21:45 (1991); "Labor and the Corporate Structure: Changing Conceptions and Emerging Possibilities," *U. Chi. L. Rev.* 55:73 (1988).
21. See, generally, Simon, supra note 20.
22. See, generally, Roman Frydman and Andrzej Rapaczynski, *Markets and Institutions in Large Scale Privatizations: An Approach to Economic and Social Transformations in Eastern Europe*, Working Paper no. 49, Center for Law and Economic Studies, Columbia University School of Law (no date).
23. See Frydman and Rapaczynski, supra, note 22. This article contains an informative survey of the technical and policy issues involved in large-scale privatization in Central and Eastern Europe.
24. Id., p. 38–39.
25. In theory, a conventional Western business corporation is owned and controlled by its shareholders. The directors and managers are merely agents of the shareholders, acting in a fiduciary capacity. But for a variety of reasons, the officers are often in a position to effectuate policies geared more to serve their own interests than those of the general shareholder ("agency problems"). Supposedly this difficulty is kept under control by the shareholders' right to remove officers who disserve them. However, where there is a large number of small shareholders, it is often difficult to achieve sustained coordination and cohesive policy-making ("shareholder coordination problems"). The dilemmas these problems pose for corporate law, and the range of conventional solutions, are surveyed in William Simon, "Contract versus Politics in Corporation Doctrine," in *The Politics of Law: A Progressive Critique* ed. David Kairys, rev. ed. (New York: Pantheon Books, 1990), pp. 387–409.

26. For detailed discussions of the structure of the Mondragon cooperatives, see David Ellerman & Peter Pitegoff, "The Democratic Corporation: The New Worker Cooperative Statute in Massachusetts," *N.Y.U. Rev. of L. and Social Change* 11:44 (1982–83); and Keith Bradley and Alan Gelb, *Cooperation at Work: The Mondragon Experience* (London: Heinemann Educational Books, 1983).

27. Alan Hyde has written an exceedingly interesting reexamination of the question of employee ownership. See Alan Hyde, "Employee Ownership," supra note 20. For a more pessimistic view, see Henry Hansmann, "When Does Worker Ownership Work? ESOPS, Law Firms, Codetermination and Economic Democracy," *Yale L. J.* 99:1749 (1990). This article includes some skeptical comments on Mondragon. See id., pp. 1790–94. For Hyde's response to Hansmann's thesis, see Hyde, "Employee Ownership," supra note 20, particularly p. 169 n. 35.

28. This might mean one shareholder, one vote, or there might be some enhanced voting and institutional deference to members with larger or longer-term commitments. But participation rights should not turn solely on the value of one's investment stake.

29. For a creative effort to propose such innovations in the context of public administration, see Gerald Frug, "Administrative Democracy," *Univ. of Toronto L.J.* 40:559 (1990).

30. Prof. Rapaczynski has indicated that legal nontransferability could be used to prevent concentration of voucher ownership. See Lawrence Wechsler, "A Reporter at Large: Shock," *The New Yorker* (December 10, 1990) pp. 89, 119.

31. See generally, Duncan Kennedy, "Neither the Market nor the State: Housing Privatization Issues," in this volume.

32. See generally, Fred Block, *Postindustrial Possibilities: A Critique of Economic Discourse* (Berkeley, CA: Univ. of California Press, 1990).

33. Even conservative business observers agree: "Much of [the U.S.'s overseas competitors'] success in the global arena stems from public and private investments in maintaining and modernizing their infrastructures and in the health, education, and training of their 'human capital.' Public investment is a crucial factor of production in the global economy. . . . The key to strong economic growth, healthy corporate profits, and higher living standards over the long pull is productivity. And that, as our competitors know well, means investing in people and improving their social welfare." "Special Report: Why We Should Invest in Human Capital," *Business Week*, (December 17, 1990) pp. 88, 88–90.

34. Cf. the prescient remarks of Jacek Kurczewski, "What's Good With Rights: Social Movements and Social Reconstruction in Poland" (unpublished, May, 1989). Kurczewski argues that Solidarity is both a "manifestation and organization of the new middle class," gradually coming into existence within communist society since 1945, which "links the skilled shipyard worker and university

professor who remain outside the closed barrier of the nomenklatura" (p. 9). In his view, the enlargement and diffusion of this social grouping will provide the foundation for a democratic political culture, but, as of that writing, this group lacked "economic power sufficient to counterbalance the power of the nomenklatura that controls the state" (p. 10).

Contributors

Gregory S. Alexander is Professor of Law, Cornell Law School.

Stanisław Biernat is Associate Professor of Law, Jagiellonian University, Cracow, Poland.

Maria Borucka-Arctowa is Professor of Sociology of Law and Legal Theory at the Jagiellonian University in Cracow, Poland. She also heads the Research Group on Legal Consciousness at the Polish Academy of the Sciences' Institute of Legal Sciences. She has directed many research projects and published numerous books and articles on natural law and human rights, law and social action, legal consciousness, functions of the law, efficiency, and the administration of justice. Her current research interests include legal socialization, sociolegal aspects of evolving democracies, procedural justice, and European integration.

Dariusz Chelmiński is Assistant Professor of Sociology, School of Management, University of Warsaw.

Andrzej Czynczyk is Assistant Professor of Sociology, Institute of Applied Social Sciences, University of Warsaw.

Krystyna Daniel is Assistant Professor of Law, Department of Sociology of Law, Jagiellonian University, Cracow.

Edgar L. Feige is Professor of Economics at the University of Wisconsin-Madison.

Clayton P. Gillette is the Perre Bowen Professor of Law, University of Virginia School of Law.

Duncan Kennedy is Professor of Law, Harvard University.

Karl E. Klare is Professor of Law at Northeastern University. He specializes in the law of labor relations and workplace democracy.

Lena Kolarska-Bobińska is Director, Centrum Badania Opinii Spolecznej (Center for Public Opinion Research), Warsaw, Poland.

Thomas Raiser is Professor of Law and Legal Sociology, Justus-Liebig-University, Giessen, Germany.

András Sajó is Chair, Postgraduate Legal Studies, Central European University, Budapest; Counsel to the President of Hungary.

William H. Simon is Professor of Law, Stanford University.

Grażyna Skąpska is Associate Professor of the Sociology of Law, Jagiellonian University, Cracow, Poland.

Leopold Specht is Lecturer in Law, Harvard Law School; partner, Patzak, Specht & Krauss, Vienna, Austria.

Henryk Sterniczuk is Professor of Management, Faculty of Business, University of New Brunswick; President of the International Foundation for Capital Market Development and Ownership Changes in Poland, Center for Privatization, Warsaw; President of the Institution of Privatization and Management, Moscow.

Joan C. Williams is Professor of Law at The American University, Washington, D.C.

Andrzej Wojtyna is Associate Professor and Chair, Department of Macroeconomics, Cracow Academy of Economics.